TM 10-412

US ARMY FIELD MANUAL

ARMY RECIPES

1946

WORLD WAR II
CIVILIAN REFERENCE EDITION

THE UNABRIDGED CLASSIC WARTIME COOKBOOK
FOR LARGE GROUPS, TROOPS, CAMPS, AND CAFETERIAS

U.S. WAR DEPARTMENT

Doublebit Press

The Military Outdoors Skills Series
Historic Field Manuals and Military Guides
on Outdoors Skills and Travel

Military manuals contain essential knowledge about outdoors life, thriving while in the field, and self-sufficiency. Unfortunately, many great military books, field manuals, and technical guides over the years have become less available and harder to find. These have either been rescinded by the armed forces or are otherwise out of print due to their age. This does not mean that these manuals are worthless or "out of date" – in fact, the opposite is true! It is true that the US Military frequently updates its manuals as its protocols frequently change based on the current times and combat situations that our armed services face. However, the knowledge about the outdoors over the entire history of military publications is timeless!

By publishing the **Military Outdoors Skills Series**, it is our goal at Doublebit Press to do what we can to preserve and share valuable military works that hold timeless knowledge about outdoors life, navigation, and survival. These books include official unrestricted texts such as army field manuals (the FM series), technical manuals (the TM series), and other military books from the Air Force, Navy, and texts from before 1900. Through remastered reprint editions of military handbooks and field manuals, outdoors enthusiasts, bushcrafters, hunters, scouts, campers, survivalists, nature lore experts, and military historians can preserve the time-tested skills and institutional knowledge that was learned through hard lessons and training by the U.S. Military and our expert soldiers.

Soldiers were the original campers and survivalists! Because of this, military field manuals about outdoors life contain essential knowledge about thriving in the wilds. This book is not just for soldiers!

This book is an important contribution to outdoors literature and has important historical and collector value toward preserving the American outdoors tradition. The knowledge it holds is an invaluable reference for practicing skills related to thriving in the outdoors. Its chapters thoroughly discuss some of the essential building blocks of outdoors knowledge that are fundamental but may have been forgotten as equipment gets fancier and technology gets smarter. In short, this book was chosen for Historic Edition printing because much of the basic skills and knowledge it contains could be forgotten or put to the wayside in trade for more modern conveniences and methods.

Although the editors at Doublebit Press are thrilled to have comfortable experiences in the woods and love our high-tech and light-weight equipment, we are also realizing that the basic skills taught by the old experts are more essential than ever as our culture becomes more and more hooked on digital technology. We don't want to risk forgetting the important steps, skills, or building blocks involved with thriving in the outdoors. This Civilian Reference Edition reprint represents a collection of military handbooks and field manuals that are essential contributions to the American outdoors tradition despite originating with the military. In the most basic sense, these books are the collection of experiences by the great experts of outdoors life: our countless expert soldiers who learned to thrive in the backwoods, deserts, extreme cold environments, and jungles of the world.

With technology playing a major role in everyday life, sometimes we need to take a step back in time to find those basic building blocks used for gaining mastery – the things that we have luckily not completely lost and has been recorded in books over the last two centuries. These skills aren't forgotten, they've just been shelved. *It's time to unshelve them once again and reclaim the lost knowledge of self-sufficiency.*

Based on this commitment to preserving our outdoors heritage, we have taken great pride in publishing this book as a complete original work. We hope it is worthy of both study and collection by outdoors folk in the modern era of outdoors and traditional skills life.

Unlike many other photocopy reproductions of classic books that are common on the market, this Historic Edition does not simply place poor photography of old texts on our pages and use error-prone optical scanning or computer-generated text. We want our work to speak for itself, and reflect the quality demanded by our customers who spend their hard-earned money. With this in mind, each Historic Edition book that has been chosen for publication is carefully remastered from original print books, *with the Doublebit Civilian Reference Edition printed and laid out in the exact way that it was presented at its original publication.* We provide a beautiful, memorable experience that is as true to the original text as best as possible, but with the aid of modern technology to make as beautiful a reading experience as possible for books that are typically over a century old. Military historians and outdoors enthusiasts alike are sure to appreciate the care to preserve this work!

Because of its age and because it is presented in its original form, the book may contain misspellings, inking errors, and other print blemishes that were common for the age. However, these are exactly the things that we feel give the book its character, which we preserved in this Historic Edition. During digitization, we ensured that each illustration in the text was clean and sharp with the least amount of loss from being copied and digitized as possible. Full-page plate illustrations are presented as they were found, often including the extra blank page that was often behind a plate. For the covers, we use the original cover design to give the book its original feel. We are sure you'll appreciate the fine touches and attention to detail that your Historic Edition has to offer.

For outdoors and military history enthusiasts who demand the best from their equipment, the Doublebit Press Civilian Reference Edition reprint of this military manual was made with you in mind. Both important and minor details have equally both been accounted for by our publishing staff, down to the cover, font, layout, and images. It is the goal of Doublebit Civilian Reference Edition series to preserve outdoors heritage, but also be cherished as collectible pieces, worthy of collection in any outdoorsperson's library and that can be passed to future generations.

WAR DEPARTMENT TECHNICAL MANUAL
TM 10-412

ARMY RECIPES

WAR DEPARTMENT • *AUGUST 1946*

United States Government Printing Office

Washington 1946

WAR DEPARTMENT
Washington 25, D. C., 27 August 1946

TM 10–412, Army Recipes, is published for the information and guidance of all concerned.

[AG 300.7 (12 Mar 46)]

By order of the Secretary of War:

Official: DWIGHT D. EISENHOWER
Edward F. Witsell   *Chief of Staff*
Major General
The Adjutant General

Distribution:

AAF (5); AGF (5); T (25); Base Comd (5); AAF Comd (5); Tech Sv (2) except OQMG (100); A Areas (2); FC (10); BU (2); GH (10); RH (5); SH (5); CH (10); Gen & Sp Sv Sch (2) except QM Sch (25); Bakers & Cooks Sch (50); Tng C (25); RC (10); Rehab C (10); A (5); CHQ (2); B (2); D (2); Bn (2); S Bn (3); C (5); AF (5); W (5); G (10); S (5).

For explanation of distribution formula, see FM 21–6.

CONTENTS

III

This manual supersedes TM 10–412, 15 August 1944, and TB 10–412–1, 1 September 1944.

SECTION I

INTRODUCTION

---

1. GENERAL. a. Recipes are essential for both experienced and inexperienced cooks. Even after long years of service, a cook cannot remember the exact quantities of every recipe. He needs the stimulation of new recipes if the meals he prepares are to be interesting and not monotonous. Recipes, accurate as to amounts and procedure, are important for good cooking. In this book directions for combining ingredients are given in detail to aid the cook in obtaining desirable results.

b. A cook needs more than recipes. He needs practice, imagination and, above all, a desire to please those who eat the food he prepares. The soldier who develops these qualities and follows the recipes provided for him soon becomes a skillful cook. He quickly learns to judge the consistency of a batter by the way it feels under the spoon. He knows when bread is light by the touch of his fingers. He knows when extra seasoning will make a sauce more enjoyable and when a garnish will make a dish more appetizing.

2. RECIPES. a. The recipes in this manual represent the food habits of American families. They utilize the foods which are most abundant in this country as well as those which may be found where troops may be sent. Each recipe as set up will yield food sufficient for 100 portions of the size designated.

b. The unit of 100 portions was selected because requisitions for food issues are based on amounts for 100 men. It is the responsibility of mess personnel to observe the actual number of men who will eat a certain food. If only 50 out of 100 men like a specific dish, amounts of ingredients for 50 rather than for 100 should be made the basis for requisitions. In this way waste through over-preparation can be avoided.

c. Many messes have more than 100 men assigned to them. However, some soldiers assigned to a mess may be absent for one or more meals. The number of men who will be present for each meal must be determined before supplies are ordered. If 175 men are to be there the amount for 100 is multiplied by 1¾ to get the total quantity of food needed. After a short time the cooks will be able to determine the average number of men who will be present for every meal. Each recipe can be increased or decreased accordingly and the amounts required can be written with pencil in the blank column and can be changed from time to time as necessary. (See model recipe in e below.)

1

d. A large number of recipes in this book are followed by one or more variations. These show only the ingredients or procedures which differ from the basic recipe. In preparing a variation, follow the basic recipe, making the substitutions as directed.

e. Model recipe.

NO.   BAKING POWDER BISCUITS   Yield: 25 pounds mixture, 212 biscuits, each 2½-inch diameter

Ingredients	100 servings	.... servings
Flour, sifted...............	12 pounds (12 No. 56 dippers)......	....
Baking powder..............	10 ounces (½ mess kit cup)........	....
Salt......................	3 ounces (6 mess kit spoons)........	....
Shortening.................	3 pounds (1½ No. 56 dippers)......	....
Milk, evaporated...........	4¼ —14½-ounce cans............	....
Water (for milk)*..........	2½ quarts (2½ No. 56 dippers).....	....

*The amount of water will vary according to the type of flour used.

1. Sift flour, baking powder, and salt together. Add shortening; stir until mixture resembles coarse crumbs.

2. Mix milk and water. Add to dry ingredients, mixing only enough to combine dry and liquid ingredients.

3. Place dough on floured bread board and knead lightly. Roll ¾ inch thick; cut dough into biscuits with floured biscuit cutter.

4. Place in baking pans. Bake in hot oven (450° F.) about 15 minutes.

3. APPETIZERS. a. An appetizer is a food served to stimulate the appetite. An appetizer is very light, looks attractive and tempts the eater to want more food. The most commonly served appetizers are relishes such as celery, young onions, olives, pickles and radishes. Raw vegetables such as carrot strips, flowerlets of cauliflower, green pepper rings and watercress may also be used. They must be clean, cold and crisp.

b. Fruit cocktail may be any one fruit or a mixture of fruits. Slices of cantaloup, watermelon balls, whole strawberries, pineapple wedges, orange sections and grapefruit halves are the most common fruits served. Sweeten fresh fruits; chill before serving. Chill canned fruits thoroughly. The sirup from canned fruits may be combined with lemon juice and water and served as an appetizer in summer.

c. Juices from canned vegetables may be used as appetizers. Add seasonings and chill before serving. The flavor of tomato juice may be varied by adding salt, lemon juice, Worcestershire sauce and onion juice.

4. MEASUREMENTS. a. Accuracy at all times is essential for success in cooking. Ingredients either must be weighed accurately or measured accurately. It is preferable to weigh ingredients if scales are available; otherwise it is best to measure them in graduated measures and in standard cups and spoons. If graduated measures are not available, No. 56 dippers, mess kit cups, and mess kit spoons can be used. A cook or baker can obtain satisfactory results with Army equipment if he is careful to follow the same procedure each time he prepares the recipe. He can train his eye to judge the line on the utensil that means ¼, ½, or ¾ full when an unmarked measure is used. One cupful of liquid comes approximately to the top of the date figures on a No. 56 dipper; two cupfuls to the top of the letters designating the manufacturer; three cupfuls to the top of the "U. S." letters.

b. Measure sugar, cornstarch, and other dry ingredients without packing or shaking. Pack brown sugar and shortening firmly into the measuring utensil. Sift flour *before measuring;* place lightly, without packing, in measuring utensil until level full. If ingredients are weighed, flour may be weighed before sifting but must be sifted afterwards before combining with other ingredients.

c. To measure with a spoon, fill spoon to overflowing and level with the straight edge of a knife. To measure a half spoonful, fill the spoon; level and divide it lengthwise with a knife. The Quartermaster tablespoon is slightly larger than the mess kit spoon but for practical purposes may be used as an identical measure.

5. TABLES OF INFORMATION. a. Table of equivalent measures.

3 teaspoons . . . . 1 tablespoon
4 tablespoons . . . . ¼ cup   (measuring)
5⅓ tablespoons . . . . ⅓ cup   (measuring)
8 tablespoons . . . . ½ cup   (measuring)
16 tablespoons . . . . 1 cup   (measuring)
2 cups . . . . 1 pint
2 pints . . . . 1 quart
4 cups . . . . 1 quart
4 quarts . . . . 1 gallon
8 quarts . . . . 1 peck
4 pecks . . . . 1 bushel
16 ounces . . . . 1 pound

b. Table of mess equipment measures.

1 mess kit cup . . . . 1½ liquid pints
1 No. 56 dipper . . . . 1 liquid quart
1 No. 55 dipper . . . . 1¾ liquid quarts

c. Table of weights and mess measurements of commonly used foods.

Item	M-1910 spoon ounces	Mess kit cup (1½ pints)		No. 56 dipper (1 quart)		No. 55 dipper (1¾ quarts)	
		Pounds	Ounces	Pounds	Ounces	Pounds	Ounces
Allspice, ground	¼						
Apples, evaporated			7		9	1	
Apricots, evaporated		1		1	5	2	5
Barley		1	8	2		3	8
Beans, dry, kidney		1	3	1	9	2	12
Beans, dry, lima		1	4	1	10	2	14
Beans, dry, navy		1	5	1	12	3	1
Beef, ground, raw		1	8	2		3	8
Bread crumbs, dried			12	1		1	12
Bread crumbs, moist (loose pack)			6		8		14
Butter (solid pack)		1	8	2		3	8
Carrots, cubed			14	1	3	2	1
Celery, cubed			12	1		1	12
Cheese, American cheddar, ground			14	1	3	2	1
Cheese, American cheddar, shredded			12	1		1	12
Cheese, cottage		1	8	2		3	8
Cinnamon, ground	¼						
Cloves, ground	¼						
Cocoa	¼		10		13	1	7
Coconut, shredded (loose pack)			8		11	1	3
Coffee, roasted and ground			12	1		1	12
Cornmeal		1		1	5	2	5
Cornstarch	⅓	1		1	5	2	5
Cream of tartar	⅓						
Eggs, powdered, whole	¼		9		12	1	5
Eggs, whites, fresh		1	8	2		3	8
Eggs, whole, without shell		1	8	2		3	8
Eggs, yolks, fresh		1	8	2		3	8
Extract, lemon or vanilla	½						
Farina		1	3	1	9	2	12
Flour, issue, sifted	¼		12	1		1	12
Flour, issue, unsifted	¼		15	1	4	2	3
Flour, pastry, sifted	⅓		10		13	1	7
Flour, pastry, unsifted	⅓		13	1	1	1	14
Flour, whole wheat	⅓		14	1	3	2	1
Gelatin powder, flavored	¼	1		1	5	2	5
Ginger, ground	¼						
Hominy grits		1	2	1	8	1	10
Lard substitute		1	8	2		3	8
Lentils		1		1	5	2	5
Mace	¼						
Milk, powdered, whole	¼		12	1		1	12
Molasses		2	4	3		5	4
Mustard, ground	¼						
Nutmeg, ground	¼						
Oats, rolled			9		12	1	5
Oil, salad		1	4	1	10	2	14
Onions, diced			12	1		1	12
Paprika	¼						
Parsley, chopped			9		12	1	5
Peaches, evaporated		1		1	5	2	5
Peas, dry, split		1	5	1	12	3	1
Pepper, black	¼						
Peppers, green, chopped			12	1		1	12
Powder, baking	⅜	1	2	1	8	2	10
Powder, chili	¼						
Powder, curry	¼						
Prunes, evaporated		1		1	5	2	5

c. Table of weights and mess measurements of commonly used foods. (Con't)

Item	M-1910 spoon ounces	Mess kit cup (1½ pints)		No. 56 dipper (1 quart)		No. 55 dipper (1¾ quarts)	
		Pounds	Ounces	Pounds	Ounces	Pounds	Ounces
Raisins, seedless...............	....	1	......	1	5	2	5
Rice...........................	....	1	8	2	......	3	8
Sage..........................	⅛	......	......	......	......	......	......
Salt..........................	½	1	9	2	1	3	10
Seasoning, poultry.............	¼	......	......	......	......	......	......
Soda, baking..................	½	1	8	2	......	3	8
Sugar, brown (loose pack).......	¼	1	......	1	5	2	5
Sugar, powdered...............	¼	......	14	1	3	2	1
Sugar, granulated..............	½	1	8	2	......	3	8
Tapioca, granulated............	....	1	3	1	9	2	12
Tapioca, pearl.................	....	1	......	1	5	2	5
Tea..........................	....	......	8	......	11	1	3
Vinegar.......................	½	1	9	2	1	3	10
Water........................	....	1	8	2	......	3	8

BEVERAGES

---

6. BEVERAGES. a. General. The formulas for making beverages are simple. The most important rule to remember is to serve hot those beverages which are intended to be hot, and ice those beverages intended to be cold.

b. Rules for making coffee and tea.

(1) Measure accurately.

(2) Make only amount needed.

(3) Discard used grounds or leaves.

(4) Keep equipment clean.

NO. 1 COFFEE (kettle method) Yield: 7 gallons,
100 9½-ounce servings.

Ingredients	100 servings	.... servings
Coffee, roasted and ground....	3 pounds (3 No. 56 dippers).........	....
Water, freshly drawn.........	7½ gallons (30 No. 56 dippers).......	....

1. Place coffee in a 50-pound coffee sack or other cloth bag large enough to permit free circulation of water and expansion of the coffee.*

2. Tie the bag with a cord of sufficient length to fasten to the handle of the container. This facilitates removal of the bag from the hot brew.

3. Pour freshly drawn water into a large kettle; heat to boiling point.

4. Place coffee bag in boiling water; tie cord to handle of kettle. Reduce heat to keep water below the boiling point. *Coffee must always be kept below the boiling point.*

5. Submerge the bag with a stick or paddle; push up and down to force the water through the grounds.

6. Cover kettle; brew 12 to 15 minutes.

7. Lift bag; drain thoroughly in kettle. Remove bag entirely.

8. Serve coffee at once.

*Fifteen pounds of coffee is the maximum amount that can be placed in one bag if the full extraction of flavor is to be obtained from the coffee. If 100 gallons of coffee are to be made, divide the 40 pounds of coffee evenly into three bags. This expedites extraction and facilitates the removal of the coffee bags after brewing.

Note. Remove coffee grounds from bags immediately after they are taken from the brew. Wash bags thoroughly, without soap, in cold water and place in pans of cold water until used again. Keep the bags wet all the time they are not in use. Replace the bag with a new one about once a week.

NO. 2. COFFEE (emergency method)

Pour the 7½ gallons (30 No. 56 dippers) freshly drawn water into a large kettle; heat to boiling point. Pour 3 pounds (3 No. 56 dippers) loose coffee into boiling water. Reduce heat; brew 10 to 12 minutes. If necessary, settle grounds by sprinkling a small amount of cold water over coffee (use less than ½ pint [⅓ mess kit cup] cold water to 1 pound coffee). The cold water carries the coffee grounds to the bottom of the kettle. Pour coffee carefully to avoid stirring up the grounds.

NO. 3. COFFEE (urn method) Yield: 7 gallons,
100 9½-ounce servings.

Ingredients	100 servings	.... servings
Coffee, roasted and ground....	3 pounds (3 No. 56 dippers).........	....
Water, freshly drawn.........	7½ gallons (30 No. 56 dippers).......	....

1. Pour water into jacket of urn until glass gauge registers about ¾ full.
2. Heat the water to the boiling point but avoid boiling it.
3. Replenish water whenever gauge shows less than ½ full.
4. Pour coffee into wet urn bag or basket and pour or siphon freshly boiling water evenly over the coffee.
5. Cover and let water drip completely through once.
6. If urn bag is used, pour ½ of the coffee brew back over grounds to give a full extraction and a clear brew. Remove bag or basket as any seepage from grounds impairs the delicacy of flavor and aroma.

Note. Coffee grounds will absorb about 2 quarts (2 No. 56 dippers) water. Make coffee just before using as it deteriorates on standing.

NO. 4. COFFEE (dunking method)

Heat water in urn jacket as in steps 1 and 2 in recipe for coffee (urn method). Pour the 7½ gallons (30 No. 56 dippers) freshly boiling water into the urn. Place 3 pounds (3 No. 56 dippers) coffee in cloth bag; tie with a cord long enough to facilitate removal. Drop bag into the hot water in urn; tie cord to handle of urn. Reduce heat to keep water below the boiling point. Push coffee bag up and down to force water through the grounds. Brew 10 to 12 minutes. Remove coffee bag.

NO. 5. ICED COFFEE

Prepare iced coffee as in recipe for hot coffee but make *twice* as strong. Use twice as much ground coffee to the same amount of water as is used in making hot coffee to compensate for the dilution caused by melting ice. Remove coffee brew from urn or kettle; place in a dispenser with sufficient ice to keep coffee well chilled until served.

NO. 6. BOSTON COFFEE

Use ½ recipe for coffee and prepare coffee. Scald 1½ gallons of evaporated milk with 1½ gallons of water and mix with prepared coffee. Serve hot.

NO. 7. TEA (urn method)   Yield: 8 gallons, 100 10-ounce servings.

Ingredients	100 servings	.... servings
Tea......................	8 ounces (1 mess kit cup)............	....
Water, freshly boiling........	8 gallons (32 No. 56 dippers)........	....

1. Place tea in a cloth bag large enough to hold at least three times the amount.
2. Tie top of bag with cord long enough to facilitate removal; tie cord to handle of urn.
3. Heat water in tank to boiling point; lower bag containing tea into dry urn crock.
4. Pour or siphon boiling water over bag containing tea. If siphon is used, watch water gauge on boiler to determine quantity of water.
5. Submerge tea bag with a paddle; push up and down repeatedly 5 to 7 minutes to force water through the tea leaves.
6. Lift tea bag; drain thoroughly in kettle. Remove bag entirely.

Note. Remove tea leaves from bag immediately after it is taken from the brew. Wash bag thoroughly, without soap, in cold water and place in pan of cold water until used again. Keep tea bag wet all the time it is not in use. Replace the bag with a new one about once a week.

NO. 8. TEA (kettle method)

Use amounts in receipe for urn method. Tie tea in cloth bag large enough to hold at least three times the amount. Tie cord to the container to make it easy to pull bag out of the water. Drop bag into kettle of boiling water; cover tightly. Reduce heat to prevent boiling; brew 5 to 7 minutes. Plunge bag up and down several times; remove bag from brew. If bag is not used and tea is put directly into the boiling water, strain beverage as soon as it is brewed. Otherwise, it will develop an undesirable flavor.

NO. 9. ICED TEA

Prepare iced tea as in recipe for hot tea reducing boiling water to 5 gallons (20 No. 56 dippers). Brew 1 minute longer than for hot tea. Add 5 gallons (20 No. 56 dippers) cold water; chill. If ice is to be added, reduce total water to 8 gallons (32 No. 56 dippers) as melting ice will weaken the tea.

NO. 10. COCOA

Yield: 8 gallons,
100 10-ounce servings.

Ingredients	100 servings	.... servings
Cocoa	2½ pounds (3 No. 56 dippers)	
Sugar, granulated	4½ pounds (2¼ No. 56 dippers)	
Salt	¼ ounce (½ mess kit spoon)	
Water, cold	1 gallon (4 No. 56 dippers)	
Water, hot	5 gallons (20 No. 56 dippers)	
Milk, evaporated	24—14½-ounce cans	
Vanilla (optional)	½ ounce (1 mess kit spoon)	

1. Combine cocoa, sugar, and salt.
2. Add cold water gradually. Heat to boiling point; boil 5 minutes, stirring constantly.
3. Add hot water, milk, and vanilla; heat to serving temperature.
4. Beat well before serving.

NO. 11. ICED COCOA

Prepare cocoa as in recipe for hot cocoa; chill the hot mixture. Substitute 5 gallons (20 No. 56 dippers) cold water for the 5 gallons of hot water. Add the cold water, milk, and vanilla to chilled mixture; stir until smooth. Serve with chipped ice.

NO. 12. COCOA SIRUP

Yield: 2 gallons,
100 2½-ounce servings.

Ingredients	100 servings	.... servings
Cocoa	1½ pounds (2 No. 56 dippers)	
Sugar, granulated	3 pounds (1½ No. 56 dippers)	
Salt	½ ounce (1 mess kit spoon)	
Water	6 quarts (6 No. 56 dippers)	

1. Bring water to the boiling point (212° F.).
2. Mix cocoa, sugar, and salt thoroughly.
3. Add hot water slowly, stirring constantly.
4. Bring to a boil (212° F.) and boil for 5 minutes.
5. Cool and serve.

NO. 13. LEMONADE

Yield: 8 gallons,
100 10-ounce servings.

Ingredients	100 servings	.... servings
Sugar, granulated	4¾ pounds (2⅜ No. 56 dippers)	
Water, hot	1½ gallons (6 No. 56 dippers)	
Water, cold	5½ gallons (22 No. 56 dippers)	
Lemon juice*	1 gallon (4 No. 56 dippers)	

*Use approximately 96 lemons.

1. Dissolve sugar in hot water; cool.
2. Add cold water and lemon juice.
3. Serve very cold using ice if available.

NO. 14. GRAPE LEMONADE

Substitute 1½ gallons (6 No. 56 dippers) grape juice for the 1½ gallons (6 No. 56 dippers) cold water in recipe for lemonade. Reduce sugar to 3 pounds (1½ No. 56 dippers).

NO. 15. FRUIT PUNCH

Substitute a combination of grape juice and one or more other fruit juices such as pineapple, grapefruit, or orange for ½ lemon juice in recipe for lemonade. Reduce sugar as necessary.

NO. 16. LEMONADE (made with lemon juice powder synthetic)
Yield: 8 gallons, 100 10-ounce servings.

Ingredients	100 servings	.... servings
Lemon juice powder, synthetic.	18 ounces (1 mess kit cup)............	....
Sugar, granulated............	8 pounds (4 No. 56 dippers)........	....
Water....................	8 gallons (32 No. 56 dippers)........	....

1. Mix lemon juice powder and sugar together thoroughly.
2. Add mixture slowly to water, stirring constantly.
3. Chill; serve immediately.

NO. 17. TEA PUNCH
Yield: 8 gallons, 100 10-ounce servings.

Ingredients	100 servings	.... servings
Tea........................	6½ ouncess (¾ mess kit cup)........	....
Water, fresh boiling..........	7¼ gallons (29 No. 56 dippers).......	....
Sugar, granulated............	3¼ pounds (1½ No. 56 dippers).....	....
Lemon juice*..............	2⅓ quarts (2⅓ No. 56 dippers)......	....
Fruit juice (grape, pineapple, or grapefruit).	3 quarts (3 No. 56 dippers)........	....

*Use approximately 56 lemons.

1. Tie tea loosely in a cloth bag.
2. Pour freshly boiled water over tea leaves; brew 4 to 6 minutes. Remove tea bag.
3. Add sugar; stir until sugar is dissolved. Chill; add fruit juices.
4. Serve very cold.

Note. If ice is added to the punch, reduce water to 6 gallons (24 No. 56 dippers.)

NO. 18. EGG NOG
Yield: 7 gallons, 100 9½-ounce servings.

Ingredients	100 servings	.... servings
Eggs......................	48 eggs.................	....
Salt......................	½ ounce (1 mess kit spoon).........	....
Sugar, granulated............	1½ pounds (1 mess kit cup)........	....
Milk, evaporated............	7½ quarts (7½ No. 56 dippers).....	....
Water (for milk)*..........	7½ quarts (7½ No. 56 dippers).....	....
Nutmeg...................		....

*Fresh milk may be used instead of evaporated milk and water.

1. Break and separate egg yolks from egg whites.
2. Beat egg yolks until thick and lemon colored.
3. Add salt and sugar and stir until well dissolved.
4. Add milk and water.
5. Fold in stiffly beaten egg whites.
6. Pour into glasses and sprinkle with nutmeg.

NO. 19. GRAPEFRUIT NOG

Yield: 4 gallons,
100 5-ounce servings.

Ingredients	100 servings	.... servings
Milk, evaporated	1½ gallons (6 No. 56 dippers)	
Water (for milk)*	2 quarts (2 No. 56 dippers)	
Sugar, granulated	2 pounds (1 No. 56 dipper)	
Grapefruit juice	8 quarts (8 No. 56 dippers)	

*Fresh milk may be used in lieu of evaporated milk and water.

1. Thoroughly mix milk, water, and sugar.
2. Stir in the grapefruit juice slowly.

Note. All ingredients must be cold; canned or fresh juice may be used.

BREADS

---

7. QUICK BREADS. a. General. Quick breads are flour mixtures which can be baked immediately after mixing. They are leavened by baking powder, soda, or steam. Mix all quick breads as rapidly as possible and with a minimum amount of handling to prevent development of the gluten in the flour.

b. Batters. A batter is a flour mixture that is thin enough to be poured or dropped from a spoon. Batters may be thick or thin depending upon the proportion of flour to liquid. Muffins, fritters, and drop biscuits are made from thick batters. Waffles, griddle cakes, and popovers are made from thin batters.

c. Doughs. A dough is a flour mixture containing a much smaller proportion of liquid than a batter. It contains sufficient flour to enable handling. Baking powder biscuits, rolled cobblers, and shortcakes are made from quick doughs.

8. YEAST BREADS. a. Yeast breads are leavened by the gas released during the growth of yeast plants. Yeast needs moisture, air, and warmth. Moisture is supplied by milk or water; air by kneading; warmth by controlling the temperature of the ingredients and the atmosphere where the dough is placed to rise. The most satisfactory temperature is about 80° F.

b. Yeast doughs are kneaded to develop gluten in the flour. This makes the dough elastic and enables it to hold the gasses which give the bread a satisfactory texture.

NO. 20. WHITE BREAD

Yield: Approximately 20 1-pound loaves.

Ingredients	100 servings	.... servings
Milk, evaporated.............	1—14½-ounce can.......................	....
Water (for milk).............	1 gallon (4 No. 56 dippers)...........	....
Yeast......................	6 ounces...........................	....
Salt.................·......	5 ounces (10 mess kit spoons)........	....
Sugar, granulated............	1 pound (½ No. 56 dipper)...........	....
Flour, sifted*...............	15 pounds (15 No. 56 dippers).......	....
Shortening, softened..........	1 pound (½ No. 56 dipper)...........	....

*The amount of water will vary according to the type of flour used.

1. Mix milk and water. Scald; cool to 80° F.
2. Soften yeast in milk; add salt and sugar.
3. Add flour and shortening; mix about 10 minutes to make a smooth and elastic dough.

4. Place dough in a warm place (80° F.) ; allow to rise 2 hours. Punch dough; allow to rise 20 minutes more.

5. Cut dough into 1½-pound pieces; mould evenly into loaves and place in greased 1-pound pans.

6. Allow to rise until double in volume.

7. Bake in hot oven (425° to 450° F.) approximately 30 to 40 minutes.

NO. 21. WHITE RAISIN BREAD

Prepare basic dough as in recipe for white bread, increasing yeast to 1 pound. Add 10 pounds raisins during the last 2 or 3 minutes of mixing. Make dough slightly softer by reducing the quantity of flour if raisins are quite dry.

NO. 22. BASIC DOUGH FOR HOT ROLLS AND BUNS

Yield: 25 pounds mixture, 225 2½-ounce rolls.

Ingredients	100 servings	.... servings
Flour, sifted................	14 pounds (11 No. 56 dippers).......	....
Yeast.....................	8 ounces (½ cake)....................	....
Salt......................	4 ounces (8 mess kit spoons).........	....
Water (for milk)...........	4 quarts (4 No. 56 dippers).........	....
Milk, evaporated...........	1—14½-ounce can....................	....
Sugar, granulated...........	1 pound (½ No. 56 dipper).........	....
Lard.....................	1 pound (½ No. 56 dipper).........	....

1. Dissolve yeast in 1 quart of water.

2. Dissolve sugar and salt in 3 quarts of water.

3. Add 1 can of evaporated milk.

4. Add all of lard or shortening.

5. Add ½ of flour and mix well.

6. Add remaining water with dissolved yeast.

7. Add remaining flour and mix until a smooth dough is obtained.

8. Dough temperature should be 78°-82° F.

9. Give one rising of 1¾ hours. Punch well.

10. Let stand for 20 minutes and take to make-up bench.

NO. 23. PLAIN ROLLS

Yield: Approximately 300 rolls.

Prepare basic dough as in recipe for hot rolls and buns. Divide into pieces weighing 3 to 4 pounds each. Roll each piece into a long strip. Cut strips into pieces about 1 inch thick; shape into rolls. Place ½ inch apart on greased sheet pans. Cover pans; allow dough to rise until double in volume. Handle rolls carefully after rising as jarring will cause them to fall. Protect rolls from drafts to prevent formation of a crust on the dough. Bake in hot oven (425° to 450° F.) about 20 minutes.

NO. 24. FINGER ROLLS

Prepare basic dough as in recipe for hot rolls and buns. Divide into pieces weighing 3 to 4 pounds each. Roll each piece into a long strip. Divide the elongated pieces of dough into pieces of about 1½ to 1¾ ounces. Instead of rounding as for plain rolls, roll the pieces into cigar shapes, about 4 to 4½ inches long. Place in greased sheet pan about ½ inch apart and proof until doubled in size, and bake for about 15 minutes in a hot oven (425°-450° F.) or to a golden brown.

NO. 25. HARD ROLLS
Yield: 35 pound mixture, 250 3-ounce rolls.

Ingredients	100 servings	.... servings
Flour, sifted	23 pounds (23 No. 56 dippers)	
Water or milk	7¼ quarts (7¼ No. 56 dippers)	
Yeast	8 ounces	
Salt	8 ounces (16 mess kit spoons)	
Sugar, granulated	8 ounces (16 mess kit spoons)	
Shortening	4 ounces	
Cornstarch	1 ounce (3 mess kit spoons)	

1. Proceed as in mixing roll dough.
2. Allow dough to ferment or raise until it is more than double its original size.
3. Make up dough as for soft rolls.
4. Wash rolls with a hot cornstarch solution made by mixing one ounce of cornstarch in one pint of boiling water. This wash is applied just before placing the rolls in the oven, and immediately upon their removal from the oven.
5. Bake at 425° to 450° F. for 25 or 30 minutes, or until light brown in color.

NO. 26. PARKERHOUSE ROLLS
Yield: Approximately 300 rolls.

Prepare basic dough as in recipe for white bread. Shape into plain rolls. Brush with melted fat. Crease each roll across the center on greased side with a small rolling pin. Fold rolls on the crease. Place close together in greased pans with creased side up. Cover pans; allow to rise until double in size. Bake in hot oven (425° to 450° F.) about 20 minutes.

NO. 27. WHOLE WHEAT BREAD
(100 per cent)
Yield: Approximately 20 1-pound loaves.

Ingredients	100 servings	.... servings
Milk, evaporated	1—14½-ounce can	
Water (for milk)	1 gallon (4 No. 56 dippers)	
Yeast	6 ounces	
Salt	5 ounces (10 mess kit spoons)	
Sugar, granulated	1 pound (½ No. 56 dipper)	
Flour, whole wheat*	15 pounds (13 No. 56 dippers)	
Shortening, softened	1 pound (½ No. 56 dipper)	

*The amount of water will vary according to the type of flour used.

1. Mix milk and water. Scald; cool to 80° F.
2. Soften yeast in milk; add salt and sugar.
3. Add flour and shortening; mix about 10 minutes to make a smooth and elastic dough.
4. Place dough in a warm place (80° F.); allow to rise 2 hours. Punch dough; allow to rise 20 minutes more.
5. Cut dough into 1½-pound pieces; mould evenly into loaves and place in greased 1-pound pans.
6. Allow to rise until double in volume.
7. Bake in hot oven (425° to 450° F.) approximately 30 to 40 minutes.

Note. This recipe may be made by using ⅓ whole wheat flour and ⅔ sifted white flour.

NO. 28. WHOLE WHEAT RAISIN BREAD

Prepare basic dough as in recipe for whole wheat bread, increasing yeast 1 pound. Add 10 pounds raisins during the last 2 or 3 minutes of mixing. Make dough slightly softer by reducing the quantity of flour if raisins are quite dry.

NO. 29. RYE BREAD

Yield: Approximately 20 1-pound loaves.

Ingredients	100 servings	.... servings
Yeast...........................	4 ounces.......................	....
Water, cool..................	1 gallon (4 No. 56 dippers)...........	....
Salt...........................	4 ounces (8 mess kit spoons)...........	....
Sugar, granulated............	3 ounces (6 mess kit spoons).........	....
Caraway seeds, ground (optional).	½ ounce (1½ mess kit spoons).......	....
Flour, white, sifted...........	12 pounds (12 No. 56 dippers).......	....
Flour, rye...................	3 pounds (2¼ No. 56 dippers).......	......'...
Shortening, softened..........	6 ounces (12 mess kit spoons)........	....
Cornmeal......................		....

1. Soften yeast in water; add salt, sugar, and caraway seeds.
2. Add white flour, rye flour and shortening; mix until a smooth dough is obtained. The dough will be somewhat stiffer than that for other breads.
3. Place dough in a warm place (80° F.); allow to rise about 1½ hours. Punch dough; allow to rise 20 minutes more.
4. Cut dough into 1½-pound pieces; mould evenly into loaves.
5. Sprinkle shallow sheet pans with cornmeal. Place loaves 6 inches apart on top of cornmeal. Allow to rise 30 to 40 minutes.
6. Cut the surface of each loaf several times across the width with a sharp knife or razor blade.
7. Bake in hot oven (425° to 450° F.) 35 to 40 minutes.

Note. If a glossy crust is desired, brush loaves before baking with a mixture of boiled cornstarch. Use ⅔ ounce (2 mess kit spoons) cornstarch and 1 quart (1 No. 56 dipper) water.

NO. 30. BOSTON BROWN BREAD

Yield: 100 servings,
2 ounces each

Ingredients	100 servings	.... servings
Graham flour	1⅔ pounds (1½ No. 56 dippers)	
Rye flour	1⅓ pounds (1¼ No. 56 dippers)	
Cornmeal	2 pounds (1⅔ No. 56 dippers)	
Baking soda	1⅓ ounces (2¼ mess kit spoons)	
Salt	1½ ounces (3 mess kit spoons)	
Vinegar	4½ ounces (9 mess kit spoons)	
Milk, evaporated	1½ quarts (1½ No. 56 dippers)	
Water (for milk)	1½ quarts (1½ No. 56 dippers)	
Molasses	4½ pounds (1½ No. 56 dippers)	
Raisins	2 pounds (1⅔ No. 56 dippers)	

1. Sift together the dry ingredients.
2. Add the bran remaining in the sifter to dry ingredients.
3. Mix together the vinegar, milk, water, and molasses.
4. Make a well in the dry ingredients, pour in the liquid mixture and mix as quickly as possible.
5. Add the raisins last.
6. Fill greased molds, or 1-pound cans ⅔ full.
7. Place cans in double roaster or steamer and steam for 3 hours.

NO. 31. BASIC SWEET DOUGH

Yield: 35 pound mixture

Ingredients	100 servings	.... servings
Sugar, granulated	4 pounds (2 No. 56 dippers)	
Shortening	4 pounds (2 No. 56 dippers)	
Salt	5 ounces (10 mess kit spoons)	
Eggs, beaten	30 eggs (1½ No. 56 dippers)	
Milk, evaporated	2—14½-ounce cans	
Water (for milk)	3 quarts (3 No. 56 dippers)	
Yeast	1½ pounds	
Vanilla		
Flour, Sifted	16 pounds (16 No. 56 dippers)	

1. Combine sugar, shortening, and salt; mix thoroughly.
2. Add eggs; beat well.
3. Mix milk and water. Scald; cool to 80° F. Add yeast and vanilla; stir until well mixed. Add to egg mixture.
4. Add flour; mix thoroughly.
5. Place dough in a warm place (80° F.); allow to rise 2 hours or until double in volume. Punch down; allow to rise 15 minutes more.

NO. 32. CINNAMON ROLLS

Divide basic sweet dough into seven pieces of equal size. Roll each into an oblong shape ½ inch thick. Grease each piece with melted shortening. Mix 4 pounds (2 No. 56 dippers) granulated sugar and 1 ounce (4 mess kit spoons) cinnamon together. Sprinkle mixture over pieces of dough. Roll each piece tightly like jelly roll. Cut into pieces ¾ inch thick. Place close together in greased baking pans. Allow to rise until double in size. Bake in hot oven (400° to 450° F.) about 20 minutes.

NO. 33. CINNAMON TWISTS

Divide basic sweet dough into seven pieces of equal size. Form into oblong shapes and allow 10 to 15 minutes recovery periods. Roll each piece into a long thin sheet similar to that used for cinnamon rolls. Grease well with melted fat and cover with sugar and cinnamon mixture (see cinnamon rolls), chopped dried fruit may be added. Fold the dough, forming three layers. Cut the folded dough strips crosswise with a knife or dough scraper into pieces about 1 inch wide. Then twist each piece by placing hands, one on the left and one on the right end of piece, and rolling each end in opposite directions. Proof or let rise to double volume and bake at 400° - 450° F. about 15 to 20 minutes. Serve plain or iced.

NO. 34. RAISED COFFEE CAKE (streussel cake)

Roll 32 to 36 pounds basic sweet dough into sheet approximately ½ inch thick. Place on baking sheet pans. Combine 2 pounds (one No. 56 dipper) granulated sugar, 1 pound (½ No. 56 dipper) butter, 1 pound (½ No. 56 dipper) shortening and ½ ounce (1 mess kit spoon) salt for streussel mixture; mix well. Add 6 ounces (8 mess kit spoons) honey or sirup and 3 pounds (3 No. 56 dippers) sifted flour; stir until a crumb-like mixture is obtained. Sprinkle mixture over dough in baking pans. Bake in hot oven (400° F.) about 30 minutes.

NO. 35. RAISED DOUGHNUTS

Divide basic sweet dough into seven pieces. Allow to rise 15 to 20 minutes. Roll each piece into sheet ½ inch thick. Cut with floured doughnut cutter. Place in pans; cover pans and allow dough to rise about 30 minutes. Place doughnuts, a few at a time, into a kettle of hot fat.* Fry in hot deep fat (350° to 360° F.) until golden brown on under side. Turn and fry on other side. See directions (par. 16) for deep fat frying.

*Use screen if available.

NO. 36. BAKING POWDER BISCUITS   Yield: 25 pounds mixture, 212 biscuits, each 2½ inches diameter

Ingredients	100 servings	.... servings
Flour, sifted	12 pounds (12 No. 56 dippers)	
Baking powder	10 ounces (½ mess kit cup)	
Salt	3 ounces (6 mess kit spoons)	
Shortening	3 pounds (1½ No. 56 dippers)	
Milk, evaporated	4¼—14½-ounce cans	
Water (for milk)*	2½ quarts (2½ No. 56 dippers)	

*The amount of water will vary according to type of flour used.

18

1. Sift flour, baking powder, and salt together. Add shortening; stir until mixture resembles coarse crumbs.
2. Mix milk and water. Add to dry ingredients, mixing only enough to combine dry and liquid ingredients.
3. Place dough on floured bread board and knead lightly. Roll ¾ inch thick; cut dough into biscuits with floured biscuit cutter.
4. Place in baking pans. Bake in hot oven (450° F.) about 15 minutes.

Note. Biscuits may be brushed with melted shortening or milk before baking.

NO. 37. BUTTER BISCUITS

Divide the basic dough into four equal parts. Shape into elongated form and allow to rest on work bench for 15 to 20 minutes so that dough will roll more easily. Roll the pieces of dough to a thickness of about ¼ inch. Keep the dough piece of uniform shape and thickness. Grease the top surface with melted fat. Use sufficient fat to give a well-greased surface. Fold the greased dough to make two layers. Dock or prick the dough with a fork or a regular docker. Force the docker completely through the dough. Cut the biscuits with a biscuit cutter and place close together on a greased sheet pan. Proof until doubled in size, and bake 15 to 20 minutes in hot oven (425° - 450° F.), or to a golden brown.

NO. 38. BUTTERSCOTCH BISCUITS

Prepare biscuit dough as in recipe for baking powder biscuits. Divide dough into 2-pound pieces. Roll each piece into an oblong shape, 20 by 9 by ¼ inches. Combine 12 ounces (⅓ mess kit cup) butter, 3 pounds (2 No. 56 dippers) brown sugar and 1½ pounds (1½ No. 56 dippers) chopped raisins *or* nut meats; mixed well. Sprinkle mixture over dough and roll each piece like jelly roll beginning on long side. Slice into 1-inch pieces. Place in lightly greased baking pans. Bake in hot oven (450° F.) about 15 minutes. Nuts or raisins may be omitted.

NO. 39. CHEESE BISCUITS

Add 3 pounds (3 No. 56 dippers) chopped cheese to recipe for plain biscuits after shortening has been combined with dry ingredients. Add liquid and proceed as for plain biscuits.

NO. 40. CINNAMON BISCUITS

Prepare and roll biscuit dough as in recipe for baking powder biscuits. Combine 3 pounds (1½ No. 56 dippers) sugar ¾ pound (½ mess kit cup) soft butter and 6 ounces (12 mess kit spoons) cinnamon. Spread over dough; sprinkle 3 pounds (2¼ No. 56 dippers) seedless raisins over surface; press into dough lightly with rolling pin. Roll, cut, and bake as for butterscotch biscuits.

NO. 41. SHORTCAKE BISCUITS

Prepare recipe for plain baking powder biscuits using 1 pound (½ No. 56 dipper) granulated sugar and 2 pounds (1 No. 56 dipper) shortening and ½ of all other ingredients. Mix, roll, cut, and bake as for plain biscuits. Split and serve with fruit between the halves and on top.

NO. 42. PLAIN MUFFINS

Yield: Approximately 25 pounds mixture, 250 muffins, each 2¼ inches diameter.

Ingredients	100 servings	.... servings
Flour, sifted	9 pounds (9 No. 56 dippers)	
Sugar, granulated	2½ pounds (1¼ No. 56 dippers)	
Baking powder	7½ ounces (¼ No. 56 dipper)	
Salt	3 ounces (6 mess kit spoons)	
Milk, evaporated	4½—14½-ounce cans	
Water (for milk)	2⅔ quarts (2⅔ No. 56 dippers)	
Eggs, beaten	20 eggs (1 No. 56 dipper)	
Shortening, melted	1½ pounds (¾ No. 56 dipper)	

1. Sift flour, sugar, baking powder, and salt together.
2. Mix milk and water; add beaten egg.
3. Combine dry ingredients, milk mixture, and shortening. Stir only until liquid and dry ingredients are combined. Avoid overmixing.
4. Fill greased muffin pans ⅔ full. Bake in hot oven (400° F.) about 25 minutes.

NO. 43. BLUEBERRY MUFFINS

Add 4 pounds (3 No. 56 dippers) blueberries to sifted dry ingredients in recipe for plain muffins. Add liquid ingredients. mix carefully to prevent mashing blueberries. Bake as for plain muffins.

NO. 44. RAISIN, NUT, OR DATE MUFFINS

Add 4 pounds (3 No. 56 dippers) raisins, 3 pounds (3 No. 56 dippers) chopped nut meats, or 4½ pounds (3 No. 56 dippers) chopped dates to sifted dry ingredients in recipe for plain muffins. Add liquid and proceed as for plain muffins.

NO. 45. SPICE MUFFINS

Sift 2 ounces (8 mess kit spoons) cinnamon and 2 ounces (5½ mess kit spoons) ground cloves with dry ingredients in recipe for plain muffins. Proceed as for plain muffins.

NO. 46. BRAN MUFFINS

Yield: 26 pounds mixture, approximately 250 muffins each 2¼ inches in diameter.

Ingredients	100 servings	.... servings
Milk, evaporated.............	5—14½-ounce cans.................	....
Water (for milk).............	3 quarts (3 No. 56 dippers).........	....
Bran, prepared.............	3 pounds (6 No. 56 dippers).........	....
Sugar, granulated...........	2 pounds (1 No. 56 dipper).........	....
Shortening..............	1½ pounds (¾ No. 56 dipper).......	....
Eggs, beaten................	24 eggs (1¼ No. 56 dippers)........	....
Flour, sifted...............	6 pounds (6 No. 56 dippers).........	....
Baking powder.............	8 ounces (⅓ No. 56 dipper)........	....
Salt.......................	4 ounces (8 mess kit spoons)........	....

1. Mix milk and water. Add bran; soak about 10 minutes.
2. Mix sugar and shortening; stir until smooth. Add beaten egg; mix well.
3. Add soaked bran; mix well.
4. Sift flour, baking powder, and salt together; add to bran mixture, stirring only until dry and liquid ingredients are combined.
5. Spread in greased muffin pans. Bake in hot oven (425° F.) about 20 minutes.

Note. Bran muffin mixture may be baked in sheet pans and cut into pieces. It will yield four pans, each 17 by 24 by 1 inches, 60 pieces per pan, each piece 2½ by 2¾ by 1 inches.

NO. 47. CORNBREAD

Yield: 12 pounds mixture, 120 pieces, each 2⅓ by 2¾ by 1 inches.

Ingredients	100 servings	.... servings
Flour, sifted...............	2 pounds (2 No. 56 dippers).........	....
Sugar, granulated...........	6 ounces (¼ mess kit cup)..........	....
Cornmeal.................	3 pounds (3 mess kit cups).........	....
Baking powder.............	3 ounces (8 mess kit spoons)........	....
Salt.......................	2 ounces (4 mess kit spoons)........	....
Milk, evaporated...........	2—14½-ounce cans.............	....
Water (for milk)...........	1 quart (1 No. 56 dipper)........	....
Eggs, beaten...............	10 eggs (½ No. 56 dipper)........	....
Shortening, melted..........	1 pound (½ No. 56 dipper).........	....

1. Sift flour, sugar, cornmeal, baking powder, and salt together.
2. Mix milk and water; add beaten egg.
3. Add milk and egg mixture to dry ingredients; partially mix. Add melted shortening. Stir only until dry and liquid ingredients are combined. Avoid overmixing.
4. Spread mixture in greased baking pans. Bake in hot oven (425° F.) about 20 minutes.

NO. 48. BACON CORNBREAD

Prepare cornbread reducing the amount of melted shortening to 4 ounces (8 mess kit spoons). Place 2 pounds (1¼ No. 56 dippers) chopped raw bacon over surface of batter in baking pans. Bake as for cornbread. Bacon will be more crisp and brown if mixture is placed under broiler for a few minutes after the bread is baked.

SECTION IV

BREAKFAST FOODS

9. CEREAL COOKERY. a. Table for cooking cereals.

Cereal	Amount	Water[1] (gallons)	Salt[2] (mess kit spoons)	Cooking time (minutes)	Approximate size of serving
Cornmeal.......	6 pounds (4½ No. 56 dippers)	5	6	30	6 ounces (¼ mess kit cup)
Hominy grits.....	6 pounds (4 No. 56 dippers)	6	6	40	6 ounces (¼ mess kit cup)
Oats, rolled.......	6 pounds (8 No. 56 dippers)	6	6	20	6 ounces (¼ mess kit cup)
Rice............	8 pounds (4 No. 56 dippers)	9	6	20	6 ounces (¼ mess kit cup)
Wheat cereal.....	6 pounds (3¾ No. 56 dippers)	4	6	20	6 ounces (¼ mess kit cup)
Whole wheat cereal	6 pounds (4¼ No. 56 dippers)	4	6	20	6 ounces (¼ mess kit cup)

[1]The amount of water needed will vary according to the method of cooking, the type of utensil used, and the length of the cooking period.

[2]It may be necessary to increase the amount of salt.

b. Directions for cooking cereals. (1) Add salt to water; heat to boiling point.

(2) Add cereal slowly to boiling water. Heat to boiling point; reduce heat and simmer until thick, stirring constantly to prevent lumping. When large quantities are cooked, lumping may be prevented by adding the cereal to cold water. Heat to boiling point; stir constantly until mixture thickens.

c. Cooked cereals. (1) Hot cooked cereals may be served with milk and sugar. Raisins, chopped, seeded dates or chopped, dried figs may be added to the cereal a few minutes before serving.

(2) Cooked cornmeal, oatmeal, or hominy grits may be fried. Pour the cooked cereal into well-greased pans to a depth of about 1 inch; cool. Cut into squares and fry. Serve with sirup or jelly. If the squares are moist, dip in flour or batter before frying.

NO. 49. WHEAT GRIDDLE CAKES

Yield: 6 gallons mixture,

100 servings, 4 cakes

per serving, each 4 mess kit

spoons mixture.

Ingredients	100 servings	.... servings
Flour, sifted................	15 pounds (15 No. 56 dippers).......	....
Sugar, granulated...........	1½ pounds (1 mess kit cup)........	....
Baking powder.............	10 ounces (½ mess kit cup)........	....
Salt......................	5 ounces (10 mess kit spoons)........	....
Milk, evaporated...........	11½—14½-ounce cans............	....
Water (for milk)...........	1¾ gallons (7 No. 56 dippers)........	....
Eggs, well beaten...........	50 eggs (2½ No. 56 dippers)........	....
Shortening, melted..........	2¼ pounds (1⅛ No. 56 dippers).....	....

1. Sift flour, sugar, baking powder, and salt together.
2. Mix milk and water; add beaten egg.
3. Combine dry ingredients, milk mixture, and shortening. Stir only until dry and liquid ingredients are mixed and most of the lumps beaten out.
4. Drop batter by spoonfuls onto hot, greased griddle. Cook cakes on one side until top is full of bubbles. Turn and cook on other side. Turn cakes only once.

NO. 50. BUCKWHEAT GRIDDLE CAKES

Yield: 4¾ gallons mixture,
100 servings, 4 cakes per serving, each 3 mess kit spoons mixture.

Ingredients	100 servings	.... servings
Flour, sifted...............	6¼ pounds (6¼ No. 56 dippers).....	....
Flour, buckwheat...........	7¼ pounds (6 No. 56 dippers).......	....
Sugar, granulated..........	2½ pounds (1¼ No. 56 dippers).....	....
Baking powder.............	6⅔ ounces (¼ No. 56 dipper).......	....
Salt......................	5 ounces (10 mess kit spoons)........	....
Milk, evaporated...........	10¼—14½-ounce cans..............	....
Water (for milk)...........	5¾ quarts (5¾ No. 56 dippers).....	....
Eggs, well beaten..........	33 eggs (1½ No. 56 dippers)........	....
Shortening, melted.........	1 pound (½ No. 56 dipper)........	....

1. Sift flour, buckwheat flour, sugar, baking powder, and salt together.
2. Mix milk and water; add beaten egg.
3. Combine dry ingredients, milk mixture, and shortening. Stir only until all dry and liquid ingredients are mixed and most of the lumps beaten out.
4. Drop batter onto hot, greased griddle. Cook cakes on one side until top is full of bubbles. Turn and cook on other side. Turn cakes only once.

NO. 51. CORNMEAL GRIDDLE CAKES

Yield: 4¾ gallons mixture,
100 servings, 4 cakes per serving, each 3 mess kit spoons mixture.

Ingredients	100 servings	.... servings
Flour, sifted...............	11 pounds (11 No. 56 dippers)......	....
Cornmeal..................	3½ pounds (2¾ No. 56 dippers).....	....
Sugar, granulated..........	3 pounds (1½ No. 56 dippers).......	....
Baking powder.............	8¼ ounces (⅓ No. 56 dipper).......	....
Salt......................	5 ounces (10 mess kit spoons)........	....
Milk, evaporated...........	9—14½-ounce cans................	....
Water (for milk)...........	1¼ gallons (5 No. 56 dippers).......	....
Eggs, well beaten..........	45 eggs (2¼ No. 56 dippers)........	....
Shortening, melted.........	1 pound (½ No. 56 dipper)........	....

1. Sift flour, cornmeal, sugar, baking powder, and salt together.
2. Mix milk and water; add beaten egg.
3. Combine dry ingredients, milk mixture, and shortening. Stir only until all dry and liquid ingredients are mixed and most of the lumps beaten out.
4. Drop batter by spoonfuls onto hot, greased griddle. Bake cakes on one side until top is full of bubbles. Turn and bake on other side. Turn cakes only once.

NO. 52. QUICK COFFEE CAKE

Yield: 12 pounds mixture, 120 pieces, each 2⅓ by 2¾ by 1 inches.

Ingredients	100 servings	.... servings
Flour, sifted	3½ pounds (3½ No. 56 dippers)	
Sugar, granulated	3 pounds (1½ No. 56 dippers)	
Baking powder	2½ ounces (7 mess kit spoons)	
Salt	1 ounce (2 mess kit spoons)	
Milk, evaporated	1½—14½-ounce cans	
Water (for milk)	1¾ pints (⅞ No. 56 dipper)	
Eggs, beaten	10 eggs (½ No. 56 dipper)	
Shortening, melted	1 pound (½ No. 56 dipper)	
Butter, melted	½ pound (¼ No. 56 dipper)	
Sugar, brown	1½ pounds (¾ No. 56 dipper)	
Flour, sifted	4 ounces (⅓ mess kit cup)	
Cinnamon	1 ounce (4 mess kit spoons)	

1. Sift flour, sugar, baking powder, and salt together.
2. Mix milk and water; add beaten egg.
3. Combine dry ingredients, milk mixture, and shortening. Stir only until liquid and dry ingredients are combined. Avoid overmixing.
4. Spread mixture in greased baking pans.
5. Mix melted butter, brown sugar, flour, and cinnamon together. Stir until a crumb-like mixture is obtained. Sprinkle over dough in baking pans.
6. Bake in moderate oven (375° F.) about 25 minutes.

NO. 53. APPLE COFFEE CAKE

Prepare quick coffee cake and spread in baking pans. Arrange 4 pounds (4 No. 56 dippers) sliced apples over the top. Mix 1½ pounds (1 No. 56 dipper) brown sugar, 1 ounce (3½ mess kit spoons) cinnamon and ¾ pound (½ mess kit cup) butter together. Sprinkle mixture over apples. Bake in moderate oven (375° F.) 30 to 35 minutes.

NO. 54. POPOVERS

Yield: 100 servings, 2 popovers each.

Ingredients	100 servings	.... servings
Milk, evaporated...........	6—14½-ounce cans...............	....
Water (for milk)...........	3 quarts (3 No. 56 dippers)........	....
Eggs, slightly beaten........	50 eggs (2½ No. 56 dippers).......	....
Flour, sifted...............	6 pounds (6 No. 56 dippers).......	....
Salt......................	1 ounce (2 mess kit spoons)........	....

1. Mix milk and water; add beaten egg. Beat thoroughly.
2. Add flour and salt; continue beating until mixture is smooth.
3. Pour mixture into hot, greased muffin pans. Bake in hot oven (450° F.) 30 minutes. Reduce heat to moderate (350° F.) and continue baking 10 to 15 minutes.
4. Remove from pans and puncture the surface of each popover to allow steam to escape.
5. Serve as soon as possible.

Note. Popovers are done if they feel light when lifted from the pan.

NO. 55. FRENCH TOAST

Yield: 3¾ gallons mixture, 100 servings, 3 slices toast each.

Ingredients	100 servings	.... servings
Milk, evaporated............	13—14½-ounce cans...............	....
Water (for milk)............	6 quarts (6 No. 56 dippers)........	....
Eggs, slightly beaten........	60 eggs (3 No. 56 dippers).........	....
Salt.......................	1 ounce (2 mess kit spoons)........	....
Sugar, granulated..........	¾ pound (½ mess kit cup)........	....
Bread, dry, sliced...........	300 slices.......................	....

1. Mix milk and water; add beaten egg, salt, and sugar. Mix well.
2. Dip slices of bread in milk and egg mixture.
3. Fry on greased griddle until brown on one side. Turn and fry on other side.

NO. 56. MOCK MAPLE SIRUP

Yield: 1 gallon

Ingredients	100 servings	.... servings
Sugar, brown...............	6 pounds (4½ No. 56 dippers)......	....
Water, boiling..............	2½ quarts (2½ No. 56 dippers)......	....
Vanilla.....................	....	....

1. Add sugar to boiling water; stir until sugar is dissolved.
2. Heat to boiling point; boil 10 minutes or until a thin sirup is formed, without stirring. Remove from heat.
3. Add vanilla; cool.

NO. 57. PLAIN SIRUP

Yield: 1 gallon.

Ingredients	100 servings	.... servings
Sugar, granulated............	6 pounds (3 No. 56 dippers)........	....
Water.....................	2 quarts (2 No. 56 dippers).........	....
Salt.......................	.........(⅓ mess kit spoon)........	....
Corn sirup.................	1 pint (½ No. 56 dipper)...........	....

1. Mix sugar, water, salt, and corn sirup together.
2. Heat to boiling point; reduce heat and simmer about 10 minutes or until thin sirup is formed. Cool; cover and store until needed.

NO. 58. MAPLE SIRUP

Add 2⅔ mess kit spoons maple flavoring to recipe for plain sirup after it is removed from the heat.

SECTION V

CAKES AND COOKIES

---

10. "BUTTER" CAKES. a. General. There is an unlimited variety of "butter" cakes, but the same basic ingredients and mixing procedures are used for all of them. The texture and tenderness of the cake depends on the shortening. Use a type of shortening that softens easily and mixes well with other ingredients.

b. Mixing. The quality of a cake is dependent upon the method of handling and combining ingredients. Sift the flour to insure accurate measurement and reduce the amount of mixing required to make a smooth batter. The flour and liquid are added to the shortening and sugar mixture alternately, beginning and ending with flour. The addition of liquid first tends to separate the fat from the other ingredients while the flour binds the ingredients together. Unnecessary beating after the liquid and flour are added will toughen the cake by developing the elasticity of the gluten (the toughening property of the flour).

c. Temperature control. Temperature control is important. Have sugar and shortening at room temperature (70° to 73° F.) to enable easier mixing. Eggs and milk may be colder (about 65° F.) but not at refrigerator temperature. If the batter is too warm, the fat becomes oily; if too cold, the fat hardens and gives the batter a curdled appearance. Under both conditions the cakes will have poor grain and small volume.

d. Baking. Bake cakes at temperatures recommended in the recipes. Too rapid baking gives cakes a hard crust and poor volume; slow baking causes coarse grain and may give cakes a gummy or sticky quality. Over-baking will make dry cakes with hard crusts. When the cake shrinks and pulls away from the sides of the pan it is done. Test the cake by inserting a toothpick; if it comes out clean the cake has been cooked sufficiently. The cake is done if it springs back when pressed with the finger.

e. Care of cakes after baking. Remove cakes from pans while warm. If cakes remain in pans until cold, rust resulting from water condensing on the pan may discolor the cake and affect the flavor. When cool, replace cakes in pans lined with paper and cover tightly to prevent evaporation of moisture when exposed to air. Frost cakes only when cold to prevent frosting from softening and running off the cake. Frosting seals the top surface and prevents loss of moisture.

f. Characteristics. A well mixed and baked cake has a soft golden brown crust which is only slightly rounded. It has a fine, uniform sized grain, and is moist and feels light when lifted. The cake holds its shape when cut.

11. SPONGE CAKE. a. General. Angel food, jelly roll, and sponge cakes are made without shortening. They are leavened by air incorporated into beaten eggs. The quality of this type of cake is dependent upon the number of eggs used and the degree to which they are beaten. The tenderness of the cake depends upon the amount of air incorporated into the mixture as there is no fat added to separate the particles of flour and prevent them from forming a tough product.

b. Angel food cake. (1) *Eggs.* If possible use thin egg whites as they will produce a larger cake than the thicker ones. Have eggs at room temperature. They will yield a larger volume than when at refrigerator temperature. Beat whites until just stiff but not dry. Stiffly beaten egg whites will cause a tough cake with poor volume and grain. Cream of tartar is added to the cake to prevent shrinkage during baking and to bleach the cake, thus making it very white.

(2) *Mixing.* Sift flour several times until fluffy, thereby decreasing the amount of mixing necessary to distribute it. Mix flour with eggs by folding the flour into the eggs rather than by stirring or beating. The flour or sugar prevents the air cells from being broken. Great care must be taken in folding in the flour, otherwise the air cells will be broken and the air lost. After the last amount of flour has been added, mix only until flour disappears.

(3) *Baking.* Bake angel food cakes in ungreased pans. If pan is not greased, the cake will stick to the pan until cold, thus aiding the cake to support its weight. The cake is done when it is brown and pulls away from the sides of the pan. Avoid overbaking as this toughens the cake. After baking, invert pans on racks or rest the edges on props to permit circulation of air around the cake. Prevent the surface of the cake from resting on the rack or props. Remove from pans when cool.

c. Sponge cakes. A true sponge cake differs from an angel food in that the yolks of the eggs are used. Beat the egg yolks until they are light, thick, and fluffy. Overbeating at this stage is impossible. Underbeating produces a compact and soggy cake. Follow the same methods and precautions for sponge cakes as for angel food cakes.

d. Jelly roll. Heat eggs and sugar to 100° F. to hasten the beating and insure a firmer cell structure. This makes a lighter roll as less of the foamy mass will break down when the flour is added. If cake is used for cream roll, turn upside down on cloth covered with sugar, loosen paper, and cover with pan; cool. Thus, the moisture is retained in the cake, making it less likely to crack when rolled.

12. COOKIES. Cookies are easy to mix but need constant attention while baking. Drop cookies can be made from cake dough if more flour or less liquid is added so as to make a stiff batter. A soft cookie dough suitable for rolling can be made from cake dough if still further increase in flour or decrease in liquid is made. Use sheet pans smaller than the oven rack for baking cookies to permit the hot air to circulate around the cookies. Fill pans and stack criss-cross; bake as many as the ovens will hold at one time. Use knife or spatula to remove cookies from pans. Place cookies in single layers on racks or clean paper to cool. Avoid stacking or piling cookies while cooling.

NO. 59. PLAIN CAKE

Yield: 15 pounds mixture,
100 servings, each $3\frac{1}{3}$
by $2\frac{1}{3}$ by $1\frac{1}{4}$ inches.

Ingredients	100 servings	.... servings
Shortening	$1\frac{3}{4}$ pounds ($\frac{7}{8}$ No. 56 dippers)	
Sugar, granulated	$3\frac{3}{4}$ pounds ($1\frac{7}{8}$ No. 56 dippers)	
Eggs	23 eggs ($1\frac{1}{2}$ mess kit cups)	
Flour, sifted	4 pounds (4 No. 56 dippers)	
Baking powder	$2\frac{1}{2}$ ounces ($6\frac{2}{3}$ mess kit spoons)	
Salt	$\frac{1}{2}$ ounce (1 mess kit spoon)	
Milk, evaporated	$1\frac{3}{4}$—$14\frac{1}{2}$-ounce cans	
Water (for milk)	$1\frac{1}{2}$ pints (1 mess kit cup)	
Vanilla	$1\frac{1}{2}$ ounces (3 mess kit spoons)	

1. Stir shortening until soft and smooth.
2. Add sugar gradually; mix thoroughly.
3. Add unbeaten eggs, a few at a time, beating after each addition until well mixed. Beat thoroughly at this stage to insure a light, tender cake.
4. Sift flour, baking powder, and salt together twice.
5. Mix milk and water; add vanilla.
6. Add dry ingredients and milk alternately to sugar and egg mixture, first adding about $\frac{1}{3}$ dry ingredients, then $\frac{1}{2}$ milk, then another $\frac{1}{3}$ dry ingredients and remaining milk and dry ingredients.
7. Mix thoroughly but avoid overmixing.
8. Place in greased sheet pans. Bake in moderate oven (350° F.) 30 to 35 minutes or until done.

Note. This recipe makes two sheet pans (17 by 24 by 1 inches) or eight loaf pans ($9\frac{7}{8}$ by $4\frac{1}{4}$ by $2\frac{3}{4}$ inches) or 200 individual cakes each 3 inches in diameter.

NO. 60. BANANA CAKE

Prepare plain cake reducing baking powder to $1\frac{1}{2}$ ounces (4 mess kit spoons) and adding $\frac{3}{4}$ ounce ($1\frac{1}{2}$ mess kit spoons) baking soda. Reduce evaporated milk to one $14\frac{1}{2}$-ounce can and water to 1 pint ($\frac{1}{2}$ No. 56 dipper). Add $3\frac{3}{4}$ pounds ($1\frac{3}{4}$ No. 56 dippers) peeled, crushed bananas to shortening and sugar. Frost cake with banana or lemon butter cream frosting (recipes Nos. 106 and 108) or cover before baking with cinnamon topping. (See recipe No. 119.)

NO. 61. BOSTON CREAM CAKE

Prepare plain cake; bake in pie tins. Use two thin layers for each cake or if layers are thick, cool and split each in half. Spread cornstarch pudding (recipe No. 132 or 411) between halves or layers. Sprinkle with confectioners or granulated sugar or frost with butter frosting. (See recipe No. 105.)

NO. 62. CHOCOLATE CREAM CAKE

Prepare plain cake; bake in pie tins. Use two thin layers for each cake or if layers are thick, cool and split each in half. Spread chocolate custard (recipe No. 413) between halves or layers. Sprinkle with confectioners or granulated sugar or frost with chocolate butter frosting. (See recipe No. 107.)

NO. 63. GOLD CAKE

Substitute 21 egg yolks* (½ No. 56 dipper) for whole eggs in recipe for plain cake. Use 2 additional ounces (4 mess kit spoons) evaporated milk and 2 additional ounces (4 mess kit spoons) water. Frost with marshmallow or lemon butter frosting (recipes No. 115 and 108) or cover before baking with crumb or cinnamon topping. (See recipes Nos. 125 and 119.)

*Use egg whites for frosting or pie meringue.

NO. 64. LEMON CAKE

Substitute either 2 ounces (4 mess kit spoons) lemon extract or 2½ ounces (10 mess kit spoons) grated lemon rind for vanilla in recipe for plain cake. Frost with lemon butter or banana cream frosting. (See recipes Nos. 108 and 106.)

NO. 65. MAPLE CAKE

Substitute 1¼ ounces (2½ mess kit spoons) maple extract for vanilla in recipe for plain cake. Frost with marshmallow frosting. (See recipe No. 115.)

NO. 66. ORANGE CAKE

Substitute either 2 ounces (4 mess kit spoons) orange extract or 2½ ounces (10 mess kit spoons) grated orange rind for vanilla in recipe for plain cake. Frost with orange butter or banana cream frosting. (See recipes Nos. 110 and 106.)

NO. 67. RAISIN SPICE CAKE

Add 2½ pounds raisins with the last amount of flour in recipe for plain cake. Serve plain or frost with banana cream frosting. (See recipe No. 106.)

NO. 68. SPANISH CAKE

Sift 1¼ ounces (5 mess kit spoons) cinnamon with dry ingredients in recipe for plain cake. Frost with lemon butter or mocha butter frosting (recipes Nos. 108 and 109) or cover before baking with cinnamon topping. (See recipe No. 119.)

NO. 69. SPICE CAKE

Substitute ½ pint (¼ No. 56 dipper) molasses for 9 ounces of the sugar in recipe for plain cake. Add molasses with the milk. Sift ¼ ounce (1 mess kit spoon) cinnamon with dry ingredients. Serve plain or frost with lemon butter or marshmallow frosting. (See recipes Nos. 108 and 115.)

NO. 70. WASHINGTON PIE

Prepare plain cake; bake in pie tins. Use two thin layers for each cake or if layers are thick, cool and split each in half. Spread jam or jelly between halves or layers. Sprinkle with confectioners or granulated sugar or frost with jelly frosting. (See recipe No. 112.)

NO. 71. WHITE CAKE

Substitute 20 egg whites* (½ No. 56 dipper) for whole eggs in recipe for plain cake. Frost with chocolate butter frosting, or peanut butter frosting (recipe No. 107 or 111) or cover before baking with toasted nut topping. (See recipe No. 121.)

*Use egg yolks in custard, scrambled eggs, or mayonnaise.

NO. 72. APPLESAUCE CAKE

Yield: 15¼ pounds mixture, 100 servings, each 3⅓ by 2⅓ by 1 inches.

Ingredients	100 servings	.... servings
Shortening	1¾ pounds (⅞ No. 56 dipper)	
Sugar, granulated	3¼ pounds (1⅝ No. 56 dippers)	
Eggs	9 eggs (½ No. 56 dipper)	
Flour, sifted	3½ pounds (3½ No. 56 dippers)	
Baking powder	1¼ ounces (3⅓ mess kit spoons)	
Baking soda	¾ ounce (1½ mess kit spoons)	
Salt	½ ounce (1 mess kit spoon)	
Cinnamon	½ ounce (2 mess kit spoons)	
Cloves, ground	¼ ounce (1 mess kit spoon)	
Applesauce	2¼ quarts (2¼ No. 56 dippers)	
Raisins	1¾ pounds (1⅓ No. 56 dippers)	

1. Stir shortening until soft and smooth.
2. Add sugar gradually; mix thoroughly.

3. Add unbeaten eggs a few at a time, beating after each addition until well mixed. Beat thoroughly at this stage to insure a light, tender cake.
4. Sift flour, baking powder, soda, salt, cinnamon, and cloves together twice.
5. Add dry ingredients and applesauce alternately to egg and sugar mixture, first adding about ⅓ dry ingredients, then ½ applesauce, then another ⅓ dry ingredients, and remaining applesauce and dry ingredients. Add raisins with last amount of dry ingredients.
6. Mix thoroughly but avoid overmixing.
7. Place in greased sheet pans. Bake in moderate oven (350° F.) 30 to 35 minutes or until done.

Note. This recipe makes two sheet pans (18 by 26 by 1 inches) or 7 loaf pans (9⅞ by 4¼ by 2¾ inches). Serve cake plain or frost with lemon or banana butter cream frosting. (See recipes Nos. 108 or 106.)

NO. 73. DEVIL'S FOOD CAKE

Yield: 15½ pounds mixture, 100 servings, each 3⅓ by 3⅓ by 1¼ inches.

Ingredients	100 servings	.... servings
Shortening	1⅛ pounds (¾ No. 56 dipper)	
Sugar, granulated	4½ pounds (2¼ No. 56 dippers)	
Eggs	17 eggs (¾ No. 56 dipper)	
Flour, sifted	3½ pounds (3½ No. 56 dippers)	
Baking powder	½ ounce (1⅓ mess kit spoons)	
Baking soda	¾ ounce (1½ mess kit spoons)	
Salt	½ ounce (1 mess kit spoon)	
Cocoa	1⅛ pounds (1⅓ No. 56 dippers)	
Vinegar	2 ounces (4 mess kit spoons)	
Milk, evaporated	1—14½-ounce can	
Water (for milk)	1 quart (1 No. 56 dipper)	
Vanilla	1 ounce (2 mess kit spoons)	

1. Stir shortening until soft and smooth.
2. Add sugar gradually; mix thoroughly.
3. Add unbeaten eggs a few at a time, beating after each addition until well mixed. Beat thoroughly at this stage to insure a light, tender cake.
4. Sift flour, baking powder, soda, salt, and cocoa together twice.
5. Combine vinegar, milk, water, and vanilla.
6. Add dry ingredients and liquid alternately to egg and sugar mixture, first adding about ⅓ dry ingredients, then ½ liquid, then another ⅓ dry ingredients and remaining milk and dry ingredients.
7. Mix thoroughly but avoid overmixing.
8. Place in greased sheet pans. Bake in moderate oven (350° F.) 30 to 35 minutes or until done.

Note. This recipe makes 2 sheet pans (18 by 26 by 1 inches) or 8 loaf pans (9⅞ by 4¼ by 2¾ inches) or 200 individual cakes each 3 inches in diameter. Frost devil's food cake with butter cream, fudge, peanut butter, or marshmallow frostings (recipes Nos. 105, 113, 111, or 115) or cover before baking with coconut topping. (See recipe No. 120.)

NO. 74. MARBLE CAKE

Prepare ½ recipe for devil's food cake and ½ recipe for plain or white cake. Drop small amounts of cake mixture into greased loaf pans, alternating dark and light mixtures. Bake as directed for devil's food cake. Serve plain or frost with butter cream, marshmallow, or fudge frostings. (See recipes Nos. 105, 115 or 113.)

NO. 75. GINGERBREAD

Yield: 15¼ pounds mixture, 100 servings, each 3⅛ by 2⅛ by 1¼ inches.

Ingredients	100 servings	.... servings
Shortening	1 pound (½ No. 56 dipper)	....
Sugar, granulated	1½ pounds (¾ No. 56 dipper)	....
Eggs	5 eggs (¼ No. 56 dipper)	....
Molasses	1¾ quarts (1¾ No. 56 dippers)	....
Flour, sifted	4½ pounds (4½ No. 56 dippers)	....
Baking powder	¾ ounce (2 mess kit spoons)	....
Baking soda	1½ ounces (2½ mess kit spoons)	....
Salt	½ ounce (1 mess kit spoon)	....
Ginger	1¼ ounces (5 mess kit spoons)	....
Cinnamon	½ ounce (2 mess kit spoons)	....
Water	1½ quarts (1½ No. 56 dippers)	....

1. Stir shortening until soft and smooth.
2. Add sugar gradually; mix thoroughly.
3. Add unbeaten eggs a few at a time, beating after each addition until well mixed. Beat thoroughly at this stage to insure a light, tender cake.
4. Add molasses and beat well.
5. Sift flour, baking powder, soda, salt, ginger, and cinnamon together twice.
6. Add dry ingredients and water alternately to egg and sugar mixture, first adding about ⅓ dry ingredients, then ½ water, then another ⅓ dry ingredients and remaining water and dry ingredients.
7. Mix thoroughly but avoid overmixing.
8. Place in greased sheet pans. Bake in moderate oven (350° F.) 30 to 35 minutes or until done.

Note. This recipe makes 2 sheet pans (18 by 26 by 1 inches) or 7 loaf pans (9⅞ by 4¼ by 2¾ inches) or 200 individual cakes each 3 inches in diameter.

NO. 76. UPSIDE DOWN CAKE

Yield: 17½ pounds mixture, 100 servings, each 2 by 2¼ by 1¾ inches.

Ingredients	100 servings	.... servings
Shortening	1 pound (½ No. 56 dipper)	
Sugar, granulated	2¾ pounds (1⅜ No. 56 dippers)	
Eggs	9 eggs (½ No. 56 dipper)	
Flour, sifted	3½ pounds (3½ No. 56 dippers)	
Baking powder	2½ ounces (6⅔ mess kit spoons)	
Salt	¼ ounce (½ mess kit spoon)	
Milk, evaporated	2—14½-ounce cans	
Water	1¾ pints (⅞ No. 56 dipper)	
Vanilla	¼ ounce (½ mess kit spoon)	
Butter	1 pound (½ No. 56 dipper)	
Sugar, granulated	1½ pounds (¾ No. 56 dipper)	
Fruit, crushed, sliced or halved, drained	1½ quarts (1½ No. 56 dippers)	
Fruit juice or sirup	1 pint (½ No. 56 dipper)	

1. Stir shortening until soft and smooth.
2. Add sugar gradually; mix thoroughly.
3. Add unbeaten eggs, a few at a time, beating after each addition until well mixed; continue beating until light and fluffy. Beat thoroughly at this stage to insure a light, tender cake.
4. Sift flour, baking powder, and salt together twice.
5. Mix milk and water; add vanilla.
6. Add dry ingredients and milk alternately to egg and sugar mixture, first adding about ⅓ dry ingredients, then ½ milk, then another ⅓ dry ingredients and remaining milk and dry ingredients.
7. Mix thoroughly but avoid overmixing.
8. Stir butter until soft and smooth; add sugar gradually and mix well.
9. Spread butter and sugar mixture generously in shallow pans.
10. Cover with fruit and sirup or juice making ½-inch layer.
11. Pour layer of cake batter ½ inch thick over fruit. Bake in moderate oven (350° F.) 30 to 40 minutes or until done.
12. Cool slightly; loosen from sides of pans and turn out upside down on trays.

Note. Bake upside down cake in pans which are at least 2 inches deep.

NO. 77. APRICOT UPSIDE DOWN CAKE

Use canned or freshly cooked apricots and apricot juice for the fruit and fruit juice in recipe for upside down cake.

NO. 78. PEACH UPSIDE DOWN CAKE

Use canned, sliced peaches, and peach juice for the fruit and fruit juice in recipe for upside down cake.

NO. 79. PINEAPPLE UPSIDE DOWN CAKE

Use canned, crushed pineapple, and pineapple juice for the fruit and fruit juice in recipe for upside down cake.

NO. 80. RAISIN UPSIDE DOWN CAKE

Prepare upside down cake. Combine ¾ pound (½ mess kit cup) soft butter 1¼ pounds (¾ No. 56 dipper) granulated sugar and ¾ ounce (3 mess kit spoons) grated orange rind; mix well. Spread in bottom of shallow pans. Combine 2¼ pounds (1¾ No. 56 dippers) raisins ¾ pound (½ mess kit cup) granulated sugar and 2¼ pints (1⅛ No. 56 dippers) water; heat to boiling point and boil 5 minutes. Cool. Cover butter and sugar mixture with cooked raisins. Add cake batter and bake as directed for upside down cake.

NO. 81. PRUNE AND APRICOT UPSIDE DOWN CAKE

Use equal amounts of cooked, dried apricots, and cooked prunes, and apricot and prune juice for the fruit and fruit juice in recipe for upside down cake.

NO. 82. HOLIDAY FRUIT CAKE
Yield: 19 pounds mixture, 100 servings, 2¾ ounces each.

Ingredients	100 servings	.... servings
Raisins, seedless	1½ pounds (1⅛ No. 56 dippers)	
Currants	1½ pounds (1¼ No. 56 dippers)	
Pineapple, candied, diced	1½ pounds (¾ No. 56 dipper)	
Citron	1½ pounds (1¼ No. 56 dippers)	
Cherries, candied	1½ pounds (1¼ No. 56 dippers)	
Lemon juice	3 ounces (6 mess kit spoons)	
Orange rind, grated	4 ounces (⅓ mess kit cup)	
Cider or fruit juice	1 pint (½ No. 56 dipper)	
Butter or shortening	2 pounds (1 No. 56 dipper)	
Sugar, brown	2 pounds (1½ No. 56 dippers)	
Eggs	20 eggs (1 No. 56 dipper)	
Molasses	4 ounces (8 mess kit spoons)	
Flour, sifted	2¼ pounds (2¼ No. 56 dippers)	
Baking powder	¼ ounce (⅔ mess kit spoon)	
Cinnamon	1 ounce (4 mess kit spoons)	
Cloves, ground	½ ounce (2 mess kit spoons)	
Allspice	¼ ounce (1 mess kit spoon)	

1. Combine fruits, lemon juice, orange rind, and cider. Cover and allow to stand overnight.
2. Stir shortening until soft and smooth.
3. Add brown sugar gradually, beating until light and fluffy.
4. Add unbeaten eggs a few at a time, beating after each addition until well mixed; continue beating until light and fluffy. Add molasses and mix well.

5. Sift flour, baking powder, and spices together twice; add gradually to sugar mixture, beating after each addition until well mixed. Add fruit with last amount of dry ingredients; mix well.
6. Mix thoroughly but avoid overmixing.
7. Place in greased loaf pans lined with greased paper. Bake in slow oven (200° F.). Increase heat gradually to moderate (325° F.) during last half of baking period. Time will vary from 3 to 4 hours according to the size of the loaves.

Note. This recipe makes 7 loaf pans (9⅞ by 4¼ by 2¾ inches).

NO. 83. PRUNE CAKE

Yield: 14¾ pounds mixture, 100 servings, each 3⅓ by 3⅛ by 1¼ inches.

Ingredients	100 servings	.... servings
Shortening	1⅓ pounds (¾ No. 56 dipper)	
Sugar, granulated	3½ pounds (1¾ No. 56 dippers)	
Eggs	13 eggs (⅔ No. 56 dipper)	
Flour, sifted	4½ pounds (4½ No. 56 dippers)	
Baking powder	2½ ounces (6⅔ mess kit spoons)	
Baking soda	½ ounce (1 mess kit spoon)	
Salt	½ ounce (1 mess kit spoon)	
Cloves, ground	¼ ounce (1 mess kit spoon)	
Allspice	½ ounce (2 mess kit spoons)	
Cinnamon	1½ ounces (6 mess kit spoons)	
Milk, evaporated	1¾—14½-ounce cans	
Water (for milk)	1½ pints (¾ No. 56 dipper)	
Prunes, cooked, chopped	1⅓ quarts (1⅓ No. 56 dippers)	

1. Stir shortening until soft and smooth.
2. Add sugar gradually; mix thoroughly.
3. Add unbeaten eggs, a few at a time, beating after each addition until well mixed. Continue beating until light and fluffy. Beat thoroughly at this stage to insure a light, tender cake.
4. Sift flour, baking powder, soda, and spices together twice.
5. Mix milk and water; add vanilla.
6. Add dry ingredients and milk alternately to egg and sugar mixture, first adding about ⅓ dry ingredients, then ½ milk, then another ⅓ dry ingredients and remaining milk and dry ingredients.
7. Add prunes. Mix thoroughly but avoid overmixing.
8. Place in greased sheet pans. Bake in moderate oven (350° F.) about 30 to 35 minutes.

Note. This recipe makes 2 sheet pans (18 by 26 by 1 inches) or 8 loaf pans (9⅞ by 4¼ by 2¾ inches) or 200 individual cakes each 3 inches in diameter.

NO. 84 OLD FASHIONED RAISIN CAKE   Yield: 19 pounds mixture, 100 3-ounce servings.

Ingredients	100 servings	.... servings
Raisins, seedless	4 pounds (4 mess kit cups)	
Salt	1 ounce (2 mess kit spoons)	
Allspice	¼ ounce (1 mess kit spoon)	
Cinnamon	½ ounce (2 mess kit spoons)	
Cloves, ground	¼ ounce (1 mess kit spoon)	
Nutmeg	¼ ounce (1 mess kit spoon)	
Water, boiling	2 quarts (2 No. 56 dippers)	
Sugar, brown	4 pounds (4 mess kit cups)	
Shortening	1¼ pounds (⅞ mess kit cup)	
Flour, sifted	4 pounds (4 No. 56 dippers)	
Baking soda	1¼ ounces (2½ mess kit spoons)	

1. Wash raisins. Combine raisins, salt, allspice, cinnamon, cloves, nutmeg and water. Heat to boiling point. Remove from heat.
2. Add sugar and shortening; stir until sugar is dissolved. Cool.
3. Sift flour and soda together; add slowly to liquid mixture. Mix well.
4. Pour batter into well-greased and floured pans. Bake in moderate oven (350° F.) about 45 minutes.

Note. Frost with sea foam frosting (recipe No. 118) or serve hot or cold with hard sauce (recipe No. 539) or lemon sauce. (See recipe No. 540.)

NO. 85. ANGEL FOOD CAKE   Yield: 11½ pounds mixture, 100 servings, 1¾ ounces each.

Ingredients	100 servings	.... servings
Egg whites	80 eggs (4 No. 56 dippers)	
Cream of tartar	1¼ ounces (3¾ mess kit spoons)	
Salt	½ ounce (1 mess kit spoon)	
Vanilla	½ ounce (1 mess kit spoon)	
Sugar, granulated	5 pounds (2½ No. 56 dippers)	
Flour, sifted	1¾ pounds (1¾ No. 56 dippers)	

1. Have egg whites at room temperature (70° F.); add cream of tartar and salt. Beat 2 to 3 minutes or until egg whites are foamy.*
2. Add flavoring and ½ sugar slowly, beating constantly.
3. Continue beating until just stiff enough to hold up in peaks but not dry.
4. Sift flour and remaining sugar together five times.
5. Fold flour and sugar mixture carefully into egg whites, mixing just enough to combine well.
6. Fill ungreased angel food tins ⅔ full. Bake in slow oven (325° F.) 25 to 30 minutes or until done.
7. Cool before serving.

*The slightest quantity of grease or egg yolk in the egg whites will injure the beating of the white and cause baking failure.

Note. Serve plain or frost with jelly frosting, chocolate, orange, or lemon butter frosting. (See recipes Nos. 112, 107, 110, or 108.)

NO. 86. SPONGE CAKE

Yield: 11½ pounds mixture,
100 servings, 1¾
ounces each.

Ingredients	100 servings	.... servings
Egg yolks...........	36 yolks (4/5 No. 56 dipper)........	....
Sugar, granulated...........	3½ pounds (1¾ No. 56 dippers).....	....
Water, hot..............	1⅛ pints (⅝ No. 56 dipper)........	....
Vanilla................	1 ounce (2 mess kit spoons)........	....
Lemon extract...........	¾ ounce (1½ mess kit spoons)......	....
Flour, sifted............	2¼ pounds (2¼ No. 56 dippers).....	....
Salt.................	½ ounce (1 mess kit spoon)........	....
Egg whites.............	36 whites (4/5 No. 56 dipper)	....

1. Mix egg yolks and ½ sugar; beat 15 to 20 minutes.
2. Combine water, vanilla, and lemon extract; add to egg mixture. Mix thoroughly.
3. Sift flour and salt together twice. Add to egg mixture, mixing only enough to combine.
4. Beat egg whites until light and foamy; add remaining sugar gradually. Continue beating until stiff enough to hold up in peaks but not dry.
5. Fold egg whites carefully into egg yolk mixture, mixing only enough to combine well.
6. Fill ungreased 50-ration pans ⅔ full. Bake in slow oven (325° F.) 25 to 30 minutes or until done.
7. Cool before serving.

Note. This recipe makes three 50-ration pans, 3¾ pounds mixture each.
Serve plain or frost with lemon or orange butter cream frostings. (See recipes Nos. 108 or 110.)
Sponge cakes also may be served with ice cream (recipe No. 152) or with a fruit sauce. (See recipes Nos. 536 or 537.)

NO. 87. JELLY ROLL

Yield: 8 pounds mixture,
100 servings, 1¼
ounces each, 25 portions
to each roll.

Ingredients	100 servings	.... servings
Eggs......................	32 eggs (1½ No. 56 dippers)........	....
Sugar, granulated...........	2 pounds (1 No. 56 dipper)........	....
Water, hot..............	¾ pint (½ No. 56 dipper)........	....
Vanilla...............	½ ounce (1 mess kit spoon)........	....
Flour, sifted..............	2 pounds (2 No. 56 dippers)........	....
Baking powder..............	2 ounces (5⅓ mess kit spoons).......	....
Salt.....................	1 ounce (2 mess kit spoons)........	....

1. Mix eggs and sugar; heat over hot water until warm (110° F.), stirring constantly.
2. Beat rapidly 15 to 20 minutes or until mixture is fluffy and thick.

40

3. Mix water and vanilla; add to egg mixture.
4. Sift flour, baking powder, and salt together twice; fold carefully into egg mixture, mixing only enough to combine ingredients.
5. Spread on greased baking sheets lined with greased paper. Bake in hot oven (400° F.) 5 to 6 minutes.
6. Turn at once from pans onto cloth covered with powdered sugar.
7. Remove paper; spread with jelly* and roll.

*A cream filling such as vanilla or chocolate (recipes Nos. 105, 107) may be used instead of jelly.

Note. This recipe makes four sheet pans (18 by 26 by 1 inches).

NO. 88. CAKE DOUGHNUTS

Yield: 30-pound mixture, 225 2-ounce pieces.

Ingredients	100 servings	.... servings
Sugar, granulated	5½ pounds (2¾ No. 56 dippers)	
Shortening	1½ pounds (¾ No. 56 dippers)	
Salt	2 ounces (4 mess kit spoons)	
Eggs	40 eggs (2 No. 56 dippers)	
Milk, evaporated	1 pound 12 ounces (1 No. 56 dipper)	
Water (for milk)	2 pounds (1 No. 56 dipper)	
Flour, sifted	14 pounds (14 No. 56 dippers)	
Baking powder	14 ounces (½ No. 56 dipper)	

1. Cream the shortening, sugar, and salt thoroughly.
2. Add the eggs to the above mixture and mix until smooth.
3. Blend the milk and water together and add to the mixture.
4. Sift flour and baking powder together at least three times and add to the mixture and mix until smooth.
5. Roll the mixture on a floured table to a thickness of ½ inch, and cut with a doughnut cutter. Fry in deep fat at 360° F. until brown.

NO. 89. SUGAR COOKIES

Yield: 8½ pounds mixture, 204 cookies, each 3½ inches in diameter.

Ingredients	100 servings	.... servings
Flour, sifted	3 pounds (3 No. 56 dippers)	
Baking powder	1⅛ ounces (3 mess kit spoons)	
Salt	½ ounce (1 mess kit spoon)	
Shortening	1½ pounds (1 mess kit cup)	
Sugar, granulated	2¾ pounds (2¼ mess kit cups)	
Eggs, beaten	6 eggs (⅓ No. 56 dipper)	
Vanilla	½ ounce (1 mess kit spoon)	
Milk, evaporated	2—14½-ounce cans	
Water (for milk)	½ pint (⅓ mess kit cup)	
Sugar, granulated (for topping)	8 ounces (⅓ mess kit cup)	
Cinnamon (for topping)	1 ounce (4 mess kit spoons)	

1. Sift flour, baking powder, and salt together.
2. Mix shortening and sugar; stir until light and fluffy.

3. Add beaten egg gradually, mixing well after each addition; add vanilla.

4. Mix milk and water. Add flour mixture and milk alternately to sugar mixture, mixing well after each addition.

5. Mix sugar and cinnamon.

6. Drop cookie mixture by spoonfuls onto ungreased baking pans. Sprinkle with sugar and cinnamon mixture.

7. Bake in moderate oven (375° F.) 12 to 15 minutes.

8. Remove from pans at once.

Note. Cookie dough may be rolled ⅛ inch thick on lightly floured board and cut with floured cookie cutter.

NO. 90. CHOCOLATE COOKIES

Substitute 10 ounces (1 mess kit cup) cocoa for ¾ pound (1 mess kit cup) flour in recipe for suger cookies. Sift cocoa with remaining flour and other dry ingredients.

NO. 91. CHOCOLATE NUT COOKIES

Substitute 10 ounces (1 mess kit cup) cocoa for ¾ pound (1 mess kit cup) flour in recipe for sugar cookies. Sift cocoa with remaining flour and other dry ingredients. Add ¾ pound (1 mess kit cup) broken nut meats to the sifted flour mixture. Mix well.

NO. 92. GINGER COOKIES

Sift 1½ ounces (3 mess kit spoons) soda, ¾ ounce (3 mess kit spoons) ginger and ¼ ounce (1 mess kit spoon) cinnamon with flour in recipe for sugar cookies. Substitute 1⅛ pounds (½ mess kit cup) molasses for the evaporated milk and water; mix well.

NO. 93. PEANUT COOKIES

Add 1½ pounds (1 No. 56 dipper) chopped peanuts to the sifted flour in recipe for sugar cookies.

NO. 94. SPICE COOKIES

Sift ½ ounce (2 mess kit spoons) cinnamon, ¼ ounce (1 mess kit spoon) nutmeg and ⅛ ounce (½ mess kit spoon) ground cloves with flour in recipe for sugar cookies.

NO. 95. RAISIN COOKIES

Add 3 pounds (3 mess kit cups) seedless raisins to sifted flour in recipe for sugar cookies.

NO. 96. APPLESAUCE COOKIES

Yield: 11 pounds mixture, 200 cookies, each 3 inches in diameter.

Ingredients	100 servings	.... servings
Flour, sifted..................	3 pounds (3 No. 56 dippers).........	....
Baking powder..............	¾ ounce (2 mess kit spoons)........	
Salt.......................	½ ounce (1 mess kit spoon).........	....
Baking soda................	¼ ounce (½ mess kit spoon)........	
Cinnamon..................	(½ mess kit spoon).................	
Nutmeg...................	(⅛ mess kit spoon)................	
Raisins....................	1 pound (1 mess kit cup)...........	
Shortening.................	1 pound (½ No. 56 dipper).........	
Sugar, granulated...........	2 pounds (1 No. 56 dipper)........	
Eggs, beaten...............	5 eggs (¼ No. 56 dipper)..........	......
Applesauce, thick...........	1⅛ quarts (1⅛ No. 56 dipper)......	

1. Sift flour, baking powder, salt, soda, and spices together. Add raisins; mix well.
2. Mix shortening and sugar; stir until light and fluffy.
3. Add beaten egg gradually, mixing well after each addition. All applesauce.
4. Add flour mixture gradually, mix well.
5. Drop by spoonfuls on ungreased baking pans. Bake in hot oven (400° F.) 8 to 10 minutes.
6. Remove from pans at once.

NO. 97. BANANA DROP COOKIES

Yield: 14¼ pounds mixture, 225 cookies, each 3 inches in diameter.

Ingredients	100 servings	.... servings
Flour, sifted..................	3¾ pounds (3¾ No. 56 dippers).....	....
Baking powder..............	1¾ ounces (3½ mess kit spoons).....	
Baking soda................	⅙ ounce (⅓ mess kit spoon)........	
Salt.......................	¾ ounce (1½ mess kit spoons).......	
Shortening.................	2½ pounds (1¼ No. 56 dippers).....	
Sugar, granulated...........	3¼ pounds (2¼ mess kit cups)......	
Eggs......................	15 eggs (¾ No. 56 dipper)..........	
Vanilla....................	1½ ounces (3 mess kit spoons)......	
Bananas, ripe, peeled, mashed.	3¾ pounds (2½ mess kit cups)....	
Sugar, granulated (for topping)	....	
Cinnamon (for topping).......		

1. Sift flour, baking powder, soda, and salt together.
2. Mix shortening and sugar; stir until light and fluffy.
3. Add eggs gradually, mixing well after each addition; add vanilla.
4. Add flour mixture and bananas alternately, mixing well after each addition.
5. Mix sugar and cinnamon.
6. Drop cookie mixture by spoonfuls on ungreased baking pans. Sprinkle with cinnamon mixture. Bake in hot oven (400° F.) 10 to 12 minutes.
7. Remove from pans at once.

NO. 98. BROWNIES

Yield: 17 pounds mixture,
218 cookies, each 2
inches square.

Ingredients	100 servings	.... servings
Flour, sifted..................	2⅛ pounds (2⅛ No. 56 dippers).....	....
Baking powder..............	¾ ounce (2 mess kit spoons)........	....
Salt......................	½ ounce (1 mess kit spoon)........	....
Cocoa.....................	1 pound (1¼ No. 56 dippers).......	....
Raisins, seedless............	3 pounds (3 mess kit cups)........	....
Shortening.................	2½ pounds (1¼ No. 56 dippers).....	....
Sugar, granulated...........	5½ pounds (2¾ No. 56 dippers).....	....
Eggs, beaten...............	26 eggs (1¼ No. 56 dippers).......	....
Vanilla...................	2 ounce (4 mess kit spoons)........	....

1. Sift flour, baking powder, salt, and cocoa together. Add raisins; mix well.
2. Mix shortening and sugar; stir until light and fluffy.
3. Add beaten egg gradually, mixing well after each addition; add vanilla.
4. Add flour mixture and mix only enough to dampen flour.
5. Spread mixture about ¾ inch thick in well-greased baking pans. Bake in slow oven (325° F.) 35 minutes.
6. Cut into 2-inch squares at once. Turn out onto rack to cool.

NO. 99. NUT BROWNIES

Substitute 1¾ pounds (1½ No. 56 dippers) broken nut meats for raisins in recipe for brownies.

NO. 100. FRUIT BARS

Yield: 18 pound mixture,
225 cookies.

Ingredients	100 servings	.... servings
Sugar, granulated...........	2½ pounds (1¼ No. 56 dippers).....	....
Salt.....................	1¼ ounces (2½ mess kit spoons).....	....
Cinnamon.................	1¼ ounces (5 mess kit spoons).....	....
Ginger...................	⅝ ounce (2½ mess kit spoons)......	....
Baking soda...............	1¼ ounces (2½ mess kit spoons).....	....
Shortening................	1¾ pounds (⅞ No. 56 dipper)......	....
Eggs.....................	16 eggs (¾ No. 56 dipper).......	....
Molasses or brown sugar......	2½ pounds (⅞ No. 56 dipper)......	....
Raisins, seedless, or other fruit.	3¾ pounds (2½ No. 56 dippers).....	....
Flour, sifted...............	5 pounds (5 No. 56 dippers).......	....

1. Combine sugar, salt, cinnamon, ginger, soda, and shortening; stir until light and fluffy.
2. Mix eggs and molasses or brown sugar; beat well.
3. Add egg and molasses mixture to sugar mixture in three parts, beating until light after each addition.
4. Add fruit and flour; mix until a smooth dough is formed.

5. Place dough on sheet cakepans, using ½ No. 56 dipper dough to each pan; flatten with spatula until ½ inch thick. Bake in hot oven (380° to 400° F.) 18 to 20 minutes.
6. Cool. Cut each strip into 12 pieces.

NO. 101. MOLASSES CRUMB COOKIES
Yield: 14½ pounds mixture, 232 cookies, each 3½ inches in diameter.

Ingredients	100 servings	.... servings
Flour, sifted	4 pounds (4 No. 56 dippers)	
Baking powder	1½ ounces (4 mess kit spoons)	
Baking soda	1 ounce (2 mess kit spoons)	
Salt	1 ounce (2 mess kit spoons)	
Ginger	½ ounce (2 mess kit spoons)	
Cinnamon	½ ounce (2 mess kit spoons)	
Cloves, ground	½ ounce (2 mess kit spoons)	
Cake crumbs	1½ pounds (2½ mess kit cups)	
Shortening	1½ pounds (1 mess kit cup)	
Sugar, granulated	3 pounds (1½ No. 56 dippers)	
Eggs, beaten	10 eggs (½ No. 56 dipper)	
Molasses	2¾ pounds (1⅛ mess kit cup)	
Water	¾ pint (½ mess kit cup)	

1. Sift flour, baking powder, baking soda, salt, and spices together. Add cake crumbs; mix well.
2. Mix shortening and sugar; stir until light and fluffy.
3. Add beaten egg and molasses gradually, mixing well after each addition.
4. Add flour mixture and water alternately, mixing well after each addition.
5. Drop by spoonfuls onto greased baking pans. Bake in moderate oven (350° F.) 10 to 12 minutes.
6. Remove from pans at once.

NO. 102. OATMEAL COOKIES
Yield: 12½ pounds mixture, 200 cookies, each 3 inches in diameter.

Ingredients	100 servings	.... servings
Flour, sifted	2¼ pounds (2¼ No. 56 dippers)	
Baking powder	1¼ ounces (2¾ mess kit spoons)	
Salt	¾ ounce (1½ mess kit spoons)	
Cinnamon	⅜ ounce (1½ mess kit spoons)	
Nutmeg	(½ mess kit spoon)	
Cloves, ground	(¼ mess kit spoon)	
Shortening	2¼ pounds (1⅛ No. 56 dippers)	
Sugar, granulated	2¼ pounds (1⅛ No. 56 dippers)	
Eggs	7 eggs (⅓ No. 56 dipper)	
Oats, rolled	1¼ pounds (1⅔ No. 56 dippers)	
Raisins, seedless	1½ pounds (1⅛ No. 56 dippers)	
Milk, evaporated	1—14½-ounce can	
Water (for milk)	1¼ pints (¾ mess kit cup)	

1. Sift flour, baking powder, salt, and spices together.
2. Mix shortening and sugar; stir until light and fluffy.

3. Add eggs gradually, mixing well after each addition.
4. Add rolled oats and raisins; mix thoroughly.
5. Mix milk and water. Add flour mixture and milk alternately to oatmeal mixture, mixing well after each addition.
6. Drop by spoonfuls onto ungreased baking pans. Bake in hot oven (400° F.) 12 to 15 minutes.
7. Remove from pans at once.

NO. 103. BANANA OATMEAL COOKIES

Substitute ½ ounce (1 mess kit spoon) baking soda for baking powder and 3 pounds (2 mess kit cups) peeled, mashed ripe bananas for evaporated milk and water in recipe for oatmeal cookies.

NO. 104. VANILLA WAFERS

Yield: 10 pound mixture, 175 wafers.

Ingredients	100 servings	.... servings
Flour, sifted..................	3¾ pounds (3¾ No. 56 dippers).....	....
Salt.......................	1 ounce (2 mess kit spoons).........	....
Shortening..................	2¼ pounds (1½ mess kit cups).......	....
Sugar, granulated............	1¾ pounds (⅞ No. 56 dipper).......	....
Eggs, beaten................	12 eggs (⅔ No. 56 dipper)..........	....
Vanilla....................	2 ounces (4 mess kit spoons)........	....

1. Sift flour and salt together.
2. Mix shortening and sugar; beat until light and fluffy.
3. Add beaten egg gradually, mixing well after each addition.
4. Add vanilla. Add flour mixture gradually; mix well.
5. Drop onto ungreased baking pans and flatten with a spatula. Bake in moderate oven (375° F.) 8 to 10 minutes.
6. Remove from pans at once.

NO. 105. BUTTER CREAM FROSTING

Yield: 6¼ pounds frosting

Ingredients	100 servings	.... servings
Butter or shortening..........	1⅛ pounds (⅝ No. 56 dipper).......	....
Milk, evaporated.............	½—14½-ounce can................	....
Water (for milk).............	¼ pint (8 mess kit spoons).........	....
Vanilla....................	2 ounces (4 mess kit spoons)........	....
Sugar, confectioners..........	4½ pounds (4 No. 56 dippers).......	....
Salt.......................	½ ounce (1 mess kit spoon).........	....

1. Stir butter or shortening until soft and smooth.
2. Mix milk and water; and vanilla.

3. Sift sugar and salt together. Add sugar and milk gradually to butter or shortening, beating constantly. Beat until mixture is smooth.

4. Spread carefully on cakes.

Note. This recipe makes enough frosting for 2 sheet cakes (18 by 26 by 1 inches) or for 200 individual cakes.

Frosting may be stored in tightly covered containers in refrigerator and used as needed. Warm frosting slightly and stir until smooth before spreading on cakes. Add a little hot water if necessary.

NO. 106. BANANA CREAM FROSTING

Substitute ¾ pint (½ mess kit cup) mashed bananas and 1¼ ounces (2½ mess kit spoons) lemon juice for the liquid in recipe for butter cream frosting. Omit vanilla.

NO. 107. CHOCOLATE BUTTER FROSTING

Sift ¾ pound (1 No. 56 dipper) cocoa with the sugar and salt in recipe for butter cream frosting. Increase water to ½ pint (¼ No. 56 dipper).

NO. 108. LEMON BUTTER FROSTING

Substitute 3 mess kit spoons grated lemon rind for vanilla and 2 ounces (4 mess kit spoons) lemon juice for an equal amount of water in recipe for butter cream frosting.

NO. 109. MOCHA BUTTER FROSTING

Substitute cold coffee for the water in recipe for chocolate butter frosting.

NO. 110. ORANGE BUTTER FROSTING

Substitute 3 mess kit spoons grated orange rind for vanilla and 4 ounces (8 mess kit spoons) orange juice for an equal amount of water in recipe for butter cream frosting. Two and one quarter mess kit spoons orange extract may be used instead of the orange rind and juice.

NO. 111. PEANUT BUTTER FROSTING

Mix ¾ pound peanut butter with the butter in recipe for butter cream frosting.

NO. 112. JELLY FROSTING Yield: 5½ pounds frosting.

Ingredients	100 servings	.... servings
Butter or shortening..........	13 ounces (½ mess kit cup)..........	....
Peanut butter...............	5 ounces (⅙ No. 56 dipper)..........	....
Salt......................	....	....
Sugar, confectioners..........	2¾ pounds (2⅓ No. 56 dippers).....	....
Jelly, currant...............	1¾ pounds (⅝ No. 56 dipper).......	....

1. Mix butter or shortening, peanut butter, and salt together; stir until smooth.

2. Add ½ sugar gradually.

3. Add remaining sugar and currant jelly alternately.

4. Mix thoroughly; spread on cakes.

Note. This recipe makes frosting for two sheet cakes (18 by 26 by 1 inches). Other flavors of jelly may be substituted for the currant jelly. Use on plain cake, spice cake, angel food, or sponge cake.

NO. 113. FUDGE FROSTING NO. I   Yield: 6 pounds frosting

Ingredients	100 servings	.... servings
Gelatin, plain	1¼ ounces (5 mess kit spoons)	
Water, cold	¼ pint (8 mess kit spoons)	
Cocoa	10 ounces (1 mess kit cup)	
Sugar, granulated	2 pounds (1 No. 56 dipper)	
Salt	¼ ounce (½ mess kit spoon)	
Butter	½ pound (¼ No. 56 dipper)	
Water, boiling	¾ pint (½ mess kit cup)	
Egg yolks, beaten	6 yolks (⅛ mess kit cup)	
Vanilla	1 ounce (2 mess kit spoons)	
Sugar, confectioners	2½ pounds (2 No. 56 dippers)	

1. Soak gelatin in cold water 5 minutes.

2. Mix cocoa, sugar, and salt together; add butter and boiling water.

3. Heat to boiling; boil about 5 minutes, stirring constantly. Remove from heat.

4. Add gelatin; beat well.

5. Add a small amount of cocoa and gelatin mixture to beaten egg yolk; mix well.

6. Add remaining cocoa and gelatin mixture; mix well.

7. Add vanilla and confectioners sugar; beat until smooth.

8. Spread on cakes.

Note. This recipe makes frosting for 2 sheet cakes (18 by 26 by 1 inches) or for 200 individual cakes.

NO. 114. FUDGE FROSTING NO. II   Yield: 5 quarts.

Ingredients	100 servings	.... servings
Sugar, granulated	4 pounds (2 No. 56 dippers)	
Chocolate, chopped	¾ pound	
or		
Cocoa	7 ounces (⅔ mess kit cup)	
Salt	½ ounce (1 mess kit spoon)	
Milk, evaporated	1—14½-ounce can	
Water (for milk)	1 quart (1 No. 56 dipper)	
Corn sirup	1 pound (¾ mess kit cup)	
Butter	½ pound (¼ No. 56 dipper)	
Vanilla	1 ounce (2 mess kit spoons)	

1. Mix sugar, chocolate, *or* cocoa and salt together.

2. Mix milk and water. Combine sugar mixture, milk, corn sirup, and butter; mix well.

3. Heat to boiling over low heat; boil until sugar is dissolved, stirring constantly.

4. Boil, without stirring, to 238° F. or until sirup spins a long thread when dropped from a spoon or forms a soft ball when a spoonful is dropped into a little cold water. Remove from heat.
5. Cool to 110° to 120° or until pans can be touched without discomfort. Add vanilla.
6. Beat vigorously with a paddle or large spoon. Scrape sides of pan occasionally and continue beating until frosting is creamy and thick enough to spread.

Note. If the humidity is high, boil fudge frosting to 240° to 242° F.

NO. 115. MARSHMALLOW FROSTING Yield: 4½ quarts frosting

Ingredients	100 servings	.... servings
Sugar, granulated	2½ pounds (1¼ No. 56 dippers)	
Cream of tartar*	⅙ ounce (½ mess kit spoon)	
Water, hot	¾ pint (½ mess kit cup)	
Egg whites, stiffly beaten	12 whites (⅓ No. 56 dipper)	
Vanilla	½ ounce (1 mess kit spoon)	

*If cream of tartar is not available use ½ mess kit cup corn sirup.

1. Mix sugar, cream of tartar, and water together.
2. Heat to boiling over low flame; stir constantly until sugar is dissolved.
3. Boil, without stirring, to 238° F. or until sirup spins a long thread when dropped from a spoon or forms a soft ball when a spoonful is dropped in a little cold water.
4. Pour sirup in fine stream over egg whites, beating constantly.
5. Continue beating until cold and stiff enough to spread on cake; add vanilla.
6. Spread on cakes.

Note. This recipe makes frosting for 2 sheet cakes (18 by 26 by 1 inches) or for 200 individual cakes.

NO. 116. CHOCOLATE MARSHMALLOW FROSTING

Add 6 ounces (½ mess kit cup) sifted cocoa to the cooled frosting in recipe for marshmallow frosting. Mix thoroughly.

NO. 117. RAISIN MARSHMALLOW FROSTING

Add ½ pound (½ mess kit cup) chopped seedless raisins to marshmallow frosting recipe.

NO. 118. SEA FOAM FROSTING Yield: 5 pounds frosting.

Ingredients	100 servings	.... servings
Sugar, brown	3 pounds (3 mess kit cups)	
Water, boiling	¾ pint (½ mess kit cup)	
Salt	¼ ounce (½ mess kit spoon)	
Egg whites	16 whites (⅜ No. 56 dipper)	

1. Combine sugar, water and salt.

2. Cover and heat to boiling; boil, without stirring, to 238° or until sirup spins a long thread when dropped from a spoon.

3. Beat egg whites until stiff but not dry. Pour sirup in a fine stream over beaten egg white. Continue beating until the frosting is cold and stiff enough to spread.

Note. Clean cooking utensils thoroughly before preparing sea foam frosting. If utensils are greasy, the grease will interfere with the beating of the egg whites.

NO. 119. CINNAMON TOPPING   Yield: 2¼ pounds mixture.

Ingredients	100 servings	.... servings
Cinnamon..................	1¼ ounces (5 mess kit spoons).......	....
Sugar, granulated...........	2¼ pounds (1½ mess kit cups).......	....

1. Mix cinnamon and sugar.
2. Sprinkle generously over cake batter before baking.

NO. 120. COCONUT TOPPING   Yield: 4½ pounds mixture.

Ingredients	100 servings	.... servings
Butter, melted...............	10 ounces (⅓ No. 56 dipper)........	....
Coconut, shredded...........	2½ pounds (3⅔ No. 56 dippers).....	....
Sugar, granulated...........	1 pound (½ No. 56 dipper).......	....
Cocoa.....................	7 ounces (½ No. 56 dipper)........	....

1. Combine melted butter, coconut, sugar, and cocoa; mix well.
2. Sprinkle generously over cake batter before baking.

Note. This recipe makes topping for two sheet cakes (18 by 26 by 1 inches).

NO. 121. TOASTED NUT TOPPING   Yield: 4½ pounds mixture.

Ingredients	100 servings	.... servings
Nuts, chopped...............	3 pounds (3 No. 56 dippers)........	....
Sugar, granulated...........	1½ pounds (¾ No. 56 dipper).......	....

1. Mix nuts and sugar.
2. Sprinkle generously over cake batter before baking.

NO. 122. WHITE ICING   Yield: 4½ quarts icing.

Ingredients	100 servings	.... servings
Sugar, confectioners.........	4¾ pounds (3¼ No. 56 dippers).....	....
All butter or lard, or ½ and ½.	1⅛ pounds (½ No. 56 dipper)......	....
Sirup.....................	3 pounds (1¼ No. 56 dippers).......	....
Water, hot.................	3 ounces (1½ mess kit spoons).......	....
Salt......................	½ ounce (1 mess kit spoon).........	....
Vanilla...................	To taste....................	....

1. Cream 1 pound 2 ounces sugar and butter (or lard, or ½ and ½) until light.
2. Add sirup to above and mix thoroughly.
3. Add remainder of sugar to above and mix thoroughly.
4. Dissolve salt in water and add salt, water, and vanilla to above. Mix thoroughly.

NO. 123. WHITE FUDGE ICING
Yield: 5 quarts icing.

Ingredients	100 servings	.... servings
Sugar, confectioners.........	9½ pounds (4¾ No. 56 dippers).....	....
Milk, evaporated.............	4—14½-oz. cans (1⅞ No. 56 dippers)..	....
Vinegar (45-grain)............	6 ounces (8 mess kit spoons)........	....
Salt.......................	¼ ounce (½ mess kit spoon)........	....
All butter or lard, or ½ and ½.	12 ounces (⅜ No. 56 dipper)........	....
Vanilla....................	To taste.................	....

1. Stir sugar, milk, vinegar, and salt until mixture starts to boil, then boil without stirring to 238° F., or until soft ball forms in cold water. Remove from fire. Do not stir. If 90-grain vinegar is used, ½ the amount called for in formula is required.

2. Add butter (or lard, or ½ and ½) to above and cool to lukewarm. Then beat until stiff. Thin down with simple sirup (2 parts sugar and 1 part hot water).

NO. 124. COCOA ICING
Yield: 4½ quarts icing.

Ingredients	100 servings	.... servings
Cocoa.....................	9 ounces (⅔ No. 56 dipper)..........	....
All butter or lard (melted), or ½ each	1 pound 2 ounces (⅝ No. 56 dipper)....	....
Sirup......................	2⅝ pounds (⅞ No. 56 dipper).......	....
Sugar, confectioners.........	4½ pounds (3¼ No. 56 dippers).....	....
Water, hot.................	2 ounces (4 mess kit spoons)........	....
Salt.......................	½ ounce (½ mess kit spoon)........	....
Vanilla....................	To taste.................	....

1. Place melted butter in mixing bowl and add cocoa. Mix thoroughly.
2. Add sirup to above and mix thoroughly.
3. Sift sugar, add to above and mix until smooth.
4. Add hot water, salt, and vanilla to above and mix until smooth.

NO. 125. STREUSSEL TOPPING
Yield: 4 quarts topping.

Ingredients	100 servings	.... servings
Sugar, granulated............	2 pounds (1 No. 56 dipper).........	....
Butter....................	1 pound (½ No. 56 dipper).........	....
Lard or fat................	1 pound (½ No. 56 dipper..........	....
Salt......................	½ ounce (1 mess kit spoon)........	....
Honey or sirup.............	6 ounces (8 mess kit spoons).......	....
Flour.....................	4 pounds (3 No. 56 dippers)........	....

1. Cream slightly sugar, butter, lard, and salt.
2. Add honey or sirup and flour. Blend to a crumb-like mixture.

SECTION VI

DESERTS

13. PUDDINGS AND MISCELLANEOUS DESSERTS. The most commonly used desserts are cakes, pies, fruits, and puddings. Cakes, pies, and fruit are discussed in other sections; puddings and miscellaneous desserts are in this section.

NO. 126. APPLE BROWN BETTY   Yield: 100 servings,
½ cup (4 ounces)
each.

Ingredients	100 servings	.... servings
Apples, fresh*	20 pounds	
Bread, cubed	6 pounds	
Sugar, granulated	7 pounds (3½ No. 56 dippers)	
Salt	¾ ounce (1½ mess kit spoons)	
Cinnamon	1½ ounces (6 mess kit spoons)	
Raisins, seedless	3 pounds (3 mess kit cups)	
Lemon juice	½ pint (⅓ mess kit cup)	
Molasses	1 quart (1 No. 56 dipper)	
Water	1 gallon (4 No. 56 dippers)	
Butter, melted	2 pounds (1 No. 56 dipper)	

*Three No. 10 cans apples may be substituted for the 20 pounds fresh apples.

1. Wash apples; pare and core. Slice apples.
2. Mix all ingredients together and place in greased baking pans.
3. Bake in moderate oven (375° F.) about 1 hour.

Note. Serve with hard sauce (recipe No. 539) or lemon sauce (recipe No. 540), or with evaporated milk.

NO. 127. APPLE CRISP   Yield: 3¾ gallons,
100 servings,
½ cup (5½ ounces)
each.

Ingredients	100 servings	.... servings
Apples, fresh*	40 pounds	
Nutmeg	1 ounce (4 mess kit spoons)	
Sugar, granulated	3 pounds (1½ No. 56 dippers)	
Sugar, brown	7½ pounds (5¾ No. 56 dippers)	
Flour, sifted	4 pounds (4 No. 56 dippers)	
Butter	4 pounds (2 No. 56 dippers)	

*Six No. 10 cans apples may be substituted for the 40 pounds fresh apples.

1. Wash apples; pare and core. Slice apples.
2. Spread apples in greased baking pans.
3. Mix nutmeg and granulated sugar; sprinkle over apples.
4. Mix brown sugar, flour, and butter together; stir until crumbly. Sprinkle over apples.
5. Bake in moderate over (350° F.) 1½ hours or until apples are tender.

NO. 128. BAKED CUSTARD

Yield: 100 servings, approximately 6 ounces each.

Ingredients	100 servings	.... servings
Eggs	60 eggs (3 No. 56 dippers)	
Sugar, granulated	2 pounds (1 No. 56 dipper)	
Salt	½ ounce (1 mess kit spoon)	
Vanilla	1 ounce (2 mess kit spoons)	
Milk, evaporated	16—14½-ounce cans	
Water (for milk)	2 gallons (8 No. 56 dippers)	
Nutmeg (optional)	¼ ounce (1 mess kit spoon)	

1. Combine eggs, sugar, salt, and vanilla; beat thoroughly.
2. Mix milk and water; add to egg mixture. Mix well.
3. Pour mixture into sheet pans. Sprinkle nutmeg over top of mixture.
4. Bake in slow oven (300° F.) about 30 minutes or until firm.

NO. 129. BANANA PUDDING

Yield: 100 servings, 5 ounces each.

Ingredients	100 servings	.... servings
Milk, evaporated	13—14½-ounce cans	
Water (for milk)	1½ gallons (6 No. 56 dippers)	
Cornstarch	1¾ pounds (1¾ mess kit cups)	
Sugar, granulated	4 pounds (2 No. 56 dippers)	
Salt	1 ounce (2 mess kit spoons)	
Eggs, well beaten	24 eggs (1¼ No. 56 dippers)	
Vanilla	1 ounce (2 mess kit spoons)	
Bananas, sliced	12 pounds	

1. Mix milk and water.
2. Mix constarch, ½ sugar and a small amount of cold milk together, stir until smooth.
3. Combine the other 2 pounds sugar, the salt and remaining milk; heat to boiling point.
4. Add cornstarch mixture very slowly to hot milk. Simmer until thick and clear, stirring constantly. Remove from heat.
5. Pour hot mixture slowly onto beaten egg; mix well. Add vanilla.
6. Cool, stirring occasionally.
7. Add bananas just before serving.

NO. 130. FRUIT PUDDING

Substitute diced peaches or other diced fruit for bananas in recipe for banana pudding.

NO. 131. BREAD PUDDING
Yield: 100 servings, 4 ounces each.

Ingredients	100 servings	.... servings
Bread, cubed...............	5 pounds........................	....
Raisins, seedless.............	2½ pounds (2½ mess kit cups).......	....
or		
Coconut, shredded..........	2½ pounds (3½ No. 56 dippers).....	
Sugar, granulated...........	2½ pounds (1¼ No. 56 dippers).....	
Cinnamon..................	¾ ounce (3 mess kit spoons)......	
Salt......................	1½ ounces (3 mess kit spoons)......	
Milk, evaporated............	11—14½-ounce cans...............	
Water (for milk).............	5¼ quarts (5¼ No. 56 dippers)......	
Butter, melted..............	¾ pound (½ mess kit cup).........	
Eggs, beaten................	40 eggs (2 No. 56 dippers).........	

1. Place bread cubes in greased baking pans. Sprinkle with raisins *or* coconut.

2. Mix sugar, cinnamon, and salt together.

3. Mix milk and water; heat. Add melted butter.

4. Combine sugar mixture, milk, and beaten egg; mix well.

5. Pour over bread. Allow to stand ½ hour before baking.

6. Bake in moderate oven (325° F.) 1½ hours or until firm.

Note. Serve with lemon sauce or hard sauce (recipes Nos. 540 and 539), or with evaporated milk.

NO. 132. CORNSTARCH PUDDING
Yield: 100 servings, 5 ounces each.

Ingredients	100 servings	.... servings
Milk, evaporated............	15½—14½-ounce cans...............	....
Water (for milk).............	7½ quarts (7½ No. 56 dippers)......	....
Cornstarch.................	2¼ pounds (2¼ mess kit cups)......	
Sugar, granulated...........	5 pounds (2½ No. 56 dippers).......	
Salt......................	2½ ounces (5 mess kit spoons)......	
Eggs, well beaten...........	30 eggs (1½ No. 56 dippers).......	
Vanilla....................	1½ ounces (3 mess kit spoons).......	

1. Mix milk and water.

2. Mix cornstarch, ½ of the sugar and a small amount of cold milk together; stir until smooth.

3. Combine the other 2½ pounds sugar, salt, and remaining milk; heat to boiling point.

4. Add cornstarch mixture to hot milk very slowly. Reduce heat; simmer until thick and clear, stirring constantly.

5. Remove from heat and pour slowly onto beaten egg; mix well. Add vanilla.

6. Cool before serving.

NO. 133. COTTAGE PUDDING

Yield: 14½ pounds mixture,
100 servings, each
3⅓ by 2⅓ by 1 inches.

Ingredients	100 servings	.... servings
Shortening	1½ pounds (¾ No. 56 dipper)	
Sugar, granulated	3 pounds (1½ No. 56 dippers)	
Eggs	12 eggs (½ No. 56 dipper)	
Flour, sifted	5 pounds (5 No. 56 dippers)	
Baking powder	3½ ounces (9⅓ mess kit spoons)	
Salt	1 ounce (2 mess kit spoons)	
Milk, evaporated	2½—14½-ounce cans	
Water (for milk)	1 quart (1 No. 56 dipper)	
Vanilla	1 ounce (2 mess kit spoons)	

1. Stir shortening until soft and smooth.
2. Add sugar gradually; mix thoroughly.
3. Add unbeaten eggs a few at a time, beating after each addition until well mixed; continue beating until light and fluffy.
4. Sift flour, baking powder, and salt together twice.
5. Mix milk and water; add vanilla.
6. Add dry ingredients and milk alternately to sugar mixture, first adding about ⅓ dry ingredients, then ½ milk, then another ⅓ dry ingredients and remaining milk and dry ingredients.
7. Mix thoroughly until smooth.
8. Pour into greased sheet pans. Bake in moderate oven (350° F.) about 30 to 35 minutes or until done.

Note. This recipe makes two sheet cakes (17 by 24 by 1 inches).

Serve with chocolate sauce, hard sauce, or a fruit sauce. (See recipes Nos. 538, 539 or 537.)

NO. 134. CHOCOLATE COTTAGE PUDDING

Yield: 15¼ pounds mixture,
100 servings, each
3⅓ by 2⅓ by 1¼ inches.

Ingredients	100 servings	.... servings
Shortening	2¼ pounds (1½ mess kit cups)	
Sugar, granulated	3¾ pounds (2½ mess kit cups)	
Eggs	15 eggs (¾ No. 56 dipper)	
Flour, sifted	3¾ pounds (3¾ No. 56 dippers)	
Baking powder	2½ ounces (6⅔ mess kit spoons)	
Salt	½ ounce (1 mess kit spoon)	
Baking soda	¾ ounce (1½ mess kit spoon)	
Cocoa	14 ounces (1 No. 56 dipper)	
Milk, evaporated	2—14½-ounce cans	
Water (for milk)	1½ pints (¾ No. 56 dipper)	
Vanilla	1 ounce (2 mess kit spoons)	

1. Stir shortening until soft and smooth.
2. Add sugar gradually; mix thoroughly.

3. Add unbeaten eggs, a few at a time, beating after each addition until well mixed; continue beating until light and fluffy.

4. Sift flour, baking powder, salt, soda, and cocoa together twice.

5. Mix milk and water; add vanilla.

6. Add dry ingredients and milk alternately to sugar mixture, first adding about ⅓ dry ingredients, then ½ milk, then another ⅓ dry ingredients and remaining milk and dry ingredients.

7. Mix thoroughly until smooth.

8. Pour into greased sheet pans. Bake in moderate oven (350° F.) about 30 to 35 minutes or until done.

Note. This recipe makes two sheet cakes (17 by 24 by 1 inches). Serve with chocolate sauce or hard sauce. (See recipes Nos. 538 or 539.)

NO. 135. FRUIT ROLL

Yield: 100 servings, 5½ ounces each.

Ingredients	100 servings	.... servings
Flour, sifted..............	9 pounds (9 No. 56 dippers)........	....
Salt..................	1½ ounces (3 mess kit spoons).......	....
Shortening...............	3 pounds (1½ No. 56 dippers)......	....
Water, cold..............	1¼ quarts (1¼ No. 56 dippers).....	....
Butter, melted............	1 pound (½ No. 56 dipper)........	....
Apples, sliced*...........	14 pounds................	....
Sugar, granulated..........	4½ pounds (2¼ No. 56 dippers).....	....
Nutmeg................	¾ ounce (3 mess kit spoons)........	....
Cinnamon...............	¾ ounce (3 mess kit spoons)........	....

*Two No. 10 cans apples may be substituted for the 14 pounds fresh apples.

1. Sift flour and salt together.

2. Add shortening; stir until a crumbly mixture is obtained.

3. Add water gradually; stir until mixture is moistened just enough to hold together. Stir lightly until smooth.

4. Divide dough evenly into 11 portions. Roll each piece of dough into strips about ¼ inch thick, 8 inches wide, and a little longer than length of baking pan to be used.

5. Brush each strip of dough with melted butter.

6. Mix apples, sugar, nutmeg, and cinnamon together. Spread over dough.

7. Roll up lengthwise like a jelly roll.

8. Place rolls in pan seam side down and close together so that rolls will retain their shape.

9. Bake in moderate oven (375° to 400° F.) about 1 hour or until apples are tender and dough is well baked.

Note. Drained, canned cherries may be used as the fruit in this recipe. Use two No. 10 cans. Omit apples, nutmeg, and cinnamon. Serve with cherry sauce. (See recipe No. 537.)

NO. 136. INDIAN PUDDING

Yield: 100 servings, 5 ounces each.

Ingredients	100 servings	.... servings
Milk, evaporated	23—14½-ounce cans	
Water (for milk)	10½ quarts (10½ No. 56 dippers)	
Cornmeal	3½ pounds (3½ mess kit cups)	
Sugar, granulated	5 pounds (2½ No. 56 dippers)	
Ginger	1¾ ounces (7 mess kit spoons)	
Cinnamon	⅞ ounce (4 mess kit spoons)	
Salt	2¼ ounces (4½ mess kit spoons)	
Molasses	4¾ quarts (4¾ No. 56 dippers)	
Butter, melted	2 pounds (1 No. 56 dipper)	

1. Mix milk and water; heat slowly until a slight film forms on top of the milk.
2. Add cornmeal slowly, stirring constantly. Cook, stirring constantly, 20 minutes or until thick.
3. Add remaining ingredients; mix thoroughly.
4. Pour into baking pans. Bake in slow oven (250° to 300° F.) 3 hours without stirring.
5. Serve warm or cool.

NO. 137. PINEAPPLE RICE CREAM

Yield: 6 gallons.

Ingredients	100 servings	.... servings
Milk, evaporated	17½—14½-ounce cans	
Water (for milk)	7 quarts (7 No. 56 dippers)	
Rice	3¾ pounds (2½ mess kit cups)	
Sugar, granulated	5 pounds (2½ No. 56 dippers)	
Salt	1¼ ounces (2½ mess kit spoons)	
Butter	1¼ pounds (⅚ mess kit cup)	
Pineapple, crushed	3 No. 10 cans	

1. Mix milk and water; heat slowly until a slight film forms on top.
2. Add rice, sugar, salt, and butter; mix thoroughly.
3. Cook slowly, stirring frequently, about 2⅓ hours or until rice is soft and has absorbed most of the milk. Remove from heat.
4. Cool. Add pineapple just before serving.

Note. If available, use double boiler for cooking rice mixture.

NO. 138. PRUNE PUDDING

Yield: 4½ gallons.

Ingredients	100 servings	.... servings
Prunes, dried	10½ pounds	
Water, cold	4½ gallons (18 No. 56 dippers)	
Sugar, granulated	6 pounds (3 No. 56 dippers)	
Cinnamon	1 ounce (4 mess kit spoons)	
Salt	1 ounce (2 mess kit spoons)	
Cornstarch	1⅞ pounds (1⅓ No. 56 dippers)	
Water, cold	1½ quarts (1½ No. 56 dippers)	
Lemon juice	¾ pint (½ mess kit cup)	

1. Wash prunes; add water. Heat to boiling; reduce heat and simmer 45 minutes or until soft.

2. Drain and remove pits.

3. Measure prune juice and if necessary add water to make 9 quarts (9 No. 56 dippers) liquid.

4. Combine prunes, prune juice, sugar, cinnamon, and salt; heat to boiling.

5. Mix cornstarch, cold water, and lemon juice together; stir until smooth. Add slowly to hot prune mixture. Reheat to boiling; boil 5 minutes, stirring frequently.

Note. Serve with cream or evaporated milk.

NO. 139. PRUNE WHIP

Yield: 4 gallons,
100 servings, ¾ cup each.

Ingredients	100 servings	.... servings
Prunes, dried...............	11½ pounds......................	....
Water, cold................	4 gallons (16 No. 56 dippers).........	....
Egg whites.................	28 whites (¾ No. 56 dipper).........	....
Sugar, granulated...........	3½ pounds (1¾ No. 56 dippers)......	....
Salt......................	½ ounce (1 mess kit spoon)..........	....
Lemon juice...............	½ pint (⅓ mess kit cup)...........	....

Note. Use prune liquid in fruit drinks.

1. Wash prunes; add cold water. Heat to boiling without draining; reduce heat and simmer 45 minutes or until soft.

2. Drain and remove pits; press pulp through a sieve. Cool.

3. Beat egg whites until stiff; add sugar and salt gradually.

4. Add lemon juice and prune pulp; mix carefully but thoroughly.

5. Serve cold.

NO. 140. APRICOT WHIP

Substitute 9½ pounds dried apricots, 2½ gallons (10 No. 56 dippers) cold water, and 56 egg whites (1⅓ No. 56 dippers) for similar ingredients in recipe for prune whip. Omit lemon juice. Use apricot liquid in fruit drinks.

NO. 141. RICE PUDDING

Yield: 4½ gallons,
4 ounces each.

Ingredients	100 servings	.... servings
Milk, evaporated...........	20—14½-ounce cans................	....
Water (for milk)............	2¼ gallons (9 No. 56 dippers).......	....
Rice.....................	4½ pounds (3 mess kit cups)........	....
Sugar, granulated..........	4½ pounds (2¼ No. 56 dippers).....	....
Salt.....................	1½ ounces (3 mess kit spoons).......	....
Vanilla...................	3 ounces (6 mess kit spoons)........	....
Raisins...................	2 pounds (2 mess kit cups)..........	....

1. Mix milk and water. Heat 3 gallons (12 No. 56 dippers) milk slowly until slight film forms on top.

2. Add rice, sugar, and salt; mix thoroughly.

3. Cook, stirring occasionally, about 2 hours or until rice has absorbed most of the milk.
4. Remove from heat and add remainder of milk, vanilla, and raisins; mix thoroughly.
5. Pour into greased baking pans. Bake in moderate oven (350° F.) about 1 hour or until rice is soft.
6. Serve hot or cold.

NO. 142. TAPIOCA PUDDING

Yield: 100 servings, 4½ ounces each.

Ingredients	100 servings	.... servings
Milk, evaporated	17½—14½ ounce cans	
Water (for milk)	1¾ gallons (7 No. 56 dippers)	
Tapioca, quick cooking	2 pounds	
Sugar, granulated	5 pounds (2½ No. 56 dippers)	
Salt	2½ ounces (5 mess kit spoons)	
Eggs, beaten	30 eggs (1½ No. 56 dippers)	
Vanilla	1½ ounces (3 mess kit spoons)	

Note. Serve plain or with a sauce (recipes Nos. 537 to 541) or with evaporated milk.

1. Mix milk and water. Heat ⅔ milk slowly until a slight film forms on top.
2. Combine remaining cold milk, tapioca, sugar, and salt; stir until smooth.
3. Add tapioca mixture gradually to hot milk, stirring constantly. Cook, stirring constantly, until tapioca granules are transparent.
4. Remove from heat. Pour slowly onto beaten egg; mix well. Add vanilla; chill.
5. Cool; stirring occasionally.

NO. 143. COFFEE JELLY

Yield: 100 servings, 4 ounces each.

Ingredients	100 servings	.... servings
Water, cold	1 quart (1 No. 56 dipper)	
Gelatin, plain	5½ ounces (⅓ mess kit cup)	
Coffee, hot, strong	1½ gallons (6 No. 56 dippers)	
Sugar, granulated	3 pounds (1½ No. 56 dippers)	
Salt	⅓ ounce (⅔ mess kit spoon)	
Lemon juice	½ pint (⅓ mess kit cup)	

1. Pour cold water over gelatin; allow to stand 5 minutes.
2. Add hot coffee, sugar, salt, and lemon juice; stir until sugar is dissolved.
3. Chill.

Note. Serve with whipped cream or whipped evaporated milk.

NO. 144. CHOCOLATE SPONGE

Yield: 100 servings,
4 ounces each.

Ingredients	100 servings	.... servings
Water, cold..................	1¾ quarts (1¾ No. 56 dippers)......	....
Gelatin, plain................	7 ounces (½ mess kit cup)...........	....
Water, hot..................	1¾ quarts (1¾ No. 56 dippers)......	....
Sugar, granulated............	4¾ pounds (2⅓ No. 56 dippers).....	....
Salt.......................	½ ounce (1 mess kit spoon)..........	....
Chocolate..................	1¼ pounds......................	....
or		
Cocoa.....................	1 pound (1½ mess kit cups)........	....
Egg yolks, slightly beaten.....	84 yolks (1⅘ No. 56 dippers).......	....
Egg whites, stiffly beaten.....	84 whites (2 No. 56 dippers)........	....
Vanilla....................	3 ounces (6 mess kit spoons)........	....

1. Pour cold water over gelatin; mix and allow to stand 5 minutes.
2. Mix hot water, sugar, salt, and chocolate or cocoa together, Heat to boiling point; boil about 3 minutes or until smooth.
3. Add gelatin; stir until thoroughly dissolved.
4. Add slightly beaten egg yolks. When mixture begins to thicken, add stiffly beaten egg whites and vanilla.
5. Chill.

Note. Serve with whipped cream or whipped evaporated milk.

NO. 145. GELATIN BREAD PUDDING

Yield: 100 servings,
4 ounces each.

Ingredients	100 servings	.... servings
Milk, evaporated.............	9—14½-ounce cans................	....
Water (for milk).............	4¼ quarts (4¼ No. 56 dippers)......	....
Gelatin, plain...............	3 ounces (12 mess kit spoons).......	....
Sugar, granulated............	3 pounds (1½ No. 56 dippers).......	....
Salt.......................	¾ ounce (1½ mess kit spoons)......	....
Bread cubes, white..........	10½ quarts (10½ No. 56 dippers)....	....
Eggs, slightly beaten........	30 eggs (1½ No. 56 dippers).......	....
Vanilla....................	¾ ounce (1½ mess kit spoons)......	....

1. Mix milk and water; pour 1 quart (1 No. 56 dipper) milk over gelatin and allow to stand 5 minutes, stirring frequently.
2. Combine remaining milk, sugar, and salt. Heat over low fire until slight film forms on top.
3. Add gelatin; stir until gelatin is thoroughly dissolved.
4. Pour hot milk mixture slowly over beaten egg, stirring constantly.
5. Add bread cubes; cook until thick.
6. Remove from fire; add vanilla and beat until frothy.
7. Chill.

Note. Serve with a sauce (recipes Nos. 537 to 541) or with cream.

NO. 146. FRUIT GELATIN

Yield: 4½ gallons,
100 servings, ¾
cup each.

Ingredients	100 servings	.... servings
Gelatin, flavored.............	5 pounds (5 mess kit cups)...........	....
Water, boiling...............	1½ gallons (6 No. 56 dippers).......	....
Water, cold..................	1½ gallons (6 No. 56 dippers).......	....
Fruit, sliced and fruit juice....	1½ gallons (6 No. 56 dippers).......	....

1. Dissolve gelatin in boiling water; add cold water.
2. Chill until mixture begins to thicken; add mixed fruit. Chill until firm.
3. Cut in squares.

NO. 147. LEMON GELATIN

Yield: 4 gallons,
100 servings, ¾
cup each.

Ingredients	100 servings	.... servings
Water, cold.................	1¼ quarts (1¼ No. 56 dippers)......	....
Gelatin, plain...............	1 pound (1 mess kit cup)...........	....
Water, boiling..............	2½ gallons (10 No. 56 dippers)......	....
Sugar, granulated...........	10 pounds (5 No. 56 dippers).......	....
Lemon juice................	3⅓ quarts (3⅓ No. 56 dippers).....	....

1. Pour cold water over gelatin; mix and allow to stand 5 minutes.
2. Add boiling water and sugar; stir until sugar is dissolved.
3. Add lemon juice; mix thoroughly.
4. Pour into pans and chill until firm.
5. Cut into squares.

Note. Serve with cream or evaporated milk.

NO. 148. ORANGE GELATIN

Yield: 5 gallons,
100 servings, ¾
cup each.

Ingredients	100 servings	.... servings
Water, cold.................	2 quarts (2 No. 56 dippers).........	....
Gelatin, plain...............	1 pound (1 mess kit cup)...........	....
Water, boiling..............	2½ gallons (10 No. 56 dippers)......	....
Sugar, granulated...........	5 pounds (2½ No. 56 dippers)......	....
Lemon juice................	1¼ quarts (1¼ No. 56 dippers)......	....
Orange juice...............	1¾ gallons (7 No. 56 dippers)......	....

1. Pour cold water over gelatin; mix and allow to stand 5 minutes.
2. Add boiling water and sugar; stir until sugar is dissolved.
3. Add lemon juice and orange juice; mix thoroughly.
4. Pour into pans; chill until firm.
5. Cut into squares.

Note. Orange sections may be added to the gelatin if desired.

NO. 149. PINEAPPLE GELATIN

Yield: 5 gallons,
100 servings, ¾
cup each.

Ingredients	100 servings	.... servings
Water, cold	2 quarts (2 No. 56 dippers)	
Gelatin, plain	1 pound (1 mess kit cup)	
Water, boiling	2½ gallons (10 No. 56 dippers)	
Sugar, granulated	5 pounds (2½ No. 56 dippers)	
Lemon juice	1¼ quarts (1¼ No. 56 dippers)	
Pineapple juice	2 No. 10 cans	

1. Pour cold water over gelatin; mix and allow to stand 5 minutes.
2. Add boiling water and sugar; stir until sugar is dissolved.
3. Add lemon juice and pineapple juice; mix thoroughly.
4. Pour into pans; chill until firm.
5. Cut into squares.

NO. 150. ORANGE CHARLOTTE

Yield: 100 servings,
4 ounces each.

Ingredients	100 servings	.... servings
Water, cold	1 pint (½ No. 56 dipper)	
Orange juice and pulp	2 quarts (2 No. 56 dippers)	
Gelatin, plain	3 ounces (12 mess kit spoons)	
Water, boiling	1 quart (1 No. 56 dipper)	
Sugar, granulated	4 pounds (2 No. 56 dippers)	
Salt	⅓ ounce (⅔ mess kit spoon)	
Lemon juice	½ pint (⅓ mess kit cup)	
Egg whites	24 whites (⅗ No. 56 dipper)	

1. Pour cold water and ½ pint (⅓ mess kit cup) orange juice over gelatin; allow to stand 5 minutes.
2. Add boiling water, sugar, and salt; stir until sugar is dissolved.
3. Add lemon juice and remaining orange juice; mix thoroughly.
4. Cool. When mixture begins to stiffen, beat until light and frothy.
5. Beat egg whites until stiff; add carefully to gelatin.
6. Chill.
Note. Serve on stale cake.

NO. 151. PINEAPPLE SPONGE

Yield: 4½ gallons,
4 ounces each.

Ingredients	100 servings	.... servings
Water, cold	2 quarts (2 No. 56 dippers)	
Gelatin, plain	½ pound (½ mess kit cup)	
Egg yolks, beaten	32 yolks (⅔ No. 56 dipper)	
Sugar, granulated	8 pounds (4 No. 56 dippers)	
Lemon juice	1 pint (½ No. 56 dipper)	
Salt	½ ounce (1 mess kit spoon)	
Water, boiling	3 quarts (3 No. 56 dippers)	
Pineapple, crushed	2 No. 10 cans	
Vanilla	4 ounces (8 mess kit spoons)	
Egg whites	32 whites (⅘ No. 56 dipper)	

1. Pour cold water over gelatin; mix and allow to stand 5 minutes.
2. Mix beaten egg yolk and ¾ sugar. Add lemon juice and salt; mix well.

3. Pour boiling water over gelatin; stir until gelatin is dissolved.
4. Pour gelatin into egg mixture slowly, stirring constantly.
5. Chill until mixture begins to thicken; add pineapple and vanilla.
6. Beat egg whites until stiff; add remaining sugar gradually.
7. Add egg white to gelatin mixture. Pour into pans; chill until firm.

NO. 152. VANILLA ICE CREAM

Yield: 4 gallons,
100 servings,
3½ ounces each.

Ingredients	100 servings	.... servings
Cornstarch	8 ounces (½ mess kit cup)	
Salt	½ ounce (1 mess kit spoon)	
Sugar, granulated	5 pounds (2½ No. 56 dippers)	
Milk, evaporated	13—14½-ounce cans	
Water (for milk)	1½ gallons (6 No. 56 dippers)	
Eggs, slightly beaten	24 eggs (1¼ No. 56 dippers)	
Cream, thin	1 pint (½ No. 56 dipper)	
Vanilla	2½ ounces (5 mess kit spoons)	

1. Mix cornstarch, salt, and ½ sugar together.
2. Mix milk and water; add to cornstarch mixture. Mix well.
3. Heat to boiling point; reduce heat and simmer until thick, stirring constantly.
4. Mix beaten egg and remaining sugar; add to cooked mixture a little at a time, beating after each addition.
5. Cool; add cream and vanilla. Mix well.
6. Place can in freezer; put in dasher and fill can ⅔ full of mixture. Cover and adjust crank.
7. Pack with alternate layers of ice and coarse salt to within 3 inches of top. Use six parts ice to one part salt.
8. Turn crank steadily and slowly. The mixture is frozen when the crank turns hard. While freezing, add more salt and ice if necessary.
9. Remove dasher and pack with additional ice and salt; allow to stand 2 hours before serving.

NO. 153. CHOCOLATE ICE CREAM

Add 1¼ pounds (2 mess kit cups) cocoa to dry ingredients in recipe for vanilla ice cream. Increase sugar to 7 pounds (3½ No. 56 dippers).

NO. 154. COFFEE ICE CREAM

Substitute 2 quarts (2 No. 56 dippers) strong coffee for an equal amount of water in recipe for vanilla ice cream. Increase sugar to 6 pounds (3 No. 56 dippers).

NO. 155. FRUIT ICE CREAM

Increase sugar to 6 pounds (3 No. 56 dippers) in recipe for vanilla ice cream. Omit vanilla. Add 1 gallon (4 No. 56 dippers) crushed fruit such as peaches, raspberries, or strawberries.

NO. 156. ORANGE ICE

Yield: 6 gallons,
100 servings,
5 ounces each.

Ingredients	100 servings	.... servings
Gelatin, orange flavored.......	26 ounces (1¼ No. 56 dippers).......	....
Sugar, granulated............	8 pounds (4 No. 56 dippers)........	....
Water, boiling...............	2 gallons (8 No. 56 dippers).........	....
Water, cold.................	2 gallons (8 No. 56 dippers).........	....
Orange juice................	1 gallon (4 No. 56 dippers).........	....
Lemon juice................	½ pint (⅓ mess kit cup)...........	....

1. Mix gelatin and sugar. Pour boiling water over gelatin mixture; stir until gelatin and sugar are dissolved.
2. Add cold water; cool.
3. Add orange juice and lemon juice; mix thoroughly.
4. Freeze, following directions for freezing vanilla ice cream. (See recipe No. 152).

NO. 157. LEMON ICE

Substitute lemon-flavored gelatin for orange-flavored gelatin in recipe for orange ice. Omit orange juice and increase lemon juice to 1 quart (1 No. 56 dipper).

NO. 158. RASPBERRY ICE

Substitute raspberry-flavored gelatin for orange-flavored gelatin in recipe for orange ice. Omit orange juice and increase lemon juice to 1 pint (½ No. 56 dipper).

EGGS

14. **COOKING.** Eggs are a protein food and must be cooked at low temperatures. High temperature toughens egg whites and darkens the yolks.

NO. 159. "BOILED" EGGS
Yield: 100 servings,
2 eggs per serving.

Ingredients	100 servings	.... servings
Eggs......................	200 eggs...............................	....
Water, boiling...............	....	....

1. Place 100 eggs at a time in large wire basket or other similar utensil with long handle.

2. Lower basket into boiling water; reduce heat and simmer 3 to 5 minutes for soft cooked eggs and 12 to 15 minutes for hard cooked eggs.

3. Remove from water. Plunge hard cooked eggs in cold water.

Note. If hard cooked eggs are to be used in salads or other dishes, remove shells immediately after plunging in cold water.

NO. 160. CREAMED EGGS
Yield: 100 servings,
1 egg per serving.

Ingredients	100 servings	.... servings
Eggs, hard-cooked...........	100 eggs.............................	....
White sauce.................	2¼ gallons (9 No. 56 dippers)........	....
Parsley, minced.............	5 ounces (½ mess kit cup)..........	....
Worcestershire sauce.........	3 ounces (6 mess kit spoons)........	....
Bread, toasted...............	100 slices...........................	....

1. Remove shells from eggs; cut eggs into quarters or slices.

2. Prepare white sauce. (See recipe No. 548.)

3. Combine white sauce, parsley, Worcestershire sauce, and eggs; mix well.

4. Heat slowly to serving temperature.

5. Pour creamed eggs over toast.

NO. 161. DEVILED EGGS

Yield: 100 servings,
1 egg per serving.

Ingredients	100 servings	.... servings
Eggs, hard-cooked	100 eggs	
Milk, evaporated	½—14½-ounce cans	
Water (for milk)	½ pint (⅓ mess kit cup)	
Mayonnaise	1½ pints (1 mess kit cup)	
Salt	1 ounce (2 mess kit spoons)	
Mustard, dry	½ ounce (2 mess kit spoons)	
Vinegar	½ pint (⅓ mess kit cup)	

1. Remove shells from eggs; cut eggs in half lengthwise.
2. Remove yolks from eggs; mash thoroughly.
3. Combine mashed yolks and remaining ingredients; mix thoroughly.
4. Refill whites with yolk mixture, using approximately one mess kit spoon filling for each half of egg white.

NO. 162. FRIED EGGS

Yield: 100 servings, 2 eggs per serving.

Ingredients	100 servings	.... servings
Eggs	200 eggs	
Shortening, melted	2½ pounds (1¼ No. 56 dippers)	
Salt		
Pepper		

1. Break eggs one at a time into a saucer.
2. Place eggs in hot fat; cook slowly until eggs are firm.
3. Sprinkle with salt and pepper.
4. Turn eggs and cook on other side if desired.

NO. 163. POACHED EGGS

Yield: 100 servings, 2 eggs per serving.

Ingredients	100 servings	.... servings
Eggs	200 eggs	
Water, boiling		
Salt	5½ ounces (11 mess kit spoons)	

1. Break eggs one at a time into a saucer.
2. Place eggs carefully one at a time in greased pans containing enough boiling salted water to cover eggs.
3. Cover pan and allow eggs to cook without boiling about 5 minutes or until firm.

NO. 164. SCRAMBLED EGGS

Yield: 100 servings, 3 to 4 ounces each.

Ingredients	100 servings	.... servings
Eggs	150 eggs	
Milk, evaporated	3—14½-ounce cans	
Water (for milk)	1½ quarts (1½ No. 56 dippers)	
Shortening, melted	1½ pounds (1 mess kit cup)	
Salt	3 ounces (6 mess kit spoons)	
Pepper	¼ ounce (1 mess kit spoon)	

1. Break eggs; beat slightly.
2. Mix milk and water; add beaten egg. Add salt and pepper.
3. Pour egg mixture into hot fat.
4. Cook slowly to desired firmness, stirring occasionally when eggs begin to thicken.

NO. 165. SHIRRED EGGS

Yield: 100 servings, 2 eggs per serving.

Ingredients	100 servings	.... servings
Eggs	200 eggs	
Salt		
Pepper		

1. Break eggs into greased muffin pans.
2. Sprinkle with salt and pepper.
3. Bake in moderate oven (375° F.) about 15 minutes or until eggs are firm. Remove from pans with a spatula.

NO. 166. PLAIN OMELET

Yield: 15 quarts mixture, ⅔ cup (4¾ ounces) per serving.

Ingredients	100 servings	.... servings
Milk, evaporated	8—14½-ounce cans	
Water (for milk)	3¾ quarts (3¾ No. 56 dippers)	
Eggs, beaten	150 eggs (7½ No. 56 dippers)	
Salt	5 ounces (10 mess kit spoons)	
Pepper	⅓ ounce (1 mess kit spoon)	
Fat, melted	4 ounces (8 mess kit spoons)	

1. Mix milk and water: add beaten egg, salt, and pepper.
2. Pour egg mixture 2 to 2½ inches deep into melted fat in baking pans.
3. Bake in slow oven (325° F.) about 35 to 40 minutes.

Note. Omelet may be cooked on griddle instead of in the oven.

NO. 167. CHEESE OMELET

Add 3½ pounds (3½ No. 56 dippers) finely chopped cheese to egg mixture in recipe for plain omelet.

NO. 168. HAM OMELET

Add 4½ pounds (3½ No. 56 dippers) finely chopped ham to egg mixture in recipe for plain omelet.

NO. 169. BACON OMELET

Cut 4 pounds sliced bacon into small pieces. Fry until crisp; pour fat from bacon. Add bacon to egg mixture in recipe for plain omelet.

NO. 170. SPANISH OMELET

Serve plain omelet with Spanish sauce. (See recipe No. 552.)

FISH AND
OTHER SEA FOOD

---

15. FISH COOKERY. a. Fish are of two general types; fat and lean. Fat fish are best for baking and broiling and lean fish for steaming, simmering, and for chowder. Either fat or lean fish may be fried. The retention of the shape of the fish is a problem in cooking. The muscle fibers separate during cooking due to the small amount of connecting tissue. For this reason baking and steaming give the best results.

b. Sprinkle both sides of the raw fish with salt 5 to 10 minutes before cooking. The packaged fillets and steaks are usually lightly salted before packing. Cook at low temperature until well done but not tough and dry. The time required for cooking depends upon the depth of the fish in the pan. Press the fish lightly with a fork. If it separates into flakes, it is cooked sufficiently.

NO. 171. CREAMED CODFISH   Yield: Approximately 3½ gallons, 100 servings, approximately ½ cup fish over 1 slice toast each.

Ingredients	100 servings	.... servings
Codfish, salt*	16 pounds	
Milk, evaporated	9—14½-ounce cans	
Water (for milk)	4½ quarts (4½ No. 56 dippers)	
Butter, melted	2 pounds (1 No. 56 dipper)	
Flour, sifted	¾ pound (¾ No. 56 dipper)	
Mustard, dry		
Salt	1½ ounces (3 mess kit spoons)	
Pepper		
Toast	100 slices	

*Tuna fish, salmon, or mackerel may be substituted for codfish in recipe above.

1. Wash codfish and remove bones; soak 4 hours or overnight in cold water. Drain.

2. Mix milk and water; heat to boiling.

3. Mix melted butter, flour, mustard, salt, and pepper together; stir until smooth. Add to hot milk, stirring constantly. Heat to boiling point; reduce heat and simmer until thick, stirring constantly.

4. Add codfish; reheat, and serve on toast.

NO. 172. BAKED CREAMED CODFISH

Add 1 pound (1 No. 56 dipper) chopped onions, 2 quarts (2 No. 56 dippers) cubed toast, 1 pound (⅔ mess kit cup) chopped pickles to mixture in recipe for creamed codfish. Place in baking pans. Bake in moderate oven (375° F.) 30 minutes.

NO. 173. CODFISH CAKES
Yield: 200 cakes,
100 servings, 2
3-inch cakes each.

Ingredients	100 servings	.... servings
Codfish, salt..................	16 pounds............................	....
Water, boiling................		....
Potatoes, mashed, without seasoning.	16 pounds (8 No. 56 dippers)........	....
Eggs, beaten.................	16 eggs (¾ No. 56 dipper)..........	....
Shortening, melted...........	½ pound (⅓ mess kit cup)..........	....
Salt.........................	½ ounce (1 mess kit spoon).........	....
Pepper......................		....
Flour, sifted.................	13 ounces (⅔ No. 56 dipper)........	....
Fat (for frying)..............	2 pounds (1 No. 56 dipper)..........	....

1. Wash codfish and remove bones; soak fish 4 hours or overnight in cold water. Drain.
2. Cover with boiling water. Heat to boiling point; reduce heat and simmer 20 minutes. Drain.
3. Mix codfish, potatoes, beaten egg, melted shortening, salt, and pepper, beat until well mixed.
4. Form into cakes weighing about 3 ounces each (3 inches in diameter, ½ inch thick); roll in flour.
5. Fry until brown.

Note. Codfish mixture may be rolled into balls and fried in deep fat.

NO. 174. CRAB CAKES
Yield: 100 servings,
approximately 5 ounces
or 2 cakes each.

Ingredients	100 servings	.... servings
Crab meat...................	24 pounds............................	....
Butter or other fat..........	1½ pounds (1 mess kit cup).........	....
Onions, chopped.............	¾ pounds (¾ No. 56 dipper)........	....
Bread crumbs...............	3 pounds (3 No. 56 dippers).........	....
Eggs, well beaten...........	24 eggs (1¼ No. 56 dippers)........	....
Mustard, dry................	2 ounces (8 mess kit spoons)........	....
Salt........................	2 ounces (4 mess kit spoons)........	....
Pepper......................	½ ounce (2 mess kit spoons)........	....
Flour, sifted.................	1 pound (1 No. 56 dipper)..........	....

1. Remove any shell or cartilage from the crab meat.
2. Melt butter, add onions, and cook until yellow.

3. Mix crab meat, cooked onions, bread crumbs, eggs, and seasonings.
4. Form into small cakes, and roll in flour.
5. Fry in fat until brown, and serve with a sauce.

Note. Cakes may be breaded and fried in deep fat heated to 375° F. for 4 minutes, or until brown.

NO. 175. CRAB COCKTAIL

Yield: 100 servings,
approximately ¾ ounces
or ⅔ cup each.

Ingredients	100 servings	.... servings
Crab meat, flaked	15 pounds	
Catsup	2 quarts (2 No. 56 dippers)	
Vinegar or lemon juice	1 pint (½ No. 56 dipper)	
Celery, finely chopped	1 pound (1 No. 56 dipper)	
Horseradish	½ pint (¼ No. 56 dipper)	
Salt	1 ounce (2 mess kit spoons)	
Tabasco sauce	1 mess kit spoon	
Lettuce		

1. Remove any shell or cartilage from crab meat.
2. Chill and place in lettuce cup.
3. Make sauce by mixing remaining ingredients together.
4. Immediately before serving put sauce on cocktails.

NO. 176. DEVILED CRABS

Yield: 100 servings,
approximately 5 ounces each.

Ingredients	100 servings	.... servings
Crab meat	18 pounds	
Butter	1 pound (1½ No. 56 dipper)	
Flour	1 pound (1 No. 56 dipper)	
Milk	1 gallon (4 No. 56 dippers)	
Eggs, beaten	12 eggs (¾ No. 56 dipper)	
Salt	1½ ounces (3 mess kit spoons)	
Pepper, cayenne		
Mustard	¾ ounce (3 mess kit spoons)	
Worcestershire sauce	1 ounce (2 mess kit spoons)	
Bread crumbs	2 pounds (2 No. 56 dippers)	

1. Examine crab meat for any cartilage or shell.
2. Make a white sauce of butter, flour, and milk.
3. Add beaten eggs, seasonings, and mix well.
4. Mix in the crab meat, and fill thoroughly cleaned and scrubbed crab shells with mixture, or place in a greased baking pan.
5. Sprinkle with bread crumbs.
6. Bake in moderate oven (375° F.) for about 10 minutes, or until brown.

NO. 177. FRIED SOFT SHELL CRABS   Yield: 100 servings, 2 crabs each.

Ingredients	100 servings	.... servings
Soft shell crabs	200	
Salt	2½ ounces (5 mess kit spoons)	
Eggs	24 eggs (1¼ No. 56 dippers)	
Water	1 pint (½ No. 56 dipper)	
Bread crumbs	3 pounds (3 No. 56 dippers)	
Flour	3 pounds (2⅖ No. 56 dippers)	

1. Dress crabs.

2. Salt each crab on both sides.

3. Dip crabs in well-beaten eggs to which water has been added.

4. Roll crabs in mixture of bread crumbs and flour.

5. Fry in deep fat heated to 360° F. for about 3 minutes on each side, or until golden brown.

6. Drain on absorbent paper.

7. Serve with a tartar sauce.

NO. 178. BAKED FRESH FISH   Yield: Two No. 50 baking pans, 100 servings, 2½ by 4½ inches each.

Ingredients	100 servings	.... servings
Bacon or salt pork, thinly sliced.	4 pounds	
Fish, fresh, dressed	35 pounds	
Salt	2½ ounces (5 mess kit spoons)	
Pepper	(¼ mess kit spoon)	

1. Cut 1 pound bacon or salt pork into small pieces. Place in baking pans and fry until crisp.

2. Wash fish and remove bones; cut into servings about 2½ by 4½ inches in size.

3. Place fish over fried bacon in pans; sprinkle with salt and pepper. Cover with thin slices of remaining bacon or salt pork.

4. Bake in moderate oven (325° F.) about 1 hour. Baste occasionally with melted fat.

Note. If there is enough oven space, place the fish in single layers in pans and bake for 30 minutes instead of 1 hour.

NO. 179. BAKED FISH WITH STUFFING   Yield: Two No. 50 baking
pans, 100 servings,
2 by 3 inches each,
⅓ cup dressing each.

Ingredients	100 servings	.... servings
Shortening, melted............	2 pounds (1 No. 56 dipper)..........	....
Bread cubes, dry.............	2 gallons (8 No. 56 dippers).........	....
Onions, finely chopped........	½ pound (⅔ mess kit cup)..........	....
Salt.......................	1¼ ounces (2½ mess kit spoons).....	....
Pepper.....................	(¼ mess kit spoon)................	....
Poultry seasoning (optional)..	1 ounce (4 mess kit spoons)........	....
Parsley, chopped (optional)...	6 ounces (⅔ mess kit cup)..........	....
Fish, fresh, dressed..........	35 pounds........................	....
Salt.......................	2 ounces (4 mess kit spoons)........	....

1. Combine melted shortening, bread cubes, onions, salt, pepper, poultry
seasoning, and parsley; mix well.

2. Wash fish and remove bones. If whole fish are used, stuff with bread
and onion mixture. If fillets are used, spread mixture in bottom of
greased baking pans and place fish slices on top. Sprinkle fish with
salt.

3. Bake in moderate oven (325° F.) 1 hour or until fish are flaky.

Note. The fish is improved if basted several times during baking with a small
amount of hot water and butter. Use 1 quart (1 No. 56 dipper) hot water and
¼ pound (8 mess kit spoons) butter.

NO. 180. BREAD STUFFING FOR FISH   Yield: 100 servings,
approximately 1½
ounces each.

Ingredients	100 servings	.... servings
Onions, chopped..............	½ pound (½ No. 56 dipper)........	....
Celery, chopped..............	½ pound (½ No. 56 dipper)........	....
Butter or other fat, melted....	2 pounds (1 No. 56 dipper)........	....
Bread crumbs, soft..........	8 pounds (16 No. 56 dippers).......	....
Lemon juice.................	½ pint (¼ No. 56 dipper).........	....
Salt.......................	1¼ ounces (2½ mess kit spoons).....	....
Pepper.....................	⅛ ounce (½ mess kit spoon).......	....
Poultry seasoning (optional)...	1 ounce (4 mess kit spoons)........	....
Parsley, chopped (optional)...	6 ounces (½ No. 56 dipper)........	....

1. Fry onions and celery in fat until tender but not brown.

2. Combine bread crumbs, lemon juice, seasonings, onions, celery and
fat; mix well.

Note. If too dry, a small amount of water may be added.

75

NO. 181. FISH BAKED WITH TOMATO SAUCE

Yield: Two No. 50 baking pans,
100 servings, 2½ by 4½
inches each.

Ingredients	100 servings	.... servings
Fish, fresh, dressed..........	35 pounds......................	....
Onions, finely chopped........	1 pound (1 No. 56 dipper)...........	....
Celery, diced.................	1 pound (1 No. 56 dipper)...........	....
Peppers, green, diced.........	¾ pound (¾ No. 56 dipper)........	....
Shortening, melted...........	1 pound (½ No. 56 dipper)........	....
Flour, sifted.................	8½ ounces (⅔ mess kit cup).......	....
Salt.......................	1¼ ounces (2½ mess kit spoons).....	....
Pepper.....................		
Tomatoes...................	1 No. 10 can...................	....
Parsley, finely chopped (optional).	4½ ounces (½ mess kit cup)........	....

1. Wash fish and remove bones; cut fish into servings and place in well-greased baking pans.

2. Fry onions, celery, and green peppers in shortening until tender but not brown. Add flour, salt, and pepper; mix well. Add tomatoes and parsley.

3. Heat to boiling; reduce heat and simmer slowly about 20 minutes, stirring frequently.

4. Pour over fish. Bake in moderate oven (325° F.) about 1 hour. Serve sauce from pan with the fish.

NO. 182. FISH BIRDS

Yield: 100 servings,
approximately 6½ ounces each.

Ingredients	100 servings	.... servings
Fish fillets..................	30 pounds......................	....
Salt.......................	2 ounces (4 mess kit spoons)........	....
Pepper.....................	¼ ounce (1 mess kit spoon)........	....
Bacon, sliced...............	1 pound.......................	....
Bread stuffing...............	12 pounds......................	....

1. Remove skin, and cut fillets into serving size portions.

2. Stuff with bread stuffing (recipe No. 180), roll and tie with string or fasten with toothpicks.

3. Place in well-greased baking pan.

4. Sprinkle with salt and pepper.

5. Place ⅓ strip of bacon on each roll.

6. Bake at 375° F. for 30 minutes.

7. Serve with a sauce. (See tartar sauce recipe No. 561.)

NO. 183. BROILED FISH   Yield : 100 servings,
approximately 5 ounces each.

Ingredients	100 servings	.... servings
Fish, fillets or steaks..........	30 pounds.............................	....
Salad oil....................	1 pint (⅔ mess kit cup).............	....
Salt.......................	2½ ounces (5 mess kit spoons).......	....
Pepper.....................	¼ ounce (1 mess kit spoon)..........	....
Parsley....................	3 ounces (⅓ mess kit cup)...........	....

1. Cut fish into serving size pieces.
2. Combine oil, seasonings, and flavorings, and dip each piece of fish in the mixture.
3. Place on preheated broiler pan about 2 inches from flame. If skin is left on fish, fish should be placed on pan, skin side down.
4. Broil until fish is browned, about 15 minutes; baste while cooking.
5. Serve with a sauce. (See tartar sauce recipe No. 561.)

NO. 184. DEEP-FAT FRIED FISH   Yield : 100 servings,
approximately 5 ounces each.

Ingredients	100 servings	.... servings
Fish, fillets or steaks..........	30 pounds.............................	....
Salt.......................	2½ ounces (5 mess kit spoons).......	....
Pepper.....................	¼ ounce (1 mess kit spoon)..........	....
Eggs.......................	18 eggs (¾ No. 56 dipper)..........	....
Milk.......................	1 pint (½ No. 56 dipper)...........	....
Dry bread crumbs............	2 pounds (2 No. 56 dippers).........	....

1. Cut fish into serving size pieces.
2. Dip fish in mixture of egg, milk, salt, and pepper.
3. Roll fish in bread crumbs.
4. Fry in deep fat heated to 375° F. (a temperature at which a piece of day old bread will brown in 60 seconds) for 4 to 6 minutes, or until brown.
5. Drain on absorbent paper.
6. Serve immediately with a sauce.

Note. Fish may be pan fried following directions for saute fish (See recipe No. 186.)

NO. 185. DEEP-FAT FRIED FISH FILLETS   Yield : 100 servings,
5½ ounces each.

Ingredients	100 servings	.... servings
Fish fillets..................	35 pounds............................	....
Salt.......................	To taste.............................	....
Pepper.....................	To taste	....
Flour......................	Sufficient to cover fillets...........	....
Eggs.......................	10 eggs..............................	....
Milk, evaporated............	1—14½-ounce can (½ No. 56 dipper).	....
Water (for milk)............	1 pint (½ No. 56 dipper)...........	....
Bread crumbs or corn meal....	Sufficient to cover fillets...........	....

1. Cut fillets into portions of desired size.
2. Season.
3. Roll in flour.
4. Dip in mixture of eggs, milk, and water.
5. Fry in deep lard at 350° F. about 7 to 10 minutes or until golden brown.

Note. Small, whole fish may be fried by the same method. Both the frying temperature and the time are variable, according to the thickness of fish.

NO. 186. SAUTE FISH   Yield: 100 servings, approximately 5 ounces each.

Ingredients	100 servings	.... servings
Fish, fillets or steaks..........	30 pounds............................	....
Salt......................	2½ ounces (5 mess kit spoons).......	....
Pepper.....................	¼ ounce (1 mess kit spoon)..........	....
Flour......................	1 pound (1 No. 56 dipper)..........	....
Cornmeal or bread crumbs....	1⁵⁄₁₆ pound (1 No. 56 dipper)........	....

1. Cut fish into serving size portions.
2. Sprinkle with salt and pepper.
3. Dip into mixture of flour and cornmeal.
4. Heat fat over slow fire in a heavy metal pan. At first sign of fat cooking, place fish in pan.
5. Fry fish 3 to 4 minutes, turn and fry until evenly browned. Cooking time about 10 minutes depending on thickness of fish.
6. Drain on absorbent paper.
7. Serve immediately with a sauce.

Note. Fish may be deep-fat fried following directions for fried fish. (See recipe No. 184.)

NO. 187. FRIED HADDOCK FILLETS   Yield: 100 servings, 2½ by 4½ inches each.

Ingredients	100 servings	.... servings
Fish, dressed, fillets..........	35 pounds........................	....
Salt......................	3 ounces (6 mess kit spoons).........	....
Flour, sifted.................	1 pound (1 No. 56 dipper)..........	....
Cornmeal or dry bread crumbs.	1 pound (1 mess kit cup)............	....
Fat (for frying)..............	1 pound (⅔ mess kit cup)..........	....

1. Wash fish; cut into servings.
2. Sprinkle with salt.
3. Mix flour and cornmeal or bread crumbs; roll fish in mixture.
4. Fry in hot fat (375° F.) until brown.

Note. Two pounds of flour or 2 pounds cornmeal may be used instead of 1 pound flour and 1 pound cornmeal.

Serve fried haddock with hot tomato sauce. (See recipe No. 559.)

NO. 188. BROILED SPINY LOBSTER TAILS

Yield: 100 servings, 1 tail each.

Ingredients	100 servings	.... servings
Spiny lobster tails............	100......................	....
Butter, melted...............	1 pound (½ No. 56 dipper).........	....
Salt.......................	2 ounces (4 mess kit spoons)........	....
Pepper.....................	⅛ ounce (½ mess kit spoon)........	....
Paprika....................	⅛ ounce (½ mess kit spoon)........	....

1. Clean, wash and cut tails in half lengthwise.
2. Brush the flesh with melted butter and season with salt, pepper, and paprika.
3. Place on greased broiler rack and broil 8 to 10 minutes on the flesh side, and 6 to 8 minutes on the shell side.
4. Serve with melted butter.

NO. 189. LOBSTER NEWBURG

Yield: 100 servings, approximately 5½ ounces each.

Ingredients	100 servings	.... servings
Lobster meat...............	15 pounds..................	....
Butter.....................	1 pound (½ No. 56 dipper).........	....
Flour, sifted................	¼ pound (¼ No. 56 dipper)........	....
Cream.....................	2 gallons (8 No. 56 dippers)........	....
Egg yolks..................	48 eggs (2½ No. 56 dippers)........	....
Salt.......................	½ ounce (1 mess kit spoon)........	....
Pepper, cayenne............	Dash......................	....
Lemon juice................	1 pint (½ No. 56 dipper)...........	....
Paprika....................	Dash......................	....
Toast......................	....	....

1. Cut lobster meat into cubes and cook in melted butter for 5 minutes.
2. Add flour. Gradually add cream and bring mixture slowly to boiling point. Let simmer gently for 2 or 3 minutes.
3. Add well-beaten egg yolks, salt, and cayenne and cook over very low heat for 2 minutes longer.
4. Add lemon juice, and remove from heat.
5. Serve on toast. Garnish with paprika.
   Note. For crab Newburg use crab meat instead.

NO. 190. BAKED MACKEREL

Substitute canned mackerel for salmon in recipe for baked salmon hash. (See recipe No. 197.)

NO. 191. MACKEREL CAKES

Substitute canned mackerel for salmon in recipe for salmon cakes. (See recipe No. 196.)

NO. 192. OYSTER COCKTAIL   Yield: 100 servings,
approximately 6 oysters each.

Ingredients	100 servings	.... servings
Oysters, raw	2 gallons (8 No. 56 dippers)	
Catsup	2 quarts (2 No. 56 dippers)	
Vinegar or lemon juice	1 pint (½ No. 56 dipper)	
Celery, finely chopped	1 pound (1 No. 56 dipper)	
Horseradish, grated	½ pint (¼ No. 56 dipper)	
Salt	1 ounce (2 mess kit spoons)	
Tabasco sauce	(1 mess kit spoon)	
Lettuce		

1. Drain the oysters and remove all pieces of shell.
2. Chill and place in a lettuce cup.
3. Make sauce by mixing remaining ingredients together.
4. Serve sauce with cocktail.

NO. 193. DEEP-FAT FRIED OYSTERS   Yield: 100 servings,
6 to 8 oysters each.

Ingredients	100 servings	.... servings
Oysters, large	4 gallons (16 No. 56 dippers)	
Salt	To taste	
Pepper	To taste	
Flour	Sufficient to cover oysters	
Eggs	16 eggs (¾ No. 56 dipper)	
Oyster liquid	1 quart (1 No. 56 dipper)	
Bread crumbs or corn meal	Sufficient to cover oysters	

1. Drain oysters and season.
2. Roll in flour.
3. Dip in mixture of eggs and oyster liquid.
4. Cover with bread crumbs or corn meal.
5. Fry in deep lard at 350° F. for approximately 3 minutes, or until golden brown.

NO. 194. SCALLOPED OYSTERS   Yield: Approximately 6 gallons,
100 servings, 1 cup
(6 oysters) each.

Ingredients	100 servings	.... servings
Bacon, sliced	3 pounds	
Oysters, standards or shucked	3 gallons (12 No. 56 dippers)	
Bread, diced, toasted or crackers	4 gallons (16 No. 56 dippers)	
Salt	2 ounces (4 mess kit spoons)	
Pepper	(½ mess kit spoon)	
Milk, evaporated	6—14½-ounce cans	

1. Cut bacon into ½ pieces; fry until crisp. Add oysters with juice; heat to boiling.
2. Add bread or crackers, salt, and pepper. Heat to boiling point; reduce heat and simmer 10 minutes.
3. Add undiluted milk just before serving. Heat thoroughly.

NO. 195. BAKED SCALLOPED OYSTERS

Prepare mixture as in recipe for scalloped oysters. Place in baking pans. Bake in moderate oven (350° F.) about 30 minutes.

NO. 196. SALMON CAKES

Yield: 200 cakes,
100 servings, 2 cakes
per serving, each 3 inches in
diameter.

Ingredients	100 servings	.... servings
Salmon....................	20—1-pound cans...................	....
Potatoes, mashed, without seasonings.	20 pounds (10 No. 56 dippers).......	....
Eggs.......................	16 eggs (¾ No. 56 dipper)...........	....
Bread or cracker crumbs......	2¾ pounds (2¾ No. 56 dippers).....	....
Salt.......................	3 ounces (6 mess kit spoons)........	....
Pepper, black..............	....	....
Pepper, cayenne...........	....	....
Fat (for frying).............	2 pounds (1 No. 56 dipper).........	....

1. Remove skin from salmon.

2. Combine salmon, salmon liquid, potatoes, eggs, crumbs, salt, pepper, and cayenne.

3. Make into cakes each weighing 3 ounces (3 inches in diameter, 1 inch thick). Fry in fat until brown.

Note. Serve with tomato sauce. (See recipe No. 559.)

NO. 197. BAKED SALMON HASH

Yield: Two No. 50 baking pans,
100 servings, approxi-
mately ¾ cup each.

Ingredients	100 servings	.... servings
Salmon....................	20—1-pound cans...................	....
Potatoes, mashed, without seasonings.	15 pounds (8 No. 56 dippers).......	....
Onions, chopped.............	10 pounds (10 No. 56 dippers)......	....
Salt.......................	2½ ounces (5 mess kit spoons)......	....
Pepper....................	(½ mess kit spoon)................	....

1. Remove skin from salmon. Mix salmon, salmon liquid, and remaining ingredients together.

2. Spread mixture in greased baking pans. Bake in moderate oven (375° F.) about 1¼ hours.

Note. If hash is too dry, small lumps of butter or shortening may be placed on top of fish before baking.

NO. 198. SALMON LOAF

Yield: 100 servings,
5 ounces each.

Ingredients	100 servings	.... servings
Salmon	20—1-pound cans	
Eggs, beaten	24 eggs (1¼ No. 56 dippers)	
Bread crumbs, soft	1 pound (2 No. 56 dippers)	
Butter	1 pound (½ No. 56 dipper)	
Milk, evaporated	2—14½-ounce cans	
Water (for milk)	1 quart (1 No. 56 dipper)	

1. Drain salmon; reserve juice.
2. Combine salmon, beaten egg, bread crumbs, butter, milk, and water; mix well. Shape into loaves.
3. Place in well-greased bread pans. Bake in slow oven (300° F.) about 1 hour or until slightly brown.

Note. Serve with salmon sauce (recipe No. 560) made with juice drained from salmon.

NO. 199. SCALLOPED SALMON

Substitute salmon for oysters in recipe for scalloped oysters. (See recipe No. 194.) Use salmon liquid and oil.

NO. 200. BAKED SALMON OR MACKEREL AND NOODLES

Substitute either salmon or mackerel for tuna fish in recipe for baked tuna fish and noodles. (See recipe No. 206.)

NO. 201. DEEP-FAT FRIED SCALLOPS

Yield: 100 servings,
8 to 10 each.

Ingredients	100 servings	.... servings
Scallops	4 gallons (16 No. 56 dippers)	
Salt	To taste	
Pepper	To taste	
Flour	Sufficient to cover scallops	
Eggs	10 eggs (½ No. 56 dipper)	
Milk, evaporated	½—14½-ounce can (½ No. 56 dipper)	
Water (for milk)	½ pint (¼ No. 56 dipper)	
Bread crumbs	Sufficient to cover scallops	

1. Wash and drain scallops.
2. Season.
3. Roll in flour.
4. Dip in mixture of eggs, milk, and water.
5. Roll in bread crumbs.
6. Fry in deep lard at 350° F. for approximately 4 minutes or until golden brown.

NO. 202. SHRIMP COCKTAIL

Yield: 100 servings,
approximately 3½ ounces
or ⅓ cup each.

Ingredients	100 servings	.... servings
Shrimp, cooked	15 pounds	
Catsup	2 quarts (2 No. 56 dippers)	
Vinegar, or lemon juice	1 pint (½ No. 56 dipper)	
Celery, diced	1 pound (1 No. 56 dipper)	
Horseradish	½ pint (¼ No. 56 dipper)	
Salt	1 ounce (2 mess kit spoons)	
Tabasco sauce	(1 mess kit spoon)	
Lettuce		

1. Clean the shrimp by removing any shell and the sand vein running along the back.

2. Chill and place in lettuce cup.

3. Make a sauce by mixing the remaining ingredients together.

4. Immediately before serving put sauce on cocktails.

NO. 203. SHRIMP CREOLE WITH RICE

Yield: 100 servings,
approximately 9½ ounces each.

Ingredients	100 servings	.... servings
Shrimp, raw	20 pounds	
Onions, chopped	2 pounds (2 No. 56 dippers)	
Celery, chopped	1 pound (1 No. 56 dipper)	
Green pepper, chopped	1 pound (1 No. 56 dipper)	
Butter or other fat	1 pound (½ No. 56 dipper)	
Flour, sifted	¼ pound (¼ No. 56 dipper)	
Tomatoes	2½ No. 10 cans (8 No. 56 dippers)	
Salt	2½ ounces (5 mess kit spoons)	
Worcestershire sauce	2½ ounces (5 mess kit spoons)	
Pepper	¼ ounce (1 mess kit spoon)	
Rice, dry	6 pounds (3 No. 56 dippers)	

1. Cover shrimp with boiling salted water.

2. Cook 15 minutes. Drain. Plunge into cold water to cool quickly.

3. Remove shell, remove black vein with a sharp pointed knife.

4. Fry onions, celery, and green pepper in melted fat till golden brown.

5. Add flour and tomatoes and cook until smooth and slightly thick.

6. Add shrimp and seasoning and heat.

7. Cook rice and drain.

8. Serve shrimp creole over rice.

NO. 204. FRENCH FRIED SHRIMP

Yield: 100 servings,
approximately 5 ounces each.

Ingredients	100 servings	.... servings
Shrimp, fresh	30 pounds	
Salt	2½ ounces (5 mess kit spoons)	
Eggs, beaten	12 eggs (½ No. 56 dipper)	
Water, cold	½ pint (½ No. 56 dipper)	
Bread crumbs	2 pounds (2 No. 56 dippers)	
Flour	2 pounds (2 No. 56 dippers)	

1. Remove shells and sand vein, and wash shrimp.
2. Cut them almost through lengthwise and salt on both sides.
3. Dip the shrimp in well-beaten eggs to which the water has been added.
4. Roll shrimp in a mixture of bread crumbs and flour.
5. Fry in deep fat heated to 350° F. for about 3 minutes or until golden brown.
6. Drain on absorbent paper.

NO. 205. CREAMED SHRIMP AND PEAS

Yield: Approximately 3 gallons,
100 servings, approximately ½ cup each over 1 slice
of toast.

Ingredients	100 servings	.... servings
Peas	2 No. 10 cans	
Flour, sifted	6 ounces (½ mess kit cup)	
Salt	2 ounces (4 mess kit spoons)	
Mustard, dry		
Pepper		
Butter	8 ounces (⅓ mess kit cup)	
Milk, evaporated	6—14½-ounce cans	
Shrimp*	16—5¾-ounce cans	
Toast	100 slices	

*Nine pounds fresh shrimp may be substituted for the 16 cans shrimp. Cover shrimp with water; heat to boiling point; reduce heat and simmer 20 minutes. Peel, remove sand vein, and wash. Leave shrimp whole or cut into pieces.

1. Drain peas; heat 2 quarts (2 No. 56 dippers) liquid to boiling point.
2. Mix flour, salt, mustard, pepper, and butter together; stir untl smooth.
3. Add to hot liquid gradually. Heat to boiling point; boil until thick, stirring constantly. Add milk and continue cooking slowly about 5 minutes.
4. Add peas and shrimp; simmer slowly until heated through. Serve on toast.

NO. 206. BAKED TUNA FISH AND NOODLES

Yield: Two No. 50 baking pans,
approximately 100
servings, ½ cup each.

Ingredients	100 servings	.... servings
Noodles....................	6 pounds........................	....
Salt......................	3 ounces (6 mess kit spoons).........	....
Water, boiling..............	3 gallons (12 No. 56 dippers)........	....
Celery, diced..............	2 pounds (2 No. 56 dippers).........	....
Onions, chopped...........	(4 mess kit spoons)..............	....
Pimiento, chopped (optional)..	2—4-ounce cans.................	....
Corn flakes................	2 quarts (2 No. 56 dippers).........	....
Salt......................	2 ounces (4 mess kit spoons)........	....
Pepper...................	....	....
Tuna fish, flaked...........	12—12-ounce cans...............	....
Fat, melted...............	1 pound (½ No. 56 dipper).........	....
Flour, sifted..............	8 ounces (½ No. 56 dipper).........	....
Milk, evaporated...........	6—14½-ounce cans.............	....
Water (for milk)...........	3 quarts (3 No. 56 dippers).........	....

1. Add noodles to boiling salted water; boil 10 minutes. Drain well.
2. Combine noodles, celery, onions, pimiento, corn flakes, salt, pepper, tuna fish, and fish liquid and oil.
3. Mix melted fat and flour; stir until smooth.
4. Mix milk and water; add to flour mixture. Heat to boiling point; boil 5 minutes or until thick, stirring constantly. Pour over fish and noodle mixture; mix well.
5. Pour into well-greased baking pans. Bake in moderate oven (375° F.) 40 minutes.

NO. 207. TUNA A LA KING

Yield: 100 servings,
approximately 7½ ounces each.

Ingredients	100 servings	.... servings
Tuna.......................	24—13-ounce cans..............	....
Oil drained from tuna.......	1½ quarts (1½ No. 56 dippers)......	....
Flour, sifted...............	1½ quarts (1½ No. 56 dippers)......	....
Milk......................	3 gallons (12 No. 56 dippers)........	....
Eggs, beaten..............	18 eggs (¾ No. 56 dipper)........	....
Green pepper.............	¾ pound (1 mess kit cup).........	....
Celery....................	¾ pound (1 mess kit cup).........	....
Salt......................	2 ounces (4 mess kit spoons)........	....
Paprika...................	½ ounce (2 mess kit spoons).......	....

1. Drain tuna and flake.
2. Make a white sauce by mixing tuna oil and flour, add milk and cook until slightly thick.
3. Cook celery and green pepper until tender in salted water.
4. Add beaten eggs to white sauce.
5. Add remining ingredients to white sauce, and serve immediately on toast or biscuits.

SECTION IX

FRITTERS AND CROQUETTES

16. DEEP-FAT FRYING. a. It is customary to use lard, hydrogenated fat, or oil for deep-fat frying; however, carefully rendered beef fat will give satisfactory results. Rendered lamb fat can be used in combination with lard, lard substitute or beef fat.

b. Melt fat in fryer or deep kettle, using enough to fill the kettle to within 3 inches of the rim. If the kettle is too full the fat will bubble over when the food is added. Drain moist foods well before frying as the moisture forms steam when in contact with hot fat. The steam may cause the fat to boil over and catch fire. Set thermostat on the fryer or test fat with a thermometer or by frying a cube of stale bread. A 1-inch cube of bread will become brown as follows:

Temperature	Time
350° F.	1½ minutes
360° F.	1 minute
370° F.	40 seconds

Food will become grease soaked if the temperature is too low. Heat fat to required temperature before each addition of food. Cook a small amount of food at one time, otherwise the fat will be cooled. Flavors and odors left in fat after frying strong foods may be removed by frying several slices of potatoes. The potatoes will absorb the flavors and odors.

c. Foods most often cooked in deep fat are breaded meats, fish, fritters, croquettes, potatoes, and doughnuts. The recipes for fritters and croquettes are found in this section.

NO. 208. BANANA FRITTERS   Yield: Approximately 11¼ pounds mixture, 100 servings, 2 fritters each.

Ingredients	100 servings	.... servings
Flour, sifted..................	4¼ pounds (4¼ No. 56 dippers).....	....
Sugar, granulated............	1¾ pounds (⅞ No. 56 dipper).....	....
Baking powder..............	4 ounces (10½ mess kit spoons)......	....
Salt.......................	3 ounces (6 mess kit spoons)........	....
Milk, evaporated............	2—14½-ounce cans................	....
Water (for milk)............	1½ pints (1 mess kit cup)........	....
Eggs, beaten................	12 eggs (⅔ No. 56 dipper)........	....
Shortening, melted..........	6 ounces (¼ mess kit cup)........	....
Bananas....................	50 to 60 bananas................	....
Flour, sifted (for rolling).....	1 pound (1 No. 56 dipper)..........	....
Shorening (for frying)	....	....

1. Sift flour, sugar, baking powder, and salt together.

87

2. Combine milk, water, beaten egg, and shortening; mix well. Add to flour mixture; stir until smooth.
3. Cut each banana into three or four diagonal pieces. Roll each piece lightly in flour.
4. Drop pieces of bananas into batter; stir lightly until each piece is completely covered.
5. Fry bananas in deep hot fat (375° F.) 4 to 6 minutes, turning frequently to cook them evenly.
6. Drain on absorbent paper or a rack.
7. Serve very hot.

NO. 209. BANANA BRAN FRITTERS

Add 14 ounces (2 No. 56 dippers) bran to sifted flour mixture in recipe for banana fritters; mix well. Add ½ pint (⅓ mess kit cup) water to liquid ingredients.

NO. 210. PINEAPPLE FRITTERS

Substitute 3¾ quarts (5 mess kit cups) or 1 No. 10 can thoroughly drained, diced pineapple for the bananas in recipe for banana fritters. Use the juice for sauce to serve on fritters.

NO. 211. PEACH FRITTERS

Substitute 3¾ quarts (5 mess kit cups) or 1 No. 10 can thorouhly drained, sliced peaches for the bananas in recipe for banana fritters. Use the juice in sauce to serve on fritters.

NO. 212. APPLE FRITTERS

Substitute 4¾ quarts (4¾ No. 56 dippers) or 1 No. 10 can thoroughly drained, sliced apples for the bananas in the recipe for banana fritters. Use the juice in sauce to serve on fritters.

NO. 213. BEEF FRITTERS

Yield: 100 servings, 2 fritters (3 ounces each) per serving.

Ingredients	100 servings	.... servings
Bread	8 pounds	
Beef, cooked, ground	20 pounds	
Onions, finely chopped	3 pounds (3 No. 56 dippers)	
Salt	1 ounce (2 mess kit spoons)	
Pepper	¼ ounce (1 mess kit spoon)	
Milk, evaporated	1—14½-ounce can	
Water (for milk)	1 pint (½ No. 56 dipper)	
Eggs, slightly beaten	10 eggs (½ No. 56 dipper)	
Flour, sifted (for rolling)	1 pound (1 No. 56 dipper)	
Fat (for frying)		

1. Soak bread in water; press and discard water.

2. Combine bread, meat, onions, salt, and pepper; mix thoroughly.
3. Make into 3-ounce cakes.
4. Combine milk and water; add beaten egg. Dip meat cakes in mixture. Roll in flour.
5. Fry in deep hot fat (350° F.) until golden brown.

NO. 214. LAMB, HAM, VEAL, CHICKEN, OR TURKEY FRITTERS

Substitute lamb, ham, veal, chicken, or turkey for beef in recipe for beef fritters. Use same weight of cooked lamb, ham, or veal or 12 pounds cooked chicken or turkey.

NO. 215. CORN FRITTERS
(Using cream-style corn)

Yield: Approximately 18 pounds mixture, 100 servings, 2 fritters each.

Ingredients	100 servings	.... servings
Flour, sifted	5 pounds (5 No. 56 dippers)	
Sugar, granulated	2½ ounces (5 mess kit spoons)	
Baking powder	2½ ounces (7 mess kit spoons)	
Salt	2½ ounces (5 mess kit spoons)	
Eggs, beaten	10 eggs (½ No. 56 dipper)	
Shortening, melted	7½ ounces (⅓ mess kit cup)	
Corn, cream-style	9 No. 2 cans	
Fat (for frying)		

1. Sift flour, sugar, baking powder, and salt together.
2. Combine beaten egg, shortening, and corn; add to flour mixture and stir until smooth.*
3. Drop by spoonfuls into deep hot fat (375° F.) and fry about 6 or 7 minutes, turning fritters frequently to cook them evenly.
4. Drain on absorbent paper or a rack.
5. Serve very hot.

*If necessary, add water to make batter of proper consistency.

Note. Serve corn fritters with sirup or jelly.

NO. 216. CORN FRITTERS (Using kernel corn)

Yield: Approximately 20 pounds mixture, 100 servings, 2 fritters each.

Ingredients	100 servings	.... servings
Flour, sifted	4¼ pounds (4¼ No. 56 dippers)	
Sugar, granulated	2¼ ounces (4½ mess kit spoons)	
Baking powder	2¼ ounces (6 mess kit spoons)	
Salt	2¼ ounces (4½ mess kit spoons)	
Milk, evaporated	2—14½-ounce cans	
Water (for milk)	1 quart (1 No. 56 dipper)	
Eggs, beaten	9 eggs (½ No. 56 dipper)	
Shortening, melted	6 ounces (¼ mess kit cup)	
Corn, kernel, drained	2 No. 10 cans	
Fat (for frying)		

1. Sift flour, sugar, baking powder, and salt together.
2. Combine milk, water, beaten egg, and shortening; add to flour mixture and stir until smooth.
3. Add corn and mix well.
4. Drop by spoonfuls into deep hot fat (375° F.) and fry about 6 or 7 minutes, turning fritters frequently to cook them evenly.
5. Drain on absorbent paper or rack.
6. Serve very hot.

Note. Serve with sirup or jelly.

NO. 217. CARROT FRITTERS

Substitute 6½ quarts (6½ No. 56 dippers) cooked, diced carrots, or 2 No. 10 cans diced carrots for corn in recipe for corn fritters.

NO. 218. CORN AND HAM FRITTERS

Substitute 4½ pounds (4 No. 56 dippers) cooked, finely chopped ham for ½ corn in recipe for corn fritters.

NO. 219. HAM FRITTERS

Yield: Approximately 14 pounds mixture, 100 servings, 2 fritters each.

Ingredients	100 servings	.... servings
Flour, sifted	¾ pound (¾ No. 56 dipper)	
Baking powder	2¼ ounces (6 mess kit spoons)	
Pepper	⅔ ounce (2 mess kit spoons)	
Milk, evaporated	1—14½-ounce can	
Water (for milk)	1 pint (½ No. 56 dipper)	
Eggs, beaten	32 eggs (1½ No. 56 dippers)	
Ham, cooked, chopped	9 pounds (8 No. 56 dippers)	
Onions, chopped	2⅔ ounces	
Fat (for frying)		

1. Sift flour, baking powder and salt together.
2. Combine milk, water, and beaten egg; add to flour mixture and stir until smooth.
3. Add ham and onions; mix well.
4. Drop by spoonfuls into deep hot fat (375° F.) and fry about 2 to 3 minutes, turning fritters frequently to cook them evenly.
5. Drain on absorbent paper or rack.
6. Serve very hot.

Note. Serve with sirup.

NO. 220. OATMEAL FRITTERS — Yield: Approximately 18¼ pounds mixture, 100 servings, 2 fritters each.

Ingredients	100 servings	.... servings
Flour, sifted	6 pounds (6 No. 56 dippers)	
Sugar, granulated	3 pounds (1½ No. 56 dippers)	
Baking powder	6 ounces (⅓ mess kit cup)	
Salt	3½ ounces (7 mess kit spoons)	
Cinnamon	¾ ounce (3 mess kit spoons)	
Nutmeg	3½ ounces (14 mess kit spoons)	
Oats, rolled	2¾ pounds (4 No. 56 dippers)	
Milk, evaporated	3—14½-ounce cans	
Water (for milk)	1½ pints (¾ No. 56 dipper)	
Eggs, beaten	14 eggs (¾ No. 56 dipper)	
Shortening, melted	10 ounces (½ mess kit cup)	
Fat (for frying)		

1. Sift flour, sugar, baking powder, salt, cinnamon, and nutmeg together. Add rolled oats; mix well.

2. Combine milk, water, beaten egg, and shortening; add to flour mixture and mix well.

3. Drop by spoonfuls into deep hot fat (375° F.) and fry about 4 minutes, turning fritters frequently to cook them evenly.

4. Drain on absorbent paper or a rack.

5. Serve very hot.

Note. Serve with sugar, sugar and cinnamon, sirup, or a sauce.

NO. 221. VEGETABLE FRITTERS — Yield: 100 servings, 2 fritters each.

Ingredients	100 servings	.... servings
Celery, cooked, diced	2¾ pounds (2¾ No. 56 dippers)	
Carrots, cooked, diced	2½ pounds (2 No. 56 dippers)	
Peas, shelled, cooked	2 pounds (2½ No. 56 dippers)	
Flour, sifted	8½ pounds (8½ No. 56 dippers)	
Baking powder	6 ounces (⅓ mess kit cup)	
Salt	2 ounces (4 mess kit spoons)	
Milk, evaporated	5—14½-ounce cans	
Water (for milk)	1¾ quarts (1¾ No. 56 dippers)	
Eggs, beaten	18 eggs (1 No. 56 dipper)	
Fat (for frying)		

1. Combine cooked vegetables.

2. Sift flour, baking powder, and salt together.

3. Combine milk, water, and beaten egg; add to flour mixture and stir until smooth.

4. Add cooked vegetables and mix lightly.

5. Drop by spoonfuls into deep hot fat (375° F.). Fry about 6 or 7 minutes, turning fritters frequently to cook them evenly.

6. Drain on absorbent paper or a rack.

7. Serve very hot.

Note. Serve very hot with a meat gravy, cheese, or tomato sauce. (See recipe Nos. 562, 547, and 559.) Use liquid from vegetables in soups.

NO. 222. BEEF CROQUETTES   Yield: 100 servings, 2 croquettes each.

Ingredients	100 servings	.... servings
Beef, cooked, ground.........	25 pounds........................	....
Salt......................	2 ounces (4 mess kit spoons).........	....
Pepper.....................	¼ ounce (1 mess kit spoon).......	....
Onions, finely chopped........	5 pounds (5 No. 56 dippers).........	....
Fat (for frying)..............	2½ pounds (1¼ No. 56 dippers).....	....
Flour, sifted................	2 pounds (2 No. 56 dippers).........	....
Meat stock, hot.............	2 quarts (2 No. 56 dippers).........	....
Eggs, slightly beaten.........	30 eggs (1½ No. 56 dippers)........	....
Bread crumbs, dry..........	5 pounds (5 No. 56 dippers).........	....
Mace (optional)..............	¼ ounce (½ mess kit spoon)........	....
Milk, evaporated.............	1—14½-ounce can................	....
Water (for milk).............	1 pint (½ No. 56 dipper)..........	....
Eggs, slightly beaten.........	10 eggs (½ No. 56 dipper).........	....
Flour, sifted (for rolling).....		
Bread crumbs................		
Fat (for frying).............		

1. Mix ground beef, salt, and pepper together.

2. Fry onions until brown; add flour and mix well.

3. Add hot stock gradually; heat to boiling point, stirring constantly

4. Cool; add slightly beaten egg, bread crumbs, mace, and ground beef; mix thoroughly. Refrigerate until thoroughly chilled.

5. Mix milk and water; add beaten egg and mix well.

6. Shape meat into croquettes; roll in flour and dip in egg and milk mixture. Roll in crumbs.

7. Fry in deep fat (350° F.) 12 to 15 minutes or until golden brown. Serve hot.

NO. 223. LAMB OR VEAL CROQUETTES

Substitute lamb or veal for beef in recipe for beef croquettes.

NO. 224. BEEF, LAMB, OR VEAL CROQUETTE LOAF

Prepare croquette mixture as in recipe for beef croquettes. Place in well-oiled baking pans. Bake in slow oven (325° F.) 1 hour. Cut in squares.

NO. 225. CHICKEN OR TURKEY CROQUETTES

Yield: 100 servings, 2 croquettes each.

Ingredients	100 servings	.... servings
Chicken or turkey, cooked, finely chopped	16 pounds	
Salt	2 ounces (4 mess kit spoons)	
Pepper	½ ounce (2 mess kit spoons)	
Onions, finely chopped	4 pounds (4 No. 56 dippers)	
Fat (for frying)	2 pounds (1 No. 56 dipper)	
Flour, sifted	1½ pounds (1½ No. 56 dippers)	
Chicken or turkey stock, hot	2 quarts (2 No. 56 dippers)	
Eggs, slightly beaten	24 eggs (1¼ No. 56 dippers)	
Bread crumbs, dry	3 pounds (3 No. 56 dippers)	
Flour, sifted (for rolling)		
Eggs, slightly beaten	10 eggs (½ No. 56 dipper)	
Milk, evaporated	1—14½-ounce can	
Water (for milk)	1 pint (½ No. 56 dipper)	
Bread crumbs (for rolling)		

1. Mix turkey or chicken, salt, and pepper together.

2. Fry onions until brown; add flour and mix well.

3. Add hot stock gradually; heat to boiling point, stirring constantly.

4. Cool; add slightly beaten egg, bread crumbs, and chicken or turkey; mix thoroughly. Refrigerate until thoroughly chilled.

5. Mix milk and water; add beaten egg and mix well.

6. Shape meat into croquettes; roll in flour and dip in egg and milk mixture. Roll in crumbs.

7. Fry in deep hot fat (350° F.) 12 to 15 minutes or until brown.

NO. 226. BAKED CHICKEN OR TURKEY CROQUETTE LOAF

Prepare croquette mixture as in recipe for chicken or turkey croquettes. Place in well-oiled baking pans. Bake in slow oven (325° F.) 1 hour. Cut in squares.

NO. 227. HAM CROQUETTES

Yield: 100 servings, 2 croquettes each.

Ingredients	100 servings	.... servings
Ham, cooked, finely chopped	25 pounds	
Salt	2 ounces (4 mess kit spoons)	
Pepper	½ ounce (2 mess kit spoons)	
Mace (optional)	¼ ounce (1 mess kit spoon)	
Parsley (optional)	2 ounces	
Onions, finely chopped	5 pounds (5 No. 56 dippers)	
Fat (for frying)	2 pounds (1 No. 56 dipper)	
Flour, sifted	2 pounds (2 No. 56 dippers)	
Ham stock, hot	5 quarts (5 No. 56 dippers)	
Eggs, slightly beaten	30 eggs (1½ No. 56 dippers)	
Bread crumbs, dry	5 pounds (5 No. 56 dippers)	
Flour, sifted		
Milk, evaporated	1—14½-ounce can	
Water (for milk)	1 pint (½ No. 56 dipper)	
Eggs, slightly beaten	10 eggs (½ No. 56 dipper)	
Bread crumbs		
Fat (for frying)		

1. Combine ham, salt, pepper, mace, and parsley.

2. Fry onions until brown; add flour and mix well.

3. Add hot ham stock gradually; heat to boiling point, stirring constantly.

4. Cool; add slightly beaten egg, bread crumbs, and ham; mix thoroughly. Refrigerate until thoroughly chilled.

5. Mix milk and water; add beaten egg and mix well.

6. Shape meat into croquettes; roll in flour and dip in egg and milk mixture. Roll in crumbs.

7. Fry in deep hot fat (350° F.) 12 to 15 minutes or until golden brown. Serve hot.

NO. 228. MEAT CROQUETTES

Yield: 25½ pounds mixture, 100 servings, 2 croquettes each.

Ingredients	100 servings	.... servings
Onions, finely chopped........	½ pound (½ No. 56 dipper).........	....
Fat (for frying)...............	¾ pound (½ mess kit cup).........	....
Flour, sifted.................	¾ pound (¾ No. 56 dipper)........	....
Salt.......................	3 ounces (6 mess kit spoons)........	....
Pepper.....................		
Worcestershire sauce.........	4 ounces (7 mess kit spoons)........	....
Milk, evaporated.............	4—14½-ounce cans..............	....
Water (for milk).............	1½ quarts (1½ No. 56 dippers)......	.........: ..
Meat, left-over, finely ground..	16 pounds (14 No. 56 dippers).......	....
Bread crumbs, soft...........	2¼ pounds (4½ No. 56 dipper).....	....
Eggs, beaten................	10 eggs (½ No. 56 dipper)..........	....
Bread crumbs...............		
Fat (for frying)..............		....

1. Fry onions until tender. Add flour, salt, pepper, and Worcestershire sauce. Mix well.

2. Mix milk and water; add to onions. Heat to boiling; boil until thick, stirring constantly. Remove from heat.

3. Add meat and bread crumbs; mix well. Refrigerate until thoroughly chilled.

4. Shape mixture into croquettes; dip in beaten egg. Roll in crumbs.

5. Fry in deep hot fat (375° F.) about 3 to 5 minutes.

6. Drain on absorbent paper.

7. Serve very hot.

Note. Serve with brown gravy (recipe No. 562) or tomato sauce. (See recipe No. 559.)

NO. 229. POTATO CROQUETTES

Yield: Approximately 23½ pounds mixture, 100 servings, 2 croquettes each.

Ingredients	100 servings	.... servings
Potatoes, mashed............	22 pounds........................	....
Eggs, beaten...............	27 eggs (1⅓ No. 56 dippers)........	....
Bread crumbs...............		....
Fat (for frying).............		....

1. Mix potatoes and ⅔ beaten egg.* Refrigerate until thoroughly chilled.
2. Shape potato mixture into croquettes; dip in remainder of beaten egg. Roll in crumbs.
3. Fry in deep hot fat (375° F.) 3 to 5 minutes or until brown.
4. Drain on absorbent paper.
5. Serve very hot.

*If mixture is too soft to handle, add small amount of sifted flour.

Note. Serve with tomato sauce. (See recipe No. 559.)

NO. 230. POTATO AND ONION CROQUETTES

Add 1 pound (1 mess kit cup) finely chopped onions to the potato mixture in recipe for potato croquettes.

NO. 231. POTATO AND GREEN PEPPER CROQUETTES

Add 1½ pounds (1½ No. 56 dippers) finely diced green peppers to the potato mixture in recipe for potato croquettes.

NO. 232. TOMATO, CHEESE AND RICE CROQUETTES

Yield: 22¼ pounds mixture, 100 servings, 2 croquettes each.

Ingredients	100 servings	.... servings
Flour, sifted.................	½ pound (½ No. 56 dipper)........	....
Salt.........................	5½ ounces (11 mess kit spoons)......	....
Pepper......................		....
Worcestershire sauce........	1½ ounces (2½ mess kit spoons).....	....
Mustard, dry................	1⅔ ounces (4¾ mess kit spoons).....	....
Shortening, melted..........	½ pound (⅓ mess kit cup)..........	....
Tomatoes....................	2 No. 3 cans.....................	....
Cheese, finely chopped........	2 pounds (2 No. 56 dippers)........	....
Rice, cooked................	12¾ quarts (12¾ No. 56 dippers)....	....
Eggs, beaten................	10 eggs (½ No. 56 dipper)..........	....
Bread crumbs...............		....
Fat (for frying).............		....

1. Combine flour, salt, pepper, Worcestershire sauce, mustard, and melted shortening; mix well.

2. Strain tomatoes through a coarse sieve; add to flour mixture. Heat to boiling point; reduce heat and simmer until smooth and thick, stirring constantly.

3. Add cheese and heat until cheese is melted. Remove from heat.

4. Add cooked rice and mix lightly. Refrigerate until thoroughly chilled.

5. Shape mixture into croquettes; dip in beaten egg. Roll in crumbs.

6. Fry in deep hot fat (375° F.) 2 to 3 minutes.

7. Drain on absorbent paper.

8. Serve very hot.

Note. Serve with tomato sauce. (See recipe No. 559.)

NO. 233. CHEESE AND RICE CROQUETTES

Substitute three 14½-ounce cans evaporated milk and 1½ pints (1 mess kit cup) water for strained, canned tomatoes in recipe for tomato, cheese, and rice croquettes.

SECTION X

FRUIT

17. **FRESH FRUITS. a. Preparation.** Wash all fresh fruits thoroughly to remove any inspect sprays which might be present. If possible pare fresh fruits immediately before using. When pared and left in contact with the air, some fresh fruits become discolored. Discoloration may be partially prevented by covering the fruit with a thin sirup or lemon juice until ready for use.

b. Uses for fresh fruits. (1) *Apples*. Serve raw and whole for breakfast; sliced or cubed in salads or fruit cocktail; baked, stewed, or as applesauce for breakfast or dessert. Leave skin on raw apples if it is tender.

(2) *Bananas*. Serve whole for breakfast; sliced for breakfast, dessert, salads, or fruit cocktail. Peel and slice bananas as short a time as possible before using to prevent discoloration.

(3) *Berries*. Wash and drain; handle carefully to avoid crushing. Serve raw for breakfast or dessert; cooked in shortcake, cobblers, or pies.

(4) *Dates*. Wash and seed. Serve on cereals or in cakes, cookies, or puddings.

(5) *Grapes*. Wash. Serve raw in bunches; if firm, slice, seed, and serve in salads or fruit cocktail.

(6) *Grapefruit*. Cut into halves crosswise; cut around rind to loosen pulp; remove seeds and loosen pulp from each section with a knife. Serve raw for breakfast or dessert; baked or broiled with sugar at low temperature for dessert. Pare thickly and remove each section of pulp by cutting carefully between membranes for salads.

(7) *Lemons*. Cut into halves; squeeze juice for use in fruit drinks, pies, or puddings. Slice or cut into eighths lengthwise for use in tea.

(8) *Melons*. Cut into halves or quarters; remove seeds. Serve for breakfast or dessert. Slice and pare or remove pulp with a teaspoon and shape into balls for salads or fruit cocktail.

(9) *Oranges*. Serve whole, cut into halves, or pared, sliced, and segmented for breakfast, dessert, salads, or fruit cocktail. Cut into halves; squeeze juice for use in fruit drinks or desserts.

(10) *Peaches*. Serve raw and whole or peeled, stoned, and sliced for breakfast or dessert; cooked in shortcake, cobblers, or pies. Peel and slice peaches as short a time as possible before using to prevent discoloration.

(11) *Pears.* Serve raw and whole or pared, cored, and sliced for breakfast or dessert; stewed with sugar, cinnamon, cloves, or lemon.

(12) *Pineapple.* Pare pineapple with long, sharp knife, beginning at top and cutting down. Remove eyes with pointed knife; slice. Serve for breakfast, dessert, salads, or fruit cocktail. Shred pineapple by cutting in slices before paring; shred with a fork.

(13) *Plums.* Serve raw and whole for breakfast or dessert; stewed with sugar for sauce or pies.

(14) *Rhubarb.* Serve stewed or baked with sugar for breakfast, dessert, or pies.

(15) *Watermelons.* Serve sliced and cut in large wedge-shaped pieces for dessert.

18. DRIED FRUITS. Wash thoroughly before using. Dried fruits may be soaked to reduce cooking time. Avoid a long soaking period as it produces a watery, tasteless fruit. Cook raisins and dates without soaking. Cook dried fruits slowly in the water used for soaking. Add sugar at the end of the cooking period. When added at the beginning, sugar interferes with the absorption of water by the fruit.

NO. 234. APPLESAUCE   Yield: 5½ gallons,
100 servings, approximately
¾ cup each.

Ingredients	100 servings	.... servings
Apples, fresh	35 pounds	
Water	8½ quarts (8½ No. 56 dippers)	
Sugar, granulated	7½ pounds (3¾ No. 56 dippers)	
Nutmeg *or* cinnamon	¾ ounce (3 mess kit spoons)	

1. Wash apples; remove cores. Cut apples into quarters.
2. Add water. Heat to boiling point; reduce heat and simmer about 25 minutes or until soft.
3. Press through a sieve. Add sugar and nutmeg or cinnamon; mix well.

Note. Six sliced lemons may be added to the applesauce to improve the flavor.

NO. 235. BAKED APPLES   Yield: 100 servings,
1 apple each.

Ingredients	100 servings	.... servings
Apples	100 apples	
Sugar, granulated	6¼ pounds (3⅛ No. 56 dippers)	
Cinnamon (optional)		
Water	4¾ quarts (4¾ No. 56 dippers)	

1. Wash apples; remove cores. Remove 1 inch of skin from top of apples.
2. Place apples in baking pans.

3. Mix sugar, cinnamon, and water together; pour over apples.
4. Bake in moderate oven (375° F.) about 1 hour.

NO. 236. BAKED PEACHES OR PEARS
Substitute 100 peaches or pears for apples in recipe for baked apples.
Leave whole or cut in halves.

NO. 237. STEWED APPLES
Yield: 100 servings,
5 ounces each.

Ingredients	100 servings	.... servings
Apples....................	35 pounds........................	....
Sugar, granulated............	8 pounds (4 No. 56 dippers)........	....
Water....................	2 gallons (8 No. 56 dippers)........	....
Orange rind *or* lemon rind.....	....	....

1. Wash apples; pare and remove cores. Cut apples into eighths.
2. Mix sugar and water. Heat to boiling point; boil until sugar is dissolved, stirring constantly.
3. Continue boiling 5 minutes. Reduce heat and add grated rind.
4. Add apples to sirup; simmer until transparent. If sirup thickens during cooking, add more water.

NO. 238. CRANBERRY SAUCE
Yield: 100 servings,
approximately
3 ounces each.

Ingredients	100 servings	.... servings
Sugar, granulated............	5 pounds (2½ No. 56 dippers)......	....
Water, boiling..............	2 quarts (2 No. 56 dippers)........	....
Cranberries...............	5 pounds (5 No. 56 dippers)........	....

1. Mix sugar and hot water. Heat to boiling point; boil 5 minutes.
2. Wash cranberries; add to boiling sirup. Heat to boiling point; reduce heat and simmer, without stirring, 5 minutes or until all skins pop open. Remove from heat.
3. Cool before serving.

NO. 239. CRANBERRY JELLY
Force cooked cranberries in recipe for cranberry sauce through a coarse sieve. Heat the juice to boiling point; boil 5 minutes or until jellied. Chill until firm.

NO. 240. CRANBERRY APPLE RELISH
Yield: 100 servings,
2 ounces each.

Ingredients	100 servings	.... servings
Oranges....................	7 oranges........................	....
Lemons....................	3 lemons........................	....
Apples....................	2½ pounds........................	....
Cranberries.................	3½ pounds (3½ No. 56 dippers).....	....
Sugar, granulated............	4 pounds (2 No. 56 dippers)........	....

1. Wash oranges and lemons; cut into quarters without peeling.
2. Remove seeds. Chop pulp and rind.
3. Wash apples; remove seeds and cores. Cut into quarters; chop.
4. Wash cranberries; chop.
5. Combine chopped oranges, lemons, apples, and cranberries. Add sugar; mix well.
6. Refrigerate a few hours before serving.

NO. 241. CRANBERRY ORANGE RELISH

Yield: 100 servings, approximately 2 ounces each.

Ingredients	100 servings	. . . servings
Oranges	10 oranges	
Cranberries	5 pounds (5 No. 56 dippers)	
Sugar, granulated	5 pounds (2½ No. 56 dippers)	

1. Wash oranges; cut into quarters without peeling. Remove seeds. Chop pulp and rind.
2. Wash cranberries; chop.
3. Combine oranges, cranberries, and sugar, mix well.
4. Refrigerate a few hours before serving.

NO. 242. STEWED DRIED APRICOTS

Yield: 100 servings, 5 ounces each.

Ingredients	100 servings	. . . . servings
Apricots, dried	7 pounds	
Water, cold	2 gallons (8 No. 56 dippers)	
Sugar, granulated	3 pounds (1½ No. 56 dippers)	

1. Wash apricots. Cover with cold water; soak 2 hours.
2. Heat to boiling; reduce heat and simmer 30 minutes or until tender.
3. Add sugar; continue cooking 5 minutes.

NO. 243. STEWED DRIED PEACHES

Substitute an equal amount of dried peaches for the dried apricots in recipe for stewed dried apricots. Increase water to 3 gallons (12 No. 56 dippers).

NO. 244. STEWED PRUNES.

Yield: 100 servings, 5 ounces each.

Ingredients	100 servings	. . . . servings
Prunes, dried	8 pounds	
Water, cold	2¾ gallons (11 No. 56 dippers)	
Sugar, granulated	1½ pounds (¾ No. 56 dipper)	
Lemons, sliced	3 lemons	

1. Wash prunes. Cover with cold water; soak 2 hours.
2. Heat to boiling point; reduce heat and simmer 45 minutes or until soft.
3. Add sugar and lemon slices. Continue simmering 5 minutes.

MACARONI, SPAGHETTI, NOODLES, AND RICE

19. USE IN MEAL. Macaroni, spaghetti, noodles, and rice are sometimes served instead of potatoes. If combined with meat, cheese, or eggs, they may be used as a main dish. The recipes in this chapter yield 8- to 12-ounce portions which can be reduced when served as a vegetable.

NO. 245. BOILED MACARONI Yield: 100 servings, 8 ounces (1½ cups) each.

Ingredients	100 servings	.... servings
Macaroni.................	15½ pounds.......................	....
Salt......................	7½ ounces (⅓ mess kit cup)........	....
Water, boiling............	15 gallons (60 No. 56 dippers).......	....
Butter...................	3 pounds (1½ No. 56 dippers).......	....

1. Break macaroni into 2- to 3-inch pieces.
2. Add macaroni slowly to boiling salted water; boil 10 to 15 minutes or until tender. Drain well.
3. Add butter; mix lightly.

NO. 246. MACARONI AU GRATIN Yield: 100 servings, 12 ounces (1½ cups) each.

Ingredients	100 servings	.... servings
Macaroni.................	11¼ pounds......................	....
Salt......................	5 ounces (10 mess kit spoons).......	....
Water, boiling............	10 gallons (40 No. 56 dippers).......	....
Cheese, shredded..........	10 pounds (10 No. 56 dippers).......	....
Fat, melted...............	1 pound (½ No. 56 dipper).........	....
Flour, sifted..............	8 ounces (½ No. 56 dipper).........	....
Salt......................	4 ounces (8 mess kit spoons)........	....
Pepper...................		
Milk, evaporated..........	15—14½-ounce cans...............	
Water (for milk)..........	7½ quarts (7½ No. 56 dippers)......	
Butter, melted............	2 pounds (1 No. 56 dipper).........	
Bread crumbs, dry.........	3 pounds (3 No. 56 dippers)........	

1. Break macaroni into 2- to 3-inch pieces.
2. Add macaroni slowly to boiling salted water; boil 10 to 15 minutes or until tender. Drain well.
3. Place macaroni in well-greased baking pans; cover with shredded cheese.
4. Mix melted fat, flour, salt, and pepper together; stir until smooth.
5. Mix milk and water; add to flour mixture. Heat to boiling point; boil until thick, stirring constantly. Pour sauce over macaroni and cheese.
6. Pour melted butter over crumbs; sprinkle crumbs over macaroni.
7. Bake in moderate oven (350° F.) 25 minutes or until crumbs are brown.

NO. 247. MACARONI AU GRATIN WITH CORN AND BACON

Add two No. 10 cans cream-style corn to macaroni in recipe for macaroni au gratin. Omit buttered crumbs and reduce cheese to 4 pounds (4 No. 56 dippers). Place strips of broiled bacon (2½ pounds) on top.

NO. 248. MACARONI AU GRATIN WITH MEAT

Add 10 to 12 pounds chopped cooked ham or corned beef to white sauce in recipe for macaroni au gratin. Shredded cheese and buttered crumbs may be omitted.

NO. 249. MACARONI AU GRATIN WITH PIMIENTOS

Add 1½ pints (1 mess kit cup) chopped pimientos to white sauce in recipe for macaroni au gratin.

NO. 250. BAKED MACARONI AND CHEESE. (Without cream sauce)
Yield: 100 servings, 8 ounces (1½ cups) each.

Ingredients	100 servings	.... servings
Macaroni	10 pounds	
Salt	6 ounces (12 mess kit spoons)	
Water, boiling	10 gallons (40 No. 56 dippers)	
Cheese, shredded*	8 pounds (8 No. 56 dippers)	

*Add four cans evaporated milk and make cheese sauce to pour over cooked macaroni for even distribution.

1. Break macaroni into 2- to 3-inch pieces.
2. Add macaroni slowly to boiling salted water; boil 10 to 15 minutes or until tender. Drain well.
3. Place ½ macaroni in well-greased baking pans; cover with ½ cheese. Add remaining macaroni; sprinkle remaining cheese on top.
4. Bake in moderate oven (350° F.) 25 minutes or until cheese is melted.

NO. 251. MACARONI REPUBLIC
Yield: 100 servings, 12 ounces (1½ cups) each.

Ingredients	100 servings	.... servings
Macaroni	10 pounds	
Salt	8 ounces (⅔ mess kit cup)	
Water, boiling	15 gallons (60 No. 56 dippers)	
Milk, evaporated	10—14½-ounce cans	
Water (for milk)	1¼ gallons (5 No. 56 dippers)	
Butter	2½ pounds (1¼ No. 56 dippers)	
Pimientos, finely chopped	7½—14½-ounce cans	
Parsley, chopped	5 bunches	
Bread, diced	3¾ pounds (3¾ No. 56 dippers)	
Salt	10 ounces (⅝ mess kit cup)	
Pepper	¼ ounce (1 mess kit spoon)	
Celery salt	(1 mess kit spoon)	
Mustard, dry	¼ ounce (1 mess kit spoon)	
Cheese, shredded	5 pounds (5 No. 56 dippers)	
Eggs, beaten	90 eggs (4½ No. 56 dippers)	
Paprika		

1. Break macaroni into 2- to 3-inch pieces.

2. Add macaroni slowly to boiling salted water; boil 10 to 15 minutes or until tender. Drain well.

3. Mix milk and water; heat. Add butter, pimientos, parsley, bread crumbs, salt, pepper, celery salt, mustard, and cheese. Reheat and simmer until cheese is melted.

4. Add milk and crumb mixture to beaten egg.

5. Mix macaroni and crumb mixture.

6. Place in well-greased baking pans. Sprinkle with paprika. Bake in slow oven (325° F.) until firm.

NO. 252. MACARONI WITH TOMATOES AND CHEESE

Yield: 100 servings, 12 ounces
(1½ cups) each.

Ingredients	100 servings	.... servings
Macaroni	8 pounds	
Salt	4 ounces (8 mess kit spoons)	....
Water, boiling	8 gallons (32 No. 56 dippers)	
Tomato puree	2 No. 10 cans	
Water	3 quarts (3 No. 56 dippers)	
Onions, chopped	2 pounds (2 No. 56 dippers)	
Celery leaves	1 ounce	
Sugar, granulated	6 ounces (¼ mess kit cup)	
Pepper		
Butter	½ pound (⅓ mess kit cup)	
Cheese, shredded	4 pounds (4 No. 56 dippers)	

1. Break macaroni into 2- to 3-inch pieces.

2. Add macaroni slowly to boiling salted water; boil 10 to 15 minutes or until tender. Drain well.

3. Combine tomato puree, water, onions, celery leaves, sugar, and pepper. Heat to boiling point; reduce heat and simmer 20 minutes. Strain.

4. Add butter and cheese to hot tomato mixture; stir until cheese is melted.

5. Combine sauce and macaroni.

6. Place in baking pans. Bake in moderate oven (350° F.) 25 minutes.

Note. Noodles or spaghetti may be substituted for the macaroni.

NO. 253. SPAGHETTI WITH TOMATO CHEESE SAUCE

Yield: 100 servings, 12 ounces (1½ cups) each.

Ingredients	100 servings	.... servings
Tomatoes	3 No. 10 cans	
Sugar, granulated	6 ounces (¼ mess kit cup)	
Salt	3 ounces (6 mess kit spoons)	
Onions, chopped	3 pounds (3 No. 56 dippers)	
Parsley	2 ounces	
Cloves, ground	½ ounce (2 mess kit spoons)	
Fat, melted	3 pounds (1½ No. 56 dippers)	
Flour, sifted	1½ pounds (1½ No. 56 dippers)	
Soup stock or water, hot	1½ gallons (6 No. 56 dippers)	
Cheese, shredded	6 pounds (6 No. 56 dippers)	
Spaghetti	10 pounds	
Salt	5 ounces (10 mess kit spoons)	
Water, boiling	10 gallons (40 No. 56 dippers)	

1. Combine tomatoes, sugar, salt, onions, parsley, and cloves. Heat to boiling point; reduce heat and simmer until onions are tender. Press through sieve.

2. Mix melted fat and flour; stir until smooth. Add hot tomato mixture and hot soup stock.

3. Heat to boiling point; boil 5 minutes or until thick, stirring constantly. Remove from fire; add cheese. Stir until cheese is melted.

4. Break spaghetti into 2- to 3-inch pieces.

5. Add spaghetti to boiling salted water; boil 20 minutes or until tender. Drain well.

6. Add sauce to spaghetti; mix well.

NO. 254. SPAGHETTI WITH TOMATO SAUCE AND MEAT BALLS

Prepare spaghetti as in recipe for spaghetti with tomato cheese sauce, omitting cheese. Mix 10 pounds ground beef (fresh or left-over) with 12 slightly beaten eggs (⅔ No. 56 dipper); add salt and pepper. Form into balls; fry in 1 pint (⅔ mess kit cup) bacon fat until meat is done. Add to spaghetti just before serving.

NO. 255. NOODLES AND BUTTERED CRUMBS

Yield: 100 servings, 8 ounces (1½ cups) each.

Ingredients	100 servings	.... servings
Noodles	12½ pounds	
Salt	6 ounces (¼ mess kit cup)	
Water, boiling	12½ gallons (5o No. 56 dippers)	
Bread crumbs, dry	2 pounds (2 No. 56 dippers)	
Salt	1½ ounces (3 mess kit spoons)	
Pepper	¼ ounce (1 mess kit spoon)	
Butter, melted	2½ pounds (1¼ No. 56 dippers)	

1. Add noodles to boiling salted water; boil 10 to 15 minutes or until tender. Drain well.
2. Mix bread crumbs, salt, and pepper; cook in melted butter until bread crumbs are brown.
3. Mix bread and noodles together.

NO. 256. FRIED NOODLES

Boil noodles as in recipe for noodles and buttered crumbs. Drain thoroughly. Dry noodles between soft paper towels. Fry in deep hot fat (390° F.) 1 minute or until brown. Drain on slices of bread or paper towels. Sprinkle with salt.

NO. 257. SCALLOPED NOODLES WITH CHEESE, TOMATOES, AND BACON

Yield: 100 servings, 12 ounces (1½ cups) each.

Ingredients	100 servings	.... servings
Tomatoes..................	5 No. 10 cans.......................	....
Salt (for tomatoes)..........	3 ounces (6 mess kit spoons)........	....
Pepper..	¼ ounce (1 mess kit spoon)..........	....
Noodles...................	12 pounds........................	....
Salt (for noodles)...........	6 ounces (¼ mess kit cup)..........	....
Water, boiling.............	12 gallons (48 No. 56 dippers).......	....
Cheese, shredded...........	9 pounds (9 No. 56 dippers).........	....
Bacon, thinly sliced........	3 pounds........................	....

1. Mix tomatoes, salt, and pepper together. Heat to boiling point; reduce heat and simmer until slightly thick.
2. Add noodles to boiling salted water; boil 10 to 15 minutes or until tender. Drain well.
3. Arrange alternate layers of noodles, tomatoes, and cheese in well-greased baking pans. Cover with bacon slices.
4. Bake in moderate oven (350° F.) 20 minutes or until bacon is crisp.

NO. 258. BOILED RICE

Yield: 100 servings, 1 cup (8 ounces) each.

Ingredients	100 servings	.... servings
Rice......................	15 pounds (7½ No. 56 dippers)......	....
Salt......................	12 ounces (½ mess kit cup).........	....
Water, boiling..............	6 gallons (24 No. 56 dippers).......	....

1. Wash rice thoroughly several times.
2. Add rice to rapidly boiling salted water. Heat to boiling point; boil, uncovered, about 30 minutes or until nearly all the water has been absorbed. Stir occasionally with a fork.
3. Cover and reduce heat; continue cooking until all the water is absorbed and rice is tender.

NO. 259. COOKED RICE

Yield: 100 servings,
6 ounces each.

Ingredients	100 servings	.... servings
Rice	6 pounds (3 No. 56 dippers)	
Shortening	1½ pounds (¾ No. 56 dipper)	
Water	3 gallons (12 No. 56 dippers)	
Salt	To taste	

1. Wash rice enough to remove mill dust only and drain thoroughly.
2. Melt shortening in pot, add rice and heat to 212° F.
3. Combine water and salt and bring to a boil. Add rice with fat to the boiling water. When all rice has been added, cut temperature to a slow simmer. Cover container tightly and keep covered while simmering for 30 minutes.
4. DO NOT STIR.

NO. 260. BAKED RICE AND CHEESE

Yield: 100 servings, 12 ounces
(1½ cups) each.

Ingredients	100 servings	.... servings
Rice, raw	8 pounds (4 No. 56 dippers)	
Salt	8 ounces (⅓ mess kit cup)	
Water, boiling	8 gallons (32 No. 56 dippers)	
Butter, melted	4 pounds (2 No. 56 dippers)	
Flour, sifted	2 pounds (2 No. 56 dippers)	
Salt	3 ounces (6 mess kit spoons)	
Mustard, dry	1½ ounces (6 mess kit spoons)	
Milk, evaporated	16—14½-ounce cans	
Water (for milk)	2 gallons (8 No. 56 dippers)	
Cheese, shredded	16 pounds (16 No. 56 dippers)	
Butter, melted	1½ pounds (1 mess kit cup)	
Bread crumbs, moist	4 pounds (8 No. 56 dippers)	

1. Wash rice thoroughly.
2. Add rice to rapidly boiling salted water; boil 15 to 20 minutes or until tender. Drain well.
3. Combine melted butter, flour, salt, and mustard; stir until smooth.
4. Mix milk and water; add to flour mixture. Heat to boiling point; boil about 5 minutes or until thick, stirring constantly.
5. Add cheese; stir until cheese is melted.
6. Pour melted butter over bread crumbs.
7. Mix cheese sauce and cooked rice.
8. Place in well-greased baking pans. Sprinkle with buttered crumbs. Bake in moderate oven (350° F.) 25 minutes or until crumbs are brown.

NO. 261. SPANISH RICE

Yield: 7 gallons,
100 servings, approximately 1 cup each.

Ingredients	100 servings	.... servings
Tomatoes...................	4 No. 10 cans.....................	....
Water.....................	3 gallons (12 No. 56 dippers)........	....
Onions, chopped.............	3 pounds (3 No. 56 dippers)........	....
Peppers, green, chopped......	2 pounds (2 No. 56 dippers)........	....
Salt......................	8 ounces (⅓ mess kit cup)..........	....
Pepper....................	¼ ounce (1 mess kit spoon).........	....
Rice, uncooked..............	12 pounds (6 No. 56 dippers).......	....
Cheese, shredded............	9 pounds (9 No. 56 dippers).......	....

1. Combine tomatoes, water, onions, peppers, salt, and pepper; heat to boiling point.

2. Wash rice; drain thoroughly.

3. Add rice to tomato mixture. Cover and heat to boiling point; reduce heat and simmer until rice is tender, stirring frequently.

4. Remove from heat; add cheese. Stir until cheese is melted.

MEAT

20. MEAT. a. General. A large percentage of the money allotted for the ration is spent for meat; therefore it is important to exercise great care in the selection and preparation of this food. The maximum number of servings will be obtained only if the recipes in this section are followed exactly. These recipes recommend low cooking temperatures which lessen shrinkage of the meat.

b. Oversea hams. Hams packed for shipment overseas are sewed or tied in muslin cloth, packed four to the wooden box containing approximately 75 pounds net weight. Under certain conditions the spaces between the hams are filled with dry granulated salt, and when so packed, the hams become partially dehydrated and quite salty. Oversea hams in this condition must be treated in a special manner in order to be acceptable. The methods of preparation given in recipes for oversea hams will produce a product satisfactory for mess use.

NO. 262. ROAST MEAT (beef, lamb, pork, or veal)

Yield: 100 servings, 4 ounces each.

Ingredients	100 servings	.... servings
Meat, carcass...............	60 pounds.......................	....
or		
Meat, boneless..............	42 pounds.......................	....
Salt......................	10 ounces (⅓ No. 56 dipper)........	....
Pepper...................	½ ounce (2 mess kit spoons)........	....

1. Cut meat into pieces weighing 6 to 8 pounds each.
2. Rub with salt and pepper.
3. Place in baking pans with fat side up. Fill pans without stacking or crowding. Place larger roasts in oven first.
4. Roast, uncovered, at constant temperature in moderate oven (325° F.) approximately 3 hours for beef, 4 hours for lamb and veal and 4½ to 5 hours for pork.* Cook pork well.
5. Remove roasts from pans. Allow lamb, pork, and veal roasts to stand 30 minutes before carving. Carve in thin slices across the grain and serve immediately.

*The cooking time for beef is approximately 30 minutes per pound, for lamb and veal approximately 40 to 45 minutes per pound, and for pork approximately 45 to 50 minutes per pound.

NO. 263. ROAST MEAT WITH DRESSING

Prepare dressing (recipe No. 436); place in pan with roast. Roast as directed in recipe for roast meat.

NO. 264. ROAST BEEF WITH YORKSHIRE PUDDING

Serve roast beef with Yorkshire pudding. (See recipe No. 265.)

NO. 265. YORKSHIRE PUDDING

Yield: 100 servings, 2 pieces per serving, each 2 by 1 inches.

Ingredients	100 servings	.... servings
Flour, sifted..................	6 pounds (6 No. 56 dippers).........	....
Salt.......................	3 ounces (6 mess kit spoons)........	....
Eggs, unbeaten..............	48 eggs (2½ No. 56 dippers)........	....
Milk, evaporated.............	6—14½-ounce cans..............	....
Water (for milk).............	3 quarts (3 No. 56 dippers)........	....
Beef fat (from roasts), hot....	....	....

1. Sift flour; measure flour and sift again with salt.

2. Add unbeaten eggs; mix thoroughly.

3. Mix milk and water; add gradually to egg mixture. Beat until smooth and bubbles form.

4. Cover bottoms of baking pans with hot fat. Pour mixture to depth of ½ inch into the pans.

5. Bake in moderate oven (350° F.) 45 minutes.

6. Cut into squares and serve with roast beef.

NO. 266. SPICED LAMB ROAST

Yield: 100 servings, 8 to 10 ounces each.

Ingredients	100 servings	.... servings
Lamb, carcass..............	60 pounds.....................	....
Vinegar....................	1 gallon (4 No. 56 dippers)........	....
Water.....................	2 gallons (8 No. 56 dippers)........	....
Garlic, finely chopped........	2 cloves.....................	....
Onions, chopped.............	4 pounds (4 No. 56 dippers).......	....
Tomatoes...................	1 No. 10 can.................	....
Bay leaves..................	½ ounce.....................	....
Salt.......................	....	....
Pepper.....................	....	....

1. Remove bones from meat; cut meat into 4-pound pieces. Roll.

2. Add vinegar, water, and garlic; refrigerate over night.

3. Remove meat from liquid; wipe thoroughly with a clean cloth.

4. Place meat in baking pans; cover with onions, tomatoes, bay leaves, salt, and pepper.

5. Roast in slow oven (300° F.) about 2½ hours or until thoroughly done.

NO. 267. BAKED (ROAST) HAM
Yield: 100 servings, 4 to 5 ounces each.

Ingredients	100 servings	.... servings
Ham, smoked, commercial....	55 pounds............................	.............·.......
or		
Ham, boneless, commercial....	38 pounds............................	....

1. Remove hock from ham at stifle joint, leaving as much meat as possible on cushion section. Remove the skin from regular (skin-on) hams.
2. Place in baking pans with fat side up. Fill pans without stacking or crowding. Allow room for circulation of air between hams.
3. Roast, uncovered and without water, at constant temperature in slow oven (300° F.) allowing 18 to 25 minutes per pound for hams weighing 10 to 14 pounds with bone in. Larger hams will cook in fewer minutes per pound.
4. Remove aitch bone; split ham lengthwise along leg bone into knuckle and cushion sections. Remove leg bone from knuckle section. Split cushion into two equal-sized pieces. Carve the three boneless pieces of ham across the grain.

NO. 268. BAKED HAM WITH BARBECUE OR TOMATO SAUCE
Serve baked ham with barbecue sauce (recipe No. 551) or tomato sauce. (See recipe No. 559.)

NO. 269. SIMMERED HAM
Prepare hams as in recipe for baked ham. Place in kettle without stacking or overlapping. Barely cover with water; cover tightly. Heat to boiling point; reduce heat and simmer until tender. Remove from water and keep warm until ready to serve.

NO. 270. BAKED HAM SLICES
Yield: 100 servings, 6 to 9 ounces each.

Ingredients	100 servings	.... servings
Ham, bone in...............	55 pounds............................	....
or		
Ham, boneless...............	38 pounds............................	....

1. Split ham into knuckle, inside, and outside sections. Cut these pieces into slices ½ to ¾ inch thick. Cut slices into servings weighing 6 to 9 ounces each.
2. Place slices in baking pans. Roast, uncovered and without water, in slow oven (300° F.) 45 minutes or until tender.

111

NO. 271. FRIED HAM SLICES

Cut ham into servings as in recipe for baked ham slices. Cut fat edge in several places on each serving to prevent curling. Fry slowly, allowing fat to collect in pan, 10 minutes for slices ⅜ inch thick.

NO. 272. GRIDDLE BROILED HAM SLICES

Cut ham into servings as in recipe for baked ham slices. Cut fat edge in several places to prevent curling. Remove fat from griddle as it accumulates to prevent ham from frying. Broil approximately 10 minutes for slices ⅜ inch thick.

NO. 273. SMOTHERED HAM SLICES

Cut ham into servings as in recipe for baked ham slices. Place in baking pans; cover with boiling water. Heat to boiling point; reduce heat and simmer 35 to 40 minutes. Drain. Combine ¼ ounce (1 mess kit spoon) ground cloves, 1 pound (1 mess kit cup) brown sugar, 2 pounds (1½ No. 56 dippers) chopped onions, 5 pounds (5 No. 56 dippers) dry bread crumbs; place over ham slices. Mix four 14½-ounce cans evaporated milk and ½ gallon (2 No. 56 dippers) water; pour over crumb mixture. Bake in slow oven (325° F.) about 45 minutes or until top is brown and crisp.

NO. 274. HAM SLICES WITH SCALLOPED POTATOES

Reduce ham to 45 pounds bone in or 31 pounds boneless. Cut into servings as in recipe for baked ham slices. Prepare scalloped potatoes (recipe No. 684); place in baking pans. Place slices of ham on uncooked potatoes. Bake in moderate oven (375° F.) until potatoes are tender and ham is cooked.

NO. 275. SCALLOPED HAM AND CORN

Cut ham into servings as in recipe for baked ham slices. Fry slowly until brown in its own fat; drain. Mix four 14½-ounce cans evaporated milk and 2 quarts (2 No. 56 dippers) water; heat. Add fat drained from ham. Pour mixture over 4½ pounds bread or cracker crumbs. Add 3 No. 10 cans corn and 8 ounces (½ No. 56 dipper) chopped onions; mix lightly. Place mixture over slices of ham in baking pans. Pour 6 ounces (¼ mess kit cup) melted butter over 2 pounds (2 No. 56 dippers) bread crumbs. Sprinkle buttered crumbs over mixture on ham slices. Bake in moderate oven (350° F.) about 1 hour.

NO. 276. HAM STEAKS GLAZED (OVERSEA HAM)

Yield: 100 servings,
6 to 8 ounces each.

Ingredients	100 servings	.... servings
Ham........................	50 pounds........................	....
Marmalade..................	1 No. 10 can....................	....
Jam........................	1 No. 10 can....................	....

1. Remove muslin cloth and cord. Scrub, scrape, or brush ham to remove mold. Trim off excess fat and skin. Slice hams into ½-inch slices.
2. Place sliced ham in suitable container and cover with clear, cold water. Soak sliced hams for approximately 4 hours before removing from water (refrigeration optional). Remove ham slices from water and drain well.
3. Place slices of soaked ham in bake or sheet pan. Mix together marmalade and jam. Spread mixture over the ham slices. Bake in moderate oven 325° F. (16 hand counts) for approximately 45 minutes.

Note. Hams may be boned before slicing. All bones can be used for cooking stock. Fat can be rendered and used for cooking purposes. Two No. 10 cans of crushed pineapple mixed with 2 pounds (approximately 1 No. 56 dipper) of sugar may be substituted for the jam mixture.

NO. 277. SIMMERED HAM OR BOILED WHOLE HAMS
(OVERSEA HAM)
Yield: 100 servings,
4 to 6 ounces each.

Ingredients	100 servings	.... servings
Ham	50 pounds	
Sugar, granulated	1 pound (½ No. 56 dipper)	

1. Remove muslin cloth and cord. Scrub, scrape, or brush ham to remove mold. Trim off skin and excess fat. Remove bones.
2. Soak to remove salt. Place ham in suitable container and cover with clear, cold water.
3. Let hams soak overnight or approximately 18 hours. If refrigerator space is available, soaking should be handled under refrigeration.
4. Remove hams from soaking water, roll and tie with string, place in clean stockpot and cover with clear, cold water. Bring to the boiling point (212° F.), then let simmer (180° F.) for 3 hours, adding ½ No. 56 dipper of granulated sugar to water. Change water at the end of the first hour and rinse salty residue from bottom of boiler before the simmering process is continued.
5. Allow hams to set before slicing.

NO. 278. BAKED HAM (OVERSEA HAM)
Yield: 100 servings,
4 to 6 ounces each.

Ingredients	100 servings	.... servings
Ham	50 pounds	
Sugar, brown	2 pounds (1 No. 56 dipper)	

1. Prepare as previously prescribed for boiled ham, except that baked ham should be simmered 2 hours instead of 3 hours.

113

2. Place in baking and roasting pan with fat surface up, with enough unsalted stock to cover bottom of pan. Sprinkle brown sugar over top of hams. For variety, slices of pineapple may be placed on top of ham before sprinkling with sugar. Bake in moderate oven, 352° F., (16 hand counts) for approximately 45 minutes.

NO. 279. BEEF POT ROAST Yield: 100 servings, 3 to 5 ounces each.

Ingredients	100 servings	.... servings
Beef (boneless)..............	42 pounds......................	....
Fat or drippings.............	4 pounds (2 No. 56 dippers).........	....
Onions.....................	5 pounds (5 No. 56 dippers).........	....
Celery.....................	3 pounds (3 No. 56 dippers).........	....
Carrots....................	8 pounds (7 No. 56 dippers).........	....
Salt.......................	....	....
Pepper.....................	....	....
Beef stock.................	4 quarts (4 No. 56 dippers).........	....

1. Cut meat into 6- to 8-pound pieces.
2. Rub with salt and pepper.
3. Sear in bakepan, using fat to brown.
4. When well browned on all sides add the stock and cover pan.
5. Braise in 350° F. oven for approximately 3 hours. Keep pan covered.
6. During last hour of cooking add all the chopped vegetables.

Note. Tomatoes may be added if desired.

NO. 280. BRAISED MEAT (beef, lamb or veal)

Yield: 100 servings, 4 to 5 ounces each.

Ingredients	100 servings	.... servings
Meat, carcass................	60 pounds......................	....
or		
Meat, boneless...............	42 pounds......................	....
Fat........................	8 ounces (¼ No. 56 dipper).........	....
Salt.......................	6 ounces (¼ mess kit cup)..........	....
Pepper.....................	½ ounce (2 mess kit spoons)........	....
Onions, chopped.............	5 pounds (5 No. 56 dippers).........	....
Water or stock, hot..........	1 quart (1 No. 56 dipper)..........	....

1. Cut meat into pieces weighing 6- to 8-pounds each.
2. Cook meat until brown in its own fat or in the ½ pound added fat.
3. Add salt, pepper, onions*, and water or stock.
4. Cover tightly and heat to boiling point; reduce heat and simmer on top of stove or in slow oven (300° F.) 3 hours or until tender, turning meat two or three times while cooking. Add small amounts of liquid as needed.
5. Remore from pans; slice in thin slices across the grain.

*Onions may be cooked in fat until brown.

Note. Heavy utensils are best for cooking pot roasts.

NO. 281. MEAT A LA MODE

Add 3 pounds (3 No. 56 dippers) diced carrots, 2 pounds (2 No. 56 dippers) diced onions and one No. 10 can tomatoes to recipe for braised meat 30 to 45 minutes before meat is tender. Drain stock from meat and vegetables; prepare gravy (recipe No. 562) using stock. Serve gravy and vegetables over meat.

NO. 282. BRAISED MEAT AND VEGETABLES

Reduce meat to 45 pounds carcass or 31 pounds boneless in recipe for braised meat. Add 8 pounds each of sliced carrots, onions, celery, and turnips 30 to 45 minutes before meat is tender.

NO. 283. SPICED POT ROAST

Prepare recipe for braised meat using a mixture of spices and diluted vinegar, sour milk, or buttermilk as the liquid instead of water or stock.

NO. 284. SOUR POT ROAST

Prepare sour pot roast as in recipe for spiced pot roast allowing the meat to stand in the vinegar mixture 24 hours or longer before braising.

NO. 285. YANKEE POT ROAST

Add parsley, bay leaves, thyme, tomatoes, carrots, onions, and garlic to the vinegar mixture in recipe for spiced pot roasts before cooking the meat.

NO. 286. BRAISED SPARERIBS
Yield: 100 servings, 8 to 10 ounces each.

Ingredients	100 servings	.... servings
Spareribs..................	75 pounds.................................	....
Salt......................	10 ounces (⅓ No. 56 dipper)........	....
Pepper....................	½ ounce (2 mess kit spoons)........	....
Water or stock............	....	....

1. Cut spareribs into 4-rib pieces weighing about 8 to 10 ounces each.
2. Place in baking pans, stacking as little as possible. Bake, uncovered, in hot oven (400° F.) until brown.
3. Sprinkle with salt and pepper; add water or stock to cover bottom of pans.
4. Cover pans. Braise in slow oven (325° F.) 1½ to 2 hours or until meat will slip from ribs.

NO. 287. BRAISED SPARERIBS WITH BARBECUE SAUCE OR SAUERKRAUT

Prepare spareribs as in recipe for braised spareribs. Braise in barbecue sauce (recipe No. 551) instead of water or braise on top of sauerkraut in greased baking pans. Use three No. 10 cans sauerkraut.

NO. 288. BRAISED STEAKS, CHOPS, AND CUTLETS

Yield: 100 servings, 2 pieces
of meat per serving,
3½ ounces each.

Ingredients	100 servings	.... servings
Meat, carcass...............	60 pounds............................	....
or		
Meat, boneless..............	42 pounds...........................	....
Flour, sifted................	2 pounds (2 No. 56 dippers).........	....
Salt......................	7 ounces (⅛ No. 56 dipper).........	....
Pepper....................	½ ounce (2 mess kit spoons)........	....
Fat.......................	2 pounds (1 No. 56 dipper)..........	....
Water.....................	....	....

1. Slice meat into steaks, chops, or cutlets ½ to ¾ inch thick. Cut into pieces about 3 by 5 inches.
2. Mix flour, salt, and pepper; roll meat in mixture.
3. Cook meat in fat until brown. Turn occasionally. Stack chops on end in baking pans, bone side down.
4. Add small amount of water to cover bottom of pans; cover tightly and bake in slow oven (300° F.) about 1½ hours or until tender.

NO. 289. BRAISED STEAKS, CHOPS, OR CUTLETS WITH BARBECUE OR TOMATO SAUCE

Serve braised steaks, chops, or cutlets with barbecue sauce (recipe No. 551) or tomato sauce. (See recipe No. 559.)

NO. 290. COUNTRY STYLE STEAKS, CHOPS, AND CUTLETS

Serve braised steaks, chops, and cutlets with milk gravy. (See recipe No. 567.)

NO. 291. BEEF STEAKS SMOTHERED WITH ONIONS

Prepare braised steaks and cover with 50 pounds sliced and partly cooked onions instead of water. Cover tightly and braise until steaks are tender.

NO. 292. SWISS AND SPANISH BEEF STEAKS

Cut beef into 1- to 1½-inch steaks weighing about 6 ounces each. Prepare as braised beef steaks substituting three No. 10 cans tomatoes for water. Cover with 6 pounds sliced onions. Sprinkle with 4 ounces (8 mess kit spoons) salt. Cover and bake in slow oven (300° F.) 3 hours or until steaks are tender. Drain liquid from steaks. Mix 1 pound (1 No. 56 dipper) sifted flour and a small amount of water; stir until smooth. Add to liquid. Heat to boiling; boil 2 minutes, stirring constantly. Pour gravy over steaks. Prepare Spanish beef steaks by adding 6 to 8 pounds (6 to 8 No. 56 dippers) chopped green peppers to tomatoes. Proceed as for Swiss steaks.

NO. 293. BIRDS (beef, pork or veal)

Reduce meat in recipe for braised steaks, chops and cutlets to 50 pounds carcass or 35 pounds boneless; cut into slices ½ inch thick, weighing about 3 ounces each. Prepare bread stuffing. (See recipe No. 436.) Spread small amount of stuffing on each piece of meat; roll and fasten with a toothpick. Mix 4 ounces (8 mess kit spoons) salt, ¼ ounce (2 mess kit spoons) pepper and 2 pounds (2 No. 56 dippers) sifted flour together. Dip rolled meat in flour mixture. Cook as for braised meats using brown gravy (recipe No. 562) or tomato sauce (recipe No. 559) instead of water.

NO. 294. BREADED STEAKS, CHOPS AND

CUTLETS (lamb, pork or veal) Yield: 100 servings, 2 pieces meat per serving, 4 to 5 ounces each.

Ingredients	100 servings	.... servings
Meat, carcass...............	60 pounds......................	....
or		
Meat, boneless (pork or veal only).	42 pounds......................	....
Flour, sifted...............	5 pounds (5 No. 56 dippers).........	....
Salt......................	10 ounces (⅓ No. 56 dipper)........	....
Pepper....................	½ ounce (2 mess kit spoons)........	....
Milk, evaporated............	2—14½-ounce cans..............	....
Water (for milk).............	1 quart (1 No. 56 dipper)...........	....
Eggs, beaten...............	20 eggs (1 No. 56 dipper)...........	....
Bread or cracker crumbs, dry..	2 pounds (2 No. 56 dippers)........	....
Fat.......................	....	....

1. Cut meat into steaks, chops, or cutlets ⅜ to ½ inch thick, weighing 3 to 4 ounces each.

2. Mix flour, salt, and pepper; roll meat in flour mixture.

3. Mix milk and water; add beaten egg. Mix well.

4. Dip floured meat into milk and egg mixture; dip into crumbs.

5. Cook until brown in a small amount of fat. Stack on end, bone side down, in baking pans. Cover tightly. Bake in slow oven (325° F.) 45 minutes.

Note. Breaded steaks, chops, and cutlets may also be fried. Fry until tender in shallow fat, turning frequently to insure even cooking. They may also be fried in deep hot fat (350° F.) approximately 7 to 10 minutes or until done.

NO. 295. BREADED STEAKS, CHOPS, AND CUTLETS
WITH BARBECUE OR TOMATO SAUCE

Serve breaded steaks, chops, and cutlets with barbecue sauce (recipe No. 551) or tomato sauce. (See recipe No. 559.)

NO. 296. GRIDDLE-BROILED STEAKS AND CHOPS

Yield: 100 servings, 2 steaks per serving, 3½ ounces each.

Ingredients	100 servings	.... servings
Meat, carcass...............	60 pounds...........................	....
or		
Meat, boneless (beef only)....	42 pounds...........................	....
Salt...................	....	....
Pepper.................	....	....

1. Cut meat into ¾-inch steaks or chops weighing about 3½ ounces each.
2. Broil steaks or chops on griddle until brown, turning frequently to insure even cooking.*
3. Cook to the desired degree; avoid overcooking.
4. Sprinkle with salt and pepper just before serving.

*If meat lacks fat, grease griddle slightly.

Note. Steaks and chops may be cooked quickly on griddle until brown, stacked on edge in open baking pans, and baked in slow oven (300° F.) to desired degree.

NO. 297. FRIED STEAKS, CHOPS AND CUTLETS

(beef, lamb, pork and veal)   Yield: 100 servings, 2 steaks per serving, 3½ ounces each.

Ingredients	100 servings	.... servings
Meat, carcass...............	60 pounds...........................	....
or		
Meat, boneless (beef, pork, veal).	42 pounds...........................	....
Flour, sifted...............	2 pounds (2 No. 56 dippers).........	....
Salt......................	4 ounces (8 mess kit spoons)........	....
Pepper....................	½ ounce (2 mess kit spoons)........	....
Fat.......................	2 pounds (1 No. 56 dipper).........	....

1. Cut meat into ½-inch steaks, chops, or cutlets, weighing about 3½ ounces each.
2. Mix flour, salt, and pepper together; roll meat in mixture.
3. Fry in small amount of fat until light, golden brown, turning frequently to insure even cooking. Continue cooking until tender.

NO. 298. PORK CHOPS WITH STUFFING

Fry pork chops until brown as in recipe above. Prepare dressing. (See recipe No. 436.) Place dressing in baking pans; arrange pork chops on top of dressing. Bake in moderate oven (350° F.) about 1 to 1½ hours.

NO. 299. FRIED BACON

Yield: 100 servings, 4 ounces each.

Ingredients	100 servings	.... servings
Bacon.....................	25 pounds........................	....

1. Slice bacon and place in pans.

2. Fry in its own fat on top of stove or in moderate oven (350° F.).*

3. Stir or turn frequently to insure even cooking. Keep fat from smoking and avoid overcooking.

*Bacon may be fried at a higher oven temperature but constant watching is necessary to prevent burning the fat and overcooking the bacon.

Note. Use bacon fat for seasoning or frying.

NO. 300. GRIDDLE-BROILED BACON

Remove rind from slabs of bacon, cutting away as little fat as possible. Slice bacon about eight slices to the inch. Broil slowly on griddle until crisp but not brittle, turning frequently.

NO. 301. OVEN-COOKED BACON

Cut brown paper into pieces 3 inches wider and 4 inches longer than 50-ration baking pans. Place bacon slices, slightly overlapping, on pieces of paper. Place only enough slices on each piece of paper to fill length of baking pan, folding the extra paper over the bacon. Turn two papers of bacon into each baking pan. Cook in moderate oven (350° F.) until bacon is cooked to the desired degree. Avoid overcooking as the crisper the bacon, the more salty it tastes. Lift bacon from hot fat and place on hot platters for serving.

NO. 302. SIMMERED BACON

Slice bacon about ⅜ inch thick. Place bacon in kettle; cover with water. Cover tightly. Heat to boiling point; reduce heat and simmer approximately 1 hour.

NO. 303. SIMMERED BACON OR HAM HOCKS WITH VEGETABLES

Reduce bacon to 20 pounds or use 50 pounds ham hocks. Cover with water. Heat to boiling point; reduce heat and simmer approximately 1 hour. Add 12 pounds small, whole onions, 12 pounds potatoes cut in half, 8 pounds whole carrots. Continue simmering 30 minutes. Add 15 pounds cabbage cut in wedges. Simmer until cabbage is tender.

NO. 304. SIMMERED MEAT (beef, corned beef, pork hocks, ham shanks)
Yield: 100 servings, 3 ounces each.

Ingredients	100 servings	.... servings
Meat, carcass...............	60 pounds........................	....
or		
Meat, boneless...............	42 pounds.......................	....
Water, boiling...............	....	....
Salt.......................	8 ounces (¼ No. 56 dipper).........	....
Pepper.....................	1 ounce (4 mess kit spoons).........	....
Onions, peeled, whole.........	1½ pounds......................	....
Bay leaves..................	15 leaves......................	....
Garlic (optional).............	1 to 2 cloves....................	....

1. Cut meat into pieces weighing about 5 pounds each.
2. Place in kettles without stacking or overlapping; barely cover with boiling water.
3. Add salt, pepper, onions, bay leaves, and garlic.
4. Cover tightly and heat to boiling point; reduce heat and simmer about 3 to 4 hours or until meat is tender. Remove meat from water.
5. Carve across the grain.

Note. Serve simmered meat with potatoes cooked in meat broth. Chopped parsley or paprika may be added to the potatoes.

NO. 305. SIMMERED MEAT WITH HORSERADISH SAUCE OR SAUERKRAUT
Serve simmered meat with horseradish sauce (recipe No. 556) or sauerkraut. Combine 15 pounds sauerkraut, 2 quarts (2 No. 56 dippers) vinegar and ½ pound (½ mess kit cup) brown sugar; add to meat 15 minutes before it has finished cooking.

NO. 306. SIMMERED MEAT AND VEGETABLES
Reduce meat to 45 pounds carcass or 31 pounds boneless in recipe for simmered meat. Add 8 pounds each of potatoes, carrots, turnips, and parsnips to meat, allowing sufficient time for each to cook before meat is tender.

NO. 307. SIMMERED CORNED BEEF
Substitute 42 pounds boneless corned beef for meat in recipe for simmered meat. Increase cooking time to 4 to 6 hours or until meat is tender. Add cold water from time to time to solidify fat. Skim grease from top of water to prevent possibility of discoloration. Test each piece of meat after 3½ to 4 hours cooking; remove each piece from water as soon as it is tender to prevent overcooking as pieces of exactly the same size may vary 15 minutes in cooking time. Submerge all pieces in cold water, fat

side down, at least 15 minutes to bleach and solidify fat and prevent shrinkage. Serve immediately or if it is to be held several hours, immerse in lukewarm, mildly salted water and reheat before serving.

NO. 308. CORNED BEEF AND CABBAGE

Prepare corned beef as in recipe for simmered corned beef. Drain; add 25 pounds quartered cabbage to corned beef liquid. Heat to boiling point; reduce heat and simmer, uncovered, about 10 to 20 minutes or until tender.

NO. 309. CORNED BEEF WITH HORSERADISH SAUCE

Serve simmered corned beef with horseradish sauce. (See recipe No. 556.)

NO. 310. NEW ENGLAND DINNER (corned beef or ham)

Use 42 pounds boneless corned beef or ham. Prepare as in recipe for simmered meat or corned beef. Add potatoes, whole carrots, onions, and quartered cabbage when meat is nearly tender; cook until vegetables are tender.

NO. 311. SIMMERED PORK HOCKS OR SPARERIBS

Yield: 100 servings, 8 to 10 ounces each.

Ingredients	100 servings	.... servings
Pork hocks or spareribs.......	75 pounds...........................	....
Water, boiling...............		....
Salt......................	8 ounces (¼ No. 56 dipper).........	....
Pepper.....................	1 ounce (4 mess kit spoons).........	....
Onions, peeled, whole (optional).	1½ pounds.........................	....
Bay leaves (optional).........	15 leaves.........................	....
Garlic (optional).............	1 to 2 cloves......................	....

1. Cut spareribs into four-rib pieces weighing about 8 to 10 ounces each.
2. Cook ribs until brown in their own fat; barely cover with boiling water.
3. Add salt, pepper, onions, bay leaves, and garlic.
4. Cover tightly and heat to boiling point; reduce heat and simmer about 3 to 4 hours or until meat is tender. Remove from water and keep warm until ready to serve.

NO. 312. SIMMERED PORK HOCKS OR SPARERIBS WITH HORSERADISH SAUCE OR SAUERKRAUT

Serve simmered pork hocks or spareribs with horseradish sauce (recipe No. 556) or sauerkraut. Add three No. 10 cans sauerkraut to meat in sufficient time for it to become thoroughly heated before meat is tender.

NO. 313. SIMMERED PORK HOCKS OR SPARERIBS AND VEGETABLES

Reduce meat to 60 pounds in recipe for simmered pork hocks or spareribs. Add 8 pounds each of sliced carrots, onions, celery, and turnips to meat allowing sufficient time for each to cook before meat is tender.

NO. 314. BAKED MEATBURGERS (beef, lamb or veal)

Yield: 100 servings, 2 meatburgers per serving, 3½ ounces each.

Ingredients	100 servings	.... servings
Meat, carcass................	55 pounds.........................	....
or		
Meat, ground................	38 pounds.........................	....
Onions, chopped.............	5 pounds (5 No. 56 dippers)........	....
Salt.......................	6½ ounces (¼ mess kit cup)........	....
Pepper.....................	½ ounce (2 mess kit spoons)........	....
Water......................	2½ quarts (2½ No. 56 dippers)......	....

1. Cut meat into cubes; grind.

2. Mix all ingredients together lightly but thoroughly.

3. Shape into patties 1 inch thick and weighing 3 to 3½ ounces each.

4. Arrange patties in baking pans. Bake, uncovered and without water, in moderate oven about 45 minutes or until baked to the desired degree.

NO. 315. BRAISED MEATBURGERS

Prepare meatburgers as in recipe for baked meatburgers substituting 2½ quarts (2½ No. 56 dippers) tomato juice or stock for water and reducing onions to 2½ pounds (2½ No. 56 dippers). Cook until brown on both sides in baking pans in just enough fat to prevent meat from sticking. Add a small amount of water; cover. Bake in slow oven (300° F.) about 45 minutes or until tender.

NO. 316. GRIDDLE-BROILED MEATBURGERS (beef or lamb)

Prepare meatburgers as in recipe for baked meatburgers. Griddle-broil about 12 minutes or until the desired degree is reached, turning frequently to insure even cooking.

NO. 317. MEATBURGERS WITH BARBECUE OR TOMATO SAUCE

Serve meatburgers with barbecue sauce (recipe No. 551) or tomato sauce. (See recipe No. 559.)

NO. 318. MEAT CHEESEBURGERS (beef or lamb)

Reduce meat to 45 pounds carcass or 31 pounds ground meat in recipe for baked meatburgers. Form into 200 flat patties, 2½ ounces each or 5 to the pound. Split and toast 200 buns; cover lower half of each with a slice of cheese, using 10 pounds American cheddar cheese. Place under broiler or in moderate oven (350° F.) until cheese is melted. Broil meat patties on griddle. Place on top of cheese on bun; spread with pickle relish. Cover with top half of bun. Serve at once.

NO. 319. SALISBURY STEAK (beef or lamb)

Prepare meatburgers as in recipe for baked meatburgers. Shape into 50 patties 1 inch thick, each weighing 6 to 7 ounces. Broil on griddle about 12 minutes or until as well done as desired, turning frequently to insure even cooking. Serve with hot creole sauce. (See recipe No. 552.)

NO. 320. CABBAGE ROLLS

Reduce ground meat to 20 pounds in recipe for baked meatburgers. Combine meat, 5 ounces (10 mess kit spoons) salt, ½ ounce (2 mess kit spoons) pepper, 2 pounds (1½ No. 56 dippers) finely ground onions and 3 pounds (6 No. 56 dippers) cooked rice; mix thoroughly. Shape into 200 loosely formed balls. Dip 200 fresh, large cabbage leaves into hot water or wilt slightly in steamer so they will roll. Wrap each meat and rice roll in a cabbage leaf. Place in baking pans and add three No. 10 cans tomato juice; cover. Bake in moderate oven (350° F.).

NO. 321. MEAT PATTIES WITH BARBECUE OR TOMATO SAUCE

Serve meat patties with barbecue sauce (recipe No. 551) or tomato sauce. (See recipe No. 559.)

NO. 322. GRIDDLE-BROILED MEAT PATTIES (beef, lamb or sausage; ham and pork combined with other meat)

Yield: 100 servings, 2 patties per serving, 3½ ounces each.

Ingredients	100 servings	.... servings
Meat, carcass...............	45 pounds.........................	....
or		
Meat, ground...............	31 pounds.........................	....
Bread crumbs, soft..........	7 pounds.........................	....
Onions, chopped.............	5 pounds (5 No. 56 dippers)........	....
Salt......................	5 ounces (10 mess kit spoons)........	....
Pepper....................	¼ ounce (1 mess kit spoon)........	....
Water or stock.............	3 quarts (3 No. 56 dippers)........	....
or		
Milk, evaporated............	3—14½-ounce cans..........	....
Water (for milk)............	1½ quarts (1½ No. 56 dippers)......	....

1. Cut meat into cubes; grind.

2. Mix all ingredients together lightly but thoroughly.

3. Shape into patties 1 inch thick weighing 3 to 3½ ounces each.

4. Griddle-broil about 12 minutes or until the desired degree is reached, turning frequently to insure even cooking.

5. Serve at once.

NO. 323. GRIDDLE-BROILED MEAT PATTIES
WITH BARBECUE SAUCE OR CATSUP

Substitute barbecue sauce (recipe No. 551) or catsup for part or all of the water in recipe for griddle-broiled meat patties.

NO. 324. BAKED MEAT PATTIES

Prepare meat as in recipe for griddle-broiled meat patties. Arrange patties in baking pans. Bake, uncovered and without water, in slow oven (325° F.) about 45 minutes or until desired degree is reached.

NO. 325. BRAISED MEAT PATTIES
(beef, lamb, pork sausage, ham, or veal)

Prepare meat as in recipe for griddle-broiled meat patties. Cook in hot fat until brown on both sides. Add small amount of water. Cover tightly. Bake in slow oven (325° F.) approximately 1 hour or until desired degree is reached.

NO. 326. BRAISED MEAT BALLS (beef, lamb or veal)

Yield: 100 servings, 4 meat balls per serving, 2 ounces each.

Ingredients	100 servings	.... servings
Bread, dry	5 pounds	
Meat, carcass	45 pounds	
or		
Meat, ground	31 pounds	
Eggs	10 eggs (½ No. 56 dipper)	
Onions, chopped	5 pounds (5 No. 56 dippers)	
Salt	6½ ounces (¼ mess kit cup)	
Pepper	½ ounce (2 mess kit spoons)	
Meat stock	1 quart (1 No. 56 dipper)	

1. Soak bread in water; press and discard water.
2. Cut meat into small pieces; grind.
3. Mix all ingredients together thoroughly.
4. Shape into 2-ounce meat balls (8 meat balls to the pound).
5. Place in greased baking pans; cook in hot oven (400° F.) until brown on all sides.
6. Add small amount of stock; cover tightly.
7. Braise in slow oven (300° F.) about 30 minutes.

NO. 327. BRAISED MEAT BALLS WITH TOMATO SAUCE OR BROWN GRAVY

Serve braised meat balls with tomato sauce (recipe No. 559) or brown gravy. (See recipe No. 562.)

NO. 328. COMBINATION MEAT BALLS (any combination of beef, lamb, pork or veal)

Use an equal weight of any two kinds of meat. Use same amount of other ingredients and prepare as for braised meat balls.

NO. 329. MEAT BALLS WITH SPAGHETTI

Prepare braised meat balls; cook until brown. Cover 6 pounds spaghetti with 14 gallons (56 No. 56 dippers) boiling salted water (use 6 ounces salt). Heat to boiling point; boil 8 minutes or until tender. Drain. Pour 3 gallons (12 No. 56 dippers) tomato sauce (recipe No. 559) over the spaghetti; add the meat balls. Simmer spaghetti and meat balls together 20 to 30 minutes.

NO. 330. MEAT BALLS WITH RICE

Substitute 3 pounds (1½ No. 56 dippers) uncooked rice for dry bread in recipe for braised meat balls.

NO. 331. SWEDISH MEAT BALLS

Prepare braised meat balls using ground pork or veal for ⅓ meat. Substitute brown gravy (recipe No. 562) for meat stock. Increase cooking time to 1½ hours.

NO. 332. MEAT LOAF (beef or lamb)   Yield: 100 servings, 5 ounces each.

Ingredients	100 servings	.... servings
Meat, carcass................	45 pounds...........................	....
or		
Meat, ground[1]..............	31 pounds..........................	....
Onions, finely chopped........	3 pounds (3 No. 56 dippers).........	....
Celery, finely chopped........	3 pounds (3 No. 56 dippers).........	....
Garlic, finely chopped........	1 to 2 cloves......................	....
Bread crumbs, soft...........	6 pounds...........................	....
Salt......................	6 ounces (¼ mess kit cup).........	....
Pepper....................	½ ounce (2 mess kit spoons).......	....
Eggs, slightly beaten........	48 eggs (2½ No. 56 dippers).......	....
Meat stock[2]................	2 to 3 quarts (2 to 3 No. 56 dippers)..	....
Bacon fat..................		....

[1]10 to 12 pounds of the 31 pounds ground raw meat may be left-over cooked meat.
[2]Amount of stock used depends upon quantity of moisture in bread crumbs.

1. Cut meat into small pieces; grind.
2. Combine meat, onions, celery, and garlic.
3. Add bread crumbs, salt and pepper, slightly beaten egg and stock; mix well but avoid overmixing.
4. Mold into loaves about 4 inches wide by 3 inches high and as long as baking pans are wide. Place in baking pans. Brush tops of loaves with bacon fat.
5. Bake, uncovered and without water, at constant temperature in moderate oven (325° F.) 1½ hours or until desired degree is reached. Avoid overcooking.

Note. Meat loaf is a roast. Gravy may be made in pans in which meat was cooked.

NO. 333. MEAT AND PORK LOAF

Reduce ground beef or lamb to 25 pounds in recipe for meat loaf. Add 6 pounds ground fresh pork, 10 slightly beaten eggs (½ No. 56 dipper), 2 gallons (8 No. 56 dippers) cooked rolled oats, 1 pound (1 No. 56 dipper) chopped onions, 6 ounces (¼ mess kit cup) salt and ¼ ounce (1 mess kit spoon) pepper; mix thoroughly. Pack lightly into greased baking pans. Bake at constant temperature in slow oven (325° F.) about 1½ hours or until there is no trace of pink left.

NO. 334. MEAT AND HAM LOAF

Substitute an equal weight of ground smoked pork for fresh pork in recipe for meat and pork loaf. Use same weight of other ingredients. Other left-over cereals may be used instead of oatmeal.

NO. 335. VEAL AND PORK LOAF

Substitute 35 pounds carcass or 25 pounds boneless veal and 9 pounds bone-in or 6 pounds boneless pork cuts for beef or lamb in recipe for meat loaf. Cut carcass meat into cubes; grind. Combine ground veal and pork, 4 pounds soft bread crumbs, 1 pound (1 No. 56 dipper) finely chopped onions, 1 pound (1 No. 56 dipper) finely chopped celery, 1½ pounds (1½ No. 56 dippers) finely chopped green peppers, eight 14½-ounce cans evaporated milk, ½ pound (⅓ No. 56 dipper) salt, ½ ounce (2 mess kit spoons) pepper and water if bread is dry. Mix thoroughly. Shape into loaves about 4 inches wide by 3 inches high by width of 50-ration baking pans. Place in baking pans; brush tops of loaves with bacon fat. Bake, uncovered and without water, at constant temperature in slow oven (325° F.) 2 hours or until well done. The meat will be done when all pink color has disappeared. Baste loaves at 15 to 20 minute intervals. Serve hot or cold.

NO. 336. MEAT LOAF WITH BARBECUE OR TOMATO SAUCE, TOMATO, OR SPICED TOMATO GRAVY

Serve meat loaf with barbecue sauce (recipe No. 551), tomato sauce. (See recipe No. 559.)

NO. 337. QUICK PORK LOAF   Yield: 100 servings, 5 ounces each.

Ingredients	100 servings	.... servings
Tapioca, granular	1½ pounds (1½ No. 56 dippers)	
Pork, cooked, free from fat, ground.	23 pounds	
Salt	1½ ounces (3 mess kit spoons)	
Pepper, cayenne (optional)		
Pepper, black	⅛ ounce (½ mess kit spoon)	
Onions, finely chopped	8 ounces (½ No. 56 dipper)	
Parsley, finely chopped (optional).		
Tomato juice	1 No. 10 can	
Worcestershire sauce	3 ounces (6 mess kit spoons)	
Water, hot	2 quarts (2 No. 56 dippers)	
Bacon fat	10 ounces (¼ No. 56 dipper)	

126

1. Combine tapioca, ground pork, salt, cayenne, and black pepper, onions, parsley, tomato juice, and Worcestershire sauce. Mix thoroughly.
2. Shape into loaves approximately 4 inches wide by 3 inches high by width of 50-ration baking pans. Place in baking pans.
3. Bake, uncovered and without water, at constant temperature in slow oven (325° F.) 1 hour, basting frequently with mixture of water and bacon fat.
4. Serve hot or cold.

NO. 338. MEAT CROQUETTE LOAF (beef, lamb, veal, corned beef, pork, or smoked ham)

Yield: 100 servings,
5 to 6 ounces each.

Ingredients	100 servings	.... servings
Meat, cooked, ground.........	25 pounds............................	....
Salt.......................	2 ounces (4 mess kit spoons).........	....
Pepper.....................	¼ ounce (1 mess kit spoon)..........	....
Onions, finely chopped........	5 pounds (5 No. 56 dippers).........	....
Meat fat...................	2½ pounds (1¼ No. 56 dippers)......	....
Flour, sifted...............	2 pounds (2 No. 56 dippers).........	....
Meat stock, hot..............	2 quarts (2 No. 56 dippers).........	....
Eggs, slightly beaten........	30 eggs (1½ No. 56 dippers)........	....
Bread or cracker crumbs, dry..	5 pounds (5 No. 56 dippers).........	....
Mace (optional).............	¼ ounce.............................	....

1. Combine ground beef, salt, and pepper.
2. Cook onions in fat until brown. Add flour; mix well.
3. Add hot stock gradually. Heat to boiling point, stirring constantly.
4. Cool; add slightly beaten egg, crumbs, and ground mace; mix thoroughly.
5. Pour into well-greased baking pans. Bake in slow oven (325° F.) 1 hour.
6. Cut into squares.

NO. 339. MEAT TAMALE LOAF (beef, lamb, pork, veal, or ham)

Yield: 100 servings, 6 ounces each.

Ingredients	100 servings	.... servings
Milk, evaporated.............	4—14½-ounce cans....................	....
Water (for milk).............	3 quarts (3 No. 56 dippers).........	....
Cornmeal....................	5 pounds (3⅔ No. 56 dippers).......	....
Onions, finely chopped........	2 pounds (2 No. 56 dippers).........	....
Garlic, finely chopped........	4 cloves............................	....
Fat........................	2½ pounds (1¼ No. 56 dippers)......	....
Tomatoes...................	2 No. 10 cans.......................	....
Corn.......................	2 No. 10 cans.......................	....
Meat, cooked, ground........	20 pounds...........................	....
Eggs.......................	30 eggs (1½ No. 56 dippers)........	....
Chili powder................		
Salt.......................	8 ounces (¼ No. 56 dipper).........	....

1. Mix milk and water. Add cornmeal to milk. Heat to boiling point; reduce heat and cook until thick, stirring constantly.
2. Cook onions and garlic in fat until soft. Add tomatoes and corn.
3. Combine cornmeal, vegetables, cooked meat, eggs, chili powder, and salt. Heat to boiling point.
4. Pour into baking pans. Bake in moderate oven (350° to 400° F.) about 45 minutes.

NO. 340. HAM AND LIMA BEAN SCALLOP   Yield: 100 servings, 8 ounces each.

Ingredients	100 servings	.... servings
Beans, lima, dried	12 pounds	
Water		
Ham, cooked, sliced*	20 pounds	
Salt	2 ounces (4 mess kit spoons)	
Pepper	⅛ ounce (½ mess kit spoon)	

*Uncooked ham may be used instead of cooked ham. Cut ham into cubes and add to lima beans about 1½ hours before they are tender. Bake as for lima beans with cooked ham.

1. Wash lima beans. Add just enough water to cover; soak 4 hours.
2. Heat, to boiling, in water in which they were soaked; reduce heat and simmer until almost tender, being careful that the skins are not broken.
3. Add cooked ham, salt, and pepper; mix well.
4. Place mixture in greased baking pans. Bake in slow oven (325° F.) 45 minutes to 1 hour.

Note. One quart (1 No. 56 dipper) sorghum molasses or brown sugar and ¾ pound (¾ No. 56 dipper) chopped onions may be added to ham and lima beans for flavor.

NO. 341. SCALLOPED HAM AND APPLES
Yield: 100 servings.

Ingredients	100 servings	.... servings
Apples	20 pounds	
Sugar, brown	4 pounds (4 mess kit cups)	
Cloves, ground	¾ ounce (3 mess kit spoons)	
Ham, cooked, chopped	20 pounds	
Water or fruit juice	1½ quarts (1½ No. 56 dippers)	

1. Wash apples; slice.
2. Mix brown sugar and cloves together.
3. Arrange alternate layers of apples, sugar mixture, and ham in baking pans. Pour water or fruit juice over top.
4. Bake in slow oven (300° F.) 1½ hours or until apples are cooked.

NO. 342. SCALLOPED HAM, APPLES, AND SWEET POTATOES
Place layer of sweet potatoes, cut lengthwise, on top of apples in recipe for scalloped ham and apples.

NO. 343. CREAMED MEAT (beef, lamb, veal or ham)

Yield: 100 servings, 6 ounces each.

Ingredients	100 servings	.... servings
Meat, carcass...............	25 pounds............................	....
or		
Meat, ground...............	17 pounds...........................	....
Onions, chopped (optional)....	1 pound (1 No. 56 dipper)...........	....
Bacon or meat fat...........	1 pound (½ No. 56 dipper)...........	....
Flour, sifted................	1½ pounds (1½ No. 56 dippers).....	....
Milk, evaporated...........	16—14½-ounce cans.................	....
Beef stock or water (for milk).	2 gallons (8 No. 56 dippers)........	....
Salt.......................		....
Pepper.....................	¼ ounce (1 mess kit spoon).........	....
Bread, toasted..............	100 slices.........................	....

1. Cut meat into 1-inch pieces; grind.

2. Cook meat in its own fat until brown, stirring frequently.

3. Cook onions in bacon fat; add flour and mix thoroughly.

4. Mix milk and beef stock or water; heat.

5. Add hot milk to fat and flour mixture gradually. Heat to boiling point; boil 1 minute, stirring constantly. Add salt and pepper.

6. Pour sauce over meat; simmer until meat is well done but not over-cooked.

7. Serve on toast.

Note. Chopped green peppers or pimientos may be added to sauce and simmered with meat.

NO. 344. DICED MEAT IN GRAVY

Yield: 100 servings, 8 ounces (1 cup) each.

Ingredients	100 servings	.... servings
Onions, chopped.............	1 pound (1 No. 56 dipper)..........	....
Meat or bacon fat...........	2 pounds (1 No. 56 dipper).........	....
Flour, sifted................	2 pounds (2 No. 56 dippers)	....
Meat stock, hot..............	2 gallons (8 No. 56 dippers)........	....
Milk, evaporated.............	8—14½-ounce cans.................	....
Water (for milk).............	1 gallon (4 No. 56 dippers)........	....
Salt.......................	2 ounces (4 mess kit spoons).......	....
Pepper.....................	¼ ounce (1 mess kit spoon)........	....
Meat, cooked, diced.........	23 pounds.........................	....
Bread, toasted..............	200 slices.........................	....

1. Cook onions slowly in fat until tender. Add flour and mix well.

2. Add meat stock gradually. Heat to boiling point, stirring constantly.

3. Mix milk and water. Add milk, salt, and pepper to hot onion mixture. Heat to boiling point; boil about 3 minutes, stirring constantly. Remove from heat.

4. Add cooked meat; reheat to serving temperature.

5. Serve on toast.

NO. 345. MEAT A LA KING

Add 2 to 4 pounds (2 to 4 No. 56 dippers) diced celery, 1 to 2 pounds (1 to 2 No. 56 dippers) finely chopped green peppers and 24 hard-cooked eggs to recipe for diced meat in gravy. Cook celery with onions. Add eggs and peppers to the meat.

NO. 346. HAM AND CORNBREAD SHORTCAKE

Prepare recipe for diced meat in gravy using 20 pounds cooked, diced ham. Prepare cornbread. (See recipe No. 47.) Cut into servings and split. Serve the creamed ham between and over the split pieces of cornbread.

NO. 347. CREAMED DRIED BEEF

Yield: 6 gallons,
100 servings, 1 cup
(8 ounces) each.

Ingredients	100 servings	servings
Beef, dried, chipped	7 pounds	
Fat, melted	1 pound (½ No. 56 dipper)	
Flour, sifted	1¼ pounds (1¼ No. 56 dippers)	
Milk, evaporated	12—14½-ounce cans	
Water (for milk)	1½ gallons (6 No. 56 dippers)	
Pepper	¼ ounce (½ mess kit spoon)	

1. Separate beef into small pieces.
2. Mix melted fat and flour; stir until smooth.
3. Mix milk and water; heat. Add gradually to flour mixture, stirring constantly.
4. Add chipped beef and pepper. Heat to boiling point; reduce heat and simmer about 10 minutes.

Note. Serve hot over toast.

NO. 348. MEAT CURRY (beef, lamb, pork, or ham)

Yield: 100 servings, 1 pound
(2 cups) each.

Ingredients	100 servings	servings
Rice, uncooked	12 pounds (6 No. 56 dippers)	
Salt	4 ounces (8 mess kit spoons)	
Water, boiling	6 gallons (24 No. 56 dippers)	
Flour, sifted	2 pounds (2 No. 56 dippers)	
Fat	4 pounds (2 No. 56 dippers)	
Milk, evaporated	16—14½-ounce cans	
Water (for milk)	2 gallons (8 No. 56 dippers)	
Salt	6 ounces (¼ mess kit cup)	
Pepper, red		
Curry powder	6 ounces (12 mess kit spoons)	
Cinnamon		
Cloves, ground		
Nutmeg		
Allspice		
Onions, chopped	3½ pounds (3½ No. 56 dippers)	
Apples, sliced	6 pounds (3 No. 56 dippers)	
Meat, cooked, diced	23 pounds	

1. Wash rice thoroughly. Add to rapidly boiling salted water; boil 15 to 20 minutes or until tender. Drain well.
2. Mix flour and ½ melted fat; stir until smooth.
3. Mix milk and water; heat. Add to flour mixture. Heat to boiling point; boil 3 minutes, stirring constantly.
4. Mix remaining fat, salt, pepper, curry powder, cinnamon, cloves, nutmeg, and allspice together.
5. Add onions, apples, and meat. Cover and heat to boiling point; reduce heat and simmer slowly 30 to 45 minutes. Add to hot white sauce.
6. Reheat rice; serve curried meat around or over rice.

NO. 349. STEW   (beef, lamb, pork, veal or smoked ham)

Yield: 100 servings, 10 ounces (approximately 1 cup) each.

Ingredients	100 servings	.... servings
Meat, carcass...............	40 pounds............................	....
or		
Meat, boneless..............	28 pounds............................	....
Flour, sifted...............	1½ pounds (1½ No. 56 dippers).....	....
Salt......................	6 ounces (¼ mess kit cup)..........	....
Pepper...................	½ ounce (2 mess kit spoons)........	....
Fat.......................	1½ pounds (¾ No. 56 dipper).......	....
Water or beef stock.........	4 gallons (16 No. 56 dippers)........	....
Onions, small, whole........	8 pounds............................	....
Carrots, sliced or cubed.......	8 pounds............................	....
Turnips, sliced or cubed......	8 pounds............................	....
Celery, diced (optional).......	5 pounds (5 No. 56 dippers).........	....
Peas, fresh or frozen.........	5 pounds............................	....
Water, boiling..............		
Flour, sifted (for gravy).......	1 pound (1 No. 56 dipper)..........	....
Water, cold (for gravy).......		....
Salt......................		....
Pepper...................		....

1. Cut meat into 1- to 2-inch cubes.
2. Mix flour, salt, and pepper together. Roll meat in flour and cook in fat until brown.
3. Add water or stock; cover and heat to boiling point; reduce heat and simmer 2½ to 3 hours or until tender.
4. Add vegetables in the following order allowing required time for each to cook: onions 45 minutes to 1 hour; carrots, 30 minutes; turnips and celery, 15 to 20 minutes. Drain; reserve liquid.
5. Barely cover peas with boiling water. Heat to boiling point; reduce heat and simmer 20 to 30 minutes or until tender.
6. Mix flour and water; stir until smooth. Add to hot meat and vegetable stock. Heat to boiling point; boil 2 minutes, stirring constantly. Add salt and pepper.
7. Pour gravy over meat and vegetables. Add cooked peas; reheat.

NO. 350. IRISH STEW (beef, lamb or veal)

Prepare recipe for stew but simmer meat without first cooking it until brown. Any of the following combination of vegetables may be added to the stew: turnips and celery; celery, green peppers, and summer squash; lima beans and turnips; onions, apples, and celery; okra, tomatoes, and celery; carrots, onions, and green beans; onions and tomato puree; and kidney beans, celery, and onions.

NO. 351. MEAT PIE WITH BISCUIT, POTATO, OR PIE CRUST

Prepare recipe for stew, reducing cooking time to 2 hours. In ham pie omit salt and simmer meat without first cooking until brown. Place stew in baking pans; cover with biscuit crust (recipe No. 36), pie crust (recipe No. 407) or mashed potatoes. (See recipe No. 681.) Mashed sweet potatoes (recipe No. 691) may be used for ham pie. Bake in hot oven (425° F.) until brown.

NO. 352. RAGOUT (beef, lamb or veal)

Increase meat to 45 pounds carcass or 31 pounds boneless in recipe for stew. Substitute tomatoes and chopped green peppers for carrots, turnips, and peas. Paprika, Worcestershire sauce, bay leaves, and parsley may be used for seasoning.

NO. 353. STEW WITH BARLEY, RICE, CHEESE, DUMPLINGS, OR NOODLES

Prepare recipe for stew but simmer meat without first cooking it until brown. Omit salt in ham stew. Reduce cooking time to 2 hours. Stew may be served with or on cooked barley or rice. Ten pounds shredded cheese may be added to stew; heat stew until cheese is melted, being careful not to boil mixture after cheese is added. Stew may also be varied by adding dumplings (recipe No. 358) or noodles (recipe No. 255) 15 to 20 minutes before the end of cooking period.

NO. 354. SPANISH STEW

Increase meat to 45 pounds carcass or 31 pounds boneless in recipe for stew. Add one No. 10 can tomatoes, 8 pounds (8 No. 56 dippers) chopped onions, 5 pounds (5 No. 56 dippers) chopped green peppers and 2 pounds diced and cooked bacon to meat stock; cook until meat is tender. Drain; prepare gravy using meat stock. Add ½ pint (⅓ mess kit cup) Worcestershire sauce to gravy.

NO. 355. TURKISH STEW

Prepare stew as in recipe for Spanish stew, rolling meat cubes in mixture of flour, salt, and cayenne pepper before cooking until brown. Add one or two cloves and crushed garlic to gravy. Wash 9 pounds (4½ No. 56 dippers) rice thoroughly. Add to rapidly boiling salted water; boil 15 to 20 minutes'or until tender. Drain well. Serve stew over rice.

NO. 356. SPICED STEW

Increase meat to 50 pounds carcass or 35 pounds boneless in recipe for stew. Omit all vegetables. Add 2 quarts (2 No. 56 dippers) vinegar, 2 pounds (1 No. 56 dipper) brown sugar, 1 ounce (4 mess kit spoons) cinnamon, 16 bay leaves, and 1 pound (¾ No. 56 dipper) sliced onions to liquid covering meat.

NO. 357. STEW EL RANCHO

Prepare recipe for stew, substituting 15 pounds potatoes, 10 pounds tomatoes, and 8 pounds cabbage, cut in eighths, for celery and peas. Add 2 ounces (8 mess kit spoons) chili powder to liquid covering meat. Decrease onions to 5 pounds.

NO. 358. DUMPLINGS

Yield: 100 servings, 1 to 2 ounces each.

Ingredients	100 servings	.... servings
Flour, sifted	8 pounds (8 No. 56 dippers)	
Baking powder	6 ounces (⅓ mess kit cup)	
Salt	3 ounces (6 mess kit spoons)	
Water	3 to 4 quarts (3 to 4 No. 56 dippers)	

1. Sift flour, baking powder, and salt together.
2. Add water to make a stiff drop batter.
3. Drop by spoonfuls on top of meat stew.
4. Cover tightly and steam 15 minutes **without** removing cover from kettle during the cooking period.

   Note. Serve dumplings separately or on top of meat.

NO. 359. FRICASSEE (beef, lamb, pork or veal)

Yield: 100 servings, 6 to 10 ounces each.

Ingredients	100 servings	.... servings
Meat, carcass	50 pounds	
or		
Meat, boneless	35 pounds	
Salt		
Pepper		
Fat	3 pounds (1½ No. 56 dippers)	
Beef stock or water	1 gallon (4 No. 56 dippers)	
Onions, chopped	5 pounds (5 No. 56 dippers)	
Celery, chopped	3 pounds (3 No. 56 dippers)	
Carrots, diced	3 pounds (2½ No. 56 dippers)	

1. Cut meat into 2-inch pieces.
2. Sprinkle with salt and pepper; cook in fat until brown on all sides.

133

3. Add small amount of beef stock or water; cover and bake in moderate oven (325° F.) approximately 3 hours or until tender. Add more liquid as needed.

4. Add chopped vegetables about 45 minutes to 1 hour before meat has finished cooking.

NO. 360. GOULASH (beef, lamb or veal) Yield: 100 servings, 6 to 8 ounces each.

Ingredients	100 servings	.... servings
Meat, carcass...............	50 pounds.......................	....
or		
Meat, boneless...............	35 pounds.....................	....
Onions, chopped.............	5 pounds (5 No. 56 dippers)........	....
Beef or bacon fat............	1 pound (½ No. 56 dipper).........	....
Garlic, ground..............	10 cloves......................	....
Majoram, powdered*........	¾ ounce (3 mess kit spoons)........	....
Salt......................	4½ ounces (9 mess kit spoons).......	....
Paprika...................		
Water, boiling..............	1¼ gallons (5 No. 56 dippers).......	....
or		
Tomatoes..................	1½ No. 10 cans.................	....
Flour, sifted...............		....
Water (for flour)...........		....

*If available.

1. Cut meat into 1-inch cubes.

2. Cook onions in fat until light brown; add cubed meat and cook until brown.

3. Add garlic, majoram, salt, and enough paprika to color red.

4. Add water or tomatoes. Cover tightly. Heat to boiling point; reduce heat and simmer about 3 hours or until meat is tender. Add more liquid as needed. Drain.

5. Mix flour and a small amount of water; stir until smooth. Add to liquid. Heat to boiling point; boil 2 minutes, stirring constantly.

6. Combine gravy and meat; heat to serving temperature.

NO. 361. GOULASH AND RICE

Reduce meat in recipe for goulash to 40 pounds carcass or 28 pounds boneless. Reduce onions to 4 pounds (4 No. 56 dippers) and garlic to 2 cloves. Wash 6 pounds (3 No. 56 dippers) rice. Add to 6 gallons (24 No. 56 dippers) rapidly boiling salted water. (Use 6 ounces salt.) Boil 15 to 20 minutes or until tender. Drain well. Serve goulash with, or on rice.

NO. 362. CHOP SUEY (beef, lamb, pork, veal, or smoked ham)
Yield: 100 servings, 16 ounces each.

Ingredients	100 servings	.... servings
Meat, carcass..............	35 pounds...........................	....
or		
Meat, boneless..............	25 pounds...........................	....
Fat.......................	....	....
Water or stock..............	2 gallons (8 No. 56 dippers)..........	....
Salt......................	6 ounces (¼ No. 56 dipper)..........	....
Pepper....................	¼ ounce (1 mess kit spoon).........	....
Onions, thinly sliced.........	12 pounds (12 No. 56 dippers).......	....
Celery, thinly diced.........	8 to 12 pounds.....................	....
Bean sprouts...............	2 No. 10 cans.....................	....
Soy sauce.................	1 pint (½ No. 56 dipper)..........	....
Cornstarch................	1 pound (1 mess kit cup)..........	....
Water (for cornstarch).......	....	....
Rice, uncooked.............	10 pounds (5 No. 56 dippers).......	....
Salt (for rice).............	3½ ounces (7 mess kit spoons).......	....
Water, boiling (for rice)......	5 gallons (20 No. 56 dippers).......	....

1. Cut meats into cubes or strips 1 by ½ by ¼ inches. Cook in fat until brown. Cover with stock or water; add salt and pepper. Heat to boiling point; reduce heat and simmer 1 hour.
2. Add onions and celery; continue cooking 30 minutes. Drain.
3. Mix liquid from meat and liquid from bean sprouts; use as base for soy sauce.
4. Prepare soy sauce.
5. Mix cornstarch and a small amount of water; stir until smooth. Add to sauce; heat to boiling point; boil 2 minutes, stirring constantly. Add cooked meat and bean sprouts.
6. Meanwhile, cook rice in boiling salted water 15 to 18 minutes or until tender.
7. Serve chop suey over boiled rice.

NO. 363. CHOW MEIN
Omit rice in recipe for chop suey. Serve meat mixture on fried Chinese noodles.

NO. 364. MEAT AND BISCUIT ROLLS
(beef, lamb, pork, veal, or smoked ham)
Yield: 100 servings, 2 rolls per serving, each 1 inch in diameter.

Ingredients	100 servings	.... servings
Bread crumbs..............	3 pounds...........................	....
Onions, chopped............	2 pounds (2 No. 56 dippers)........	....
Fat, bacon................	2 pounds (1 No. 56 dipper)..........	....
Meat, cooked, ground........	20 pounds..........................	....
Chili powder..............	1 ounce (4 mess kit spoons)........	....
Salt.....................	4 ounces (8 mess kit spoons)........	....
Biscuit dough..............	....	....

135

1. Soak bread crumbs in water; press and discard water.
2. Cook onions in fat until brown.
3. Combine meat, bread crumbs, cooked onions, chili powder, and salt; mix well.
4. Prepare rich biscuit dough (recipe No. 36) using 8 pounds (8 No. 56 dippers) sifted flour. Roll into rectangles $\frac{1}{4}$ inch thick, 8 inches wide by length of baking pans.
5. Spread meat mixture about $\frac{1}{2}$ inch thick over each piece of dough.
6. Roll like jelly roll in length equal to that of pans and seal with water. Place in baking pans.
7. Bake in slow oven (325° F.) about 30 minutes until golden brown.
8. Slice at once into 1-inch slices.

NO. 365. CHILI CON CARNE (beef, lamb, pork or veal)

Yield: 100 servings, $\frac{1}{2}$ pound (1 cup) each.

Ingredients	100 servings	.... servings
Beans, chili, small............	8 pounds..............................	....
Meat, carcass...............	35 pounds............................	....
or		
Meat, ground...............	25 pounds............................	....
or		
Meat, cooked, ground........	18 pounds............................	....
Garlic, crushed...............	4 cloves..............................	....
Fat......................	1 pound ($\frac{1}{2}$ No. 56 dipper).........	....
Pepper, chili, ground.........	6 ounces.............................	....
Chili powder...............	2 ounces (8 mess kit spoons)........	....
Salt......................	6 ounces ($\frac{1}{4}$ mess kit cup)...........	....
Meat stock.................	2 gallons (8 No. 56 dippers)........	....
Tomatoes.................	1 No. 10 can........................	....

1. Wash beans thoroughly. Cover with cold water; soak 8 hours.
2. Cover and heat to boiling point; reduce heat and simmer $1\frac{1}{2}$ hours or until tender but not split or mushy. Drain.
3. Run $\frac{2}{3}$ beans through food chopper and leave remainder whole.
4. Cut meat into $\frac{1}{2}$-inch cubes or run through coarse meat grinder.
5. Cook crushed garlic in fat until brown; add meat and cook until brown. Add chili pepper, chili powder, salt, and enough meat stock to cover.
6. Cover tightly and heat to boiling point; reduce heat and simmer until meat is tender. Add remainder of stock as needed.
7. Mix ground beans, remaining whole beans, and tomatoes with meat.
8. Serve very hot.

NO. 366. BAKED MEAT HASH (beef, corned beef, lamb, pork, veal, or ham)

Yield: 100 servings, 8 ounces (1 cup) each

Ingredients	100 servings	.... servings
Meat, boneless, cooked.......	22 pounds...........................	....
Potatoes, cooked.............	20 pounds...........................	....
Onions.....................	5 pounds (5 No. 56 dippers).........	....
Salt......................	4 ounces (8 mess kit spoons).........	....
Pepper.....................	¼ ounce (1 mess kit spoon)..........	....
Meat stock.................	2 gallons (8 No. 56 dippers).........	....

1. Chop or cut cooked meat, potatoes, and onions into cubes. Add salt, pepper, and meat stock; mix well.

2. Spread hash in well-greased baking pans. Bake in slow oven (325° F.) about 1 hour.

3. Cut into squares.

Note. If there is an insufficient amount of cooked meat, fresh ground meat may be used to make up the deficiency. Increase cooking time. Use ⅓ more uncooked boneless meat than cooked to allow for shrinkage.

NO. 367. MEAT HASH WITH SAUCE (all except ham)

Prepare hash as in recipe for baked meat hash substituting 2 gallons (8 No. 56 dippers) barbecue sauce (recipe No. 551) for meat stock.

NO. 368. MEAT HASH AND EGGS

Prepare hash as in recipe for baked meat hash. Spread in baking pans and make 100 slight hollows on top of hash. Bake in slow oven (325° F.) about 25 minutes. Remove from oven; fill each hollow with a raw egg. Replace in oven and bake 20 minutes or until eggs are cooked. Cut in squares in such a way as to have an egg in each square.

NO. 369. SOFT MEAT HASH (beef, corned beef, lamb, pork, veal, or ham)

Yield: 100 servings, 8 ounces (1 cup) each.

Ingredients	100 servings	.... servings
Meat, cooked, diced.........	22 pounds...........................	....
Potatoes, cooked, diced.......	20 pounds...........................	....
Onions, chopped.............	5 pounds (5 No. 56 dippers).........	....
Salt (if needed).............	4 ounces (8 mess kit spoons).........	....
Pepper (if needed)..........	¼ ounce (1 mess kit spoon)..........	....
Meat stock or gravy..........	1 gallon (4 No. 56 dippers)..........	....

1. Combine diced meat, potatoes, and onions; add salt and pepper if needed.

2. Pour hash into well-greased baking pans to depth of 3 inches. Add enough stock or gravy to cover entirely and moisten thoroughly, but avoid making mixture as thin as a stew.

3. Bake in slow oven (325° F.) until mixture is thoroughly hot and slightly brown on top.

Note. All kinds of left-over potatoes except fried may be utilized in this recipe. Left-over meats, gravies, and bread stuffings may also be used.

NO. 370. STUFFED PEPPERS (beef, lamb, pork, veal, or ham)

Yield: 100 servings, 8 ounces (1 cup) filling and 1 pepper each.

Ingredients	100 servings	.... servings
Peppers, green, large.........	100 peppers.......................	....
Salt......................	....	....
Water, boiling..............		
Bread crumbs[1]...............	8 pounds (8 No. 56 dippers).........	....
Onions, chopped.............	2½ pounds (2½ No. 56 dippers).....	....
Salt......................	2 ounces (4 mess kit spoons)........	....
Pepper....................	¼ ounce (1 mess kit spoon)........	....
Meat, cooked, finely chopped..	18 pounds.....................	....
Meat stock[2]...............	2 quarts (2 No. 56 dippers)........	....

[1]Rice, 4 pounds, uncooked, may be used instead of bread crumbs. Add rice to 4 gallons (16 No. 56 dippers) rapidly boiling salted water. Use 4 ounces salt. Boil 15 to 20 minutes or until rice is tender. Drain well.

[2]The amount of meat stock needed to make the mixture pack will depend upon the dryness of the bread. Use only enough to moisten the bread.

1. Wash peppers and cut in halves. Remove seeds and tough white portions.

2. Cover with boiling salted water. Heat to boiling point; reduce heat and simmer 3 to 5 minutes.

3. Mix bread crumbs, onions, salt, and pepper together.

4. Add chopped meat; moisten with meat stock. Fill halves of peppers with mixture.

5. Place in baking pans. Bake in moderate oven (350° F.) 20 to 30 minutes.

NO. 371. JELLIED MEAT AND CHEESE

(ham, lamb, pork, or veal)   Yield: 100 servings, ½ pound each.

Ingredients	100 servings	.... servings
Gelatin, lemon flavored.......	2½ pounds (2 No. 56 dippers)......	....
Water, boiling..............	1 gallon (4 No. 56 dippers)........	....
Water, cold................	1 gallon (4 No. 56 dippers)........	....
Lemon juice................	1 pint (½ No. 56 dipper)..........	....
Mustard, dry...............	1 ounce (2 mess kit spoons)........	....
Milk, evaporated............	4—14½-ounce cans..............	....
Water (for milk)............	2 quarts (2 No. 56 dippers)........	....
Mayonnaise................	1 gallon (4 No. 56 dippers)........	....
Cheese, American, chopped....	3 pounds (3 No. 56 dippers)........	....
Ham, cooked, finely chopped..	5 pounds (4 No. 56 dippers)........	....
Parsley, chopped............	4 ounces (¾ No. 56 dipper)........	....
Onions, chopped............	8 ounces (½ No. 56 dipper)........	....
Tomatoes, fresh (optional)....	25 pounds....................	....

1. Dissolve gelatin in boiling water, add cold water, lemon juice, and mustard. Mix well.
2. Chill until mixture begins to thicken.
3. Mix milk and water. Beat milk and mayonnaise gradually into gelatin mixture.
4. Fold in remaining ingredients and pour into shallow pans. Chill until firm.

Note. Slice and serve on lettuce as a salad or on a cold meat platter, garnishing with sliced or quartered tomatoes.

NO. 372. FRIED SAUSAGE (bulk or links)

Yield: 100 servings, 5- to 6-ounce links each or 2 patties per serving, 4 ounces each.

Ingredients	100 servings	.... servings
Pork sausage, fresh, bulk or link.	35 pounds......................	....

1. Shape bulk sausage into patties, making about five to the pound.
2. Fry patties or links in their own fat on top of stove.
3. Turn frequently to insure even cooking. Prevent fat from smoking and avoid overcooking.

NO. 373. GRIDDLE-BROILED SAUSAGE

Griddle-broil link sausage slowly 10 to 12 minutes or sausage patties about 15 minutes or until cooked in the center. Keep temperature below the smoking point of fat; turn frequently to insure even cooking. Serve immediately.

NO. 374. OVEN-COOKED SAUSAGE

Bake sausage patties or links at constant temperature in moderate oven (350° F.) until thoroughly cooked.

NO. 375. PORK SAUSAGE IN ACORN SQUASH

Yield: 100 servings.

Ingredients	100 servings	.... servings
Pork, sausage, fresh..........	20 pounds......................	....
Squash, acorn...............	50 squash......................	....
Salt........................	....	....

1. Shape sausage into patties, making about five to the pound.
2. Wash the squash and split lengthwise. Sprinkle with salt.
3. Place a sausage pattie in each half of squash.
4. Place in flat baking pans. Bake in moderate oven (350° F.) about 1½ hours or until well done.

NO. 376. SCRAPPLE

Yield: 100 servings,
4 to 6 ounces each

Ingredients	100 servings	.... servings
Cornmeal	5 pounds.	
Water	16 pounds (8 No. 56 dippers)	
Salt	3 ounces (1 mess kit spoon)	
Milk, evaporated	12½ pounds (6¼ No. 56 dippers)	
Cooked meat	10 pounds	
Onions	1 pound (1 No. 56 dipper)	
Carrots	½ pound (½ No. 56 dipper)	

1. Cook cornmeal in salted water until thickened.
2. Add milk to cooked cornmeal.
3. Add finely ground or chopped cooked meat, (beef, pork, or veal) onions and carrots.
4. Season with pepper.
5. Cook slowly until thick enough to cling to side of spoon (as for mush to fry).
6. Pour into bread pans that have been rinsed with cold water.
7. Allow to cool or set, remove from pans, slice about ½ inch thick, dip in meal and fry until a golden brown.

Note. Scrapple may be prepared from meat with only enough onion to season, omitting carrots. Two quarts (2 pounds) chopped cheese may be added to above mixture if desired.

NO. 377. HAM AND MEAT IN ACORN SQUASH

Substitute 10 pounds ground ham and 10 pounds ground lamb, beef, or pork for pork sausage in recipe for pork sausage in acorn squash. Omit salt.

NO. 378. PORK SAUSAGE LINKS (PIGS) IN BLANKETS

Yield: 100 servings,
3 to 4 links each.

Ingredients	100 servings	.... servings
Biscuit dough		
Pork sausage links	35 pounds	
Eggs, slightly beaten	5 eggs (¼ No. 56 dipper)	

1. Prepare biscuit dough (recipe No. 36) reducing the amount of shortening to one-half. Roll ¼ inch thick; cut into pieces, each large enough to cover one sausage link.
2. Broil links on griddle until slightly brown.
3. Roll each link in a piece of dough and seal the edges by moistening with water.
4. Dip each roll in slightly beaten egg.
5. Bake in hot oven (400° F.) approximately 20 minutes or until golden brown.

Note. Serve hot with or without gravy or a sauce.

NO. 379. FRANKFURTERS IN BLANKETS

Substitute 30 pounds frankfurters for pork sausage links in recipe for pigs in blankets. Use same weight of other ingredients.

No. 380. VIENNA SAUSAGE IN BLANKETS

Substitute 35 pounds Vienna sausage for pork sausage links in recipe for pork sausage links in blankets. Use same weight of other ingredients.

NO. 381. PORK SAUSAGE LINKS AND
SAUERKRAUT PIE

Yield: 100 servings, 2 to 3 links each.

Ingredients	100 servings	.... servings
Pork sausage links...........	25 pounds...........................	....
Sauerkraut, hot..............	8 No. 10 cans.......................	....
Flour, sifted.................		....
Water, hot..................	2 quarts (2 No. 56 dippers).........	....
Biscuit dough..............		....

1. Broil sausage links on griddle until brown.

2. Cover bottoms of two 50-ration baking pans with ½ heated sauerkraut; sprinkle lightly with flour. Add another layer of hot sauerkraut; sprinkle with flour.

3. Place sausage links over sauerkraut and add 1 quart (1 No. 56 dipper) water to each pan.

4. Prepare biscuit dough (recipe No. 36); roll ¼ inch thick. Cover pans with biscuit dough.

5. Bake in hot oven (400° F.) 30 minutes or until brown.

Note. Serve with sweet potatoes or noodles and brown gravy made with fat from sausage.

NO. 382. PIG ENDS WITH SAUERKRAUT AND
DUMPLINGS

Yield: 100 servings, 12 ounces each.

Ingredients	100 servings	.... servings
Pig ends (feet, tails, ears, etc.).	60 pounds.........................	....
Water or soup stock.........		....
Salt.......................		....
Pepper.....................		....
Sauerkraut.................	7 No. 10 cans......................	....
Flour, sifted...............	4 pounds (4 No. 56 dippers)........	....
Baking powder.............	3½ ounces (9⅓ mess kit spoons).....	....
Salt.......................	5 ounces (10 mess kit spoons).......	....
Nutmeg (optional)..........		....
Milk, evaporated...........	3—14½-ounce cans................	....
Water (for milk)...........	1¼ quarts (1¼ No. 56 dippers)......	....
Eggs, beaten...............	20 eggs (1 No. 56 dipper)..........	....
Fat.......................	8 ounces (¼ No. 56 dipper).........	....

1. Clean pig ends; scrape and wash thoroughly.

2. Cover with water or soup stock; add salt and pepper.

3. Cover and heat to boiling point; reduce heat and simmer slowly about 2½ to 3 hours or until tender.

4. Add sauerkraut.

5. Sift flour, baking powder, salt, and nutmeg together.

6. Mix milk and water. Add beaten egg and fat; mix well. Add to flour mixture; stir until smooth.*

7. Drop batter by spoonfuls onto hot meat and sauerkraut 20 minutes before serving. Cover tightly and simmer 20 to 25 minutes.

*If necessary, more flour or liquid may be added to make batter of right consistency to drop from spoon.

NO. 383. BREADED BRAINS — Yield: 100 servings, 4 ounces each.

Ingredients	100 servings	.... servings
Brains, calf	25 pounds	
Water, cold		
Vinegar		
Salt		
Flour, sifted	4 ounces (8 mess kit spoons)	
Pepper		
Milk, evaporated	1—14½-ounce can	
Water (for milk)	1 pint (½ No. 56 dipper)	
Eggs	10 eggs (½ No. 56 dipper)	
Bread or cracker crumbs		
Fat		
Parsley		

1. Cover brains with cold water; soak approximately 30 minutes. Drain.

2. Cover with fresh water. Add vinegar and ½ salt. Heat to boiling point; reduce heat and simmer 15 to 20 minutes. Drain; drop into cold water again. Drain.

3. Remove membrane and separate brains into pieces.

4. Mix flour, pepper, and remaining salt together; roll brains in mixture.

5. Mix milk and water; add eggs. Mix thoroughly.

6. Dip brains in milk mixture; roll in crumbs.

7. Fry in deep hot fat (350° F.) until golden brown.

8. Garnish with parsley and serve at once.

NO. 384. BRAINS AND SCRAMBLED EGGS

Prepare brains as in recipe for breaded brains. Beat 120 eggs until light and fluffy; add 2 ounces (4 mess kit spoons) salt, ¼ ounce (1 mess kit spoon) pepper, four 14½-ounce cans evaporated milk and 1¾ quarts (1¾ No. 56 dippers) water; mix well. Pour brains into melted fat in frying pan; pour egg mixture over brains. Cook slowly, turning as eggs coagulate and become slightly brown. Avoid overcooking. Garnish with chopped parsley. Serve at once.

NO. 385. STUFFED AND BRAISED HEART (beef)

Yield: 100 servings, 8 ounces each.

Ingredients	100 servings	.... servings
Hearts, beef	35 pounds	
Salt	3 ounces (6 mess kit spoons)	
Pepper	¼ ounce (1 mess kit spoon)	
Onions, chopped	5 ounces (⅓ No. 56 dipper)	
Celery, diced	1 pound (1 No. 56 dipper)	
Fat	1 pound (½ No. 56 dipper)	
Bread crumbs, soft, coarse	8 pounds (16 No. 56 dippers)	
Salt	3 ounces (6 mess kit spoons)	
Pepper	¼ ounce (1 mess kit spoon)	
Poultry seasoning (optional)	1 ounce (2 mess kit spoons)	
Parsley, finely chopped (optional).	1 ounce (2 mess kit spoons)	
Eggs, slightly beaten	15 eggs (¾ No. 56 dipper)	
Meat stock, hot		
Fat		

1. Wash hearts in warm water; remove arteries and veins. Wash again; drain and sprinkle inside with salt and pepper.
2. Cook onions and celery in fat until brown. Add bread crumbs, remaining salt and pepper, poultry seasoning, and parsley. Remove from heat.
3. Add beaten egg and a little hot stock to moisten; mix lightly.
4. Fill hearts with hot stuffing; pack loosely. Tie or sew if necessary.*
5. Place hearts in a utensil that can be tightly covered. Add fat; cook until brown.
6. Add small amount of meat stock.
7. Cover pans. Braise in slow oven (300° F.) 3 to 4 hours or until tender. Add more stock during cooking if necessary.
8. Remove hearts; slice into ½-inch slices across each heart so stuffing will be in center of slice.

*Hearts may be rolled in flour if desired.

Note. Serve braised hearts with brown gravy. (See recipe No. 562.)

NO. 386. STUFFED HEARTS WITH BARBECUE OR TOMATO SAUCE

Serve stuffed hearts with barbecue sauce (recipe No. 551) or tomato sauce. (See recipe No. 559.)

NO. 387. COUNTRY STYLE HEART (pork or veal)

Increase hearts to 45 pounds in recipe for stuffed and braised hearts. Increase salt to 6 ounces (12 mess kit spoons) and pepper to ½ ounce (2 mess kit spoons.) Dredge hearts in flour. Cook until brown on all sides in hot fat. Add small amount of water. Cover tightly. Braise in slow oven (300° F.) 1½ to 2 hours or until tender. Remove hearts and prepare gravy (recipe No. 562) to serve over meat.

NO. 388. BRAISED KIDNEYS

Yield: 100 servings, 4 to 5 ounces each.

Ingredients	100 servings	.... servings
Kidneys...................	40 pounds.......................	....
Fat.......................	4 pounds (2 No. 56 dippers)..........	....
Salt......................	6 ounces (¼ mess kit cup)..........	....
Pepper....................	½ ounce (2 mess kit spoons)........	....
Worcestershire sauce.........	....	....
Water or stock.............	....	....
Onions, sliced..............	5 pounds (5 No. 56 dippers).........	....
Fat.......................	....	....

1. Slice kidneys; wash in cold water. Dry well. Cook in fat until brown.
2. Add salt, pepper, and Worcestershire sauce.
3. Add small amount of water or stock; cover tightly. Heat to boiling point; reduce heat and simmer until kidneys are tender.
4. Cook onions in fat until brown. Add to kidneys.

Note. Tomato juice may be used instead of water or stock. If the strong, odorous taste is not desired the kidneys may be soaked in cold water, preferably under refrigeration, for 2 or 3 hours before cooking.

NO. 389. KIDNEY AND BEEF PIE

Yield: 100 servings, 8 ounces each.

Ingredients	100 servings	.... servings
Kidneys...................	10 pounds.......................	....
Water....................	....	....
Beef, carcass...............	35 pounds.......................	....
or		
Beef, boneless..............	25 pounds.......................	....
Salt......................	6 ounces (¼ mess kit cup)..........	....
Pepper....................	½ ounce (2 mess kit spoons)........	....
Flour, sifted...............	2 pounds (2 No. 56 dippers).........	....
Fat.......................	1 pound (½ No. 56 dipper)..........	....
Water....................	3 quarts (3 No. 56 dippers).........	....
Biscuit dough..............	....	....

1. Slice kidneys; wash in cold water. Cover with fresh water; cover pans tightly. Heat to boiling point; reduce heat and simmer about 45 minutes or until tender. Drain.
2. Mix salt, pepper and ½ flour together.
3. Cut beef into 1-inch cubes. Roll in flour mixture; cook in fat until brown.
4. Add water; braise in slow oven (300° F.) 1 to 1½ hours or until tender. Drain.
5. Mix remaining flour and a small amount of cold water; stir until smooth. Add slowly to hot beef liquid. Heat to boiling point; boil 2 minutes, stirring constantly.
6. Combine kidneys, beef, and gravy; place in baking pans.
7. Prepare biscuit dough (recipe No. 36); cover meat mixture with dough.
8. Bake in hot oven (425° F.) until brown.

Note. Use stock drained from kidneys in soup.

NO. 390. BRAISED LIVER (beef, lamb, pork or veal)

Yield: 100 servings, 5 ounces each.

Ingredients	100 servings	.... servings
Liver.	35 pounds	
Flour, sifted	3 pounds (3 No. 56 dippers)	
Salt	5 ounces (10 mess kit spoons)	
Pepper	¼ ounce (1 mess kit spoon)	
Fat	4 pounds (2 No. 56 dippers)	
Water or stock, hot		

1. Cut liver into slices ⅜ inch thick; cut slices into pieces weighing 4 to 5 ounces each.

2. Mix flour, salt, and pepper together; roll liver in mixture. Cook in fat until brown.

3. Add enough hot water or stock to cover bottom of pans; cover tightly and braise slowly about 20 minutes or until tender on top of stove or stack in baking pans and add a small amount of water. Cover tightly and braise in slow oven (300° F.) until done.

NO. 391. FRIED LIVER (beef, lamb, or pork)

Prepare liver as in recipe for braised liver. Fry until done in bacon fat, turning frequently to insure even cooking.*

*Pork liver needs to be cooked well-done and for this reason is more often braised. Overcooking in time or temperature hardens liver and destroys its flavor.

NO. 392. FRIED LIVER WITH BACON

Reduce liver to 25 pounds. Prepare as fried liver; serve with 10 pounds bacon, fried, griddle-broiled, or oven-cooked.

NO. 393. FRIED LIVER AND ONIONS

Add 50 pounds peeled and sliced onions to recipe for fried liver. Prepare onions either by shallow frying in 4 pounds (2 No. 56 dippers) fat in uncovered pan or by dipping onion slices in Yorkshire pudding batter (recipe No. 265) and frying in deep hot fat (360° F.) until golden brown. Add salt and pepper to onions.

NO. 394. LIVER FRIED IN DEEP FAT

Remove membrane from 35 pounds liver. Cut liver into 1-inch cubes. Prepare French dressing (recipe No. 533) using twice as much oil or bacon fat as vinegar. Soak liver 30 minutes or longer in dressing. Fry in deep hot fat (350° F.) until brown.

NO. 395. GRIDDLE-BROILED LIVER (lamb or veal)

Cut liver into slices ½ inch thick. Dip in bacon fat and broil on griddle at moderate temperature, 6 to 10 minutes or until color has changed, turning frequently. Add 5 ounces (10 mess kit spoons) salt and ¼ ounce (1 mess kit spoon) pepper. Serve at once.

NO. 396. LIVER CHOP SUEY

Yield: 100 servings, 12 ounces per serving (including 4 ounces liver).

Ingredients	100 servings	.... servings
Liver, any kind, cut into ½-inch cubes.	25 pounds	
Fat	1 pound (½ No. 56 dipper)	
Celery, diced	4 pounds (4 No. 56 dippers)	
Peppers, green, chopped	2 pounds (2 No. 56 dippers)	
Tomatoes	3 No. 10 cans	
Rice, uncooked	10 pounds (5 No. 56 dippers)	
Salt (for rice)	3½ ounces (7 mess kit spoons)	
Water, boiling	5 gallons (20 No. 56 dippers)	
Vegetables, Chinese	3 No. 10 cans	
Cornstarch	1½ pounds (¾ No. 56 dipper)	
Soy sauce	1 quart (1 No. 56 dipper)	
Salt	6 ounces (12 mess kit spoons)	
Pepper	½ ounce (2 mess kit spoons)	

1. Cook diced liver in hot fat until brown; add celery, green peppers, and tomatoes. Heat to boiling point; reduce heat and simmer 20 to 25 minutes.

2. Wash rice thoroughly. Add to rapidly boiling salted water; boil 15 to 18 minutes or until tender. Drain well.

3. Drain Chinese vegetables and add to liver and other vegetables; heat.

4. Mix cornstarch and soy sauce; stir until smooth. Add enough liquid from vegetables to make a sauce of pouring consistency. Heat to boiling point; boil 2 minutes, stirring constantly. Add salt and pepper.

5. Add sauce to meat and vegetable mixture; heat to serving temperature.

6. Serve chop suey over boiled rice.

NO. 397. LIVER CHOW MEIN

Omit rice in recipe for liver chop suey and serve mixture on fried Chinese noodles.

NO. 398. LIVER AND PORK DUMPLINGS AND SAUERKRAUT

Yield: 100 servings, 8 ounces each.

Ingredients	100 servings	.... servings
Pork cuts, bone in	14 pounds	
or		
Pork, boneless	10 pounds	
Liver	20 pounds	
Bread, sliced	8 pounds	
Water		
Onions, chopped	5 pounds (5 No. 56 dippers)	
Salt	6 ounces (¾ mess kit cup)	
Pepper	½ ounce (2 mess kit spoons)	
Parsley, chopped		
Nutmeg (optional)	¼ ounce (1 mess kit spoon)	
Eggs, slightly beaten	30 eggs (1½ No. 56 dippers)	
Salt		
Bay leaves (optional)		
Sauerkraut, hot	3 No. 10 cans	

1. Cut pork into cubes.
2. Place pork and liver in separate utensils. Barely cover each with water. Heat each to boiling point; reduce heat and simmer until done. Drain and reserve pork stock.
3. Grind pork and liver together.
4. Soak bread in water; press and discard water. Chop soaked bread.
5. Combine bread, ground meat, onions, salt, pepper, parsley, and nutmeg. Add beaten egg; mix thoroughly.
6. Heat pork stock to boiling point; add salt and bay leaves.
7. Drop pork and liver dumplings from spoon into boiling stock; simmer 10 to 15 minutes.
8. Serve on bed of hot sauerkraut.

NO. 399. LIVER AND PORK LOAF

Yield: 100 servings, 6 ounces each.

Ingredients	100 servings	.... servings
Liver, pork	25 pounds	
Water	2½ quarts (2½ No. 56 dippers)	
Bread, chopped	5 pounds	
Pork, ground	5 pounds	
Salt	6 ounces (¼ mess kit cup)	
Pepper	¼ ounce (1 mess kit spoon)	
Tomato catsup	1 quart (1 No. 56 dipper)	
Eggs, slightly beaten	30 eggs (1½ No. 56 dippers)	
Lemon juice	1 pint (½ No. 56 dipper)	
Onions, finely chopped	2 pounds (2 No. 56 dippers)	

1. Barely cover liver with water. Heat to boiling point; reduce heat and simmer 10 minutes. Drain; grind liver.
2. Mix all ingredients together thoroughly.
3. Pack mixture lightly into greased baking pans.
4. Bake in slow oven (325° F.) about 2 hours or until well done.
5. Remove from pans; slice. Serve hot.

Note. Mixture may be shaped into 4-ounce patties; wrap each in bacon strip and cook in oven or braise until done.

NO. 400. LIVER AND PORK LOAF WITH TOMATO SAUCE

Serve liver and pork loaf with tomato sauce. (See recipe No. 559.)

NO. 401. CREAMED SWEETBREADS

Yield: 100 servings, 8 to 10 ounces each.

Ingredients	100 servings	.... servings
Sweetbreads	25 pounds	
Water, cold		
Onions, chopped	1 to 2 pounds (1 to 2 No. 56 dippers)	
Salt	6 ounces (¼ mess kit cup)	
Vinegar		
Water, cold		
Butter, melted	1½ pounds (¾ No. 56 dipper)	
Flour, sifted	1½ pounds (1½ No. 56 dippers)	
Milk, evaporated	12—14½-ounce cans	
Water (for milk)	1½ gallons (6 No. 56 dippers)	
Pepper	¼ ounce (1 mess kit spoon)	

1. Cover sweetbreads with cold water; soak about 30 minutes. Drain. Remove membrane and fibers.

2. Cover with fresh water; add chopped onions, ½ salt and ½ ounce (1 mess kit spoon) vinegar for each quart (1 No. 56 dipper) water used.

3. Heat to boiling point; reduce heat and simmer 15 to 20 minutes. Drain. Drop into cold water or allow cold water to run over sweetbreads. Drain.

4. Remove any remaining membrane; cut sweetbreads into ½-inch cubes.

5. Mix melted butter and flour; stir until smooth.

6. Mix milk and water. Add to flour mixture. Heat to boiling point; boil 2 minutes, stirring constantly. Add pepper and remaining salt.

7. Add sweetbreads; reheat.

NO. 402. CREAMED SWEETBREADS AND LUNCHEON MEAT

Reduce sweetbreads to 12 pounds. Add 12 pounds ground luncheon meat; mix well. Prepare as in recipe for creamed sweetbreads.

NO. 403. SIMMERED TONGUE (beef, fresh or smoked)

Yield: 100 servings, 4 ounces each.

Ingredients	100 servings	.... servings
Tongue, fresh...............	45 pounds........................	....
or		
Tongue, smoked.............	40 pounds.......................	....
Water......................		....
Salt (for fresh tongues only)...	7 ounces (¼ mess kit cup)..........	....
Pepper (optional)...........	....	....
Water......................	....	....

1. Cover tongue with water; if fresh tongue is used, add salt and pepper.

2. Cover and heat to boiling point; reduce heat and simmer until tongue is tender.

3. Plunge into cold water. Remove skin and cut away roots.

4. If tongue is to be served cold, cool in water in which it was cooked; if tongue is to be served hot, trim and return to cooking water. Heat to serving temperature.

Note. Spices and chopped onions, carrots, or green peppers may be added to the cooking water.

NO. 404. TONGUE A LA MARYLAND

Add spices, bay leaves, and one No. 10 can cherries to recipe for simmered tongue. Heat and thicken sauce if desired. Serve sauce over hot sliced tongue.

NO. 405. SLICED COLD TONGUE

Prepare tongue as in recipe for simmered tongue. Allow tongue to cool in water in which it was cooked. Remove from water and slice.

NO. 406. TONGUE WITH HORSERADISH SAUCE

Serve sliced tongue with horseradish sauce. (See recipe No. 556.)

PIES

21. PASTRY. a. Ingredients. The ingredients of pastry are flour, shortening, salt, and water. Successful pastry can be made with hard wheat flour if the correct proportion of fat to flour is used and the ingredients are carefully combined. Soft wheat flour sometimes produces a crust that is too tender and crumbly to handle easily. For best results use a solid fat. Lard or hydrogenated vegetable fat makes tender pastry. Butter produces a flaky pastry. A combination of the two is often used. Use ice cold water and keep the mixture in the refrigerator.

b. Mixing. Handle pastry as lightly as possible. In combining the shortening and flour, mix only enough to distribute the ingredients evenly. Overmixing must be avoided; otherwise the gluten will become too well developed. The development of the gluten is prevented by coating each particle of fat with flour. If overmixed, the flour becomes coated with fat, thus preventing absorption of sufficient water to form a dough. Add only enough water to the flour mixture to make the dough hold together. If the water is added all at one time, excessive mixing will be required to incorporate it into the flour. As the flour becomes moist enough to form lumps, push it aside and dampen other particles of flour. When the entire mixture sticks together, enough water has been added. Avoid the use of excess water as unnecessary flour will be required to prepare the dough for rolling, thereby increasing the possibility of a tough pie crust.

c. Characteristics. Pastry can be made into one crust pies, two crust pies, or baked as pie shells. A good pastry when baked has a blistery, pebbly surface and is tender when cut. It is easily cut with a fork but not crumbly. The entire crust is light brown in color.

22. FILLINGS. Pies may be filled with fruit, custard, or cream fillings. Fruit fillings are thickened with a mixture of water and cornstarch or flour. The amount of cornstarch or flour varies according to the acidity and juiciness of the fruit and the amount of sugar. The more acid the fruit, the more starch is needed as the acid may liquefy the starch during cooking. More starch is required if a large amount of juice and sugar are used. Chill filling before placing in pie shells. Chilling helps to preserve the natural color of the fruit. If the filling is cold when pies are placed in the oven, the crust will have time to cook before the filling reaches the boiling point. Both custard and cream pie fillings contain milk and eggs—two protein foods that are very perishable. Because of the danger of spoilage, custard and cream pies are unsatisfactory in hot weather.

NO. 407. PIE CRUST (two crust)   Yield: Crust for 18
                                                    9-inch pies.

Ingredients	100 servings	.... servings
Flour, sifted..................	7½ pounds (7½ No. 56 dippers).....	....
Salt.......................	4 ounces (8 mess kit spoons)........	....
Shortening..................	4½ pounds (2¼ No. 56 dippers).....	....
Water (variable)*...........	1½ quarts (1½ No. 56 dippers)......	....

*The amount of water needed will vary according to the strength of the flour and the amount of fat used.

1. Combine flour, salt and shortening by cutting with a knife or rubbing between the fingers until shortening is in particles about the size of dried peas.

2. Add water to flour, sprinkling a small amount at a time over the mixture; mix lightly with a fork until all particles are moistened and in small lumps. Place portions that stick together to one side of the bowl before adding more water.

3. Mix ingredients as little as possible to form a stiff dough (*if dough is undermixed, the finished crust will have raw spots; if overmixed, the crust will be tough.*)

4. Place dough on floured board or table top. Divide into as many portions as there are pies to be made. Cut each portion into two pieces, each about 3 inches in diameter. Use one piece for bottom crust and the other for the top.

5. Work with one piece of dough at a time; keep remainder in refrigerator. Sprinkle flour on dough to be used for bottom crust. Roll dough, with floured rolling pin, into circular shape, 3/16 inch thick and slightly larger than pie pan. Use light, even strokes, rolling from center of dough out in every direction.

6. Roll dough onto rolling pin and unroll onto pie pan; press out all air between pan and dough.

7. Dampen outer rim of bottom crust with water to help seal top and bottom crusts together.

8. Roll out top crust in same way as bottom crust. Pierce dough with a fork in several places, making an attractive pattern, to allow steam to escape during baking.

9. Roll crust onto rolling pin and unroll onto filled lower crust.

10. Remove excess dough by pressing hands against rim of pie pan. Press the two layers of dough together and crimp with a fork or crimp between thumb and forefinger. This seals the two crusts together and helps to keep juicy pies from running over. Reserve excess dough for bottom crust of next pie. (*Always use fresh dough for top crusts.*)

11. Bake pies in hot oven (425° to 450° F.) 40 to 45 minutes. Remove from oven when filling reaches boiling point and crust is golden brown.

NO. 408. PIE CRUST. (One-crust pie)

Prepare ⅔ recipe for two-crust pies and follow directions for rolling bottom crusts. Pie crust may be baked with or without filling. If baked without filling, prick crust all over with tines of a fork before baking.

NO. 409. COBBLERS

Prepare ⅔ recipe for two-crust pies. Roll into rectangular shape to fit shallow baking pans. Fill with fruit filling. Cover with pastry if desired. Bake in hot oven (400° to 425° F.) 55 to 60 minutes. Cut each cobbler into 56 servings by dividing it into 8 portions lengthwise and 7 portions crosswise.

NO. 410. TURNOVERS

Prepare recipe for two-crust pies. Cut dough into individual servings, each 6 inches square. Place 4 ounces of filling (fruit pie fillings, recipes Nos. 418 and 424) in center of each square. Fold opposite corners of dough together; seal by crimping edges. Place on sheet pans. Brush tops with melted butter. Bake in hot oven (425° F.) about 20 minutes or until brown.

NO. 411. CREAM PIE FILLING

Yield: Filling for 18 9-inch pies, serving, 6 cuts per pie.

Ingredients	100 servings	.... servings
Milk, evaporated.............	13—14½-ounce cans................	....
Water (for milk).............	6 quarts (6 No. 56 dippers).........	....
Cornstarch.................	2½ pounds (2 No. 56 dippers).......	....
Sugar, granulated...........	7 pounds (3½ No. 56 dippers).......	....
Salt......................	1½ ounces (3 mess kit spoons)......	....
Butter....................	14 ounces (½ No. 56 dipper)........	....
Eggs, slightly beaten........	60 eggs (3 No. 56 dippers).........	....
Vanilla...................	4 ounces (8 mess kit spoons)........	....

1. Mix milk and water.
2. Mix cornstarch and ½ sugar. Add ½ milk; stir until smooth.
3. Mix salt, remaining sugar, and remaining milk together; heat to boiling point.
4. Add cornstarch mixture very slowly to hot milk. Heat to boiling point; boil 2 minutes or until thick, stirring constantly.
5. Add butter; mix well.
6. Pour about ¼ cooked mixture over beaten egg; stir until well mixed.
7. Pour egg mixture slowly into remaining cooked mixture; mix thoroughly. Heat to boiling point,* stirring constantly.
8. Cool slightly; add vanilla and mix well.
9. Pour into baked pie shells.

*Heat only to boiling point. If mixture boils, the eggs will be overcooked and the mixture will be curdled.

153

NO. 412. BANANA CREAM PIE FILLING

Pour ½ cooked filling in recipe for cream pie filling into baked pie shells. Cover with layer of sliced bananas using 20 pounds (15 No. 56 dippers) for the 18 pies. Pour remaining filling over bananas. Cover with meringue (recipe No. 432) if desired.

NO. 413. CHOCOLATE CREAM PIE FILLING

Add 1½ pounds (1¾ No. 56 dippers) cocoa to salt, sugar, and milk mixture in recipe for cream pie filling.

NO. 414. LEMON PIE FILLING Yield: Filling for 18 9-inch pies, serving, 6 cuts per pie.

Ingredients	100 servings	.... servings
Cornstarch...................	2 pounds (2 mess kit cups)..........	....
Sugar, granulated............	9 pounds (4½ No. 56 dippers).......	....
Water, cold.................	2¼ gallons (9 No. 56 dippers)......	....
Salt......................	¾ ounce (1½ mess kit spoons)......	....
Butter.....................	¾ pound (½ mess kit cup)..........	....
Egg yolks, slightly beaten.....	54 yolks (1½ mess kit cups)........	....
Lemons, juice and grated rind.	30 lemons............................	....

1. Mix cornstarch and ½ sugar together. Add ½ water; stir until smooth.
2. Mix salt, remaining sugar, and remaining water together; heat to boiling point.
3. Add cornstarch mixture very slowly. Heat to boiling point; boil 2 minutes or until thick, stirring constantly.
4. Add butter; mix well.
5. Pour about ¼ cooked mixture over beaten eggs; mix well.
6. Pour egg mixture into remaining cooked mixture; mix well. Heat to boiling point,* stirring constantly.
7. Add lemon juice and rind; mix well.
8. Pour into baked pie shells.

*Heat only to boiling point. If mixture boils, the eggs will be overcooked and the mixture will be curdled.

Note. Cover pies with meringue (recipe No. 432) if desired.

NO. 415. PINEAPPLE CREAM PIE FILLING Yield: Filling for 18 9-inch pies, serving, 6 cuts per pie.

Ingredients	100 servings	.... servings
Cornstarch.................	2¾ pounds (2 No. 56 dippers)......	....
Corn sirup.................	1½ quarts (1½ No. 56 dippers)......	....
Sugar, granulated............	10 pounds (5 No. 56 dippers).......	....
Salt......................	1 ounce (2 mess kit spoons)........	....
Pineapple juice.............	5½ quarts (5½ No. 56 dippers)......	....
Butter.....................	½ pound (¼ No. 56 dipper)........	....
Egg yolks, beaten...........	20 yolks (1 No. 56 dipper)........	....
Lemon juice................	12 ounces (½ mess kit cup)........	....
Lemon rind................	1 ounce................................	....

1. Mix cornstarch, corn sirup, sugar, and salt together. Add 1 quart (1 No. 56 dipper) pineapple juice; stir until smooth.
2. Heat 3 quarts (3 No. 56 dippers) of the remaining pineapple juice to boiling point.
3. Add cornstarch mixture very slowly to hot juice. Heat to boiling point; boil 2 minutes or until thick, stirring constantly.
4. Add butter; mix well.
5. Pour about ¼ cooked mixture slowly over beaten eggs; stir until well mixed.
6. Pour egg mixture slowly into remaining cooked mixture; mix thoroughly. Heat to boiling point,* stirring constantly.
7. Add lemon juice, lemon rind, and remaining 1½ quarts (1½ No. 56 dippers) pineapple juice; mix well.
8. Pour into baked pie shells.

*Heat only to boiling point. If mixture boils, the eggs will be overcooked and the mixture will be curdled.

NO. 416. CUSTARD PIE FILLING   Yield: Filling for 18 9-inch pies, serving, 6 cuts per pie.

Ingredients	100 servings	.... servings
Sugar, granulated............	6 pounds (3 No. 56 dippers).........	....
Cornstarch..................	1½ ounces (4 mess kit spoons).......	....
Salt........................	¾ ounce (1½ mess kit spoons).......	....
Eggs, slightly beaten........	70 eggs (3½ No. 56 dippers)........	....
Milk, evaporated............	11—14½-ounce cans...............	....
Water (for milk)............	1 gallon (4 No. 56 dippers).........	....
Butter, melted..............	6 ounces (¼ mess kit cup).........	....
Vanilla.....................	3 ounces (6 mess kit spoons).......	....
Nutmeg.....................		

1. Sift sugar, cornstarch, and salt together.
2. Add beaten eggs and mix thoroughly.
3. Mix milk and water; add vanilla, butter, and nutmeg. Stir slowly into egg mixture; mix thoroughly.
4. Place unbaked pie shells in oven. Pour one No. 56 dipper filling into each pie shell.
5. Bake in hot oven (400° to 425° F.) about 15 minutes. Reduce heat and continue baking 15 minutes or until center of pie filling has risen level with crust. Remove immediately from oven.

NO. 417. PUMPKIN PIE FILLING   Yield: Filling for 18 9-inch pies, serving, 6 cuts per pie.

Ingredients	100 servings	servings
Sugar, brown...............	6½ pounds (5 No. 56 dippers).......	....
Cinnamon..................	1½ ounces (6 mess kit spoons).......	....
Mace (optional)............	½ ounce (2 mess kit spoons)........	....
Salt.......................	1½ ounces (3 mess kit spoons).......	....
Eggs, slightly beaten........	30 eggs (1½ No. 56 dippers)........	....
Milk, evaporated............	6—14½-ounce cans...............	....
Water (for milk)............	3 quarts (3 No. 56 dippers)........	....
Pumpkin...................	2 No. 10 cans...................	....

1. Mix sugar, cinnamon, mace, and salt together.

2. Add beaten egg; mix thoroughly.

3. Mix milk and water; heat. Add hot milk and pumpkin to egg mixture; mix thoroughly.

4. Place unbaked pie shells in oven. Pour one No. 56 dipper filling into each pie shell.

5. Bake in hot oven (400° to 425° F.) about 15 minutes. Reduce heat and continue baking 15 minutes or until center of pie filling has risen level with crust. Remove immediately from oven.

NO. 418. FRESH APPLE PIE FILLING

Yield: Filling for 18 9-inch pies, serving, 6 cuts per pie.

Ingredients	100 servings	.... servings
Apples, fresh	35 pounds	
Sugar, granulated	9 pounds (4½ No. 56 dippers)	
Salt	3 ounces (6 mess kit spoons)	
Cinnamon	1½ ounces (6 mess kit spoons)	
or		
Nutmeg	¾ ounce (3 mess kit spoons)	
Butter	¾ pound (½ mess kit cup)	

1. Pare apples; core and slice.

2. Mix sugar, salt, cinnamon, or nutmeg together.

3. Fill unbaked pie shells with alternate layers of apples and sugar mixture.

4. Place small pieces of butter on top of apples; cover with pastry. (See recipe No. 407.)

5. Bake in hot oven (425° F.) 10 minutes; reduce heat and continue baking slowly until apples are tender and transparent.

Note. Other fresh fruits such as peaches or apricots may be substituted for apples in recipe for fresh apple pie filling. The amount of sugar and spices needed will vary according to the sweetness of the fruit used.

NO. 419. APPLE PIE FILLING

Yield: Filling for 18 9-inch pies, serving, 6 cuts per pie.

Ingredients	100 servings	.... servings
Apples, solid pack	3 No. 10 cans	
Water	2½ quarts (2½ No. 56 dippers)	
Cornstarch	15 ounces (1 mess kit cup)	
Water (for cornstarch)	1 quart (1 No. 56 dipper)	
Sugar, granulated	9 pounds (4½ No. 56 dippers)	
Salt	¼ ounce (½ mess kit spoon)	
Butter	¾ pound (½ mess kit cup)	
Cinnamon	¼ ounce (1 mess kit spoon)	
Lemon juice	3 lemons	

1. Drain juice from apples. Add water to juice; heat to boiling point.
2. Mix cornstarch and water; stir until smooth. Add slowly to hot juice. Heat to boiling point; boil 2 minutes or until thick, stirring constantly.
3. Add sugar and salt; stir until sugar is dissolved. Remove from heat.
4. Add butter, cinnamon, lemon juice, and apples; mix well. Cool before placing in unbaked pie shells.

NO. 420. APRICOT PIE FILLING

Yield: Filling for 18 9-inch pies, serving, 6 cuts per pie.

Ingredients	100 servings	.... servings
Apricots	4 No. 10 cans	
Cornstarch	1¼ pounds (1 No. 56 dipper)	
Water (for cornstarch)	1¼ quarts (1¼ No. 56 dippers)	
Sugar, granulated	12 pounds (6 No. 56 dippers)	
Salt	¼ ounce (½ mess kit spoon)	

1. Drain juice from apricots. Heat juice to boiling point.
2. Mix cornstarch and water; stir until smooth. Add slowly to hot juice. Heat to boiling point; boil 2 minutes or until thick, stirring constantly.
3. Add sugar and salt; stir until sugar is dissolved. Remove from heat.
4. Add apricots; mix well. Cool before placing in unbaked pie shells.

NO. 421. CHERRY PIE FILLING

Substitute four No. 10 cans sour cherries for apricots in recipe for apricot pie filling. Add enough water to cherry juice to make a total of 5 quarts (5 No. 56 dippers) liquid.

NO. 422. PEACH PIE FILLING

Yield: Filling for 18 9-inch pies, serving, 6 cuts per pie.

Ingredients	100 servings	.... servings
Peaches	4 No. 10 cans	
Cornstarch	¾ pound (¾ mess kit cup)	
Water (for cornstarch)	¾ quart (¾ No. 56 dipper)	
Sugar, granulated	8 pounds (4 No. 56 dippers)	
Salt	¼ ounce (½ mess kit spoon)	

1. Drain juice from peaches. Heat juice to boiling point.
2. Mix cornstarch and water; stir until smooth. Add slowly to hot juice. Heat to boiling point; boil 2 minutes or until thick, stirring constantly.
3. Add sugar and salt; stir until sugar is dissolved. Remove from heat.
4. Add peaches; mix well. Cool before placing in unbaked pie shells.

NO. 423. FRESH PEACH PIE

Yield: Seventeen
9-inch pies, serving,
6 cuts per pie.

Ingredients	100 servings	.... servings
Fresh peaches...............	25 pounds (½ bushel)...............	....
Water.....................	3 quarts (3 No. 56 dippers)..........	....
Flour......................	1 pound 5 ounces (1 No. 56 dipper)...	....
Sugar.....................	4½ pounds (2¼ No. 56 dippers).....	....
Salt......................	¾ ounce (1½ mess kit spoons).......	....

1. Slice peaches and set aside in a separate container.
2. Bring ½ water to a good boil.
3. Combine the remainder of the water and flour to make a batter and add to boiling water. When above is boiling, cook for 10 minutes, stirring constantly.
4. Add sugar and salt to above and stir until dissolved. Remove from fire and pour over fruit. Chill and use in pies.

NO. 424. PINEAPPLE PIE FILLING

Yield: Filling for 18
9-inch pies, serving,
6 cuts per pie.

Ingredients	100 servings	.... servings
Pineapple, shredded..........	4 No. 10 cans.....................	....
Cornstarch.................	1 pound (1 mess kit cup)...........	....
Water (for cornstarch)........	1 quart (1 No. 56 dipper)..........	....
Sugar, granulated...........	8 pounds (4 No. 56 dippers)........	....
Salt......................	¼ ounce (½ mess kit spoon)........	....

1. Drain juice from pineapple. Heat juice to boiling point.
2. Mix cornstarch and water; stir until smooth. Add slowly to hot juice. Heat to boiling point; boil 2 minutes or until thick, stirring constantly.
3. Add sugar and salt; stir until sugar is dissolved. Remove from heat.
4. Add pineapple; mix well. Cool before placing in unbaked pie shells.

NO. 425. RAISIN PIE FILLING

Yield: Filling for 18
9-inch pies, serving,
6 cuts per pie.

Ingredients	100 servings	.... servings
Raisins....................	12 pounds (9 No. 56 dippers)........	....
Sugar, brown...............	2½ pounds (2½ mess kit cups).......	....
Sugar, granulated...........	2½ pounds (1¼ No. 56 dippers).....	....
Water, boiling..............	2 gallons (8 No. 56 dippers)........	....
Salt......................	1 ounce (2 mess kit spoons)........	....
Cornstarch.................	4 ounces (¼ mess kit cup)..........	....
Water (for cornstarch)........	1 quart (1 No. 56 dipper)..........	....
Butter....................	4 ounces (8 mess kit spoons)........	....
Lemon juice................	1 ounce (2 mess kit spoons)........	....
Cinnamon..................	½ ounce (2 mess kit spoons)........	....

1. Combine raisins, brown sugar, granulated sugar, water, and salt. Heat to boiling point; reduce heat and simmer until raisins are tender.
2. Mix cornstarch and water; stir until smooth. Add slowly to hot raisin mixture. Heat to boiling point; boil 2 minutes or until thick, stirring constantly. Remove from heat.
3. Add butter, lemon juice, and cinnamon; mix well. Cool before placing in unbaked pie shells.

NO. 426. RHUBARB PIE FILLING Yield: Filling for 18 9-inch pies, serving, 6 cuts per pie.

Ingredients	100 servings	.... servings
Rhubarb	25 pounds	
Sugar, granulated	12½ pounds (6¼ No. 56 dippers)	
Salt	2½ ounces (5 mess kit spoons)	
Water	½ pint (⅓ mess kit cup)	
Cornstarch	4½ ounces (¼ mess kit cup)	

1. Wash rhubard; cut into ½-inch cubes.
2. Combine rhubarb, 10 pounds (5 No. 56 dippers) sugar, salt, and water.
3. Heat to boiling point; reduce heat and simmer 20 minutes or until rhubarb is tender, stirring frequently. Drain.
4. Mix cornstarch, the remaining 2½ pounds (1¼ No. 56 dippers) sugar and 1 quart (1 No. 56 dipper) rhubarb liquid together; stir until smooth.
5. Add cornstarch mixture slowly to hot liquid. Heat to boiling point; boil 5 minutes or until thick, stirring constantly.
6. Add rhubarb. Cool before placing in unbaked pie shells.

NO. 427. MINCEMEAT PIE FILLING Yield: Filling for 18 9-inch pies, serving, 6 cuts per pie.

Ingredients	100 servings	.... servings
Beef, lean, cooked, ground	3 pounds (2 No. 56 dippers)	
Beef suet, ground	2 pounds (2 No. 56 dippers)	
Raisins, cooked, drained	5 pounds (3½ No. 56 dippers)	
Sugar, brown	5 pounds (4 No. 56 dippers)	
Apples, chopped	10 pounds (8 No. 56 dippers)	
Apple cider	2½ quarts (2½ No. 56 dippers)	
Molasses	¾ quart (¾ No. 56 dipper)	
Lemon, juice and grated rind	4 lemons	
Cinnamon, ground	3 ounces (12 mess kit spoons)	
Cloves, ground	1 ounce (4 mess kit spoons)	
Mace, ground	1 ounce (4 mess kit spoons)	
Allspice	1 ounce (4 mess kit spoons)	
Ginger	1 ounce (4 mess kit spoons)	
Salt	3 ounces (6 mess kit spoons)	
Water	1½ quarts (1½ No. 56 dippers)	

1. Combine all ingredients; mix thoroughly.
2. Heat to boiling point; reduce heat and simmer 1 hour or until apples and raisins are tender.
3. Refrigerate approximately 1 week before using.

NO. 428. CARROT PIE FILLING

Yield: Filling for 18 9-inch pies, serving, 6 cuts per pie.

Ingredients	100 servings	.... servings
Carrots	35 pounds	
Water, boiling		
Sugar, brown[1]	6¼ pounds (4¾ No. 56 dippers)	
Salt	4 ounces (8 mess kit spoons)	
Allspice	1 ounce (4 mess kit spoons)	
Cinnamon	1 ounce (4 mess kit spoons)	
Ginger	1 ounce (4 mess kit spoons)	
Nutmeg	1 ounce (4 mess kit spoons)	
Cornstarch	5 ounces (¼ No. 56 dipper)	
Eggs	40 eggs (2 No. 56 dippers)	
Milk, evaporated	10—14½-ounce cans	
Water (for milk)	1¼ gallons (5 No. 56 dippers)	

[1] If brown sugar is not available, white sugar may be used.

1. Scrub carrots thoroughly and scrape to remove outer layer of skin; cover with boiling water.
2. Heat to boiling point; reduce heat and simmer 10 to 15 minutes or until tender. Drain.
3. Mash carrots; rub through sieve to remove lumps.[2]
4. Combine sugar, salt, spices and cornstarch; mix well. Add to carrot puree.
5. Mix milk and water. Add to carrot mixture; stir until smooth.
6. Add eggs; mix thoroughly.
7. Allow mixture to stand 1 to 2 hours before placing in pie shells.

[2] 35 pounds carrots will yield 10 quarts (10 No. 56 dippers) carrot puree.

NO. 429. DRIED APPLE PIE FILLING

Yield: Filling for 18 9-inch pies, serving, 6 cuts per pie.

Ingredients	100 servings	.... servings
Apples, dried	12 pounds	
Water, cold	4½ gallons (18 No. 56 dippers)	
Sugar, granulated	12 pounds (6 No. 56 dippers)	
Salt	2 ounces (4 mess kit spoons)	
Nutmeg	¼ ounce (1 mess kit spoon)	
Cornstarch	10 ounces (½ No. 56 dipper)	
Water (for cornstarch)	1 pint (½ No. 56 dipper)	
Lemon juice	4 ounces (8 mess kit spoons)	

1. Wash apples. Cover with cold water; soak 2 hours.
2. Add sugar, nutmeg, and salt; mix well.
3. Heat to boiling point; reduce heat and simmer until apples are tender. Drain.

4. Mix cornstarch and water; stir until smooth.
5. Add cornstarch mixture slowly to hot apple juice. Heat to boiling point; boil 5 minutes or until thick, stirring constantly.
6. Add apples and lemon juice; mix well. Pour into unbaked pie shells.

NO. 430. DRIED APRICOT PIE FILLING   Yield: Filling for 18 9-inch pies, serving, 6 cuts per pie.

Ingredients	100 servings	.... servings
Apricots, dried...............	8 pounds........................	....
Water, cold.................	2 gallons (8 No. 56 dippers).........	....
Sugar, granulated............	8 pounds (4 No. 56 dippers)........	....
Nutmeg......................	....	....
Salt.......................	1½ ounces (3 mess kit spoons).......	....
Cornstarch.................	12 ounces (¾ mess kit cup).........	....
Water (for cornstarch).......	1 quart (1 No. 56 dipper)..........	....
Lemon juice................	4 ounces (8 mess kit spoons)........	....

1. Wash apricots. Cover with cold water; soak 2 hours.
2. Add sugar, nutmeg, and salt; mix well.
3. Heat to boiling point; reduce heat and simmer until apricots are tender. Drain.
4. Mix cornstarch and water; stir until smooth.
5. Add cornstarch mixture slowly to apricot liquid. Heat to boiling point; boil 5 minutes or until thick, stirring constantly.
6. Add apricots and lemon juice; mix well. Cool before placing in unbaked pie shells.

NO. 431. DRIED PEACH PIE FILLING

Substitute 8 pounds dried peaches for dried apricots in recipe for dried apricot pie filling. Omit nutmeg.

NO. 432. MERINGUE   Yield: Meringue for 18 9-inch pies, serving, 6 cuts per pie.

Ingredients	100 servings	.... servings
Salt.......................	¼ ounce (½ mess kit spoon)........	....
Egg whites.................	50 whites (1¼ No. 56 dippers).......	....
Sugar, granulated............	4 pounds (2 No. 56 dippers)........	....
Vanilla....................	2¼ ounces (4½ mess kit spoons).....	....

1. Combine salt and egg whites; beat until stiff but not dry.
2. Add sugar gradually; continue beating until light and the meringue stands in peaks; add flavoring.
3. Pile lightly onto filling in pie shell using approximately 6 ounces per pie. Shape meringue over pie shell to depth of ½ inch, touching rim on all sides; leave in peaks.
4. Bake in slow oven (325° F.) 15 minutes or until meringue is a golden brown.

SECTION XIV

POULTRY

NO. 23. POULTRY. Chicken is one of the most universally popular foods. It is the kind of poultry most frequently served in the Army. However, turkey and duck are occasionally served.

NO. 433. ROAST CHICKEN
Yield: 100 servings,
12 to 16 ounces each.

Ingredients	100 servings	.... servings
Chicken, young, fat*........	100 pounds.........................	....
Salt......................	8 ounces (⅓ mess kit cup)..........	....
Pepper....................	1 ounce (4 mess kit spoons).........	....

*Select chickens weighing 4 to 5 pounds each.

1. Clean chickens. Wash inside and out; dry thoroughly.
2. If chickens are large, tie legs together and tie string around chicken to hold wings close to the body.
3. Rub cavity with salt and pepper; stuff with poultry dressing (recipe No. 436) if desired.
4. Brush chickens with melted fat; place in baking pans without stacking or crowding.
5. Bake, uncovered and without water, at constant temperature in moderate oven (350° F.) 2 to 2½ hours or until thoroughly cooked and juice is no longer pink. Turn chickens frequently to insure even cooking. Baste at regular intervals with the juice.

NO. 434. ROAST DUCK
Substitute 75 pounds young fat ducks for chickens in recipe for roast chicken. Reduce salt to 5 ounces (10 mess kit spoons) and pepper to ¼ ounce (1 mess kit spoon). Increase baking time to 3½ hours.

NO. 435. ROAST TURKEY
Substitute 100 pounds young fat turkeys for chickens in recipe for roast chicken. Reduce salt to 6 ounces (12 mess kit spoons) and pepper to ¾ ounce (3 mess kit spoons). Bake turkeys weighing up to 16 pounds in moderate oven (325° F.) approximately 4 hours, turkeys weighing 16 to 20 pounds in slow oven (300° F.) and turkeys over 20 pounds in slow oven (250° F.). Bake turkeys until all traces of pink juice have disappeared from the meat. Allow turkeys to stand at least 30 minutes before carving.

NO. 436. POULTRY DRESSING

Yield: 100 servings,
3 to 4 ounces each.

Ingredients	100 servings	.... servings
Celery, chopped............	5 pounds (5 No. 56 dippers)........	
Onions, finely chopped........	2½ pounds (2½ No. 56 dippers).....	
Fat (for frying).............	3 pounds (1½ No. 56 dippers)......	
Bread crumbs, soft...........	24 pounds (48 No. 56 dippers)......	
Poultry seasoning............	1½ ounces (3 mess kit spoons)......	
Salt......................	2 ounces (4 mess kit spoons)......	
Pepper....................	½ ounce (2 mess kit spoons)........	
Parsley, finely chopped.......	8 ounces (1 mess kit cup)..........	

1. Fry celery and onions until partially cooked.
2. Add bread crumbs, poultry seasoning, salt, pepper, and parsley; mix well.
3. Place in greased baking pans; cover with buttered parchment paper.
4. Bake in moderate oven (350° F.) about 1 to 1½ hours.

NO. 437. CORNBREAD DRESSING

Substitute an equal quantity of crumbled cornbread for the bread crumbs in recipe for poultry dressing.

NO. 438. NUT DRESSING

Add any desired kind of nuts to recipe for poultry dressing. Chop or leave whole according to size and kind.

NO. 439. MUSHROOM DRESSING

Add mushrooms, chopped or whole, to recipe for poultry dressing. If mushrooms are fresh, fry in fat with celery and onions.

NO. 440. OYSTER DRESSING

Heat oysters over low heat in their own liquid until edges begin to curl. Drain; add to recipe for poultry dressing. Mix carefully.

NO. 441. BAKED CHICKEN AND NOODLES

Yield: 100 servings,
10 to 12 ounces each.

Ingredients	100 servings	servings
Chicken (stewing fowl).......	4 chickens...................	
Salt (for chicken)...........		
Water, boiling (for chicken)...		
Noodles....................	5 pounds....................	
Salt (for noodles)...........	2 ounces (4 mess kit spoons)........	
Water, boiling (for noodles)...	5 gallons (20 No. 56 dippers).......	
White sauce.................	1½ gallons (6 No. 56 dippers).......	
Onions, chopped.............	2 onions....................	
Salt......................	1 ounce (2 mess kit spoons)........	
Pepper....................		
Flour, sifted................		
Butter, melted..............		
Bread crumbs...............	2 pounds (2 No. 56 dippers)........	
Cheese, diced...............	1 pound (1 No. 56 dipper)..........	

1. Clean chickens. Add boiling salted water. Heat to boiling point; reduce heat and simmer until tender.
2. Cool. Skim fat from broth. Remove meat from bones; leave meat in large pieces.
3. Add noodles to boiling salted water; boil 10 to 15 minutes or until tender. Drain well.
4. Prepare white sauce (recipe No. 548); add onions, salt, and pepper.
5. Mix flour and melted fat; stir until smooth. Add 1½ gallons (6 No. 56 dippers) chicken broth. Heat to boiling point; boil 2 minutes or until thick, stirring constantly. Add noodles.
6. Combine white sauce and cooked chicken.
7. Spread layer of noodles on bottom of greased baking pans; add layer of creamed chicken.
8. Pour melted butter over bread crumbs; mix crumbs and diced cheese. Sprinkle over chicken.
9. Bake in hot oven (400° F.) until mixture is heated through and crumbs are light brown.

NO. 442. BRAISED CHICKEN OR TURKEY

Yield: 100 servings,
12 to 14 ounces each.

Ingredients	100 servings	.... servings
Chicken or turkey, New York dressed, or	80 pounds..........................	....
Chicken or turkey, full drawn.	60 pounds..........................	....
Flour, sifted....................		....
Salt.........................	6 ounces (¼ mess kit cup)...........	....
Pepper........................	¾ ounce (3 mess kit spoons).........	....
Chicken or turkey fat.........		
Stock or water...............		

1. Clean chicken or turkey; cut into servings or leave whole.
2. Mix flour, salt, and pepper; roll chicken or turkey in flour.
3. Cook until brown in hot fat. Place in baking pans and add enough hot stock to moisten bottom of pans.
4. Cover tightly; braise in moderate oven (350° F.) 2½ to 3½ hours, depending upon kind of poultry.

NO. 443. BRAISED CHICKEN OR TURKEY WITH DRESSING

Reduce chicken or turkey to 70 pounds New York dressed or 52 pounds full drawn in recipe for braised chicken or turkey. Serve with dressing. (See recipe No. 436.)

NO. 444. BRAISED CHICKEN OR TURKEY WITH VEGETABLES

Reduce chicken to 60 pounds New York dressed or 45 pounds full drawn in recipe for braised chickey or turkey. Combine cooked chicken or turkey, brown gravy (recipe No. 562), and 8 pounds cooked whole onions, 8 pounds cooked carrots, and 10 pounds cooked, diced potatoes. Heat to serving temperature.

NO. 445. SIMMERED CHICKEN Yield: 100 servings, 12 to 14 ounces each.

Ingredients	100 servings	.... servings
Chicken, New York dressed...	80 pounds..............................	....
or		
Chicken, full drawn..........	60 pounds.............................	....
Celery, leaves and stalks......	2 pounds (2 No. 56 dippers).........	....
Onions, chopped.............	4 pounds (4 No. 56 dippers).........	....
Salt.......................	6 ounces (¼ mess kit cup)..........	....
Water......................		

1. Clean chicken; cut into suitable servings or leave whole.
2. Add celery, onions, salt, and enough water to cover chicken.
3. Cover tightly and heat to boiling point; reduce heat and simmer 3½ to 4½ hours or until tender.

Note. If meat and stock are cooked for future use, cool meat quickly, and refrigerate. Cool stock; strain if necessary and pour into clean cans or jars. The fat layer which congeals on top will help to keep stock 2 or 3 days under refrigeration. When only part of stock is used, heat remaining stock with fat layer to boiling point. Cool quickly and refrigerate.

NO. 446. SIMMERED CHICKEN WITH VEGETABLES

Reduce chicken to 65 pounds New York dressed or 49 pounds full drawn in recipe for simmered chicken. Add 8 pounds whole, small onions, 8 pounds sliced or cubed carrots, 10 pounds cubed potatoes, and 8 pounds diced celery, allowing 45 minutes to 1 hour for onions to cook; 30 minutes for carrots and potatoes, and 15 to 20 minutes for celery. Drain stock from chicken and vegetables; thicken stock with flour mixture. Simmer 10 to 15 minutes. Add salt and pepper. Combine gravy, chicken, and vegetables; heat to serving temperature. Add cooked peas or asparagus just before serving.

NO. 447. FRIED CHICKEN (MARYLAND STYLE)

Yield: 100 servings, 12 to 14 ounces each.

Ingredients	100 servings	.... servings
Chicken, New York dressed*..	80 pounds..............................	....
or		
Chicken, full drawn*.........	60 pounds.............................	....
Flour, sifted.................		
Salt.......................	6 ounces (¼ mess kit cup)..........	....
Pepper.....................	¾ ounce (3 mess kit spoons)........	....
Milk, evaporated.............	2—14½-ounce cans................	....
Water (for milk).............	1 quart (1 No. 56 dipper)..........	....
Eggs, slightly beaten.........	20 eggs (1 No. 56 dipper)..........	....
Bread crumbs, dry...........	4 pounds (4 No. 56 dippers)........	....
Fat, melted.................		
Water, boiling..............		

*Broilers or fryers.

1. Clean chicken; cut into suitable servings.
2. Mix flour, salt, and pepper together; roll chicken in flour.

3. Mix milk and water; add beaten egg and mix well. Dip floured chicken in milk and egg mixture. Roll in bread crumbs.
4. Place in well-greased baking pans. Pour small amount of melted fat over chicken.
5. Bake in moderate oven (350° F.) 1 to 2½ hours or until tender, depending upon size of chickens. Baste with mixture of hot fat and water several times during cooking.

NO. 448. COUNTRY STYLE CHICKEN (SOUTHERN FRIED)

Yield: 100 servings,
12 to 14 ounces each

Ingredients	100 servings	.... servings
Chicken, New York dressed...	80 pounds............................	....
or		
Chicken, full drawn..........	60 pounds............................	....
Flour or flour and bread crumbs	....	....
Salt.........................	6 ounces (¼ mess kit cup)...........	....
Pepper......................	¾ ounce (3 mess kit spoons).........	....
Chicken fat (for frying).......	....	....

1. Clean chicken; disjoint chicken or cut into halves or quarters according to size.
2. Mix flour, salt, and pepper together; roll chicken in flour or flour and bread crumbs.
3. Place chicken in pan of hot fat without crowding. Place largest pieces in first and on hottest part of pan.
4. Fry until brown, turning occasionally. Reduce heat after 10 to 15 minutes of cooking or when chicken begins to brown.*

*Keep temperature below smoking point of fat.

NO. 449. OVEN-FRIED CHICKEN

Clean chickens as in recipe above. Fry until brown. Place one or two layers of chicken in baking pans. Pour enough stock over chicken to keep it from sticking to bottom of pan. Bake in moderate oven (350° F.) 1½ to 2½ hours or until tender. Add additional stock in small amounts if necessary during baking.

NO. 450. CHICKEN FRIED IN DEEP FAT   Yield: 100 servings,
12 to 14 ounces each.

Ingredients	100 servings	.... servings
Chicken, New York dressed*..	80 pounds............................	....
or		
Chicken, full drawn*.........	60 pounds............................	....
Flour, sifted.................	....	....
Salt.........................	6 ounces (¼ mess kit cup)...........	....
Pepper......................	¾ ounce (3 mess kit spoons).........	....
Milk, evaporated............	2—14½-ounce cans..................	....
Water (for milk)............	1 quart (1 No. 56 dipper)...........	....
Eggs, slightly beaten.........	20 eggs (1 No. 56 dipper)...........	....
Bread crumbs, dry...........	....	....
Fat (for frying).............	....	....

*Broilers or fryers.

167

1. Clean chicken; cut into suitable servings.

2. Mix flour, salt, and pepper, together; roll chicken in flour.

3. Mix milk and water; add beaten egg and mix well. Dip floured chicken in milk and egg mixture; roll in bread crumbs.

4. Fill frying basket with chicken, leaving space between pieces. Lower chicken carefully into deep hot fat (350° F.). Fry 15 to 20 minutes after the temperature has dropped to 320° to 325° F.

5. Place cooked pieces of chicken on paper in heated pans. Keep hot in slow oven (300° to 325° F.).

Note. Unless chicken is very tender and small, it is best to simmer it in water until tender. (See recipe No. 445.) Drain and fry as in recipe above.

NO. 451. CHICKEN FRICASSEE Yield: 100 servings, 6 to 8 ounces each.

Ingredients	100 servings	.... servings
Chicken, New York dressed*..	70 pounds............................	....
or		
Chicken, full drawn*.........	52 pounds............................	....
Flour, sifted.................		....
Salt.......................	6 ounces (¼ mess kit cups).........	....
Pepper.....................	¾ ounce (3 mess kit spoons)........	....
Fat (for frying).............		....
Water.....................		....
Flour, sifted................		....
Milk, evaporated...........		....
Salt.......................		....
Pepper.....................		....

*Stewing hens.

1. Clean chicken; cut into suitable servings.

2. Mix flour, salt, and pepper together; roll chicken in flour.

3. Fry until brown. Place in kettle and cover with water. Heat to boiling point; reduce heat and simmer until tender. Drain and reserve stock.

4. Mix flour and a small amount of stock; mix thoroughly. Add remaining stock slowly. Heat to boiling point; boil 2 minutes or until thick, stirring constantly.

5. Add milk; continue simmering 10 to 15 minutes, stirring constantly. Add salt and pepper.

6. Remove meat from chicken bones if cooked whole; cut into chunks. If chicken was disjointed before cooking, bones may be left with meat.

7. Combine meat and gravy; heat to serving temperature.

Note. Serve very hot over split baking powder biscuits.

NO. 452. CREAMED CHICKEN OR TURKEY

Yield: 100 servings, approximately 6 ounces (⅔ cup) each.

Ingredients	100 servings	.... servings
Onions, chopped............	1 pound (1 No. 56 dipper)...........	....
Celery, finely chopped........	5 pounds (5 No. 56 dippers)........	....
Chicken fat (for frying).......	2 pounds (1 No. 56 dipper).........	....
Flour, sifted.............	2 pounds (2 No. 56 dippers)........	....
Chicken or turkey stock, hot..	2 gallons (8 No. 56 dippers)........	....
Milk, evaporated............	8—14½-ounce cans...............	....
Water (for milk).............	1 gallon (4 No. 56 dippers)........	....
Salt......................	....	....
Pepper....................	¼ ounce (1 mess kit spoon)........	....
Chicken or turkey, cooked, diced.	15 pounds (15 No. 56 dippers).......	....

1. Fry onions and celery in chicken fat until tender.

2. Add flour; mix thoroughly. Add hot stock slowly. Heat to boiling point; boil 2 minutes or until thick, stirring constantly. Add milk, water, salt, and pepper; mix well.

3. Add chicken or turkey. Heat to serving temperature, stirring constantly.

Note. Serve very hot over toast or split baking powder biscuits (recipe No. 36) cornbread (recipe No. 47) boiled noodles (recipe No. 255) or boiled rice. (See recipe No. 258.)

NO. 453. CHICKEN OR TURKEY A LA KING

Add 1 to 2 pounds (1 to 2 No. 56 dippers) finely chopped green peppers and pimientos to recipe for creamed chicken or turkey. Heat thoroughly. Mix 1½ cups egg yolks with enough cream or milk to make a smooth mixture. Pour slowly into creamed chicken or turkey, stirring constantly. Heat about 5 minutes. Remove from heat to prevent simmering after egg yolks are added. Serve at once.

NO. 454. CREAMED CHICKEN OR TURKEY WITH HAM

Reduce cooked diced chicken or turkey to 10 pounds (10 No. 56 dippers) in recipe for creamed chicken or turkey. Add 10 pounds cooked, diced ham.

NO. 455. CREAMED CHICKEN WITH EGGS

Add 2 dozen coarsely chopped hard-cooked eggs to recipe for creamed chicken.

NO. 456. CHICKEN STEW

Yield: 100 servings,
6 to 8 ounces each.

Ingredients	100 servings	.... servings
Chicken, New York dressed...	65 pounds..................................	....
or		
Chicken, full drawn..........	49 pounds...........................	....
Celery, coarsely chopped......	2 pounds (2 No. 56 dippers)........	....
Onions, coarsely chopped......	2 pounds (2 No. 56 dippers)........	....
Carrots, diced..............	2 pounds (1½ No. 56 dippers)......	....
Salt......................	6 ounces (¼ mess kit cup).........	....
Water.....................	7 gallons (28 No. 56 dippers).......	....
Flour, sifted...............	....	....
Water, cold................	....	....

1. Clean chicken; cut into suitable servings or leave whole.

2. Add celery, onions, carrots, salt, and enough water to cover chicken.

3. Cover tightly and heat to boiling point; reduce heat and simmer 3½ to 4½ hours or until tender.

4. Drain stock from meat; heat stock to boiling point. Mix flour and small amount of stock; stir until smooth. Pour slowly into remaining stock. Heat to boiling point; reduce heat and simmer about 10 minutes, stirring constantly.

5. Remove meat from chicken bones; cut into small pieces.

6. Combine meat and gravy. Heat to serving temperature.

NO. 457. CHICKEN PIE WITH BISCUITS OR BISCUIT CRUST

Pour chicken stew into baking pans. Cover with biscuits or biscuit crust (recipe No. 36). Bake in hot oven (425° F.) until mixture bubbles and biscuits or biscuit crust are brown.

NO. 458. CHICKEN PIE WITH MASHED POTATO CRUST

Pour chicken stew into baking pans. Cover with layer of mashed potatoes. (See recipe No. 681.) Bake in hot oven (425° F.) until mixture bubbles and potatoes are brown.

NO. 459. CHICKEN PIE WITH PIE CRUST

Pour chicken stew into baking pans. Cover with pie crust. (See recipe No. 407.) Bake in hot oven (425° F.) until mixture bubbles and crust is brown.

NO. 460. CHICKEN STEW WITH BARLEY OR RICE

Reduce chicken to 60 pounds New York dressed or 45 pounds full drawn in recipe for chicken stew. Serve stew with or on cooked barley or rice.

NO. 461. CHICKEN STEW WITH DUMPLINGS OR NOODLES

Reduce chicken to 60 pounds New York dressed or 45 pounds full drawn in recipe for chicken stew. Drop dumplings (recipe No. 358) by spoonfuls or noodles (recipe No. 255) into hot gravy and meat. Cover tightly; simmer 15 to 20 minutes.

NO. 462. CHICKEN OR TURKEY TAMALES Yield: 100 servings, 4 to 4½ ounces each.

Ingredients	100 servings	.... servings
Chicken or turkey, cooked, cubed.	15 pounds (15 No. 56 dippers)........	....
Salt......................	3 ounces (6 mess kit spoons).........	....
Pepper....................	¼ ounce (1 mess kit spoon).........	....
Chili powder...............	2 ounces (8 mess kit spoons).........	....
Garlic, crushed.............	1 clove................	....
Chicken stock..............	1 quart (1 No. 56 dipper)..........	....
Potatoes, mashed...........	5 pounds (2½ No. 56 dippers)......	....
Cornmeal..................	1½ pounds (1½ mess kit cups)......	....
Flour, sifted...............	8 pounds (8 No. 56 dippers)........	....
Water (to make sufficient dough).	....	....
Fat (for frying)...........	....	....

1. Combine meat, salt, pepper, chili powder, garlic, and chicken stock; mix well.

2. Prepare mashed potatoes. (See recipe No. 681.) Mix mashed potatoes, cornmeal, and flour together; add enough water to make a stiff dough.

3. Roll out dough ¼ inch thick. Cut into long strips, 2½ inches wide.

4. Place enough chicken mixture in center of each strip of dough to form a small core about ½ inch in diameter.

5. Moisten edges of dough and seal together. Cut rolled strips into pieces about 5 inches long.

6. Fry in deep hot fat (350° F.) until biscuit dough is cooked.

NO. 463. CHICKEN OR TURKEY AND VEAL TAMALES

Reduce cooked chicken or turkey to 10 pounds in recipe for chicken or turkey tamales. Add 10 pounds cooked veal.

SALADS

---

24. INGREDIENTS. a. A salad is any combination of raw or cooked foods served cold and crisp with a salad dressing and greens such as lettuce, watercress, chicory, or endive. Use as much of the greens as possible, discarding only those leaves which are wilted or discolored. Coarse outside leaves may be shredded for use in the salad or put aside for use in soups or stews.

b. Wash greens in a large amount of water. Remove the leaves from the water rather than pour the water from the leaves. Drain and refrigerate as soon as washed. The longer greens are allowed to remain at room temperature the more vitamins will be lost. If head lettuce is used, remove the core and allow the water to run through the head. The water forces the leaves apart without injury to the leaves. Wilted greens can be more readily revived by adding a half cup of vinegar to each gallon of water and allowing the greens to remain in the mixture several hours until refreshed.

c. Cut ingredients into small pieces, but not so small as to lose their identity. Fruits and vegetables that are easily cut may be left in large pieces. Use cooked foods that are tender but firm enough to hold their shape. Drain ingredients well before placing in mixing bowl. Mix just before serving and mix only enough to combine ingredients. Serve salad dressing separately.

25. SALAD DRESSINGS. There are three basic types of salad dressings; cooked, French, and mayonnaise. The cooked is a sauce which is thickened with starch, flour, or eggs. The French is a mixture of oil, acid, and seasonings which must be beaten just before using as the oil separates from the remainder of the ingredients if allowed to stand. Mayonnaise is a mixture of fat and oil held together by raw eggs. The oil will not separate from other ingredients in mayonnaise if care is taken to beat the mixture well and add the oil only in small amounts at the beginning. After an emulsion of the fat and oil is formed, the oil may be added in larger amounts.

NO. 464. STRING BEAN, BEET, AND PEA SALAD

Yield: Approximately 25 pounds,
100 servings, 4 mess kit spoons
(4 ounces) each.

Ingredients	100 servings	.... servings
Beets, cooked, chopped	5 pounds	
Beans, green, cooked, diced	4 pounds	
Peas, shelled, cooked	10 pounds	
Celery, diced	4 pounds (4 No. 56 dippers)	
Onions, chopped	3 pounds (3 No. 56 dippers)	
Salt	1⅔ ounces (3 mess kit spoons)	
Lettuce	6 heads	
Mayonnaise or salad dressing	1 quart (1 No. 56 dipper)	

1. Drain cooked vegetables.
2. Combine cooked vegetables, celery, onions, and salt; mix well.
3. Chill and serve on lettuce with mayonnaise or salad dressing. (See recipes Nos. 511 to 535.)

NO. 465. BEET AND HORSERADISH RELISH

Yield: Approximately 22 pounds,
100 servings, 5 mess kit
spoons (3½ ounces) each.

Ingredients	100 servings	.... servings
Beets, drained	2 No. 10 cans	
Cabbage	14 pounds	
Horseradish	1 pound (1 No. 56 dipper)	
Salt	4 ounces (8 mess kit spoons)	
Pepper		
French or other dressing	1½ pints (¾ No. 56 dipper)	

1. Chop beets and cabbage in separate containers.
2. Combine vegetables, horseradish, salt, and pepper; mix well.
3. Add French or other dressing. (See recipes Nos. 525 to 535.)
4. Allow to stand 15 minutes before serving.

Note. 13 pounds fresh beets may be substituted for the two No. 10 cans beets.

NO. 466. CABBAGE, APPLE, AND PINEAPPLE SALAD

Yield: Approximately 25 pounds,
100 servings, 5 mess kit
spoons (4 ounces) each.

Ingredients	100 servings	.... servings
Lemon juice	5 ounces (10 mess kit spoons)	
Apples, diced	6 pounds (6 No. 56 dippers)	
Pineapple, sliced	1 No. 10 can	
Cabbage, shredded	18 pounds (18 No. 56 dippers)	
Salt	2 ounces (4 mess kit spoons)	
Lettuce	6 heads	
Mayonnaise or salad dressing	1 quart (1 No. 56 dipper)	

1. Sprinkle lemon juice over diced apples to prevent discoloration of the apples.
2. Drain pineapple; cut slices into uniform pieces.
3. Combine cabbage, apples, pineapple, and salt; mix well.
4. Serve on lettuce with mayonnaise or salad dressing. (See recipes Nos. 511 to 535.)

NO. 467. CABBAGE, APPLE, AND RAISIN SALAD

Yield: Approximately 25 pounds, 100 servings, 5 mess kit spoons (4 ounces) each.

Ingredients	100 servings	.... servings
Lemon juice	3½ ounces (7 mess kit spoons)	
Apples, diced	12 pounds (12 No. 56 dippers)	
Raisins, seedless	3 pounds (2¼ No. 56 dippers)	
Cabbage, shredded	13 pounds (13 No. 56 dippers)	
Salt	½ ounce (1 mess kit spoon)	
Lettuce	6 heads	
Salad dressing, boiled	1 quart (1 No. 56 dipper)	

1. Sprinkle lemon juice over diced apples to prevent discoloration of the apples.
2. Wash raisins.
3. Combine raisins, apples, cabbage, and salt; mix well.
4. Serve on lettuce with boiled salad dressing. (See recipe No. 507.)

NO. 468. CABBAGE AND CHIPPED BEEF SALAD

Yield: Approximately 25 pounds, 100 servings, 1 piece per serving, each 2½ by 2 by 1½ inches (4 ounces).

Ingredients	100 servings	.... servings
Gelatin, lemon flavored	2½ pounds (2½ mess kit cups)	
Water, boiling	3 quarts (3 No. 56 dippers)	
Salt	1½ ounces (3 mess kit spoons)	
Vinegar	3 quarts (3 No. 56 dippers)	
Water, cold	1½ quarts (1½ No. 56 dippers)	
Milk, evaporated	1¾—14½-ounce cans	
Water (for milk)	1½ pints (¾ No. 56 dipper)	
Mayonnaise or salad dressing	1½ quarts (1½ No. 56 dippers)	
Beef, chipped	1 pound	
Cabbage, chopped	6 pounds (6 No. 56 dippers)	
Onions, chopped	¾ pound (¾ No. 56 dipper)	
Pickles, sweet, chopped	¾ pound (¾ No. 56 dipper)	
Lettuce	6 heads	

1. Dissolve gelatin in boiling water; add salt, vinegar, and cold water. Chill until it begins to thicken.
2. Mix milk and water; add mayonnaise or salad dressing. (See recipes Nos. 511 or 507.) Mix well.
3. Combine gelatin, salad dressing mixture, beef, cabbage, onions, and pickles. Pour into shallow pans; chill until firm.
4. Cut in squares and serve on lettuce.

NO. 469. CABBAGE AND GREEN PEPPER SALAD

Yield: Approximately 20 pounds, 100 servings, 4 mess kit spoons (3 ounces) each.

Ingredients	100 servings	.... servings
Cabbage, chopped............	15 pounds (15 No. 56 dippers).......	....
Peppers, green, chopped......	5 pounds (5 No. 56 dippers)........	....
Salt......................	2½ ounces (5 mess kit spoons)..:......	....
Pepper....................	(½ mess kit spoon).................	....
French or other dressing......	1 quart (1 No. 56 dipper)...........	....
Vinegar...................	½ pint (¼ No. 56 dipper).........	....

1. Combine cabbage, green peppers, salt, and pepper.
2. Mix French or other dressing (recipes Nos. 511 to 535) and vinegar; mix well.
3. Add to cabbage and pepper mixture; mix lightly.
4. Allow to stand 5 to 10 minutes before serving.

NO. 470. CLUB SALAD

Yield: Approximately 18 pounds, 100 servings, approximately 3 ounces each.

Ingredients	100 servings	.... servings
Macaroni, cooked............	5 pounds (5 No. 56 dippers)........	....
Eggs, hard cooked, diced......	20 eggs.................:........	....
Pickles, chopped.............	2 pounds (2 No. 56 dippers)........	....
Celery, diced...............	6 pounds (6 No. 56 dippers)........	....
Pimientos, chopped...........	1 pound (½ No. 56 dipper)........	....
Peppers, green, chopped......	1 pound (1 No. 56 dipper)........	....
Parsley, chopped.............	2½ ounces (12 mess kit spoons).....	....
Onions, chopped.............	½ pound (½ No. 56 dipper).......	....
Salt......................	1¼ ounces (2½ mess kit spoons).....	....
Vinegar...................	1 pint (½ No. 56 dipper)........	....
Lettuce...................	6 heads......................	....
Mayonnaise or salad dressing..	1 quart (1 No. 56 dipper)........	....

1. Combine macaroni, eggs, pickles, chopped vegetables, salt and vinegar; mix well.
2. Chill and serve on lettuce with mayonnaise or salad dressing. (See recipes Nos. 511 or 507.)

NO. 471. CRAB SALAD

Yield: 100 servings, approximately 5 ounces or ⅞ cup each.

Ingredients	100 servings	.... servings
Crab meat	15 pounds	
Celery, chopped	4 pounds (4 No. 56 dippers)	
Cucumber, chopped	4 pounds (4 No. 56 dippers)	
Eggs, hard cooked	30 eggs	
Pickles, chopped	1 pound (¾ No. 56 dipper)	
Salt	1 ounce (2 mess kit spoons)	
Lemon juice	½ pint (¼ No. 56 dipper)	
Mayonnaise or salad dressing	4 pounds (2 No. 56 dippers)	
Lettuce		

1. Remove any shell or cartilage from crab meat.
2. Mix meat with celery, cucumber, eggs, pickles, salt, and lemon juice.
3. Add mayonnaise and mix.
4. Serve on crisp lettuce leaves, and garnish with slices of hard-cooked eggs, and pickles.

NO. 472. CUCUMBER AND ONION SALAD

Yield: Approximately 25 pounds, 100 servings, 4 mess kit spoons (4 ounces) each.

Ingredients	100 servings	.... servings
Cucumbers, sliced	20 pounds	
Onions, sliced	6 pounds (6 No. 56 dippers)	
Vinegar	2¼ quarts (2¼ No. 56 dippers)	
Water	2¼ quarts (2¼ No. 56 dippers)	
Sugar, granulated	½ pound (⅓ mess kit cup)	
Salt	2¼ ounces (4½ mess kit spoons)	
Pepper	(⅓ mess kit spoon)	

1. Mix sliced cucumbers and onions.
2. Combine vinegar, water, sugar, salt, and pepper; mix well. Pour over cucumbers and onions.
3. Serve as a relish.

NO. 473. CUCUMBER AND ONION SALAD WITH OTHER VEGETABLES

Add any one or all of the following vegetables to the above recipe: sliced radishes, tomato sections, shredded green peppers, diced celery, chopped raw cauliflower, or chopped raw carrots.

NO. 474. OLD FASHIONED COLE SLAW

Yield: 20 pounds,
100 servings, 3 mess kit
spoons (3 ounces) each.

Ingredients	100 servings	.... servings
Salad dressing, boiled.........	1 gallon (4 No. 56 dippers)..........	....
Cabbage, shredded...........	15 pounds (15 No. 56 dippers).......	....
Salt.......................	1½ ounces (3 mess kit spoons).......	....

1. Prepare salad dressing. (See recipe No. 507.)
2. Pour hot salad dressing over shredded cabbage.
3. Add salt; allow to stand until cold before serving.

NO. 475. COLE SLAW WITH BACON

Yield: Approximately 20 pounds,
100 servings, 5 mess kit
spoons (4 ounces) each.

Ingredients	100 servings	.... servings
Bacon, diced...............	3 pounds......................	....
Onions, chopped.............	3 pounds (3 No. 56 dippers).......	....
Vinegar*...................	1½ pints (¾ No. 56 dipper)........	....
Sugar, granulated...........	¾ pound (½ mess kit cup).........	....
Salt.......................	1 ounce (2 mess kit spoons)........	....
Cabbage, shredded..........	15 pounds (15 No. 56 dippers).......	....

*If vinegar is too sour, dilute with water.

1. Fry bacon until crisp. Remove from pan; drain on paper
2. Fry onions in bacon fat. Add vinegar, sugar, and salt. Heat to boiling; reduce heat and simmer 5 minutes. Cool.
3. Pour onion mixture over cabbage just before serving. Add diced bacon; mix well.

NO. 476. CRISPY GARDEN SALAD

Yield: Approximately 25 pounds,
100 servings, 1 piece per
serving, each 2½ by 2 by
1½ inches (4 ounces).

Ingredients	100 servings	.... servings
Gelatin, lemon powdered......	3¼ pounds (2½ No. 56 dippers).....	....
Water, boiling..............	3 quarts (3 No. 56 dippers).........	....
Salt.......................	3 ounces (6 mess kit spoons)........	....
Tomato catsup..............	½ pint (⅓ mess kit cup)	....
Vinegar....................	1 quart (1 No. 56 dipper)..........	....
Water, cold................	1 gallon (4 No. 56 dippers).........	....
Celery, diced...............	2 pounds (2 No. 56 dippers)........	....
Lettuce, chopped............	3 heads......................	....
Radishes, cubed.............	2 bunches....................	....
Onions, green, chopped......	1½ pounds (1½ No. 56 dippers).....	....

1. Dissolve gelatin in boiling water add salt, catsup, vinegar, and cold water. Chill until slightly thickened.
2. Add celery, lettuce, radishes, and onions. Pour into shallow pans; chill until firm.
3. Cut into squares.

NO. 477. GREEN SALAD

Yield: Approximately 20 pounds, 100 servings, 3 ounces each.

Ingredients	100 servings	.... servings
Romaine, shredded..........	4 heads................................	....
Endive, shredded...........	8 heads................................	....
Lettuce, shredded...........	8 heads................................	....
Watercress, shredded........	2 pounds...............................	....
Onions, diced...............	1 pound (1 No. 56 dipper)...........	....
Salt.......................	....	....
Pepper.....................	....	....
French or other dressing......	1 quart (1 No. 56 dipper)...........	....

1. Combine shredded greens; chill until crisp. Dry thoroughly.
2. Add onions, salt, and pepper.
3. Serve with French or other dressing. (See recipes Nos. 511 to 535.)

NO. 478. LETTUCE OR MIXED GREEN SALAD

Yield: 20 pounds,
100 servings, 4 mess kit spoons (3 ounces) each.

Ingredients	100 servings	.... servings
Lettuce or mixed greens......	20 pounds.............................	....
French or other dressing......	2 quarts (2 No. 56 dippers)...........	....

1. Chill lettuce or mixed greens until crisp; dry and cut into 1½-inch pieces.
2. Serve with French or other dressing. (See recipes Nos. 511 to 535.)

NO. 479. LETTUCE AND TOMATO SALAD

Yield: Approximately 25 pounds,
100 servings, 5 mess kit spoons (4 ounces) each.

Ingredients	100 servings	.... servings
Lettuce....................	24 heads..............................	....
Tomatoes..................	10 pounds.............................	....
French dressing............	1 quart (1 No. 56 dipper).............	....

1. Chill lettuce until crisp; cut into 1½-inch pieces.
2. Cut tomatoes into quarters or eighths depending on the size; add to lettuce.
3. Serve with French dressing. (See recipe No. 525.)

179

NO. 480. LOBSTER SALAD

Yield: 100 servings, approximately 5 ounces each.

Ingredients	100 servings	.... servings
Lobster meat	15 pounds	
Gelatin	4 ounces (16 mess kit spoons)	
Water, cold	1 quart (1 No. 56 dipper)	
Mayonnaise	6 pounds (3 No. 56 dippers)	
Celery, diced	3 pounds (3 No. 56 dippers)	
Apples, diced	3 pounds (3 No. 56 dippers)	
Lemon juice	1 pint (½ No. 56 dipper)	
Salt	1 ounce (2 mess kit spoons)	
Paprika	Dash	
Lettuce		

1. Soak gelatin in cold water for 5 minutes and dissolve over boiling water.
2. Add to mayonnaise, and whip until stiff.
3. Fold in lobster meat, celery, apples, and seasoning.
4. Place in wet pans and chill.
5. Cut into squares. Serve on lettuce with mayonnaise.

NO. 481. PICCALILLI RELISH

Yield: Approximately 25 pounds, 100 servings, 4 mess kit spoons (3 ounces) each.

Ingredients	100 servings	.... servings
Cabbage, shredded	6 pounds (6 No. 56 dippers)	
Tomatoes, diced	6 pounds	
Onions, chopped	6 pounds (6 No. 56 dippers)	
Pickles, sweet, chopped	6 pounds (6 No. 56 dippers)	
Vinegar	1¼ pints (¾ No. 56 dipper)	
Cloves, ground	(⅓ mess kit spoon)	
Salt	2 ounces (4 mess kit spoons)	
Pepper	(⅔ mess kit spoon)	
Water		

1. Combine all ingredients; barely cover with water.
2. Allow to stand 1 hour; drain well.

NO. 482. POTATO SALAD NO. I

Yield: 38 pounds, 100 servings, 5 mess kit spoons (6 ounces) each.

Ingredients	100 servings	.... servings
Potatoes, cooked, sliced*	25 pounds	
Salt	6 ounces (¼ No. 56 dipper)	
Pepper	¼ ounce (1 mess kit spoon)	
Oil, salad	¾ pint (½ mess kit cup)	
Vinegar	½ pint (⅓ mess kit cup)	
Celery, diced	10 pounds (10 No. 56 dippers)	
Onions, chopped	¾ pound (¾ No. 56 dipper)	
Eggs, hard-cooked, chopped	36 eggs	
Mayonnaise or salad dressing	1 quart (1 No. 56 dipper)	
Lettuce	6 heads	

*Cook potatoes in skins; peel and slice while warm.

1. Spread layer of potatoes in bottom of shallow baking pans.
2. Mix salt, pepper, vinegar, and salad oil together; sprinkle a small amount over potatoes in baking pans. Continue filling pans with alternate layers of potatoes and oil mixture. Allow to stand 1 hour.
3. Combine celery, onions, eggs, and mayonnaise or salad dressing. (See recipes Nos. 511 to 535.) Add to potatoes; mix well.
4. Serve on lettuce.

NO. 483. POTATO SALAD NO. II   Yield: 34 pounds,
100 servings, 5 mess kit spoons (6 ounces) each.

Ingredients	100 servings	.... servings
Potatoes, cooked, diced*	25 pounds (14 No. 56 dippers)	
Onions, chopped	2 pounds (2 No. 56 dippers)	
Celery, chopped	5 pounds (5 No. 56 dippers)	
Bacon, diced	2 pounds	
Peppers, green, chopped	4¾ pounds	
Vinegar	½ pint (⅓ mess kit cup)	
Mayonnaise or salad dressing	1 quart (1 No. 56 dipper)	
Salt	8 ounces (⅓ mess kit cup)	
Pepper	¼ ounce (1 mess kit spoon)	
Lettuce	6 heads	

*Cook potatoes in skins; peel and dice while warm.

1. Mix potatoes, onions, and celery together.
2. Fry bacon; add hot bacon and bacon fat to potato mixture. Mix well.
3. Combine peppers, vinegar, mayonnaise, or salad dressing (recipes Nos. 511 to 535), salt and pepper; mix well.
4. Add to potato mixture; allow to stand until cold.
5. Serve on lettuce.

NO. 484. HOT POTATO SALAD   Yield: Approximately 32 pounds,
100 servings, 5 mess kit spoons (5 ounces) each.

Ingredients	100 servings	.... servings
Potatoes, cooked in skins	32 pounds	
Onions, chopped	1 pound (1 No. 56 dipper)	
Bacon, diced	3 pounds	
Water	1½ pints (¾ No. 56 dipper)	
Vinegar	1½ quarts (1½ No. 56 dippers)	
Salt	4 ounces (8 mess kit spoons)	

1. Peel cooked potatoes; cut crosswise into thin slices. Add chopped onions.
2. Fry bacon until crisp; remove from fat. Add bacon to potatoes; mix well.
3. Combine bacon fat, water, vinegar, and salt. Heat to boiling point; pour over potato mixture; mix well.
4. Place salad in oven and allow to remain 15 minutes before serving.

Note. One pound chopped green peppers and 4 pounds diced celery may be added to potatoes and onions in recipe above.

NO. 485. JELLIED TOMATO SALAD

Yield: 25 pounds,
100 servings, 1 piece per
serving, each 2½ by
2 by 1½ inches (4 ounces).

Ingredients	100 servings	.... servings
Water, cold...............	2 quarts (2 No. 56 dippers).........	....
Gelatin, plain..............	6 ounces......................	....
Tomatoes.................	4 No. 10 cans....	....
Onions, chopped...........	4 ounces (⅓ mess kit cup)..........	....
Salt......................	3 ounces (6 mess kit spoons)........	....
Sugar, granulated..........	½ pound (⅓ mess kit cup).........	....
Lettuce....................	6 heads......................	....

1. Pour cold water over gelatin; allow to stand 5 minutes.

2. Drain tomatoes; heat juice to boiling point.

3. Add hot tomato juice to gelatin; stir until dissolved.

4. Add onions, salt, and sugar; pour into shallow pans. Cool.

5. Add tomatoes and stir until thoroughly mixed. Chill until firm.

6. Cut into squares. Serve on lettuce.

NO. 486. TOMATO ASPIC

Yield: 25 pounds,
100 servings, 1 piece per
serving, each 2½ by 2 by
1½ inches (5 ounces).

Ingredients	100 servings	.... servings
Tomato juice...............	4 No. 10 cans...................	....
Salt......................	2 ounces (4 mess kit spoons)........	....
Sugar, granulated..........	12 ounces (½ mess kit cup).........	....
Pepper, cayenne...........		
Onions, chopped...........	5 ounces (½ mess kit cup)..........	....
Parsley, chopped..........	¼ bunch.....................	....
Water, cold...............	1⅓ quarts (1⅓ No. 56 dippers)......	....
Gelatin, plain..............	6 ounces......................	....
Lettuce....................	6 heads......................	....

1. Combine tomato juice, salt, sugar, pepper, onions, and parsley; mix well.

2. Heat to boiling point; reduce heat and simmer 20 minutes. Strain through a very fine strainer.

3. Pour cold water over gelatin; allow to stand 5 minutes.

4. Pour hot tomato juice over gelatin; stir until dissolved.

5. Pour into shallow pans. Chill until firm.

6. Cut into squares. Serve on lettuce.

NO. 487. CHOPPED RAW VEGETABLE SLAW

Yield: 22 pounds,
100 servings, 5 mess kit
spoons (3½ ounces) each.

Ingredients	100 servings	.... servings
Cabbage, shredded..........	9 pounds (9 No. 56 dippers)........	....
Carrots, chopped............	9 pounds (7½ No. 56 dippers)......	....
Radishes, chopped..........	12 bunches....................	....
Cucumbers, chopped........	3 pounds (1½ No. 56 dippers)......	....
Salt......................	1½ ounces (3 mess kit spoons)......	....
Pepper....................	¼ ounce (1 mess kit spoon).........	....
French or other dressing.....	1 quart (1 No. 56 dipper).........	....

1. Combine cabbage, carrots, radishes, cucumbers, salt, and pepper; mix well.
2. Serve with French or other dressing. (See recipes Nos. 525 to 535.)

NO. 488. COOKED VEGETABLE SALAD

Yield: 25 pounds,
100 servings, 3 mess kit
spoons (4 ounces) each.

Ingredients	100 servings	.... servings
Peas, cooked...............	15 pounds....................	....
Carrots, cooked.............	6½ pounds...................	....
Cauliflower, cooked..........	6½ pounds...................	....
Beans, string, cooked........	7 pounds.....................	....
Salt......................	½ ounce (1 mess kit spoon)......	....
Lettuce...................	6 heads......................	....
French or other dressing.....	1 quart (1 No. 56 dipper).........	....

1. Drain cooked vegetables; chill. Add salt.
2. Serve on lettuce with French or other dressing. (See recipes Nos. 525 to 535.).

NO. 489. JELLIED VEGETABLE AND EGG SALAD

Yield: Approximately 25 pounds,
100 servings, 1 piece
per serving, each 2½ by
2 by 1½ inches (4 ounces).

Ingredients	100 servings	.... servings
Beef stock, cold..............	1 gallon (4 No. 56 dippers).........	....
Gelatin, plain...............	1½ pounds (1½ mess kit cups)......	....
Beef stock, boiling...........	3 quarts (3 No. 56 dippers)........	....
Beans, string, cooked, diced...	8 pounds (7 No. 56 dippers)........	....
Celery, diced...............	4 pounds (4 No. 56 dippers)........	....
Carrots, diced..............	4 pounds (3⅓ No. 56 dippers)......	....
Eggs, hard-cooked, diced......	48 eggs......................	....
Lettuce...................	6 heads......................	....
Mayonnaise or salad dressing..	1 quart (1 No. 56 dipper)..........	....

1. Pour cold beef stock over gelatin; allow to stand 5 minutes.
2. Add boiling beef stock to gelatin; stir until dissolved. Chill until slightly thickened.
3. Add beans, celery, and carrots.
4. Add eggs last. Pour into shallow pans; chill until firm.
5. Cut into squares.
6. Serve on lettuce with mayonnaise or salad dressing. (See recipes Nos. 511 to 535.)

NO. 490. FRUIT SALAD

Yield: 25 pounds,
100 servings, 5 mess kit spoons (4 ounces) each.

Ingredients	100 servings	.... servings
Oranges......................	30 oranges........................	....
Apples, diced...............	5 pounds (5 No. 56 dippers).........	....
Pineapple, sliced, drained, diced	2½ No. 10 cans.....................	....
Lettuce.......................	6 heads...........................	....
French or other dressing......	1 quart (1 No. 56 dipper)...........	....

1. Pare oranges; cut into sections. Remove seeds and inside tough portions; dice.
2. Combine oranges, apples, and pineapple immediately after dicing to prevent discoloration of the apples. Chill.
3. Serve on lettuce with French or other dressing. (See recipes Nos. 525 to 535.)

NO. 491. FRUIT AND GARDEN GREEN SALAD

Yield: Approximately 25 pounds, 100 servings, 5 mess kit spoons (4 ounces) each.

Ingredients	100 servings	.... servings
Oranges......................	30 oranges........................	....
Grapefruit...................	12 grapefruit.....................	....
Pineapple, sliced, drained.....	3 No. 10 cans.....................	....
Apples, diced.................	3 pounds (3 No. 56 dippers)........	....
Spinach, fresh, chopped.......	4 pounds..........................	....
Lettuce......................	6 heads	....
French or other dressing......	1 quart (1 No. 56 dipper)..........	....

1. Pare oranges and grapefruit; cut into sections. Remove seeds and inside tough portions; dice.
2. Combine all fruit immediately after dicing to prevent discoloration of the apples.
3. Add chopped spinach.
4. Serve on lettuce with French or other dressing. (See recipes Nos. 525 to 535.)

NO. 492. GRAPEFRUIT, APPLE, AND BANANA SALAD

Yield: Approximately 25 pounds,
100 servings, 5 mess kit
spoons (4¼ ounces) each.

Ingredients	100 servings	.... servings
Grapefruit	16 grapefruit	
Apples, diced	11 pounds (11 No. 56 dippers)	
Bananas, sliced	4 pounds	
Lettuce	6 heads	
French or other dressing	1 quart (1 No. 56 dipper)	

1. Pare grapefruit; cut into sections. Remove seeds and inside tough portions; cut into uniform pieces.
2. Mix grapefruit and apples immediately after dicing to prevent discoloration of the apples.
3. Just before serving, peel and slice bananas; add to grapefruit and apples. Mix well.
4. Serve on lettuce with French or other dressing. (See recipes Nos. 525 to 535.)

NO. 493. ORANGE, APPLE, AND CELERY SALAD

Yield: Approximately 25 pounds,
100 servings, 5 mess kit
spoons (3½ ounces) each.

Ingredients	100 servings	.... servings
Oranges	20 oranges	
Apples, diced	13 pounds (13 No. 56 dippers)	
Celery, diced	4 pounds (4 No. 56 dippers)	
Lettuce	6 heads	
Mayonnaise or salad dressing	¾ quart (¾ No. 56 dipper)	

1. Pare oranges; cut into sections. Remove seeds and inside tough portions. Dice.
2. Combine oranges and apples immediately after dicing to prevent discoloration of the apples.
3. Add celery just before serving.
4. Serve on lettuce with mayonnaise or salad dressing. (See recipes Nos. 511 to 535.)

NO. 494. ORANGE PERFECTION SALAD

Yield: Approximately 25 pounds,
100 servings, 1 piece per
serving, each 2½ by 2 by
1½ inches (4 ounces).

Ingredients	100 servings	.... servings
Gelatin, orange flavored	3¼ pounds (2½ No. 56 dippers)	
Water, boiling	1 gallon (4 No. 56 dippers)	
Salt	2 ounces (4 mess kit spoons)	
Lemon juice	½ pint (⅓ mess kit cup)	
Water, cold	1 gallon (4 No. 56 dippers)	
Cabbage, shredded	4 pounds (4 No. 56 dippers)	
Celery, diced	2 pounds (2 No. 56 dippers)	
Carrots, finely chopped	1½ pounds (1¼ No. 56 dippers)	
Onions, finely chopped	½ pound (½ No. 56 dipper)	

1. Dissolve gelatin in boiling water. Add salt, lemon juice, and cold water; chill until slightly thickened.
2. Add cabbage, celery, carrots, and onions; mix well. Pour into shallow pans; chill until firm.
3. Cut into squares.

NO. 495. PINEAPPLE AND CHEESE SALAD

Yield: Approximately 25 pounds, 100 servings, 4 mess kit spoons (4 ounces) each.

Ingredients	100 servings	.... servings
Pineapple, sliced............	2 No. 10 cans.......................	....
Lettuce....................	10 pounds........................	....
Cheese, American, diced......	1 pound (1 No. 56 dipper)...........	....
Coconut, shredded (optional)..	1 pound (1½ No. 56 dippers)........	....
Mayonnaise or salad dressing..	1 quart (1 No. 56 dipper)...........	....

1. Drain pineapple; cut into uniform pieces.
2. Chill lettuce until crisp; cut into ½-inch pieces just before serving.
3. Combine pineapple, lettuce, and cheese; mix well. Sprinkle coconut over the top.
4. Serve with mayonnaise or salad dressing. (See recipes Nos. 511 to 535.)

Note. If soaked in milk 1 hour before using, shredded coconut will look and taste like fresh coconut. Drain carefully before using.

NO. 496. JELLIED SPICED RED CHERRIES

Yield: Approximately 25 pounds, 100 servings, 1 piece per serving, each 2½ by 2 by 1½ inches (4 ounces).

Ingredients	100 servings	.... servings
Cherries, red, sour...........	3 No. 10 cans......................	....
Sugar, brown................	2 pounds (2 mess kit cups).........	....
Cinnamon, stick.............	½ ounce..........................	....
Nutmeg, ground.............	(½ mess kit spoon)................	....
Cloves, whole...............	(⅓ mess kit spoon)................	....
Gelatin, cherry flavored.......	2½ pounds (2½ mess kit cups)......	....
Water, boiling..............	3 quarts (3 No. 56 dippers)........	....
Salt......................	1 ounce (2 mess kit spoons)........	....

1. Combine cherries, cherry juice, sugar, cinnamon, nutmeg, and cloves. Heat to boiling; reduce heat and simmer 20 minutes. Remove cinnamon and cloves.
2. Dissolve gelatin in boiling water; add salt and spiced cherry mixture.
3. Pour into shallow pans; chill until firm.
4. Cut into squares.

NO. 497. WALDORF SALAD   Yield: Approximately 25 pounds, 100 servings, 5 mess kit spoons (4 ounces) each.

Ingredients	100 servings	.... servings
Lemon juice	½ pint (⅓ mess kit cup)	
Apples, diced	14 pounds (14 No. 56 dippers)	
Celery, diced	12 pounds (12 No. 56 dippers)	
Salt	1 ounce (2 mess kit spoons)	
Lettuce	6 heads	
Mayonnaise or salad dressing	1 quart (1 No. 56 dipper)	

1. Sprinkle lemon juice over diced apples to prevent discoloration.
2. Combine apples, celery, and salt.
3. Serve on lettuce with mayonnaise or salad dressing. (See recipes Nos. 511 to 535.)

NO. 498. MACARONI SALAD   Yield: Approximately 18 pounds, 100 servings, 4 mess kit spoons (5 ounces) each.

Ingredients	100 servings	.... servings
Macaroni, cooked	5 pounds (5 No. 56 dippers)	
Celery, diced	10 pounds (10 No. 56 dippers)	
Pimientos, chopped	½—15-ounce can	
Onions, chopped	½ pound (½ No. 56 dipper)	
Parsley, chopped	½ bunch	
Salt	2 ounces (4 mess kit spoons)	
Eggs, hard-cooked, chopped	30 eggs	
Lettuce	6 heads	
Mayonnaise or salad dressing	1 quart (1 No. 56 dipper)	

1. Combine macaroni, celery, pimientos, onions, and parsley.
2. Add salt and eggs just before serving.
3. Serve on lettuce with mayonnaise or salad dressing. (See recipes Nos. 511 to 535.)

NO. 499. CHICKEN OR TURKEY SALAD   Yield: 100 servings, 5 ounces (⅔ cup) each.

Ingredients	100 servings	.... servings
Chicken or turkey, cooked, cubed.	10 pounds (10 No. 56 dippers)	
Onions, finely chopped	2 pounds (2 No. 56 dippers)	
Pineapple cubes, well drained	2 No. 10 cans	
Lemon juice		
Salt		
Pepper		
Celery, diced	12 pounds (2 No. 56 dippers)	
Lettuce	6 heads	
Mayonnaise	1 quart (1 No. 56 dipper)	

1. Mix chicken or turkey with onions and pineapple cubes.
2. Add lemon juice, salt, and pepper; mix well.

3. Chill; drain thoroughly. Add celery just before serving.
4. Serve on lettuce with mayonnaise.

Note. Garnish with pickles, tomato wedges, or hard-cooked eggs if desired.

NO. 500. MEAT SALAD (beef, lamb, pork, veal or ham)

Yield: 100 servings, 8
ounces each.

Ingredients	100 servings	.... servings
Apples.....................	6 pounds (3 No. 56 dippers).........	....
Meat, cooked, cubed..........	23 pounds (16 No. 56 dippers).......	....
Celery, cubed...............	6 pounds (6 No. 56 dippers).........	....
Carrots, shredded............	3 pounds..........................	....
Peppers, green, diced........	1 pound (1 No. 56 dipper)..........	....
Peas.......................	1 No. 10 can......................	....
Salt.......................	2 ounces (4 mess kit spoons)........	....
Mayonnaise.................	3 quarts (3 No. 56 dippers).........	....

1. Combine apples, meat, and vegetables.
2. Add salt and mayonnaise (recipe No. 511); mix lightly.

NO. 501. SALMON AND CELERY SALAD

Yield: 25 pounds,
100 servings, 4 mess kit
spoons (4 ounces) each.

Ingredients	100 servings	.... servings
Salmon, flaked...............	15—1-pound cans...................	....
Celery, diced...............	12 pounds (12 No. 56 dippers).......	....
Pickles, sweet, chopped.......	½ pound..........................	....
Eggs, hard-cooked, chopped...	24 eggs...........................	....
Salt......................	2 ounces (4 mess kit spoons)........	....
Lettuce....................	6 heads..........................	....
Mayonnaise or salad dressing..	1 quart (1 No. 56 dipper)..........	....

1. Remove skin from salmon. Combine salmon, celery, pickles, eggs, and salt; mix well.
2. Serve on lettuce with mayonnaise or salad dressing. (See recipes Nos. 511 to 535.)

Note. Other fish such as tuna, crab, halibut, cod, or any firm white fish may be substituted for salmon.

NO. 502. SALMON OR TUNA FISH SALAD   Yield: 100 servings,

4 ounces each.

Ingredients	100 servings	.... servings
Water, cold.................	1½ quarts (1½ No. 56 dippers)......	....
Gelatin, plain...............	6 ounces.........................	....
Water, boiling...............		
Salmon or tuna fish, flaked....	5—1-pound cans...................	....
Celery, finely chopped.......	3 pounds (3 No. 56 dippers)........	....
Peppers, green, chopped.....	¼ pound (¼ No. 56 dipper)........	....
Pimientos, chopped..........	¼ pound..........................	....
Lemon juice................	¾ pint (½ mess kit cup)..........	....
Salt......................	½ ounce (1 mess kit spoon)........	....
Lettuce....................	6 heads..........................	....
Mayonnaise or salad dressing..	1 quart (1 No. 56 dipper)..........	....

1. Pour cold water over gelatin; allow to stand 5 minutes.
2. Pour boiling water over gelatin; stir until dissolved.
3. Remove skin from salmon. Add salmon or tuna fish, celery, peppers, pimientos, lemon juice, salt, and mayonnaise or salad dressing (recipes Nos. 511 to 535); mix well.
4. Pour into pans; chill until firm.
5. Cut into squares. Serve on lettuce.

NO. 503. SHRIMP AND CELERY SALAD

Yield: 32 pounds,
100 servings, 5 mess kit
spoons (5 ounces) each.

Ingredients	100 servings	.... servings
Shrimps....................	40 pounds......................	....
Salt.......................	....	....
Water, boiling..............	....	....
Lemon juice................	5½ ounces (11 mess kit spoons)......	....
Celery, diced..............	14 pounds (14 No. 56 dippers)......	....
Salt......................	3 ounces (6 mess kit spoons)........	....
Pepper....................	....	....
Lettuce...................	6 heads......................	....
Mayonnaise or salad dressing..	2 quarts (2 No. 56 dippers)........	....

1. Cover shrimps with boiling salted water. Heat to boiling point; boil 15 to 20 minutes until shrimps turn pink. Drain.
2. Cover with cold water; drain. Remove shells and black intestinal vein running along the back.
3. Cut shrimps into uniform pieces; add lemon juice.
4. Combine shrimps, celery, salt, and pepper; mix well.
5. Serve on lettuce with mayonnaise or salad dressing. (See recipes Nos. 511 to 535.)

NO. 504. SHRIMP AND MACARONI OR SPAGHETTI SALAD

Substitute 6 pounds macaroni or spaghetti for celery in recipe for shrimp and celery salad.

NO. 505. SPRING TUNA FISH SALAD

Yield: 25 pounds,
100 servings, 4 mess kit
spoons (4 ounces) each.

Ingredients	100 servings	.... servings
Spinach, tender leaves........	3 pounds......................	....
Onions, green, chopped......	¾ pound (¾ No. 56 dipper)........	....
Pickles, sweet, chopped.......	1¼ pounds....................	....
Salt......................	1½ ounces (3 mess kit spoons)......	....
Tuna fish, flaked............	27—13-ounce cans..............	....
French or other dressing......	1 quart (1 No. 56 dipper)..........	....
Lettuce...................	6 heads......................	....

1. Chill spinach until crisp; shred.
2. Combine spinach, onions, pickles, salt, and tuna fish: mix well.
3. Serve on lettuce with French or other salad dressing. (See recipes Nos. 525 to 535.)

NO. 506. TUNA FISH AND CELERY SALAD

Yield: 25 pounds,
100 servings, 4 mess kit
spoons (4 ounces) each.

Ingredients	100 servings	.... servings
Tuna fish, flaked.............	20—13-ounce cans......................	....
Pimientos...................	3—15-ounce cans......................	....
Pickles, sweet, chopped......	2½ pounds (2½ No. 56 dippers).....	....
Celery, diced................	8 pounds (8 No. 56 dippers).........	....
Salt........................	3 ounces (6 mess kit spoons)........	....
Lettuce.....................	6 heads.............................	....
Mayonnaise or salad dressing..	1 quart (1 No. 56 dipper)............	....

1. Combine fish, pimientos, pickles, celery, and salt; mix well.
2. Serve on lettuce with mayonnaise or salad dressing. (See recipes Nos. 511 to 535.)

NO. 507. COOKED SALAD DRESSING   Yield: 2 quarts.

Ingredients	100 servings	.... servings
Flour, sifted................	2 ounces (8 mess kit spoons)........	....
Sugar, granulated........	6 ounces (¼ mess kit cup)..........	....
Salt.......................	¾ ounce (1½ mess kit spoons).......	....
Mustard, dry................	½ ounce (2 mess kit spoons)........	....
Milk, evaporated............	2—14½-ounce cans.................	....
Water (for milk).............	1¼ pints (⅞ mess kit cup)	....
Vinegar....................	1 pint (½ No. 56 dipper)............	....
Eggs, beaten................	8 eggs (½ mess kit cup)............	....
Butter.....................	4 ounces (8 mess kit spoons)........	....

1. Sift flour, sugar, salt, and mustard together.
2. Mix milk and water. Add slowly to dry ingredients; stir until smooth. Add vinegar slowly; mix well.
3. Heat to boiling point; boil 2 minutes or until thick, stirring constantly.
4. Add 1½ pints (1 mess kit cup) mixture slowly to beaten eggs; stir until smooth.
5. Add to remaining cooked mixture. Mix well; reheat but avoid overcooking eggs. Add butter; mix well. Cool.

NO. 508. COLE SLAW DRESSING

Add ½ pint (⅓ mess kit cup) prepared mustard to cooled dressing in recipe for cooked salad dressing.

NO. 509. PEANUT BUTTER DRESSING

Add 1 pint (⅔ mess kit cup) peanut butter to the cooled dressing in recipe for boiled salad dressing.

NO. 510. SAVORY DRESSING

Add 1 pint (⅔ mess kit cup) pickle relish or chopped sweet pickles to the cooled dressing in recipe for cooked salad dressing.

NO. 511. MAYONNAISE   Yield: 2 quarts.

Ingredients	100 servings	.... servings
Salt	¾ ounce (1½ mess kit spoons)	
Mustard, dry	¼ ounce (1 mess kit spoon)	
Eggs	5 eggs (¼ No. 56 dipper)	
Oil, salad	3½ pints (1¾ No. 56 dippers)	
Vinegar	4 ounces (8 mess kit spoons)	
Water, hot	1 ounce (2 mess kit spoons)	

1. Sift salt and mustard together.
2. Add eggs and beat until well mixed.
3. Add remaining liquid gradually, alternating vinegar and oil. Add hot water last; mix well.

NO. 512. CREAM DRESSING

Add 1¼ pints (⅞ mess kit cup) heavy whipped cream to recipe for mayonnaise.

NO. 513. HAM DRESSING

Add 1 pint (⅔ mess kit cup) tomato juice and ½ pint (⅓ mess kit cup) chopped Virginia ham to recipe for mayonnaise.

NO. 514. MARMALADE DRESSING

Add 10 mess kit spoons orange marmalade to recipe for mayonnaise.

NO. 515. MUSTARD CREAM DRESSING

Add 1 pint (⅔ mess kit cup) prepared mustard and 1 quart (1 No. 56 dipper) heavy whipped cream to recipe for mayonnaise.

NO. 516. PICKLE MAYONNAISE

Add 4 mess kit spoons catsup, 4 mess kit spoons minced parsley, 10 mess kit spoons minced sweet pickles, 10 mess kit spoons minced cucumbers and 10 mess kit spoons minced beets to recipe for mayonnaise.

NO. 517. THOUSAND ISLAND DRESSING

Add 1 quart (1 No. 56 dipper) chili sauce, 2 pounds (2 No. 56 dippers) chopped green peppers, 4 mess kit spoons chopped parsley, 4 ounces (⅓ mess kit cup) chopped onions, ⅓ mess kit spoon Worcestershire sauce and two hard-cooked eggs to recipe for mayonnaise.

NO. 518. RUSSIAN DRESSING

Add 1 quart (1 No. 56 dipper) chili sauce, 2 pounds (2 No. 56 dippers) chopped green peppers, 12 mess kit spoons chopped beets or pimientos and ⅓ mess kit spoon Worcestershire sauce to recipe for mayonnaise.

NO. 519. LAMAZE SAUCE

Yield: 100 servings, approximately 2 ounces each.

Ingredients	100 servings	.... servings
Mayonnaise or salad dressing..	8 pounds (4 No. 56 dippers).........	....
Catsup.....................	1 quart (1 No. 56 dipper)............	....
Pickle relish................	1¼ pounds (¾ No. 56 dipper).......	....
Eggs, chopped (optional)......	1½ pounds........................	....

1. Combine mayonnaise, catsup, pickles, and eggs, and mix well. Chill.
2. Serve with fish or shellfish.

NO. 520. CUCUMBER DRESSING

Yield: 100 servings, approximately 1 ounce each.

Ingredients	100 servings	.... servings
Cucumbers, diced............	3 pounds (2¼ No. 56 dippers)......	....
Mayonnaise or salad dressing..	5 pounds (2½ No. 56 dippers)......	....
Salt......................	¾ ounce (1½ mess kit spoons)......	....
Pepper....................	⅛ ounce (½ mess kit spoon)........	....
Paprika...................	¼ ounce (1 mess kit spoon).........	....
Lemon juice...............	3½ ounces (7 mess kit spoons)......	....

1. Peel, finely dice, and drain cucumbers.
2. Combine with other ingredients, and mix well.
3. Chill and serve.

NO. 521. SHELLFISH COCKTAIL SAUCE

Yield: 100 servings, approximately 1 ounce each.

Ingredients	100 servings	.... servings
Catsup....................	2 quarts (2 No. 56 dippers).........	....
Vinegar or lemon juice........	1 pint (½ No. 56 dipper)............	....
Celery, finely chopped.......	1 pound (1 No. 56 dipper)...........	....
Horseradish, grated..........	½ pint (¼ No. 56 dipper)..........	....
Salt......................	1 ounce (2 mess kit spoons).........	....
Tabasco sauce..............	(1 mess kit spoon)................	....

1. Make sauce by mixing all the ingredients together.
2. Serve with shellfish cocktails.

NO. 522. SPECIAL MAYONNAISE

Yield: 2 quarts.

Ingredients	100 servings	.... servings
Mayonnaise	1½ quarts (1½ No. 56 dippers)	
Milk, evaporated	1—14½-ounce can	
Onion juice	1 ounce (2 mess kit spoons)	
Salt	½ ounce (1 mess kit spoon)	
Pepper, cayenne		

Combine mayonnaise (recipt No. 511) and remaining ingredients; mix well.

NO. 523. HORSERADISH MAYONNAISE

Add ¾ ounce (2½ mess kit spoons) paprika and ½ pint (⅓ mess kit cup) grated horseradish to ½ of recipe for special mayonnaise.

NO. 524. PINEAPPLE MAYONNAISE

Add ½ pint (⅓ mess kit cup) pineapple juice to ½ recipe for special mayonnaise.

NO. 525. FRENCH DRESSING NO. I

Yield: 2 quarts.

Ingredients	100 servings	.... servings
Oil, salad	¾ quart (¾ No. 56 dipper)	
Vinegar	1 pint (½ No. 56 dipper)	
Salt	3 ounces (6 mess kit spoons)	
Sugar, granulated	1 ounce (2 mess kit spoons)	
Onion juice (optional)	1½ ounces (3 mess kit spoons)	

Mix all ingredients together. Shake before using.

NO. 526. CATSUP DRESSING

Add ½ pint (⅓ mess kit cup) catsup to recipe for French dressing.

NO. 527. CHEESE AND EGG DRESSING

Add 7 mess kit spoons chopped parsley, 7 mess kit spoons chopped pimiento, 1 pint (⅔ mess kit cup) chopped American cheddar cheese, and 8 hard-cooked eggs to recipe for French dressing.

NO. 528. HORSERADISH DRESSING

Add 7 mess kit spoons prepared horseradish to recipe for French dressing.

NO. 529. MUSTARD FRENCH DRESSING

Add ¾ ounce (2½ mess kit spoons) dry mustard and ¼ teaspoon cayenne pepper to recipe for French dressing.

NO. 530. MIXED PICKLE DRESSING

Add ½ pint (⅓ mess kit cup) chopped pickles to recipe for French dressing.

NO. 531. ROQUEFORT DRESSING

Add ½ pint (⅓ mess kit cup) crumbled Roquefort cheese to recipe for French dressing.

NO. 532. VINAIGRETTE DRESSING

Add 7 mess kit spoons chopped green peppers, 7 mess kit spoons chopped pickles and 7 mess kit spoons chopped parsley to recipe for French dressing.

NO. 533. FRENCH DRESSING NO. II (Thick)   Yield: 2 quarts.

Ingredients	100 servings	.... servings
Salt....................	1¾ ounces (3½ mess kit spoons).....	....
Pepper, black..............		
Sugar, granulated...........	1 ounce (2 mess kit spoons).........	
Mustard, dry...............	¾ ounce (3 mess kit spoons)........	
Pepper, cayenne............		
Mayonnaise................	½ pint (⅓ mess kit cup).........	
Vinegar...................	1 pint (½ No. 56 dipper).........	
Oil, salad.................	1⅓ quarts (1⅓ No. 56 dippers).....	
Water....................	¼ pint (4 mess kit spoons).......	

1. Sift salt, black pepper, sugar, mustard, and cayenne pepper together.
2. Add mayonnaise; mix well.
3. Add oil and vinegar alternately to mixture. Add water last; mix well.

NO. 534. SPECIAL GREEN SALAD DRESSING   Yield: 1¾ quarts.

Ingredients	100 servings	.... servings
Salt....................	1 ounce (2 mess kit spoons).........	....
Pepper...................		
Mustard, prepared..........		
Catsup...................	½ pint (⅓ mess kit cup).........	
Worcestershire sauce........		
Oil, salad.................	¾ pint (½ mess kit cup).........	
Vinegar..................	½ pint (⅓ mess kit cup).........	
Peppers, green, chopped......	4 ounces (⅓ mess kit cup).........	
Parsley, chopped...........		
Eggs, hard-cooked, chopped...	2 eggs........................	

1. Combine salt, pepper, mustard, catsup, and Worcestershire sauce; mix well.
2. Add a small amount of oil, beating continually with a wire whisk.
3. Add remaining oil and vinegar alternately in small quantities.
4. Add remaining ingredients; mix well.

Note. Serve on green salads.

NO. 535. SOUR MILK DRESSING
Yield: 1½ quarts.

Ingredients	100 servings	.... servings
Vinegar	1 pint (½ No. 56 dipper)	
Milk, evaporated	2—14½-ounce cans	
Sugar, granulated	4 ounces (8 mess kit spoons)	
Salt	⅛ ounce (⅔ mess kit spoon)	

1. Mix vinegar and evaporated milk. Add sugar and salt, stirring rapidly with a wire whip; stir until well mixed.

2. Chill.

Note. Pepper, paprika, and mustard may be added to sour milk dressing. Serve cold on green salads.

SECTION XVI

SANDWICHES

26. PREPARATION OF SANDWICHES. a. Suggestions for making sandwiches. (1) Allow butter to stand in a warm place until soft.

(2) Cut bread into slices ⅜ inches or less in thickness.

(3) Spread butter evenly over all of one side of a slice of bread. If a moist sandwich filling is used, spread both slices of bread with butter to prevent the bread from becoming soggy.

(4) Make sandwich fillings moist but not wet enough to drip when they are eaten; add seasonings carefully.

(5) Cover entire slice of bread with filling. Lettuce leaves or tender cabbage leaves may be added if sandwiches are to be served immediately.

(6) Color contrasts may be obtained by placing the filling between a slice of white and a slice of dark bread. Vary the kind of bread by using nut, raisin, whole wheat, rye, or white bread.

(7) Wrap sandwiches in wax paper immediately after making. (Commercial bread wrappers may be used.)

(8) Make sandwiches as short a time in advance as possible. If made in advance, store in refrigerator after wrapping.

(9) Avoid the use of ground meat and egg fillings in hot weather.

b. Proportions of ingredients for sandwich fillings. (1) Meat, cheese and egg fillings

Ingredients	Quantity
Bacon and baked beans:	
Bacon, cooked, chopped } Beans, baked }	5 pounds ....(8 No. 56 dippers)
Bacon and peanut butter:	
Bacon, cooked, chopped } Peanut butter }	5 pounds ....(8 No. 56 dippers)
Sliced roast beef:	
Beef, roast, sliced	....
Bologna and cheese:	
Bologna	6 pounds
Cheese, sliced	6 pounds
Cheese and mustard:	
Cheese, sliced	12 pounds
Mustard, prepared	....
Cheese and peanut butter:	
Cheese, chopped	3 pounds ....(3 No. 56 dippers)
Peanut butter	1½ gallons ....(6 No. 56 dippers)
Mustard, dry	....
Cheese and bacon:	
Cheese, chopped	6 pounds ....(6 No. 56 dippers)
Bacon, cooked, chopped	3 pounds

Ingredients	Quantity
Cottage cheese and carrot:	
Cheese, cottage	3 pounds (3 No. 56 dippers)
Carrots, chopped	3¾ pounds (3 No. 56 dippers)
Pickles, sweet, chopped	1 quart (1 No. 56 dipper)
or	
Raisins, chopped	1¼ pounds (1 No. 56 dipper)
Cottage cheese and pineapple:	
Cheese, cottage	3 pounds (3 No. 56 dippers)
Pineapple, crushed	1 No. 10 can
Chopped meat:	
Meat, cooked, ground	10 pounds (8 No. 56 dippers)
Mayonnaise	1 quart (1 No. 56 dipper)
Pickle relish	.....
Eggs, hard-cooked, chopped	28 eggs
Salt	4 ounces (8 mess kit spoons)
Deviled ham:	
Ham, cooked, ground	8 pounds
Milk, evaporated	3—14½-ounce cans
Pickle relish, sweet, well-drained	1½ pints (¾ No. 56 dipper)
Mustard, dry	1 ounce (4 mess kit spoons)
Mayonnaise	1⅓ quarts (1⅓ No. 56 dippers)
Deviled meat:	
Meat, cooked, ground	12 pounds (9¾ No. 56 dippers)
Catsup or chili sauce	1 quart (1 No. 56 dipper)
Pepper, cayenne	¼ ounce (1 mess kit spoon)
Worcestershire sauce	.....
Paprika	¾ ounce (3 mess kit spoons)
Onion juice	.....
Salt	3 ounces (6 mess kit spoons)
Mayonnaise	1½ quarts (1½ No. 56 dippers)
Dried beef and cheese:	
Cheese, chopped	5½ pounds (5½ No. 56 dippers)
Milk, evaporated	5—14½-ounce cans
Beef, dried, shredded	3 pounds
Horseradish, drained	1 pint (½ No. 56 dipper)
Pepper	(⅔ mess kit spoon)
Egg:	
Eggs, hard-cooked, chopped	75 eggs
Mayonnaise	1 quart (1 No. 56 dipper)
Add prepared mustard, minced onions, chopped pickles or celery if desired.	
Eggs, Denver:	
Eggs, beaten	75 eggs (3¾ No. 56 dippers)
Ham, cooked, chopped	5 pounds
Onions, chopped	1 pound (1 No. 56 dipper)
Fat, bacon	.....
Combine eggs, ham and onions; scramble in fat.	
Fish:	
Salmon or tuna fish	16—1-pound cans
Lemon juice	½ pint (⅓ mess kit cup)
Mayonnaise	1 quart (1 No. 56 dipper)
Pickles, chopped	2 quarts (2 No. 56 dippers)
or	
Celery, chopped	2 pounds (2 No. 56 dippers)
Sliced ham:	
Ham, sliced	15 pounds
Mustard, prepared	.....
Chopped ham:	
Ham, chopped	12 pounds
Mayonnaise	1 quart
Chopped hard-cooked eggs, chopped pickles, chopped onions, chopped meat, ground cheese, ground raisins or chopped celery may be added to the chopped ham.	

(2) Vegetable sandwich fillings.

Ingredients	Quantity
Baked bean:	
Beans, baked.....................	...............(8 No. 56 dippers)
Mustard........................	....
Salt............................	....
Pepper.........................	....
Vinegar........................	....
Bean rarebit:	
Beans, baked....................	...............(6 No. 56 dippers)
Cheese, chopped................	2 pounds.........(2 No. 56 dippers)
Onions, chopped...............	....
Salt............................	....
Pepper.........................	....
Catsup.........................	....
Baked beans and celery:	
Beans, baked....................	...............(6 No. 56 dippers)
Celery, chopped................	2 pounds.........(2 No. 56 dippers)
Mayonnaise.....................	....
Carrot and celery:	
Carrots, chopped...............	7 pounds.........(6 No. 56 dippers)
Celery, chopped................	2 pounds.........(2 No. 56 dippers)
Mayonnaise.....................	....
Carrot and raisin:	
Carrots, chopped...............	7 pounds.........(6 No. 56 dippers)
Raisins, chopped...............	2½ pounds.........(2 No. 56 dippers)
Peanut butter..................	....

(3) Sweet sandwich fillings.

Ingredients	Quantity
Apple butter:	
Butter, apple...................	
Apple butter and cottage or cream cheese:	
Butter, apple...................	...............(6 No. 56 dippers)
Cheese, cottage or cream........	...............(2 No. 56 dippers)
Date and nut:	
Dates, chopped.................	...............(6 No. 56 dippers)
Nuts, chopped.................	...............(2 No. 56 dippers)
Jam:	
Jam...........................	....
Jam and cream cheese or peanut butter:	
Jam...........................	...............(6 No. 56 dippers)
Cheese, cream	...............(2 No. 56 dippers)
or	
Peanut butter.................	....
Jelly:	
Jelly..........................	....
Jelly and cream cheese or peanut butter:	
Jelly..........................	...............(6 No. 56 dippers)
Cream cheese.................	...............(2 No. 56 dippers)
or	
Peanut butter.................	....
Nuts and raisin:	
Nuts, chopped.................	...............(2 No. 56 dippers)
Raisins, chopped..............	...............(6 No. 56 dippers)

SAUCES AND GRAVIES

27. PREPARATION OF SAUCES. The purpose of a sauce is to add flavor, moisture and nutritive value to foods. Use milk or the juice drained from cooked vegetables or fruits as the liquid in sauces. If possible prepare cream sauces in a double boiler as there is less danger of scorching. If a sauce has been thickened with eggs, avoid boiling. Serve sauces immediately after preparation if possible otherwise cover to avoid the formation of a crust on the surface.

NO. 536. APRICOT SAUCE Yield: 100 servings, 1 ounce each.

Ingredients	100 servings	.... servings
Apricots	1 No. 10 can	
Water	2 quarts (2 No. 56 dippers)	
Cornstarch	2 ounces (6 mess kit spoons)	
Sugar	4 pounds (2 No. 56 dippers)	
Salt	¼ ounce (½ mess kit spoon)	
Water	1 pint (½ No. 56 dipper)	
Lemon juice	¼ pint (8 mess kit spoons)	

1. Drain apricots; chop. Add water to apricot juice.
2. Mix cornstarch, sugar, and salt together; add water and stir until smooth.
3. Combine chopped apricots and juice; heat to boiling point. Add cornstarch mixture slowly, stirring constantly.
4. Heat to boiling point; boil 5 minutes or until clear and thick, stirring constantly. Remove from heat.
5. Add lemon juice.
6. Serve hot or cold.

NO. 537. CHERRY SAUCE Yield: 1 gallon, 100 servings, 2½ mess kit spoons each.

Ingredients	100 servings	.... servings
Cherries, sour	3 No. 10 cans	
Water		
Cornstarch	6 ounces (⅓ mess kit cup)	
Sugar, granulated	1½ pounds (1 mess kit cup)	
Salt	⅛ ounce (¼ mess kit spoon)	
Water	½ pint (⅓ mess kit cup)	
Butter	¼ pound (8 mess kit spoons)	
Lemon juice	½ ounce (1 mess kit spoon)	

1. Drain cherries. Add water to juice, if necessary, to make 3¾ quarts (3¾ No. 56 dippers) liquid.
2. Mix cornstarch, sugar, and salt together; add water and stir until smooth.
3. Heat cherry juice to boiling point; add cornstarch mixture slowly, stirring constantly.
4. Heat to boiling point; boil 5 minutes or until clear and thick, stirring constantly. Remove from heat.
5. Add butter and lemon juice; mix well.
6. Serve hot or cold.

NO. 538. CHOCOLATE SAUCE
Yield: 3½ quarts,
100 servings, 2 mess kit spoons each.

Ingredients	100 servings	.... servings
Cornstarch	4 ounces (¼ mess kit cup)	
Sugar, granulated	1½ pounds (1 mess kit cup)	
Salt	⅓ ounce (⅔ mess kit spoon)	
Cocoa	6 ounces (½ mess kit cup)	
Water	2¼ quarts (2¼ No. 56 dippers)	
Butter	¾ pound (½ mess kit cup)	

1. Mix cornstarch, sugar, salt, and cocoa together; add ¾ pint (½ mess kit cup) water. Stir until smooth.
2. Heat remaining water to boiling point; add cornstarch mixture slowly, stirring constantly.
3. Heat to boiling point; boil 5 minutes or until clear and thick, stirring frequently. Remove from heat.
4. Add butter; mix well.
5. Serve hot or cold.

NO. 539. HARD SAUCE
Yield: 100 servings,
1 ounce each.

Ingredients	100 servings	.... servings
Butter	3 pounds (1½ No. 56 dippers)	
Sugar, granulated	6½ pounds (3¼ No. 56 dippers)	
Vanilla	3 ounces (6 mess kit spoons)	

1. Stir butter until soft; add sugar gradually.
2. Stir mixture until light and fluffy. Add vanilla; mix well.

NO. 540. LEMON SAUCE
Yield: 100 servings,
1 ounce each.

Ingredients	100 servings	.... servings
Cornstarch	7 ounces (½ mess kit cup)	
Sugar, granulated	3 pounds (1½ No. 56 dippers)	
Water	2¼ quarts (2¼ No. 56 dippers)	
Butter	½ pound (⅓ mess kit cup)	
Lemon juice	¾ pint (½ mess kit cup)	

1. Mix cornstarch and sugar; add ½ pint (⅓ mess kit cup) of the water. Stir until smooth.

2. Heat remaining water to boiling point; add cornstarch mixture slowly, stirring constantly.

3. Heat to boiling point; boil 5 minutes or until clear and thick, stirring constantly. Remove from heat.

4. Add butter and lemon juice; mix well.

5. Serve hot or cold.

NO. 541. NUTMEG SAUCE

Yield: 3½ quarts,
100 servings, 2 mess kit spoons each.

Ingredients	100 servings	.... servings
Cornstarch	4 ounces (¼ mess kit cup)	
Sugar, granulated	1½ pounds (1 mess kit cup)	
Salt	⅓ ounce (⅔ mess kit spoon)	
Water	2¼ quarts (2¼ No. 56 dippers)	
Butter	¾ pound (½ mess kit cup)	
Nutmeg	⅛ ounce (½ mess kit spoon)	

1. Mix cornstarch, sugar, and salt together; add ½ pint (⅓ mess kit cup) of the water. Stir until smooth.

2. Heat remaining water to boiling point; add cornstarch mixture slowly, stirring constantly.

3. Heat to boiling point; boil 5 minutes or until clear and thick, stirring constantly. Remove from heat.

4. Add butter and nutmeg; mix well.

5. Serve hot or cold.

NO. 542. DRAWN BUTTER SAUCE

Yield: 3 quarts,
1 ounce each serving.

Ingredients	100 servings	servings
Butter, melted	1 pound (½ No. 56 dipper)	
Flour, sifted	12 ounces (1 mess kit cup)	
Water, boiling	2 quarts (2 No. 56 dippers)	
Salt	1 ounce (2 mess kit spoons)	
Cayenne (optional)		

1. Mix melted butter and flour; stir until smooth.

2. Add to hot water. Heat to boiling point; boil until slightly thick, stirring occasionally.

3. Add salt and cayenne.

Note. Vegetable juice may be used instead of water.

NO. 543. EGG SAUCE
Add 12 sliced, hard-cooked eggs to recipe for drawn butter sauce just before serving.

NO. 544. PARSLEY SAUCE
Add ½ mess kit cup minced parsley to recipe for drawn butter sauce just before serving.

NO. 545. LEMON BUTTER SAUCE
Yield: 100 servings, 1 ounce each.

Ingredients	100 servings	.... servings
Butter, melted	2¼ pounds (1⅛ No. 56 dippers)	
Flour, sifted	12 ounces (1 mess kit cup)	
Water, boiling	2 quarts (2 No. 56 dippers)	
Lemon juice	12 lemons	
Salt	½ ounce (1 mess kit spoon)	
Cayenne		
Parsley, minced	2 ounces (¼ mess kit cup)	

1. Mix melted butter and flour; stir until smooth.
2. Add to hot water. Heat to boiling point; boil 10 minutes or until thick, stirring frequently.
3. Add lemon juice, salt, cayenne, and parsley.

NO. 546. SAVORY BUTTER SAUCE
Add 1 chopped onion, 2 ounces chopped pimiento and 2 chopped green peppers to recipe for lemon butter sauce.

NO. 547. CHEESE SAUCE
Yield: 1½ gallons, 1 ounce each serving.

Ingredients	100 servings	.... servings
Flour, sifted	8 ounces (½ No. 56 dipper)	
Water, cold	1½ pints (1 mess kit cup)	
Milk, evaporated	4—14½-ounce cans	
Water (for milk)	2 quarts (2 No. 56 dippers)	
Fat	12 ounces (½ mess kit cup)	
Salt	¾ ounce (1½ mess kit spoons)	
Cheese, chopped	4 pounds (4 No. 56 dippers)	

1. Mix flour and cold water; stir until smooth.
2. Mix milk and water; heat to boiling point.
3. Pour flour mixture slowly into hot milk, stirring constantly. Heat to boiling point; boil 5 minutes or until thick, stirring constantly. Add fat and salt. Remove from heat.
4. Add chopped cheese; stir until cheese is melted.

NO. 548. WHITE SAUCE

Yield: 1 gallon, 1 ounce each.

Ingredients	100 servings	.... servings
Thin		
Fat, melted...............	8 ounces (⅓ mess kit cup)..........	
Flour, sifted...............	4 ounces (⅓ mess kit cup)..........	
Salt......................	1 ounce (2 mess kit spoons)..........	
Pepper....................		
Milk, evaporated...........	4—14½-ounce cans..........	
Water (for milk)...........	2 quarts (2 No. 56 dippers)..........	
Medium		
Fat, melted...............	14 ounces (½ mess kit cup)..........	
Flour, sifted...............	7 ounces (½ mess kit cup)..........	
Salt......................	1 ounce (2 mess kit spoons)..........	
Pepper....................		
Milk, evaporated...........	4—14½-ounce cans..........	
Water (for milk)...........	2 quarts (2 No. 56 dippers)..........	
Thick		
Fat, melted...............	1½ pounds (1 mess kit cup)..........	
Flour, sifted...............	12 ounces (1 mess kit cup)..........	
Salt......................	1½ ounces (3 mess kit spoons).......	
Pepper....................		
Milk, evaporated...........	4—14½-ounce cans..........	
Water (for milk)...........	2 quarts (2 No. 56 dippers)..........	

1. Mix melted fat, flour, salt, and pepper together; stir until smooth.
2. Mix milk and water; heat.
3. Add milk gradually to flour mixture; stir until thoroughly mixed.
4. Heat to boiling point; boil 5 minutes or until thick, stirring constantly.

NO. 549. HOLLANDAISE SAUCE

Prepare 1 gallon medium white sauce. Place 24 egg yolks (½ No. 56 dipper) in pan over hot water; add white sauce to egg yolks and beat vigorously. Add 12 ounces (½ mess kit cup) butter, ½ pint (¼ No. 56 dipper) lemon juice and a small amount of tabasco sauce or red peppers. Cook slowly, stirring constantly. Keep the temperature of the water below the boiling point. Serve hot.

NO. 550. MUSTARD SAUCE

Add ¾ pint (½ mess kit cup) prepared mustard to recipe for thin white sauce. Mix well. Serve hot on vegetables or meat.

NO. 551. BARBECUE SAUCE

Yield: 2 gallons, 100 servings, ⅓ cup each.

Ingredients	100 servings	.... servings
Onions, chopped............	1 pound (1 No. 56 dipper)..........	
Fat, bacon or ham, melted....	4 pounds (2 No. 56 dippers).........	
Vinegar...................	2 quarts (2 No. 56 dippers)..........	
Water.....................	1 quart (1 No. 56 dipper)..........	
Mustard, prepared..........	1 pint (½ No. 56 dipper)..........	
Catsup....................	1½ quarts (1½ No. 56 dippers)......	
Sugar, brown...............	4 ounces (⅛ No. 56 dipper).........	
Salt......................		
Pepper, red................		
Chili powder (optional)......		
Worcestershire sauce (optional).	2 ounces (4 mess kit spoons)........	

1. Fry onions in melted fat until tender and slightly brown.

2. Add remaining ingredients; mix thoroughly.

3. Refrigerate until ready for use.

Note. Serve on all kinds of meat.

NO. 552. CREOLE OR SPANISH SAUCE

Yield: 2 gallons, 100 servings, ⅓ cup each.

Ingredients	100 servings	.... servings
Onions, chopped	1½ pounds (1½ No. 56 dippers)	
Peppers, green, chopped	1½ pounds (1½ No. 56 dippers)	
Mushrooms	1½ pounds (1½ No. 56 dippers)	
Fat, melted	1 pound (½ No. 56 dipper)	
Tomato puree	2 quarts (2 No. 56 dippers)	
Tomatoes	8 pounds (4 No. 56 dippers)	
Meat stock	2 quarts (2 No. 56 dippers)	
Flour, sifted	1 ounce (2 mess kit spoons)	
Butter, melted	4 ounces (8 mess kit spoons)	
Salt	1 ounce (2 mess kit spoons)	
Pepper	¼ ounce (1 mess kit spoon)	
Parsley, finely chopped	3 sprigs	
Garlic, crushed	1 small clove	

1. Fry onions, green peppers and mushrooms in fat about 5 minutes; add tomato puree, tomatoes and meat stock.

2. Mix flour and melted butter; stir until smooth. Add to onion and tomato mixture. Heat to boiling point; boil 2 minutes, stirring constantly.

3. Add salt, pepper, parsley, and garlic; mix well.

NO. 553. CREOLE SAUCE WITH PIMIENTOS

Add chopped pimientos and red peppers to recipe for creole or Spanish sauce.

NO. 554. CREOLE SAUCE WITH BACON OR SALT PORK

Cut bacon or salt pork into ½-inch pieces; fry until crisp. Add fried bacon to recipe for creole or Spanish sauce. Bacon fat may be used for the fat in the sauce.

NO. 555. CREOLE SAUCE WITH CELERY

Add 1½ pounds (1½ No. 56 dippers) diced celery to recipe for creole sauce. Omit mushrooms.

NO. 556. HORSERADISH SAUCE

Yield: 2 gallons,
100 servings, ⅓
cup each.

Ingredients	100 servings	.... servings
Milk, evaporated.............	8—14½-ounce cans...............	
Water (for milk).............	1 gallon (4 No. 56 dippers)......	
Flour, sifted.................	1 pound (1 No. 56 dipper)........	
Lemon juice.................	½ pint (¼ No. 56 dipper)........	
Salt.......................	2 ounces (4 mess kit spoons).......	
Pepper.....................	(¼ mess kit spoon)...............	
Butter or fat...............	1 pound (½ No. 56 dipper).......	
Horseradish, prepared........	1 quart (1 No. 56 dipper)........	

1. Mix milk and water. Mix flour and 1 quart (1 No. 56 dipper) milk; stir until smooth. Add remaining milk.
2. Heat to boiling point; boil 2 minutes or until thick, stirring constantly.
3. Add lemon juice, salt, pepper, and horseradish; heat.
4. Keep hot over hot water until ready for use.

NO. 557. MINT SAUCE

Yield: 2 quarts,
100 servings, 1 mess kit
spoon each.

Ingredients	100 servings	.... servings
Mint, fresh, chopped.........	8 ounces (1½ No. 56 dippers).......	
Sugar, granulated............	1 pound (½ No. 56 dipper).......	
Vinegar....................	2 quarts (2 No. 56 dippers)........	

1. Wash mint thoroughly; remove stems and old leaves. Drain and chop.
2. Mix mint and sugar; allow to stand 30 to 60 minutes.
3. Add vinegar allow to stand 1 hour.

Note. Serve with roast lamb or broiled lamb chops.

NO. 558. RAISIN SAUCE

Yield: 2 gallons,
100 servings, 3 ounces
each.

Ingredients	100 servings	.... servings
Raisins....................	1½ pounds (1⅓ No. 56 dippers).....	
Water, hot (for raisins).......		
Cider or pineapple juice.......	1 gallon (4 No. 56 dippers)........	
Water.....................	1 gallon (4 No. 56 dippers)........	
Salt.......................	1 ounce (2 mess kit spoons)........	
Pepper.....................	¼ ounce (1 mess kit spoon)........	
Sugar, brown...............	1 pound (1 mess kit cup).........	
Cornstarch.................	6 ounces (18 mess kit spoons).......	
Water, cold (for cornstarch)...		
Butter.....................	1 pound (½ No. 56 dipper).......	
Lemon juice.................	4 lemons......................	
or		
Vinegar....................		

207

1. Wash raisins. Cover with hot water; soak until plump.
2. Mix cider or pineapple juice and water; add raisins, salt, pepper, and brown sugar; heat.
3. Mix cornstarch and a little cold water; add to raisin mixture. Heat to boiling point; boil 5 minutes or until thick; stirring constantly.
4. Add butter and lemon juice or vinegar; mix well.

   Note. Serve hot with baked ham or tongue.

NO. 559. TOMATO SAUCE

Yield: Approximately 2 gallons, 100 servings, approximately ⅓ cup each.

Ingredients	100 servings	.... servings
Onions, finely chopped........	1¾ pounds (1¾ No. 56 dippers)....	....
Garlic, chopped (optional).....	1 clove........................	....
Fat (for frying)..............	2 pounds (1 No. 56 dipper).........	....
Flour, sifted.................	1 pound (1 No. 56 dipper)...........	....
Cloves, ground...............	⅓ ounce (1⅓ mess kit spoons).......	....
Cinnamon, ground...........	½ ounce (2 mess kit spoons)........	....
Salt........................	1¼ ounces (2½ mess kit spoons).....	....
Cayenne....................	....	....
Water......................	2 quarts (2 No. 56 dippers)........	....
Tomatoes...................	2 No. 10 cans................	....

1. Fry chopped onions and garlic about 5 minutes but not until brown.
2. Add flour, cloves, cinnamon, salt, and cayenne; mix well.
3. Add water and tomatoes. Heat to boiling point; boil 5 minutes or until thick, stirring constantly. Reduce heat and simmer another 5 minutes, stirring frequently to prevent scorching.

   Note. Serve on spaghetti, meat balls, or fish.

NO. 560. SALMON SAUCE

Yield: 2 gallons, 2 ounces each serving.

Ingredients	100 servings	.... servings
Fat, melted.................	2 pounds (1 No. 56 dipper).........	....
Flour, sifted................	1 pound (1 No. 56 dipper)...........	....
Salt.......................	4 ounces (8 mess kit spoons)........	....
Pepper.....................	¼ ounce (1 mess kit spoon).........	....
Juice from salmon...........	....	....
Water......................	....	....
Milk, evaporated...........	8—14½-ounce cans.................	....
Catsup....................	1 quart (1 No. 56 dipper)...........	....

1. Mix melted fat, flour, salt, and pepper together; stir until smooth.
2. Place over low heat and cook about 10 minutes or until brown, stirring constantly.
3. Add enough water to salmon juice to make 1 gallon (4 No. 56 dippers) of liquid.
4. Mix milk and liquid together; heat to boiling point.
5. Add hot liquid to flour mixture. Heat to boiling point; boil 2 to 3 minutes or until thick, stirring constantly.
6. Add catsup; mix well.

NO. 561. TARTAR SAUCE

Yield: 1½ gallons,
100 servings, 3 mess kit
spoons each.

Ingredients	100 servings	.... servings
Mayonnaise, thick...........	1 gallon (4 No. 56 dippers)...........	....
Eggs, hard-cooked, chopped....	10 eggs............................	....
Pickles, dill, finely chopped....	1 pound (½ No. 56 dipper)...........	....
Onions, finely chopped........	1 pound (1 No. 56 dipper)...........	....
Parsley, finely chopped.......	4 ounces (¾ No. 56 dipper)...........	....

Mix all ingredients together thoroughly.

Note. Serve cold with corned beef hash or fish.

NO. 562. BROWN GRAVY

Yield: 2 gallons,
100 servings, ⅓ cup each.

Ingredients	100 servings	.... servings
Fat from cooked meat........	1½ pounds (¾ No. 56 dipper).......	....
Garlic, crushed (optional).....	½ clove........................	....
Flour, sifted.................	1½ pounds (1½ No. 56 dippers).....	....
Water or stock, hot..........	2 gallons (8 No. 56 dippers)........	....
Salt........................	....	....
Pepper......................	....	....

1. Pour clear fat from roasting or frying pans after meat is cooked, allowing brown particles to remain. Measure fat.
2. Return the 1½ pounds (¾ No. 56 dipper) measured fat to pans; add crushed garlic and fry until brown.
3. Add flour; stir until smooth. Continue cooking over low heat until flour is brown.
4. Add hot liquid gradually, stirring constantly.
5. Heat to boiling point; boil 2 minutes or until thick, stirring constantly. Add salt and pepper.

Note. When flour is cooked it loses some of its thickening power. The amount needed to make gravy of right consistency will depend upon how brown the flour becomes before the liquid is added.

NO. 563. TOMATO GRAVY

Increase fat to 2 pounds (1 No. 56 dipper) and flour to 2 pounds (2 No. 56 dippers) in recipe for brown gravy. Add ⅓ No. 10 can tomatoes. The acid in the tomatoes decreases the thickening power of the flour.

NO. 564. SPICED TOMATO GRAVY

Add grated nutmeg, mace, ground cinnamon, ground cloves and any other seasonings desired to recipe for tomato gravy. Add seasonings cautiously and in amounts desired.

No. 565. BROWN ONION GRAVY

Add 5 pounds (3½ No. 56 dippers) peeled and sliced onions to fat in recipe for brown gravy before the addition of the flour.

NO. 566. GIBLET GRAVY

Wash the liver, heart, and gizzard of poultry; remove any portion of the liver which may have a greenish color. Cover gizzard with cold water. Cover and heat to boiling point; reduce heat and simmer about 20 minutes. Add the heart and continue simmering 10 minutes. Add the liver and cook 10 to 15 minutes longer. Drain and chop. Add the chopped cooked giblets to recipe for brown gravy. Substitute the liquid in which giblets were cooked for part or all of the water in the gravy.

NO. 567. CREAM GRAVY
Yield: 2 gallons, 100 servings, ⅓ cup each.

Ingredients	100 servings	.... servings
Fat from cooked meat	1 pound (½ No. 56 dipper)	
Flour, sifted	1 pound (1 No. 56 dipper)	
Milk, evaporated	8—14½-ounce cans	
Water (for milk)	1 gallon (4 No. 56 dippers)	
Salt		
Pepper		

1. Pour clear fat from roasting or frying pans where meat has been cooked, allowing brown particles to remain in pan. Measure fat.

2. Return the 1 pound (½ No. 56 dipper) measured fat to pans; add flour and stir until smooth.

3. Mix milk and water; heat.

4. Add hot liquid gradually to flour and fat, stirring constantly.

5. Heat to boiling point; boil 2 minutes or until thick, stirring constantly. Add salt and pepper.

Note. The amount of salt depends upon the seasoning of the meat. Milk requires more salt than water or seasoned stock.

NO. 568. CREAM ONION GRAVY

Add 5 pounds (3½ No. 56 dippers) peeled and sliced onions to fat in recipe for cream gravy before the addition of the flour.

NO. 569. NATURAL PAN GRAVY
Yield: 100 servings, 1 ounce each.

Ingredients	100 servings	.... servings
Water, boiling	1 quart (1 No. 56 dipper)	
Fat from cooked meat	4 pounds (2 No. 56 dippers)	
Worcestershire sauce	4 ounces (6 mess kit spoons)	
Salt		
Pepper		

1. Pour hot water into hot fat in pan in which meat was cooked.

2. Add Worcestershire sauce, salt, and pepper; stir well.

Note. Serve very hot over meat. Use just enough gravy to moisten meat well.

SOUPS

28. **SOUPS.** Thin soups are best served with a heavy meal. Thick soups and chowders are used to add food value and satisfaction to a lighter meal.

NO. 570. MEAT STOCK Yield: 6¼ gallons,
100 servings, approximately 1 cup each.

Ingredients	100 servings	.... servings
Meat bones (shank).........	24 pounds............................	....
Shank meat (cut from bones)..	8 pounds.............................	....
Water......................	8¼ gallons (33 No. 56 dippers).......	....
Worcestershire sauce........	1 ounce (2 mess kit spoons)...........	....
Celery, chopped.............	8 ounces (½ No. 56 dipper)...........	....
Carrots, chopped...........	14 ounces (1 mess kit cup)...........	....
Onions, diced..............	8 ounces (½ No. 56 dipper)...........	....
Salt.......................	3 ounces (6 mess kit spoons).........	....
Cloves, ground..............	(¼ mess kit spoon)...................	....
Pepper.....................	(⅓ mess kit spoon)...................	....

1. Saw shank bones into pieces. Cut shank meat into 1-inch cubes.
2. Combine bones, meat, and water.
3. Cover and heat to boiling point; reduce heat and simmer about 3 hours, skimming as necessary.
4. Add Worcestershire sauce, celery, carrots, onions, salt, cloves, and pepper; mix well.
5. Cover and heat to boiling point; reduce heat and simmer 2 to 3 hours. Strain.
6. Cool as quickly as possible. Refrigerate until needed.
7. Before using, remove layer of hardened fat from surface of stock.

Note. Save hardened fat for frying or shortening.

NO. 571. HAM STOCK Yield: 6¼ gallons,
100 servings, approximately 1 cup each.

Ingredients	100 servings	.... servings
Ham scraps, hocks, bones or whole hams.	18 pounds............................	....
Water......................	7¾ gallons (31 No. 56 dippers).......	....
Salt.......................	....	....
Onions, diced..............	1 pound (1 No. 56 dipper)...........	....
Celery, diced...............	1 pound (1 No. 56 dipper)...........	....
Carrots, diced..............	1 pound (¾ No. 56 dipper)...........	....
Pepper.....................	(¼ mess kit spoon)...................	....

1. Combine all ingredients.
2. Cover and heat to boiling; reduce heat and simmer 4 to 5 hours or until meat is tender. Remove meat; strain stock.
3. Cool as quickly as possible. Return cooked ham to stock. Refrigerate until needed.
4. Before using, remove layer of hardened fat from surface.

Note. Save hardened fat for frying or shortening.

NO. 572. CHICKEN OR TURKEY STOCK

Yield: 6¼ gallons,
100 servings, approximately 1 cup each.

Ingredients	100 servings	.... servings
Chicken or turkey, bony parts.	30 pounds...................	....
Water.....................	7¾ gallons (31 No. 56 dippers).......	....
Carrots, diced..............	10 ounces (¾ mess kit cup).........	....
Onions, diced...............	4 ounces (¼ No. 56 dipper).........	....
Celery, diced...............	4 ounces (¼ No. 56 dipper).........	....
Salt......................	3 ounces (6 mess kit spoons)........	....
Pepper....................	(¼ mess kit spoon)................	....

1. Use all bones, backs, necks, wing tips, and feet of chicken or turkey; scrub thoroughly.
2. Add water, carrots, onions, celery, salt and pepper.
3. Cover and heat to boiling point; reduce heat and simmer about 2 hours. Strain.
4. Cool as quickly as possible. Refrigerate until needed.
5. Before using, remove layer of hardened fat from surface of stock.

Note. Save hardened fat for frying or shortening.

NO. 573. BEEF SOUP WITH BARLEY, MACARONI, NOODLES, RICE OR SPAGHETTI

Yield: 6¼ gallons,
100 servings, approximately 1 cup each.

Ingredients	100 servings	.... servings
Beef stock..................	7¼ gallons (29 No. 56 dippers).......	....
Barley, macaroni, noodles, rice *or* spaghetti.	1½ pounds....................	....
Celery, diced...............	1½ pounds (1½ No. 56 dippers).....	....
Onions, diced...............	1½ pounds (1½ No. 56 dippers).....	....
Salt......................	1½ ounces (3 mess kit spoons).......	....

1. Prepare beef stock. (See recipe No. 570.)
2. Combine all ingredients.
3. Cover and heat to boiling; reduce heat and simmer 45 minutes.

Note. Fresh or canned tomatoes may be substituted for part of the beef stock.

NO. 574. VEGETABLE BEEF SOUP

Yield: 6¼ gallons,
100 servings, approximately 1 cup each.

Ingredients	100 servings	.... servings
Beef bones.	20 pounds.	
Water.	5¼ gallons (21 No. 56 dippers).	
Pepper.		
Cloves, ground.		
Celery, diced.	2½ pounds (2½ No. 56 dippers).	
Onions, sliced.	12 ounces (¾ No. 56 dipper).	
Turnips, diced.	1½ pounds (1¼ No. 56 dippers).	
Carrots, diced.	1½ pounds (1¼ No. 56 dippers).	
Potatoes, diced.	3 pounds (2 No. 56 dippers).	
Tomatoes.	1½ No. 10 cans.	
Salt.	4 ounces (8 mess kit spoons).	

1. Remove meat from bones; saw bones into pieces.
2. Combine meat and bones; cover with water.
3. Cover and heat to boiling point; reduce heat and simmer about 1 hour.
4. Add pepper, cloves, celery, onions, turnips, carrots, potatoes, tomatoes and salt; mix well.
5. Cover and heat to boiling point; reduce heat and simmer 1 hour. Remove bones.

NO. 575. MEATLESS VEGETABLE SOUP

Yield: 6¼ gallons,
100 servings, approximately 1 cup each.

Ingredients	100 servings	.... servings
Celery, diced.	3 pounds (3 No. 56 dippers).	
Onions, diced.	1½ pounds (1½ No. 56 dippers).	
Turnips, diced.	3 pounds (2½ No. 56 dippers).	
Carrots, diced.	3 pounds (2½ No. 56 dippers).	
Fat, bacon, melted.	1½ pounds (¾ No. 56 dipper).	
Water, boiling.	4½ gallons (18 No. 56 dippers).	
Potatoes, diced.	6 pounds (4 No. 56 dippers).	
Salt.	4 ounces (8 mess kit spoons).	
Pepper.		
Paprika.		
Tomatoes.	13 pounds.	
Parsley, chopped.	10 ounces (1 mess kit cup).	

1. Fry celery, onions, turnips, and carrots in melted bacon fat about 15 minutes.
2. Add boiling water, potatoes, salt, pepper, paprika, and tomatoes; mix well.
3. Cover and heat to boiling point; reduce heat and simmer about 1 hour.
4. Add parsley just before serving.

NO. 576. CONSOMME

Yield: 6¼ gallons,
100 servings, approximately 1 cup each.

Ingredients	100 servings	.... servings
Veal bones (part knuckles)....	32 pounds..............................	....
Water.....................	8¼ gallons (33 No. 56 dippers).......	....
Salt......................	4 ounces (8 mess kit spoons)........	....
Beef cubes, raw..............	7 pounds..............................	....
Fat (for frying)..............	8 ounces (¼ No. 56 dipper).........	....
Ham cubes, raw..............	1½ pounds...........................	....
Onions, diced................	1 pound (1 No. 56 dipper)...........	....
Celery leaves................	4 ounces (½ No. 56 dippers).........	....
Carrots, diced...............	1 pound (¾ No. 56 dipper)...........	....
Pepper.....................	(⅓ mess kit spoon)...................	....
Cloves, ground..............	(¼ mess kit spoon)...................	....

1. Saw bones into pieces.
2. Cover bones with water; add salt.
3. Cover and heat to boiling; reduce heat and simmer 1 to 2 hours or until meat is tender. Remove bones.
4. Fry beef cubes in fat. Add to soup stock.
5. Add ham cubes, onions, celery leaves, carrots, pepper, and cloves; mix well.
6. Cover and heat to boiling; reduce heat and simmer about 3 hours. Strain.
7. Cool as quickly as possible. Refrigerate until needed.
8. Before using, remove layer of hardened fat from surface of soup.

Note. Save hardened fat for frying or shortening.

NO. 577. SCOTCH BROTH

Yield: 6¼ gallons,
100 servings, approximately 1 cup each.

Ingredients	100 servings	.... servings
Lamb bones and meat........	18 pounds..............................	....
Water.....................	7¾ gallons (31 No. 56 dippers).......	....
Salt......................	3 ounces (6 mess kit spoons)........	....
Pepper....................	....	....
Barley, pearl...............	1½ pounds (1 mess kit cup).........	....
Carrots, diced..............	3 pounds (2½ No. 56 dippers).......	....
Turnips, diced..............	3 pounds (2¼ No. 56 dippers)..... ..	....
Onions, sliced..............	12 ounces (¾ No. 56 dipper)........	....
Celery, diced...............	2½ pounds (2½ No. 56 dippers).....	....
Parsley, chopped...........	2 ounces (¼ mess kit cup)..........	....

1. Saw bones into pieces; cover with water.
2. Cover and heat slowly to boiling point; reduce heat and simmer 2 hours.
3. Skim: remove bones. Cut meat from bones.

214

4. Combine lamb broth, salt, pepper, barley and all vegetables except parsley; mix well.

5. Cover and heat to boiling point; reduce heat and simmer 1 hour.

6. Chop meat cut from bones; add meat to soup.

7. Add parsley just before serving.

Note. One-half mess kit spoon curry powder may be added to recipe above if desired.

NO. 578. CREOLE SOUP

Yield: 6¼ gallons,
100 servings, approximately 1 cup each.

Ingredients	100 servings	.... servings
Beef stock	6¼ gallons (25 No. 56 dippers)	
Onions, diced	1½ pounds (1½ No. 56 dippers)	
Peppers, green, chopped	6 ounces (½ mess kit cup)	
Tomatoes	1½ No. 10 cans	
Salt	2 ounces (4 mess kit spoons)	
Pepper	(⅓ mess kit spoon)	
Spaghetti	1½ pounds	

1. Prepare beef stock (recipe No. 570); heat.

2. Combine hot stock, onions, green peppers, tomatoes, salt and pepper; mix well.

3. Break spaghetti into small pieces; wash. Add to other ingredients.

4. Cover and heat to boiling point; reduce heat and simmer about 1 hour. Stir occasionally to prevent spaghetti from sticking to bottom of pan.

NO. 579. MINESTRONE SOUP

Yield: 6¼ gallons,
100 servings, approximately 1 cup each.

Ingredients	100 servings	.... servings
Beans, navy, dry	1¼ pounds	
Water	5 quarts (5 No. 56 dippers)	
Barley, noodles, rice *or* spaghetti.	1½ pounds	
Garlic	2 cloves	
Salt	2 ounces (4 mess kit spoons)	
Stock, beef, chicken, or ham	3¼ gallons (13 No. 56 dippers)*	
Onions, diced	2½ pounds (2½ No. 56 dippers)	
Potatoes, diced	2½ pounds (2½ No. 56 dippers)	
Celery strips	2½ pounds (2½ No. 56 dippers)	
Carrots, diced	4 pounds (3⅓ No. 56 dippers)	
Parsley, chopped	2 ounces (¼ mess kit cup)	
Cheese, chopped (optional)	12 ounces (¾ No. 56 dipper)	

*More stock may be added if needed for volume.

1. Wash beans. Add enough water to cover beans; soak 6 to 8 hours or overnight.

2. Add remaining water. Cover and heat to boiling point; reduce heat and simmer 1 hour or until beans are tender.

3. Add barley, noodles, rice *or* spaghetti, garlic and salt; mix thoroughly. Continue simmering 30 minutes.
4. Prepare beef stock (recipe No. 570), chicken stock (recipe No. 572) or ham stock. (See recipe No. 571.)
5. Combine beans, stock, onions, potatoes, celery, carrots, and parsley; mix well.
6. Cover and heat to boiling point; reduce heat and simmer about 1 hour.
7. Sprinkle shopped cheese over soup just before serving.

Note. Left-over vegetables may be used instead of the fresh if care is taken to prevent overcooking. Use a quantity equal to the total amount of vegetables in recipe above. Peeled fresh tomatoes may also be used.

NO. 580. OLD FASHIONED POTATO SOUP

Yield: 6¼ gallons,
100 servings, approximately 1 cup each.

Ingredients	100 servings	.... servings
Potatoes, cubed	10 pounds (6¼ No. 56 dippers)	
Water, boiling	3¼ gallons (13 No. 56 dippers)	
Salt	4 ounces (8 mess kit spoons)	
Bacon or salt pork, diced	2½ pounds	
Onions, chopped	1¼ pounds (1¼ No. 56 dippers)	
Pepper	(⅙ mess kit spoon)	
Paprika	¼ ounce (1 mess kit spoon)	
Milk, evaporated	19—14½-ounce cans	

1. Combine potatoes, boiling water and salt.
2. Cover and heat to boiling point; reduce heat and simmer about 45 minutes or until potatoes are very soft.
3. Fry bacon until crisp. Remove from pan and drain.
4. Fry onions in bacon fat about 10 minutes; drain.
5. Combine potatoes, onions, pepper, paprika, and milk; mix well.
6. Cover and heat to boiling point; reduce heat and simmer about 30 minutes.
7. Add crisp bacon just before serving.

NO. 581. ARMY BEAN SOUP

Yield: 6¼ gallons,
100 servings, approximately 1 cup each.

Ingredients	100 servings	.... servings
Beans, navy, dry	6 pounds	
Water	8¼ gallons (33 No. 56 dippers)	
Bones	18 pounds	
Onions, whole, peeled	10 ounces (½ No. 56 dipper)	
Tomatoes	½ No. 10 can	
Fat, melted	12 ounces (½ mess kit cup)	
Flour, sifted	12 ounces (¾ No. 56 dipper)	
Salt	4 ounces (8 mess kit spoons)	
Pepper	(½ mess kit spoon)	

1. Wash beans. Add enough water to cover beans; soak 6 to 8 hours or overnight.
2. Saw soup bones into pieces.
3. Combine beans, remaining water, bones and onions.
4. Cover and heat to boiling; reduce heat and simmer 4 to 5 hours or until beans are very mushy.
5. Remove soup bones.
6. Rub mixture through sieve.
7. Add tomatoes and reheat.
8. Mix melted fat, flour, salt and pepper together, stir until smooth. Add slowly to hot soup. Heat to boiling; reduce heat and simmer about 20 minutes or until soup is slightly thick, stirring constantly.

NO. 582. LIMA BEAN OR NAVY BEAN SOUP

Yield: 6¼ gallons,
100 servings, approximately 1 cup each.

Ingredients	100 servings	.... servings
Beans, lima or navy, dry......	9 pounds (3 No. 56 dippers).........	....
Water.....................	3 gallons (12 No. 56 dippers)........	....
Ham stock.................	3¼ gallons (13 No. 56 dippers)......	....
Celery, diced...............	6 ounces (½ mess kit cup)..........	....
Onions, diced..............	15 ounces (1 No. 56 dipper).........	....
Peppers, green, chopped......	6 ounces (½ mess kit cup)..........	....
Sugar, granulated...........	4 ounces (8 mess kit spoons)........	....
Pepper....................		
Flour, sifted................	12 ounces (¾ No. 56 dipper)........	....
Milk, evaporated............	8—14½-ounce cans.................	....
or		
Tomatoes..................	1 No. 10 can.....................	....
Salt......................	2 ounces (4 mess kit spoons)........	....

1. Wash beans. Add enough water to cover beans; soak lima beans 3 to 4 hours or navy beans 6 to 8 hours.
2. Add remaining water. Partially cover and heat to boiling point; reduce heat and simmer 2 hours or until skins of beans begin to burst.
3. Prepare ham stock. (See recipe No. 571.)
4. Combine beans, all but 1 pint (½ No. 56 dipper) ham stock, celery, onions, green peppers, sugar, and pepper; mix well.
5. Cover and heat to boiling point; reduce heat and simmer about 1 hour.
6. Mix the 1 pint ham stock and flour; stir until smooth. Add slowly to hot soup; mix thoroughly. Heat to boiling point; reduce heat and simmer 20 minutes or until soup is slightly thick, stirring constantly.
7. Add milk or tomatoes about 10 minutes before serving. Reheat and add salt.

NO. 583. LENTIL OR SPLIT PEA SOUP   Yield: 6¼ gallons, 100 servings, approximately 1 cup each.

Ingredients	100 servings	.... servings
Lentils or split peas	8½ pounds (5 No. 56 dippers)	
Water	1¼ gallons (5 No. 56 dippers)	
Ham stock	5 gallons (20 No. 56 dippers)	
Onions, diced	1½ pounds (1½ No. 56 dippers)	
Celery, diced	1½ pounds (1½ No. 56 dippers)	
Carrots, diced	1½ pounds (1¼ No. 56 dippers)	
Sugar, granulated	¾ ounce (1½ mess kit spoons)	
Salt	2 ounces (4 mess kit spoons)	
Pepper	(½ mess kit spoon)	
Mustard, dry	(½ mess kit spoon)	
Nutmeg, ground	(½ mess kit spoon)	
Worcestershire sauce	(½ mess kit spoon)	
Fat, melted	10 ounces (⅓ No. 56 dipper)	
Flour, sifted	12 ounces (¾ No. 56 dipper)	

1. Wash lentils or split peas. Cover with water; soak 5 hours or overnight.

2. Prepare ham stock. (See recipe No. 571.)

3. Combine lentils or split peas, ham stock, onions, celery, carrots, sugar, salt, pepper, mustard, and nutmeg; mix well.

4. Cover and heat to boiling point; reduce heat and simmer 2 hours or until lentils or split peas are very soft.

5. Rub through sieve.

6. Add Worcestershire sauce; reheat.

7. Mix melted fat and flour; stir until smooth. Add slowly to hot soup; mix thoroughly. Heat to boiling point; reduce heat and simmer about 20 minutes or until soup is slightly thick, stirring constantly.

NO. 584. CELERY AND GREEN PEA SOUP
Yield: 6¼ gallons, 100 servings, approximately 1 cup each.

Ingredients	100 servings	.... servings
Milk, evaporated	24—14½-ounce cans	
Water or liquid drained from peas (for milk).	2½ gallons (10 No. 56 dippers)	
Peas, drained	2½ No. 10 cans	
Onions, chopped	8 ounces (½ No. 56 dipper)	
Salt	1 ounce (2 mess kit spoons)	
Nutmeg		
Fat, melted	12 ounces (½ mess kit cup)	
Flour, sifted	12 ounces (¾ No. 56 dipper)	
Salt	2 ounces (4 mess kit spoons)	
Pepper	(⅓ mess kit spoon)	
Celery, finely diced	3¾ pounds (3¾ No. 56 dippers)	

1. Combine six 14½-ounce cans milk, 1 quart (1 No. 56 dipper) water, peas, onions, salt, and nutmeg; mix well.
2. Cover and heat to boiling point; reduce heat and simmer about 45 minutes.
3. Rub through sieve.
4. Mix remaining milk and remaining water; heat.
5. Mix melted fat, flour, salt, and pepper together; stir until smooth. Add slowly to hot milk; mix thoroughly. Add celery. Heat to boiling point; reduce heat and simmer until mixture is slightly thick, stirring constantly.
6. Add peas and onions; continue simmering until celery is tender.

NO. 585. CREAM OF ASPARAGUS SOUP

Yield: 6¼ gallons,
100 servings, approximately 1 cup each.

Ingredients	100 servings	.... servings
Beef stock	1¾ gallons (7 No. 56 dippers)	
Asparagus	4 No. 10 cans	
Onions, chopped	8 ounces (½ No. 56 dipper)	
Fat, melted	1 pound (½ No. 56 dipper)	
Flour, sifted	1 pound (1 No. 56 dipper)	
Salt	2 ounces (4 mess kit spoons)	
Pepper	(⅛ mess kit spoon)	
Nutmeg	(⅛ mess kit spoon)	
Milk, evaporated, heated	12—14½-ounce cans	

1. Prepare beef stock. (See recipe No. 570.)
2. Mix beef stock and asparagus including liquid from the can; heat to boiling point.*
3. Fry onions in melted fat until tender. Add flour, salt, pepper, and nutmeg; stir until smooth.
4. Add onion mixture slowly to hot milk; mix thoroughly. Heat to boiling point; reduce heat and simmer about 20 minutes or until soup is slightly thick, stirring constantly.
5. Mix asparagus and milk mixtures just before serving.

*Asparagus mixture may be rubbed through a sieve if desired.

NO. 586. CREAM OF CELERY SOUP

Yield: 6¼ gallons,
100 servings, approximately 1 cup each.

Ingredients	100 servings	.... servings
Beef stock	3¼ gallons (13 No. 56 dippers)	
Celery, finely diced	12 pounds (12 No. 56 dippers)	
Milk, evaporated	30—14½-ounce cans	
Onions, chopped	12 ounces (¾ No. 56 dipper)	
Fat, melted	1½ pounds (¾ No. 56 dipper)	
Flour, sifted	1 pound (1 No. 56 dipper)	
Salt	3 ounces (6 mess kit spoons)	
Pepper	(¼ mess kit spoon)	

1. Prepare beef stock (recipe No. 570) ; add celery.
2. Cover and heat to boiling point; reduce heat and simmer about 35 minutes or until celery is tender. Add milk.
3. Fry onions in melted fat. Add flour, salt and pepper; stir until smooth.
4. Add onion mixture slowly to hot celery mixture; mix thoroughly. Heat to boiling point; reduce heat and simmer about 20 minutes or until soup is slightly thick, stirring constantly.

NO. 587. CREAM OF CORN SOUP

Yield : 6¼ gallons, 100 servings, approximately 1 cup each.

Ingredients	100 servings	.... servings
Celery, diced	12 ounces (¾ No. 56 dipper)	
Onions, chopped	12 ounces (¾ No. 56 dipper)	
Water, boiling	1½ gallons (6 No. 56 dippers)	
Milk, evaporated	19—14½-ounce cans	
Corn, cream style	3 No. 10 cans	
Salt	4 ounces (8 mess kit spoons)	
Sugar, granulated	½ ounce (1 mess kit spoon)	
Pepper		
Paprika	¼ ounce (1 mess kit spoon)	
Fat, melted	1 pound (½ No. 56 dipper)	
Flour, sifted	1 pound (1 No. 56 dipper)	
Worcestershire sauce	½ ounce (1 mess kit spoon)	

1. Combine celery, onions, and water.
2. Cover and heat to boiling point; reduce heat and simmer until tender.
3. Combine milk, corn, salt, sugar, pepper, and paprika; mix well.
4. Cover and heat to boiling; reduce heat and simmer about 30 minutes. Add to celery and onions.*
5. Mix melted fat and flour; stir until smooth. Add to hot soup; mix thoroughly. Heat to boiling point; reduce heat and simmer about 20 minutes or until slightly thick, stirring constantly.

*Mixture may be rubbed through a sieve if desired.

NO. 588. CREAM OF GREEN PEA SOUP

Yield : 6¼ gallons, 100 servings, approximately 1 cup each.

Ingredients	100 servings	.... servings
Beef stock	1½ gallons (6 No. 56 dippers)	
Water	1 gallon (4 No. 56 dippers)	
Peas, fresh shelled, canned or frozen	2½ gallons (10 No. 56 dippers)	
Milk, evaporated	24—14½-ounce cans	
Onions, chopped	10 ounces (¾ mess kit cup)	
Fat, melted	1 pound (½ No. 56 dipper)	
Flour, sifted	1 pound (1 No. 56 dipper)	
Salt	2½ ounces (5 mess kit spoons)	
Pepper	(⅙ mess kit spoon)	
Nutmeg	(⅙ mess kit spoon)	

1. Prepare beef stock. (See recipe No. 570.)

2. Add water and peas.

3. Cover and heat to boiling; reduce heat and simmer until peas are tender.

4. Rub all but 1 quart (1 No. 56 dipper) peas through sieve.

5. Add milk to puree; continue simmering 10 minutes.

6. Fry onions in melted fat. Add flour, salt, pepper, and nutmeg; stir until smooth.

7. Add onion mixture to hot soup; mix thoroughly. Heat to boiling point; reduce heat and simmer 20 minutes or until slightly thick, stirring constantly.

8. Add remaining quart (1 No. 56 dipper) green peas just before serving.

NO. 589. CREAM OF GREEN SPLIT PEA SOUP

Yield: 6¼ gallons,
100 servings, approximately 1 cup each.

Ingredients	100 servings	.... servings
Peas, split, green.............	8 pounds (4½ No. 56 dippers).......	....
Onions, sliced...............	12 ounces (1 mess kit cup)..........	....
Pork, salt, diced............	1½ pounds.......................	....
Water.....................	4¾ gallons (19 No. 56 dippers).......	....
Salt.......................	3 ounces (6 mess kit spoons)........	....
Pepper.....................		....
Nutmeg.....................		....
Milk, evaporated.............	21—14½-ounce cans...............	....
Fat, melted.................	1 pound (½ No. 56 dipper).........	....
Flour, sifted................	1 pound (1 No. 56 dipper).........	....

1. Wash peas; add onions and salt pork. Add enough water to cover peas; soak 5 hours or overnight.

2. Add remaining water. Cover and heat to boiling point; reduce heat and simmer about 45 minutes or until peas are soft.

3. Rub through sieve; reheat.

4. Add salt, pepper, nutmeg and milk; continue simmering 20 to 30 minutes.

5. Mix melted fat and flour together; stir until smooth. Add slowly to hot soup; mix thoroughly. Heat to boiling point; reduce heat and simmer 20 minutes or until soup is slightly thick, stirring constantly.

NO. 590. CREAM OF ONION SOUP Yield: 6¼ gallons, 100 servings, approximately 1 cup each.

Ingredients	100 servings	.... servings
Onions, thinly sliced.........	10 pounds (10 No. 56 dippers).......	....
Water, boiling...............	2 gallons (8 No. 56 dippers).........	....
Beef stock..................	2¾ gallons (11 No. 56 dippers).......	....
Milk, evaporated.............	8½—14½-ounce cans...............	....
Salt........................	3 ounces (6 mess kit spoons)........	....
Pepper.....................	....	....
Fat, melted.................	1 pound (½ No. 56 dipper).........	....
Flour, sifted................	1 pound (1 No. 56 dipper).........	....

1. Add onions to ½ gallon boiling water. Heat to boiling point; reduce heat and simmer about 30 minutes.*

2. Prepare beef stock. (See recipe No. 570.)

3. Combine beef stock, milk, remaining water, salt, and pepper; add to onions.

4. Mix melted fat and flour; stir until smooth. Add slowly to hot soup; mix thoroughly. Heat to boiling point; reduce heat and simmer 20 minutes or until soup is slightly thick, stirring constantly.

*Cooked onions may be rubbed through a sieve before combining with other ingredients.

NO. 591. CREAM OF TOMATO SOUP Yield: 6¼ gallons, 100 servings, approximately 1 cup each.

Ingredients	100 servings	.... servings
Tomatoes...................	6 No. 10 cans....................	....
Parsley....................	2 ounces (¼ mess kit cup).........	....
Pepper.....................	....	....
Cloves, ground.............	....	....
Onions, chopped............	6 ounces (½ mess kit cup).........	....
Salt.......................	1 ounce (2 mess kit spoons).......	....
Sugar, granulated...........	2 ounces (4 mess kit spoons).......	....
Fat, melted................	1 pound (½ No. 56 dipper)........	....
Flour, sifted...............	1 pound (1 No. 56 dipper)........	....
Milk, evaporated............	9—14½-ounce cans...............	....
Water (for milk)............	3½ quarts (3½ No. 56 dippers)......	....
Salt.......................	½ ounce (1 mess kit spoon)........	....
Pepper.....................	....	....

1. Combine tomatoes, parsley, pepper, cloves, onions, salt, and sugar; mix well.

2. Cover and heat to boiling point; reduce heat and simmer about 40 minutes.

3. Rub through sieve; reheat.

4. Mix ½ melted fat and ½ of flour; stir until smooth. Add to hot tomato mixture; mix thoroughly. Heat to boiling point; reduce heat and simmer about 20 minutes or until slightly thick, stirring constantly.

222

5. Mix milk and water; heat slowly to boiling point.

6. Mix remaining fat and remaining flour, salt, and pepper together; stir until smooth. Add to hot milk; mix thoroughly. Heat to boiling point; reduce heat and simmer about 20 minutes or until slightly thick, stirring constantly.

7. Add hot tomato mixture slowly to hot milk mixture, stirring constantly, just before serving. Serve without reheating. If soup must be held, keep in hot water bath.

NO. 592. VEGETABLE CREAM SOUP   Yield: 6¼ gallons, 100 servings, approximately 1 cup each.

Ingredients	100 servings	.... servings
Onions, chopped	4 ounces (¼ No. 56 dipper)	
Fat, melted	1½ pounds (¾ No. 56 dipper)	
Flour, sifted	12 ounces (¾ No. 56 dipper)	
Salt	2 ounces (4 mess kit spoons)	
Pepper		
Milk, evaporated	19—14½-ounce cans	
Water (for milk)	2 gallons (8 No. 56 dippers)	
Vegetables, cooked, chopped or pureed*.	2 gallons (8 No. 56 dippers)	

*Left-over peas, carrots, cabbage, or spinach may be used.

1. Fry onions slowly in melted fat about 10 minutes. Add flour, salt and pepper; stir until smooth.

2. Mix milk and water; heat. Add onion mixture slowly to hot milk; mix thoroughly. Heat to boiling point; reduce heat and simmer about 20 minutes or until soup is slightly thick, stirring constantly.

NO. 593. BEAN CHOWDER   Yield: 6¼ gallons, 100 servings, approximately 1 cup each.

Ingredients	100 servings	.... servings
Beans, navy, dry	7 pounds (4½ No. 56 dippers)	
Water	4¼ gallons (17 No. 56 dippers)	
Pork, salt, diced	3 pounds (2 No. 56 dippers)	
Potatoes, diced	4 pounds (2½ No. 56 dippers)	
Onions, chopped	12 ounces (¾ No. 56 dipper)	
Tomatoes	2 No. 10 cans	
Sugar, granulated	3 ounces (6 mess kit spoons)	
Molasses	5 ounces (7 mess kit spoons)	
Salt	1 ounce (2 mess kit spoons)	
Pepper	(⅓ mess kit spoon)	

1. Wash beans. Add enough water to cover beans; soak 6 to 8 hours or overnight.

2. Add remaining water and ½ the salt pork. Cover and heat to boiling point; reduce heat and simmer about 2 hours or until skins of beans begin to burst.

3. Add potatoes and continue simmering.
4. Fry remaining salt pork until crisp; remove from fat and drain.
5. Fry onions in pork fat until tender. Add tomatoes, sugar, molasses, salt, and pepper; mix well.
6. Cover and heat to boiling point; reduce heat and simmer about 20 minutes.
7. Add crisp pork cubes just before serving.

NO. 594. CORN CHOWDER WITH EGGS

Yield: 6¼ gallons,
100 servings, approximately 1 cup each.

Ingredients	100 servings	.... servings
Onions, sliced................	1 pound (1 No. 56 dipper)...........	....
Peppers, green, chopped......	½ pound (½ No. 56 dipper)........	....
Water, boiling..............	1¾ gallons (7 No. 56 dippers).......	....
Corn, cream style..........	3 No. 10 cans......................	....
Milk, evaporated............	14—14½-ounce cans.................	....
Salt......................	4 ounces (8 mess kit spoons)........	....
Pepper......................		....
Eggs, hard-cooked, slices......	18 eggs...........................	....
Parsley....................	1 ounce (8 mess kit spoons)........	....

1. Combine onions, green peppers and ½ gallon (2 No. 56 dippers) water.
2. Heat to boiling; reduce heat and simmer 1 hour.
3. Combine remaining water, corn, milk, salt, and pepper. Heat thoroughly and add to onions and peppers.
4. Cover and heat to boiling; reduce heat and simmer about 40 minutes.
5. Add egg slices and parsley just before serving.

NO. 595. CORN AND TOMATO CHOWDER

Yield: 6¼ gallons,
100 servings, approximately 1 cup each.

Ingredients	100 servings	.... servings
Milk, evaporated............	13—14½-ounce cans.................	....
Water (for milk)............	1½ gallons (6 No. 56 dippers).......	....
Salt......................	4 ounces (8 mess kit spoons)........	....
Sugar, granulated..........	1½ ounces (3 mess kit spoons).......	....
Pepper......................	(⅓ mess kit spoon)...............	....
Corn, cream style..........	2½ No. 10 cans....................	....
Onions, diced...............	11 ounces (1 mess kit cup).........	....
Tomatoes...................	2½ No. 10 cans....................	....

1. Combine milk, salt, sugar, pepper, corn, and onions; mix well.
2. Cover and heat to boiling point; reduce heat and simmer about 45 minutes.
3. Heat tomatoes to boiling point.
4. Mix corn mixture and tomatoes just before serving.

NO. 596. CLAM CHOWDER (BOSTON STYLE)

Yield: 6¼ gallons,
100 servings, approximately 1 cup each.

Ingredients	100 servings	.... servings
Celery, diced	2½ pounds (2½ No. 56 dippers)	
Onions, chopped	2½ pounds (2½ No. 56 dippers)	
Potatoes, cubed	3½ pounds (2¼ No. 56 dippers)	
Salt	2 ounces (4 mess kit spoons)	
Water, boiling	1¾ gallons (7 No. 56 dippers)	
Clams	8 pounds	
Water, boiling (for clams)		
Milk, evaporated	24—14½-ounce cans	
Salt	1½ ounces (3 mess kit spoons)	
Pepper	(⅓ mess kit spoon)	
Fat, melted	1 pound (½ No. 56 dipper)	
Flour, sifted	1 pound (1 No. 56 dipper)	

1. Combine celery, onions, potatoes, salt and boiling water.

2. Cover and heat to boiling point; reduce heat and simmer about 1 hour or until vegetables are tender.

3. Scrub clams with brush; wash under running water to remove salt; cover with boiling water. Cover and heat to boiling; reduce heat and simmer about 12 to 15 minutes or until shells open.

4. Remove from shells; drain. Strain clam liquor through cheesecloth. Measure and reserve 3 quarts (3 No. 56 dippers) liquid. Chop clams.

5. Combine vegetable mixture, chopped clams, the 3 quarts (3 No. 56 dippers) clam liquor, milk, salt, and pepper. Heat slowly to boiling point.

6. Mix melted fat and flour; stir until smooth. Add slowly to hot soup; mix thoroughly. Heat to boiling; reduce heat and simmer about 15 minutes or until soup is slightly thick, stirring constantly.

NO. 597. NEW ENGLAND CLAM CHOWDER

Yield: 100 servings,
approximately 9 ounces or 1 cup each.

Ingredients	100 servings	.... servings
Bacon or salt pork, diced	2 pounds	
Onions, diced	2 pounds (2 No. 56 dippers)	
Potatoes, diced	6 pounds (5 No. 56 dippers)	
Water	4 quarts (4 No. 56 dippers)	
Salt	2 ounces (4 mess kit spoons)	
Clams, diced	3 gallons	
Pepper	¼ ounce (1 mess kit spoon)	
Milk	2 gallons (8 No. 56 dippers)	
Flour	8 ounces (¾ mess kit cup)	
Butter	8 ounces (⅓ mess kit cup)	
Parsley, chopped		

225

1. Fry bacon until crisp and brown.
2. Add onions and cook until tender.
3. Cook potatoes in salted water for 10 minutes.
4. Add bacon, onions, clams, and pepper to potatoes and simmer for 30 minutes.
5. Heat the milk and thicken slightly with flour.
6. Just before serving, add hot milk and butter and simmer 5 minutes longer.
7. Sprinkle finely chopped parsley on top and serve with crackers.

NO. 598. MANHATTAN CLAM CHOWDER

Yield: 100 servings,
approximately 9 ounces or
1 cup each.

Ingredients	100 servings	.... servings
Bacon or salt pork, diced.....	2 pounds..................	....
Onions, diced................	2 pounds (2 No. 56 dippers).........	....
Celery, diced................	2 pounds (2 No. 56 dippers).........	....
Potatoes, diced..............	6 pounds (5 No. 56 dippers).........	....
Water......................	4 quarts (4 No. 56 dippers).........	....
Salt.......................	2 ounces (4 mess kit spoons)........	....
Clams, diced...............	3 gallons................	....
Pepper.....................	¼ ounce (1 mess kit spoon)......	....
Tomatoes, strained...........	2 No. 10 cans.............	....
Butter.....................	8 ounces (⅓ mess kit cup)..........	....
Parsley, chopped...........		

1. Fry bacon until crisp and brown.
2. Add onions and celery and fry until tender.
3. Cook potatoes in salted water for 10 minutes.
4. Add bacon, onions, celery, tomatoes, clams, and pepper to potatoes and simmer for 30 minutes.
5. Just before serving add the butter and simmer 5 minutes longer.
6. Sprinkle finely chopped parsley over the top and serve with crackers.

NO. 599. FISH CHOWDER

Yield: 6¼ gallons,
100 servings, approximately 1 cup each.

Ingredients	100 servings	.... servings
Pork, salt, diced.............	1½ pounds (1 No. 56 dipper).......	....
Onions, sliced................	2 pounds (2 No. 56 dippers)........	....
Potatoes, sliced..............	6½ pounds (4 No. 56 dippers).......	....
Water, boiling...............	1¾ gallons (7 No. 56 dippers)......	....
Haddock, cleaned, boned*.....	15 pounds..................	....
Salt.......................	4 ounces (8 mess kit spoons)........	....
Pepper.....................		
Milk, evaporated.............	19—14½-ounce cans...............	....
Water (for milk).............	¾ gallon (3 No. 56 dippers)........	....

*Any similar fish may be used.

1. Fry salt pork until crisp; remove from fat and drain.
2. Fry onions slowly in pork fat until light brown. Add potatoes and water.
3. Cover and heat to boiling point; reduce heat and simmer about 10 minutes.
4. Add fish and continue simmering until fish can be easily separated into large pieces with a fork.
5. Add milk, water, salt and pepper to fish; mix well.
6. Heat to boiling point; reduce heat and simmer about 15 minutes.

NO. 600. OYSTER STEW   Yield: 6¼ gallons, 100 servings, approximately 1 cup each.

Ingredients	100 servings	.... servings
Oysters, washed and drained...	5 quarts (5 No. 56 dippers).........	....
Fat, melted.................	1¼ pounds (¾ mess kit cup)........	....
Milk, evaporated.............	22—14½-ounce cans..................	....
Water (for milk).............	2½ gallons (10 No. 56 dippers).......	....
Salt......................	4 ounces (8 mess kit spoons).........	....
Pepper....................	(¼ mess kit spoon).................	....
Worcestershire sauce........	(⅔ mess kit spoon).................	....

1. Fry oysters in melted fat until edges curl.
2. Mix milk and water; heat.
3. Combine oysters, hot milk, salt, pepper, and Worcestershire sauce; mix well.
4. Serve immediately.

SECTION XIX

VEGETABLES

29. FRESH VEGETABLES. a. Potatoes, carrots, beets and other vegetables with the edible portion grown underground are prepared for cooking by cleaning and paring before cooking or peeling after cooking. They are most often cooked in boiling salted water. Use ½ ounce (1 mess kit spoon) salt to each gallon of water.

b. Asparagus, cauliflower, greens, and other vegetables with the edible portion grown above the ground are usually delicate and need careful handling to prevent breaking and bruising. They are most often cooked in a minimum amount of boiling salted water.

c. Cook vegetables until tender but not soft. The time of cooking depends on the size and age of the vegetable. Vegetables may be served with butter or a sauce to add flavor and variety. For buttered vegetables use 1 pound (½ No. 56 dipper) butter to 20 to 25 pounds vegetables. Drain immediately after cooking and add the butter while still hot.

30. FROZEN VEGETABLES. a. Time table for cooking.

Vegetable	Issue for 100 servings (pounds)	Boiling salted water (gallons)	Cooking time (minutes)
Asparagus	20	2	6–9
Broccoli	17½	to cover	5–7
Brussel Sprouts	20	to cover	½
Cauliflower	17½	to cover	3–5
Corn	20	1	½
Beans, green	20	2	8–13
Beans, lima	20	2	10–13
Peas	20	2	4–6
Spinach	17½	2	4–6
Beans, wax	20	2	8–13

b. Directions for cooking. (1) Remove vegetables from carton; cut large frozen blocks into quarters to reduce time required for defrosting and cooking.

(2) All vegetables except spinach and corn on the cob may be cooked without defrosting. Keep spinach at room temperature 4 to 6 hours before cooking. Cook corn on the cob only until heated through. Long cooking will soften the cob, thus making it soggy.

(3) Place vegetables in small amount of boiling water. Stir while thawing to separate the particles.

(4) Allow 20 to 30 minutes for water to again reach boiling point after vegetables are added. Count the cooking time from the moment the water reaches the boiling point after the addition of the vegetables.

(5) Cook until tender; avoid overcooking.

(6) Drain vegetables if necessary. Add butter, salt, and pepper.

NO. 601. SCALLOPED ASPARAGUS   Yield: 100 servings, 2 to 3 ounces each.

Ingredients	100 servings	.... servings
Asparagus stalks.............	35 pounds*........................	....
Salt......................		....
Water, boiling.............		
Bread crumbs, coarse........	2 pounds......................	....
Onions, chopped (optional)....	6 ounces (½ No. 56 dipper).........	....
Salt......................	1¼ ounces (2½ mess kit spoons).....	....
Pepper....................		....
Milk, evaporated.............	4—14½-ounce cans............	....

*Three to four No. 10 cans asparagus may be substituted for the 35 pounds fresh aspara-
gus. Heat asparagus in liquid from the can.

1. Remove and discard the tough lower ends of the asparagus stalks. Wash remainder of stalks thoroughly.

2. Stand stalks upright in deep kettle. Add boiling salted water. Cover and heat to boiling point; reduce heat and simmer about 20 minutes or until tender. Drain.

3. Combine bread crumbs, butter, onions, salt, and pepper.

4. Spread ½ crumb mixture on bottom of well-greased baking pans.

5. Place asparagus on crumbs.

6. Mix milk and 1 quart (1 No. 56 dipper) asparagus liquid; pour over asparagus.

7. Cover with remaining crumbs.

8. Bake in moderate oven (375° F.) until thoroughly heated and crumbs are brown.

Note. Fresh asparagus may be cut into 1-inch pieces before cooking. Cook the tougher parts first and add the tender tips the last 15 minutes of cooking. Use asparagus liquid in soups.

No. 602. ASPARAGUS AND CHEESE

Yield: 100 servings, approximately ½ cup asparagus over 1 slice toast per serving.

Ingredients	100 servings	.... servings
Asparagus..................	35 pounds*........................	....
Salt......................		....
Water, boiling.............		....
Butter, melted.............	8 ounces (¼ No. 56 dipper).........	
Flour, sifted.............	6 ounces (½ No. 56 dipper).........	
Salt......................	2 ounces (4 mess kit spoons)........	
Pepper....................		
Mustard, dry.............		
Milk, evaporated.............	6—14½-ounce cans............	
Cheese, chopped.............	2 pounds (2 No. 56 dippers).........	
Bread, toasted.............	100 slices........................	

*Three to four No. 10 cans asparagus may be substituted for the 35 pounds fresh asparagus.

230

1. Remove and discard the tough lower ends of the asparagus stalks. Wash remainder of stalks thoroughly.

2. Stand stalks upright in deep kettle. Add boiling salted water. Cover and heat to boiling point; reduce heat and simmer about 20 minutes or until tender. Drain.

3. Heat 2 quarts (2 No. 56 dippers) asparagus liquid to boiling point.

4. Mix melted butter, flour, salt, pepper, and mustard together. Add hot liquid; stir until smooth. Heat to boiling point; boil 2 minutes or until thick, stirring constantly. Add milk; reheat to boiling point. Remove from heat.

5. Add cheese; stir until cheese is melted.

6. Add asparagus and heat. Serve on toast.

Note. Fresh asparagus may be broken into 1-inch pieces before cooking. Cook the tougher parts first and add the tender tips the last 15 minutes of cooking. Use any remaining asparagus liquid in soups.

NO. 603. ASPARAGUS AND BACON WITH CHEESE SAUCE

Place a slice of crisp fried bacon on top of each serving of asparagus in recipe for asparagus with cheese sauce.

NO. 604. BAKED BEANS AND TOMATOES

Yield: 100 servings, approximately 1 cup each.

Ingredients	100 servings	.... servings
Beans, navy	16 pounds (9 No. 56 dippers)	
Water, cold	4 to 5 gals. (16 to 20 No. 56 dippers)	
Salt		
Onions, quartered	2 pounds (2 No. 56 dippers)	
Molasses	¾ pint (½ mess kit cup)	
Sugar, brown	8 ounces (½ mess kit cup)	
Mustard, dry	¼ ounce (1 mess kit spoon)	
Paprika		
Salt	6 ounces (12 mess kit spoons)	
Vinegar	2 ounces (4 mess kit spoons)	
Tomato catsup or puree	2 quarts (2 No. 56 dippers)	
Pork, salt, sliced	4 pounds	
Water, hot		

1. Wash beans thoroughly. Cover with cold water; soak 6 to 8 hours.

2. Add salt. Cover and heat to boiling point; reduce heat and simmer until tender but not split or mushy. Drain.

3. Combine beans, onions, molasses, sugar, mustard, paprika, salt, vinegar and catsup or puree; mix well.

4. Arrange alternate layers of salt pork and bean mixture in baking pans, starting with pork and finishing with bean mixture.

5. Bake in slow oven (300° F.) 3 to 4 hours, adding hot water as needed.

NO. 605. BOSTON BAKED BEANS   Yield: 100 servings, approximately 1 cup each.

Ingredients	100 servings	.... servings
Beans, navy.................	16 pounds (9 No. 56 dippers)........	....
Water, cold.................	4 to 5 gals. (16 to 20 No. 56 dippers)..	....
Salt........................	....	....
Onions, quartered...........	1½ pounds (2 No. 56 dippers).......	....
Sugar, granulated...........	1 pound (½ No. 56 dipper).........	....
Salt.......................	6 ounces (12 mess kit spoons)........	....
Molasses...................	1½ quarts (1½ No. 56 dippers)......	....
Pork, salt, sliced............	6 pounds.............................	....
Water, boiling..............		

1. Wash beans thoroughly. Cover with cold water; soak 6 to 8 hours.

2. Add salt. Cover and heat to boiling point; reduce heat and simmer until beans are tender but not split or mushy. Drain.

3. Combine beans, onions, sugar, salt, and molasses; mix well.

4. Place alternate layers of salt pork and beans in baking pans, beginning and ending with salt pork. Cover pans.

5. Bake in slow oven (300° F.) at least 6 hours or as long as possible. Add boiling water as needed during baking.

NO. 606. BAKED BEANS AND HAM
Substitute 6 pounds diced smoked ham for salt pork in recipe for Boston baked beans.

NO. 607. BAKED BEANS (CANNED) AND BACON
Yield: 100 servings, approximately ⅔ cup each.

Ingredients	100 servings	.... servings
Beans, baked, plain..........	4 No. 10 cans.......................	....
Onions, chopped.............	1½ pounds (1½ No. 56 dippers).....	....
Catsup (optional)............	1 quart (1 No. 56 dipper)...........	....
Bacon, sliced................	1 pound.............................	....

1. Combine baked beans, onions and catsup; pour into baking pans.

2. Cut bacon into 2-inch pieces; place on top of beans.

3. Bake in moderate oven (375° F.) about 40 minutes or until bacon is crisp.

Note. Beans may be heated on top of stove. Fry bacon and onions; add to beans Stir occasionally.

NO. 608. SPANISH STYLE KIDNEY BEANS

Yield: 100 servings, approximately 1 cup each.

Ingredients	100 servings	.... servings
Beans, kidney...............	15 pounds (9½ No. 56 dippers)......	....
Water, cold.................	3¼ gallons (13 No. 56 dippers).......	....
Salt........................	....	....
Onions, chopped............	2½ pounds (2½ No. 56 dippers).....	....
Peppers, green, chopped	1½ pounds (1½ No. 56 dippers).....	....
Tomato puree...............	1 No. 10 can......................	....
Meat stock.................	1 quart (1 No. 56 dipper)..........	....
Pork, salt, diced...........	2¼ pounds........................	....
Salt......................	4 ounces (8 mess kit spoons)........	....
Pepper....................	....	....
Paprika...................	....	....

1. Wash beans thoroughly. Cover with·cold water; soak 3 to 4 hours.

2. Add salt. Cover and heat to boiling point; reduce heat and simmer until tender but not split or mushy.

3. Combine remaining ingredients. Add to beans; mix well.

4. Pour into well-greased baking pans.

5. Bake in moderate oven (350° F.) 1½ to 2 hours.

Note. Add hot water during baking if necessary.

NO. 609. KIDNEY BEANS AND CHILI

Yield: 100 servings, approximately 1 cup each.

Ingredients	100 servings	.... servings
Beans, kidney...............	9 pounds (5¾ No. 56 dippers)......	....
Water, cold.................	2 gallons (8 No. 56 dippers).........	....
Salt........................	....	....
Meat, cooked or raw, chopped.	15 pounds........................	....
Onions, chopped............	4 pounds (4 No. 56 dippers)........	....
Peppers, green, chopped.......	6 pounds (6 No. 56 dippers)........	....
Beef fat...................	12 ounces (½ mess kit cup).........	....
Tomatoes..................	1 No. 10 can......................	....
Chili powder*..............	3¾ ounces (15 mess kit spoons)......	....
Salt......................	....	....

*The amount of chili powder may be reduced if desired.

1. Wash beans thoroughly. Cover with cold water; soak 3 to 4 hours.

2. Add salt. Cover and heat to boiling point; reduce heat and simmer until half cooked.

3. Combine meat, onions and peppers; fry in beef fat.

4. Add beans and tomatoes; continue cooking until beans are tender.

5. Add chili powder and salt.

NO. 610. SIMMERED BEANS (lima, kidney or navy)
Yield: 100 servings, approximately 1 cup each.

Ingredients	100 servings	.... servings
Beans, lima, kidney or navy...	14 pounds................................	....
Water, cold.................	3 gallons (12 No. 56 dippers).........	....
Salt......................		....
Bacon.....................	1¾ pounds..............................	....
Onions, chopped............	1¾ pounds (1¾ No. 56 dippers).....	....
Tomatoes..................	1 No. 10 can...........................	....
Sugar, granulated...........	3 ounces (6 mess kit spoons).........	....
Salt......................	3¾ ounces (7½ mess kit spoons).....	....
Pepper....................	(½ mess kit spoon)....................	....

1. Wash beans thoroughly. Cover with cold water; soak kidney or lima beans 3 to 4 hours or navy beans 6 to 8 hours.
2. Add salt. Cover and heat to boiling point; reduce heat and simmer until tender but not split or mushy.
3. Fry bacon and onions together.
4. Add tomatoes, sugar, salt, and pepper; mix well.
5. Add tomato and bacon mixture to beans. Heat to boiling point; reduce heat and simmer about 30 minutes.

Note. Beans may be cooked in ham stock instead of water. Add ham bones and cook until beans are tender but not split or mushy. Remove bones.

NO. 611. CHEESE BEAN ROAST
Yield: 100 servings, 6 ounces each.

Ingredients	100 servings	.... servings
Beans, kidney, dry..........	7½ pounds (4¾ No. 56 dippers).....	....
Water.....................		....
Cheese, cheddar.............	12½ pounds............................	....
Onions, chopped............	1½ pounds (1½ No. 56 dippers)......	....
Fat, melted (for frying).......	12 ounces (½ mess kit cup)..........	....
Eggs, beaten...............	50 eggs (2½ No. 56 dippers).........	....
Salt......................	1½ ounces (3 mess kit spoons).......	....
Pepper....................	¼ ounce (1 mess kit spoon).........	....
Paprika....................		....
Bread crumbs, soft..........	2½ pounds.............................	....
Tomato sauce...............	2 gallons (8 No. 56 dippers).........	....

1. Wash beans. Cover with water; soak 4 hours.
2. Cover and heat to boiling point; reduce heat and simmer until tender. Drain.
3. Grind cooked beans and cheese together.
4. Fry onions until tender.
5. Combine bean mixture, onions, beaten egg, salt, pepper and paprika; mix well. Add bread crumbs; mix lightly.
6. Place in greased baking pans. Bake in moderate oven (350° F.) 40 to 50 minutes or until set.
7. Prepare tomato sauce. (See recipe No. 559.)
8. Cut roast into squares; serve with tomato sauce.

NO. 612. BAKED LIMA BEANS

Yield: 100 servings, approximately 1 cup each.

Ingredients	100 servings	.... servings
Beans, lima, dry	15 pounds (9 No. 56 dippers)	
Water, cold	2½ gallons (10 No. 56 dippers)	
Salt		
Bacon, diced	2 pounds	
Onions, chopped	2 pounds (2 No. 56 dippers)	
Peppers, green, chopped	1 pound (1 No. 56 dipper)	
Pimientos, chopped	8 ounces (⅓ mess kit cup)	
Molasses	1 pint (½ No. 56 dipper)	
Salt	4½ ounces (9 mess kit spoons)	
Pepper	(½ mess kit spoon)	
Mustard, prepared	(3¾ mess kit spoons)	

1. Wash beans thoroughly. Cover with cold water; soak 3 to 4 hours.
2. Add salt. Cover and heat to boiling point; reduce heat and simmer until tender but not split or mushy.
3. Combine bacon, onions, green peppers and pimientos; fry until tender.
4. Combine beans, onion and bacon mixture, molasses, salt, pepper and mustard.
5. Pour mixture into well-greased baking pans. Bake in moderate oven (350° F.) 1½ hours.

   Note. Add more water during baking if necessary.

NO. 613. CREOLE LIMA BEANS

Yield: 100 servings, approximately 1 cup each.

Ingredients	100 servings	.... servings
Beans, lima, dry	15 pounds	
Water, cold	2½ gallons (10 No. 56 dippers)	
Onions, quartered	12 ounces	
Salt	4½ ounces (9 mess kit spoons)	
Bacon, diced	3 pounds	
Meat stock	3 quarts (3 No. 56 dippers)	
Tomatoes	2 No. 10 cans	
Flour, sifted	1½ pounds (1½ No. 56 dippers)	
Bacon fat, melted	1½ pounds (¾ No. 56 dipper)	
Sugar, granulated	6 ounces (12 mess kit spoons)	
Pepper		
Chili sauce	1½ pints (¾ No. 56 dipper)	

1. Wash beans thoroughly. Cover with cold water; soak 3 to 4 hours.
2. Add onions. Cover and heat to boiling point; reduce heat and simmer until beans are tender but not split or mushy.
3. Fry bacon; drain. Add bacon to beans.
4. Mix stock and tomatoes; heat.
5. Mix flour and melted bacon fat. Add small amount of tomato mixture; stir until smooth. Add gradually to remaining tomato mixture. Heat to boiling point; boil 2 minutes, stirring constantly.
6. Add sugar, pepper, and chili sauce; mix well.
7. Place beans in baking pans. Pour tomato mixture over beans.
8. Bake in moderate oven (350° F.) 40 minutes to 1 hour.

NO. 614. LIMA BEANS AND BACON   Yield: 100 servings, approximately ½ cup each.

Ingredients	100 servings	.... servings
Beans, lima, dry	15 pounds (9 No. 56 dippers)	
Water, cold		
Salt		
Bacon	2 pounds	
Salt	¼ ounce (½ mess kit spoon)	
Pepper	(¼ mess kit spoon)	

1. Wash beans thoroughly. Cover with cold water; soak 3 to 4 hours.

2. Add salt. Cover and heat to boiling point; reduce heat and simmer until tender but not split or mushy. Drain.

3. Add bacon to hot liquid; heat to boiling point; simmer about 20 minutes.

4. Add beans, salt and pepper; continue simmering about 15 minutes or until heated through.

NO. 615. GREEN BEANS AND BACON   Yield: 100 servings, approximately ½ cup each.

Ingredients	100 servings	.... servings
Beans, green	25 pounds* (20 No. 56 dippers)	
Meat stock, boiling	1½ gallons (6 No. 56 dippers)	
Bacon rind or ham hocks	1 pound	
Bacon, diced	12 ounces	
Butter	8 ounces (¼ No. 56 dipper)	
Salt		
Pepper		

*Three to four No. 10 cans green beans may be substituted for the 25 pounds fresh green beans. Omit ham hocks.

1. Wash beans and remove ends. Cut into pieces or leave whole. Add boiling stock and bacon rind or ham hocks.

2. Heat to boiling point; reduce heat and simmer about 30 minutes or until beans are tender.

3. Remove bacon rinds or ham hocks. If ham hocks are used, remove meat from bones and return to stock.

4. Fry bacon. Combine bacon, bacon fat, butter, salt, pepper and cooked beans; mix well.

NO. 616. GREEN BEANS AND TOMATOES

Yield: 100 servings, approximately 1 cup each.

Ingredients	100 servings	.... servings
Beans, green..............	17 pounds........................	....
Salt......................	....	....
Water, boiling............	....	....
Bacon, sliced.............	1 pound........................	....
Onions, chopped..........	12 ounces (¾ No. 56 dipper)........	....
Peppers, green, chopped (optional).	6 ounces (½ No. 56 dipper).........	....
Flour, sifted.............	8 ounces (½ No. 56 dipper).........	....
Tomatoes.................	1 No. 10 can....................	....
Salt......................	1 ounce (2 mess kit spoons)........	....
Pepper...................	(¼ mess kit spoon)...............	....
Sugar, granulated (optional)...	2 ounces (4 mess kit spoons).......	....

1. Wash beans and remove ends. Cut into pieces. Add boiling salted water.
2. Heat to boiling point; reduce heat and simmer about 30 minutes or until tender. Drain; reserve liquid.
3. Cut bacon into ½-inch pieces: add onions and green peppers. Fry until bacon becomes slightly brown.
4. Mix flour and 1 quart (1 No. 56 dipper) bean liquid; stir until smooth. Heat to boiling point; boil 2 minutes, stirring constantly. Add to bacon mixture; mix well.
5. Add tomatoes, salt, pepper, sugar and cooked beans. Heat to boiling point; reduce heat and simmer about 15 minutes.

NO. 617. SAVORY GREEN BEANS

Yield: 100 servings, approximately ½ cup each.

Ingredients	100 servings	.... servings
Beans, green..............	25 pounds*......................	....
Salt......................	....	....
Water, boiling............	....	....
Onions, chopped...........	1¾ pounds (1¾ No. 56 dippers).....	....
Bacon fat, melted..........	8 ounces (¼ No. 56 dipper)........	....
Cloves, whole.............	....	....
Sugar, granulated..........	3 ounces (6 mess kit spoons)........	....
Salt......................	1½ ounces (3 mess kit spoons)......	....
Pepper...................	....	....
Tomatoes.................	1 No. 10 can....................	....

*Three No. 10 cans green beans may be substituted for the fresh green beans.

1. Wash beans and remove ends. Cut into pieces or leave whole. Add boiling salted water.
2. Heat to boiling point; reduce heat and simmer about 30 minutes or until tender. Drain.
3. Fry onions in bacon fat.
4. Tie cloves in cheesecloth. Combine cloves, sugar, cooked onions, salt, pepper and tomatoes. Heat to boiling point. Remove bag with cloves.
5. Combine beans and tomato mixture just before serving.

NO. 618. CREAMED BEANS AND CELERY

Yield: 100 servings, approximately ½ cup each.

Ingredients	100 servings	.... servings
Beans, green	20 pounds*	
Salt		
Water, boiling		
Celery	5 pounds	
Salt		
Water, boiling		
White sauce, hot	5½ quarts (5½ No. 56 dippers)	

*Three No. 10 cans green beans may be substituted for the 20 pounds fresh green beans. Heat beans before draining.

1. Wash beans and remove ends. Cut beans into pieces. Add boiling salted water.
2. Cover and heat to boiling point; reduce heat and simmer about 30 minutes or until tender. Drain; reserve liquid.
3. Scrub celery; dice, and cover with boiling salted water.
4. Cover and heat to boiling point; reduce heat and simmer about 10 to 15 minutes or until tender. Drain; reserve liquid.
5. Mix beans and celery.
6. Prepare white sauce (recipe No. 548) using liquids drained from beans and celery.
7. Pour white sauce over vegetables just before serving.

Note. Diced pimientos or chopped, fried bacon or ham may be added to the white sauce for variety.

NO. 619. LYONNAISE WAX BEANS

Yield: 100 servings, approximately ½ cup each.

Ingredients	100 servings	servings
Beans, wax	33 pounds*	
Salt		
Water, boiling		
Onions, chopped	12 ounces (¾ No. 56 dipper)	
Bacon fat, melted	12 ounces (½ mess kit cup)	
Salt	1½ ounces (3 mess kit spoons)	
Pepper		
Parsley, chopped	1 ounce (5 mess kit spoons)	
Lemon juice	⅛ pint (¼ mess kit cup)	

*Four No. 10 cans wax beans may be substituted for the 33 pounds fresh beans.

1. Wash beans and remove ends. Cut into pieces. Add boiling salted water.
2. Heat to boiling point; reduce heat and simmer about 30 minutes or until tender.
3. Drain all but 2 quarts (2 No. 56 dippers) water from beans.
4. Fry onions in bacon fat until tender but not brown.
5. Combine beans and onion mixture; add salt and pepper. Heat to boiling point; reduce heat and simmer 15 minutes.
6. Add parsley and lemon juice.

NO. 620. DICED BEETS AND BACON
Yield: 100 servings, approximately ¼ cup each.

Ingredients	100 servings	.... servings
Beets	25 pounds	
Water, boiling		
Bacon, sliced, chopped	2 pounds	

1. Remove beet tops about 3 inches from the beets, leaving tap root attached. Wash beets thoroughly without breaking the skin. If the skin is broken, juice will escape from the beets while cooking.

2. Add boiling water to beets. Heat to boiling point; reduce heat and simmer 30 to 35 minutes or until tender. Drain; reserve liquid.

3. Cool and remove stems and skins with fingers; slice.

4. Fry bacon crisp. Add beets and heat through.

5. Add salt and pepper; mix well.

Note. A little vinegar may be added if desired.

NO. 621. HARVARD BEETS
Yield: 100 servings, approximately ¼ cup each.

Ingredients	100 servings	.... servings
Beets	20 pounds*	
Water, boiling		
Sugar, granulated	1 pound (½ No. 56 dipper)	
Salt	1 ounce (2 mess kit spoons)	
Cornstarch	5 ounces (⅓ mess kit cup)	
Vinegar	1½ pints (¾ No. 56 dipper)	
Butter	4 ounces (8 mess kit spoons)	

*Three No. 10 cans beets may be substituted for the 20 pounds fresh beets.

1. Remove beet tops about 3 inches from the beets, leaving tap root attached. Wash beets thoroughly without breaking the skin. If the skin is broken, juice will escape from the beets while cooking.

2. Add boiling water to beets. Cover and heat to boiling point; reduce heat and simmer about 30 to 35 minutes or until tender. Drain; reserve liquid.

3. Cool and remove stems and skins with fingers. Slice.

4. Heat 3 quarts (3 No. 56 dippers) beet liquid to boiling point.

5. Combine sugar, salt, cornstarch and a small amount of cold beet liquid; stir until smooth. Add to boiling liquid; boil 2 minutes, stirring constantly.

6. Add vinegar, butter and beets. Reheat to boiling point; reduce heat and simmer 10 minutes, stirring frequently to prevent scorching. Allow to stand 10 minutes.

NO. 622. HOT SPICED BEETS

Yield: 100 servings, approximately ½ cup each.

Ingredients	100 servings	.... servings
Beets	20 pounds*	
Water, boiling		
Vinegar	1½ quarts (1½ No. 56 dippers)	
Sugar, granulated	1½ pounds (¾ No. 56 dipper)	
Salt	½ ounce (1 mess kit spoon)	
Pepper		
Cinnamon, stick	10—2½-inch sticks	
Cloves, whole	¼ ounce (1 mess kit spoon)	
Allspice, whole	¼ ounce (1 mess kit spoon)	
Onions, sliced (optional)	1 onion	
Cornstarch	1½ ounces (5 mess kit spoons)	

*Three No. 10 cans beets may be substituted for the 20 pounds fresh beets.

1. Remove beet tops about 3 inches from the beets, leaving tap root attached. Wash beets thoroughly without breaking the skin. If the skin is broken, juice will escape from the beets while cooking.

2. Add boiling water to beets. Heat to boiling point; reduce heat and simmer about 30 to 35 minutes or until tender. Drain; reserve liquid.

3. Cool and remove stems and skins with fingers; slice.

4. Combine vinegar, sugar, salt, pepper and all but ¾ pint (½ mess kit cup) beet liquid.

5. Tie spices and onion in cheesecloth; add to vinegar mixture. Heat to boiling point; reduce heat and simmer 15 minutes. Remove from heat; allow to stand 1 hour.

6. Mix cornstarch with the ¾ pint (½ mess kit cup) cold beet liquid; stir until smooth.

7. Reheat vinegar mixture to boiling point; remove spice bag. Add cornstarch mixture. Heat to boiling point; boil 2 minutes, stirring constantly.

8. Reduce heat; add beets and simmer about 10 minutes.

NO. 623. COLD SPICED BEETS

Prepare recipe for hot spiced beets, omitting cornstarch. Allow beets to chill overnight in liquid before serving.

NO. 624. BROCCOLI AU GRATIN

Yield: 100 servings, approximately ½ cup each.

Ingredients	100 servings	.... servings
Broccoli	35 pounds	
Salt		
Water, boiling		
Cheese sauce	1 gallon (4 No. 56 dippers)	
Butter, melted	6 ounces (¼ No. 56 dipper)	
Bread crumbs	1 quart (1 No. 56 dipper)	
Cheese, finely chopped	6 ounces (¼ No. 56 dipper)	

1. Wash broccoli by plunging heads up and down in cold water; soak in salted water about 30 minutes. Drain. Remove leaves and woody peeling from stalks.
2. Separate heads and stalks. Cut stalks into several pieces lengthwise; leave heads whole.
3. Place heads and stalks in separate cooking utensils. Add boiling salted water to each. Heat each to boiling point; reduce heat and simmer. Simmer heads 10 to 15 minutes. The stalks require a little longer cooking period. Drain.
4. Place broccoli in baking pans.
5. Prepare cheese sauce (recipe No. 547); pour over broccoli.
6. Pour melted butter over bread crumbs; cover broccoli with buttered crumbs and chopped cheese.
7. Bake in moderate oven (350° F.) about 15 minutes or until crumbs are brown.

NO. 625. BROCCOLI WITH HOLLANDAISE SAUCE

Pour hollandaise sauce (recipe No. 549) over broccoli in recipe for broccoli au gratin just before serving.

NO. 626. CABBAGE FRIED
Yield: 100 servings, 3 ounces each.

Ingredients	100 servings	.... servings
Cabbage	30 pounds	
Fat or drippings	4 pounds (2 No. 56 dippers)	
Salt	3 ounces (6 mess kit spoons)	

1. Remove and discard outside leaves and center core of cabbage.
2. Dice fine or shred.
3. Place in bakepan with drippings and salt. Cook on top of range about 20 to 30 minutes.
   Note. Stir frequently to avoid scorching.

NO. 627. CABBAGE AND BACON
Yield: 100 servings, approximately ½ cup each.

Ingredients	100 servings	.... servings
Cabbage	25 pounds	
Salt		
Water, boiling		
Bacon, diced	8 ounces	
White sauce	1 gallon (4 No. 56 dippers)	

1. Remove and discard outside leaves of cabbage; cut heads into quarters. Shred. Discard center core.
2. Add small amount of boiling salted water. Heat to boiling point; reduce heat and simmer, uncovered, about 10 to 20 minutes or until just tender. Drain; reserve liquid.

3. Fry bacon; drain.

4. Prepare white sauce (recipe No. 548) using bacon fat and cabbage liquid; add diced bacon.

5. Pour white sauce over cabbage just before serving.

Note. White sauce may be omitted. Add bacon, salt and pepper to cabbage and serve.

NO. 628. HOT CABBAGE SLAW   Yield: 100 servings, approximately ½ cup each.

Ingredients	100 servings	.... servings
Cabbage	25 pounds	
Bacon, diced	1½ pounds	
Water	1½ quarts (1½ No. 56 dippers)	
Vinegar	1½ quarts (1½ No. 56 dippers)	
Sugar, granulated	1 pound (½ No. 56 dipper)	
Salt	3 ounces (6 mess kit spoons)	

1. Remove and discard outside leaves of cabbage; cut heads into quarters. Shred. Discard center core.

2. Fry bacon. Drain. Add to cabbage.

3. Mix water and vinegar; heat to boiling. Add sugar, salt and bacon fat.

4. Pour sauce over cabbage about 10 minutes before serving.

Note. If old cabbage is used, cook in boiling water 5 to 10 minutes. Drain well before adding sauce.

NO. 629. CARROTS A LA KING   Yield: 100 servings, approximately ½ cup each.

Ingredients	100 servings	.... servings
Carrots	25 pounds*	
Salt		
Water, boiling		
Onions, chopped	1½ ounces (5½ mess kit spoons)	
Butter, melted	6 ounces (¼ No. 56 dipper)	
Sugar, granulated	2½ ounces (5 mess kit spoons)	
Salt	2½ ounces (5 mess kit spoons)	
Pepper		
White sauce	1½ gallons (6 No. 56 dippers)	
Pimientos, chopped	6 ounces (1 mess kit cup)	
Peppers, green, chopped	12 ounces (¾ No. 56 dipper)	

*Three No. 10 cans carrots may be substituted for the 25 pounds fresh carrots. Heat before draining.

1. Scrub carrots thoroughly and scrape to remove outer layer of skin.

2. Slice and add boiling salted water. Cover and heat to boiling point; reduce heat and simmer 10 to 15 minutes or until just tender.

3. Fry onions in melted butter until tender but not brown.

4. Combine carrots, sugar, salt, and pepper; mix well.

5. Prepare white sauce (recipe No. 548); add onions, pimientos and green peppers.

6. Pour sauce over carrots just before serving.

NO. 630. FRENCH FRIED CARROTS

Yield: 100 servings, 2 pieces each.

Ingredients	100 servings	.... servings
Carrots	40 pounds	
Flour	2 pounds (2 No. 56 dippers)	
Eggs	10 eggs (½ No. 56 dipper)	
Milk, evaporated	1 pint (½ No. 56 dipper)	
Water (for milk)	1 pint (½ No. 56 dipper)	
Salt	To taste	
Pepper	To taste	
Bread crumbs	Sufficient to cover carrots	

1. Clean carrots and boil in salted water until tender.

2. Cool quickly in cold water and drain well.

3. Roll in flour.

4. Dip in mixture of eggs, milk and water.

5. Roll in bread crumbs.

6. Fry in deep lard at 350° F. until golden brown.

NO. 631. GLAZED CARROTS

Yield: 100 servings, approximately ½ cup each.

Ingredients	100 servings	.... servings
Carrots	25 pounds*	
Salt		
Water, boiling		
Sugar, brown	2¼ pounds (1¾ No. 56 dippers)	
Water, boiling	1½ pints (¾ No. 56 dipper)	
Salt	1 ounce (2 mess kit spoons)	
Butter, melted	8 ounces (¼ No. 56 dipper)	

*Three No. 10 cans carrots may be substituted for the 25 pounds fresh carrots. Heat before draining.

1. Scrub carrots thoroughly and scrape to remove outer layer of skin.

2. Slice and add boiling salted water. Cover and heat to boiling point. Reduce heat and simmer 10 to 15 minutes or until carrots are just tender. Drain.

3. Add sugar to the 1½ pints (¾ No. 56 dipper) boiling water; stir until sugar is dissolved. Heat to boiling point; boil, without stirring, until a thin sirup is formed. Add salt and butter.

4. Place carrots in baking pans; pour sirup over carrots.

5. Bake in moderate oven (375° F.) about 20 minutes, basting frequently with sirup.

NO. 632. LYONNAISE CARROTS

Yield: 100 servings, approximately ½ cup each.

Ingredients	100 servings	.... servings
Carrots	25 pounds*	
Salt		
Water, boiling		
Onions, chopped	1 pound (1 No. 56 dipper)	
Fat, melted	1 pound (½ No. 56 dipper)	
Butter	8 ounces (¼ No. 56 dipper)	
Pepper		
Parlsey, chopped	3 ounces (⅓ mess kit cup)	
Sugar, granulated	8 ounces (¼ No. 56 dipper)	

*Three No. 10 cans carrots may be substituted for the 25 pounds fresh carrots. Heat before draining.

1. Scrub carrots thoroughly and scrape to remove outer layer of skin.
2. Slice and add boiling salted water. Cover and heat to boiling point; reduce heat and simmer 10 to 15 minutes or until carrots are just tender. Drain.
3. Fry onions in fat until light brown.
4. Combine onions, butter, pepper, parsley and sugar; mix well. Pour over carrots; mix lightly.

NO. 633. SWEET AND SOUR CARROTS

Yield: 100 servings, approximately ½ cup each.

Ingredients	100 servings	.... servings
Carrots, medium size	25 pounds	
Salt		
Water, boiling		
Butter, melted	1½ pounds (¾ No. 56 dipper)	
Flour, sifted	½ pound (½ No. 56 dipper)	
Lemon juice	½ pint (¼ No. 56 dipper)	
Sugar, granulated	6 ounces (¼ mess kit cup)	
Salt		
Pepper		

1. Scrub carrots thoroughly and scrape to remove outer layer of skin. Cut into quarters; if long, cut into two pieces. Add rapidly boiling salted water, allowing only enough water to cook the carrots so there will be approximately 2 quarts (2 No. 56 dippers) liquid left on the carrots when cooked.
2. Heat to boiling; reduce heat and simmer 10 to 15 minutes or until tender. Drain.
3. Mix melted butter and flour together; stir until smooth. Add the 2 quarts (2 No. 56 dippers) carrot liquid. Heat to boiling; boil 2 minutes, stirring constantly. Add carrots.
4. Remove from heat and add lemon juice, sugar, salt, and pepper.
5. Serve immediately.

NO. 634. CARONIP PATTIES

Yield: 100 servings, 2 patties each.

Ingredients	100 servings	.... servings
Carrots	8 pounds (6¾ No. 56 dippers)	
Turnips	8 pounds (6¾ No. 56 dippers)	
Onions	3 pounds (3 No. 56 dippers)	
Eggs (well beaten)	20 eggs (1 No. 56 dipper)	
Bread crumbs		
or		
Flour, sifted	3 pounds (3 No. 56 dippers)	
Salt	To taste	
Pepper	To taste	
Milk, evaporated	4—14½-ounce cans	

1. Peel the carrots, turnips and onions. Cut to equal size, boil until tender. Drain well and grind.
2. Add 8 well-beaten eggs to the above and mix.
3. Add bread crumbs (or flour, salt, and pepper) gradually and mix thoroughly. Form into patties ½ inch thick, 2½ inches wide.
4. Combine the remaining eggs and milk to form a batter and dip patties first into batter and then into flour or bread crumbs and place on greased sheet pans. Bake in oven at 350° F. for approximately 10 minutes or until browned.

Note. If variety is desired, instead of dipping patties into batter and flour, as patties are formed, place on sheet pan and sprinkle brown sugar over each patty and bake in oven.

NO. 635. CAULIFLOWER AU GRATIN

Yield: 100 servings, approximately ¼ cup each.

Ingredients	100 servings	.... servings
Cauliflower	35 pounds	
Salt		
Water, boiling		
White sauce	3 quarts (3 No. 56 dippers)	
Cheese, finely chopped	2 pounds (2 No. 56 dippers)	
Butter, melted	8 ounces (¼ No. 56 dipper)	
Bread crumbs	12 ounces (½ No. 56 dipper)	

1. Cover cauliflower with cold salted water; soak 30 minutes. Wash heads; remove base of stalks and discard large leaves.
2. Add boiling salted water. Heat to boiling point; reduce heat and simmer, uncovered, 8 to 10 minutes or until tender. Drain and cool. Break into pieces.
3. Prepare white sauce (recipe No. 548); add cheese and stir until cheese is melted.
4. Place cauliflower in well-greased baking pans. Pour cheese sauce over cauliflower.
5. Pour melted butter over bread crumbs; cover cauliflower with buttered crumbs.
6. Bake in moderate oven (350° F.) 30 minutes.

NO. 636. CREAMED CAULIFLOWER

Omit cheese in recipe for cauliflower au gratin.

NO. 637. CAULIFLOWER WITH BROWN CRUMBS

Cook 2 pounds (2 No. 56 dippers) dry bread crumbs in 1 pound (½ No. 56 dipper) butter until brown. Add to recipe for cauliflower au gratin. Omit cheese.

NO. 638. CAULIFLOWER WITH HOLLANDAISE SAUCE

Substitute hollandaise sauce (recipe No. 549) for white sauce in recipe for cauliflower au gratin. Omit cheese and crumbs.

NO. 639. FRENCH FRIED CAULIFLOWER

Yield: 100 servings, approximately 4 to 5 flowerettes, 3 ounces.

Ingredients	100 servings	.... servings
Cauliflower	12 pounds	
Water	4 gallons (16 No. 56 dippers)	
Salt	1 cup	

1. Parboil cauliflower in boiling salted water. When partially cooked, but still firm enough to hold its shape well, remove from cooking water and divide into flowerettes (each one weighing ½ ounce, approximately). Keep flowerettes in a long flat pan to prevent unnecessary breakage. The cauliflower may be broken into flowerettes before cooking, and placed in the steamer tray and sprinkled with salt (approximately half the amount as stated above). If this method is followed, check carefully to see that the cauliflower is *not* overcooked.
2. Sprinkle parboiled flowerettes with salt and roll lightly in flour, shaking off·excess. Dip in egg batter and roll in finely sifted dry bread crumbs.
3. Fry in deep fat, 350 to 360° F., for 1 to 2 minutes until they are a golden brown color. Sprinkle lightly with salt again.

NO. 640. BRAISED CELERY

Yield: 100 servings, approximately ½ cup each.

Ingredients	100 servings	.... servings
Celery	25 pounds	
Beef or veal stock, boiling	2 gallons (8 No. 56 dippers)	
Flour, sifted	10 ounces (½ No. 56 dipper)	
Butter, melted	8 ounces (¼ No. 56 dipper)	
Parsley, chopped	2½ ounces (¼ mess kit cup)	
Salt		
Pepper		

1. Remove discolored leaves and root ends of celery stalks; wash stalks thoroughly in cold water. Cut into 1-inch pieces.
2. Add boiling beef or veal stock to celery. Heat to boiling point; reduce heat and simmer until celery is just tender. Drain.
3. Mix flour and melted butter. Add small amount of cold water; stir until smooth. Add slowly to hot celery liquid. Heat to boiling point; boil 2 minutes, stirring constantly.
4. Add celery, parsley, salt and pepper; mix well.

Note. The amount of salt and pepper needed will depend upon how much salt and pepper has been added to the meat stock.

NO. 641. CREAMED CELERY

Substitute 1 gallon (4 No. 56 dippers) white sauce (recipe No. 548) for flour and butter in recipe for braised celery. Use water in which celery was cooked as part of the liquid in the white sauce.

NO. 642. CORN AND KIDNEY BEANS   Yield: 100 servings, approximately ½ cup each.

Ingredients	100 servings	.... servings
Beans, kidney, dry	6 pounds*	
Water, cold		
Salt		
Corn	2 No. 10 cans	
Bacon, diced	6½ ounces	
Chili sauce	½ pint (¼ No. 56 dipper)	
Salt		

*Two No. 10 cans kidney beans may be substituted for the 6 pounds dry kidney beans.

1. Wash beans thoroughly. Cover with cold water; soak 3 to 4 hours.
2. Add salt. Cover and heat to boiling point; reduce heat and simmer until tender but not split or mushy.
3. Drain part of liquid from beans and part from corn. Combine beans and corn; heat.
4. Fry bacon until crisp.
5. Combine vegetables, bacon, bacon fat, chili sauce and salt just before serving.

NO. 643. CORN A LA SOUTHERN   Yield: 100 servings, approximately ½ cup each.

Ingredients	100 servings	.... servings
Corn, cream style	3 No. 10 cans	
Eggs, slightly beaten	10 eggs (½ No. 56 dipper)	
Butter, melted	12 ounces (½ mess kit cup)	
Peppers, green, chopped	2½ pounds (2½ No. 56 dippers)	
Sugar, granulated	2¼ ounces (4½ mess kit spoons)	
Salt	1 ounce (2 mess kit spoons)	
Pepper		
Milk, evaporated	4—14½-ounce cans	
Water (for milk)	2 quarts (2 No. 56 dippers)	

1. Combine all ingredients; mix well.
2. Pour into well-greased baking pans. Bake in slow oven (300° F.) about 1 hour or until firm.

NO. 644. CORN PILAFF

Yield: 100 servings, approximately ½ cup each.

Ingredients	100 servings	.... servings
Rice, uncooked	2 pounds (1 No. 56 dipper)	
Fat	1 pound (½ No. 56 dipper)	
Water	3½ quarts (3½ No. 56 dippers)	
Salt	1¼ ounces (2½ mess kit spoons)	
Onions, chopped	11 ounces (¾ No. 56 dipper)	
Corn	3 No. 10 cans	
Pimientos, chopped	12 ounces (½ mess kit cup)	

1. Wash rice thoroughly; drain to remove excess water.

2. Cook rice in ½ the fat until brown, stirring occasionally.

3. Combine rice, water, salt, and onions. Heat to boiling point; reduce heat and simmer 30 minutes or until rice is tender.

4. Add corn, pimientos and remaining fat; mix well. Heat to serving temperature.

NO. 645. CORN SOUFFLE

Yield: 100 servings, approximately ½ cup each.

Ingredients	100 servings	.... servings
Corn	3 No. 10 cans	
Milk, evaporated	4—14½-ounce cans	
Flour, sifted	12 ounces (¾ No. 56 dipper)	
Butter, melted	12 ounces (½ mess kit cup)	
Egg yolks, slightly beaten	9 yolks (⅓ No. 56 dipper)	
Salt	1 ounce (2 mess kit spoons)	
Pepper		
Sugar, granulated	2 ounces (4 mess kit spoons)	
Egg whites	9 whites (¼ No. 56 dipper)	

1. Mix corn and milk; heat.

2. Mix flour and melted butter. Add a small amount of liquid; stir until smooth. Add hot corn and milk mixture. Heat to boiling point; boil 2 minutes, stirring constantly.

3. Add egg yolks, salt, pepper, and sugar; mix well.

4. Beat egg whites until stiff but not dry; add to corn mixture.

5. Pour into well-greased baking pans. Bake in slow oven (325° F.) about 1 hour or until firm.

NO. 646. CORN AND CHEESE SOUFFLE

Add 1½ pounds (1½ No. 56 dippers) finely chopped cheese to corn mixture in recipe for corn souffle. Sprinkle with crumbs if desired.

NO. 647. SCALLOPED CORN

Yield: 100 servings, approximately ½ cup each.

Ingredients	100 servings	.... servings
Corn	3 No. 10 cans	
Onions, diced (optional)	5 ounces (¼ No. 56 dipper)	
Milk, evaporated	2—14½-ounce cans	
Water (for milk)	¾ pint (½ mess kit cup)	
Flour, sifted	4 ounces (⅓ mess kit cup)	
Butter, melted	12 ounces (½ mess kit cup)	
Salt	1 ounce (2 mess kit spoons)	
Pepper		
Sugar, granulated	2½ ounces (5 mess kit spoons)	
Butter, melted	12 ounces (½ mess kit cup)	
Bread or cracker crumbs, dry	1¼ pounds (1¼ No. 56 dippers)	

1. Mix corn and onions; heat slowly, stirring occasionally.
2. Mix milk and water; heat.
3. Mix flour and melted butter. Add a small amount of milk; stir until smooth. Add hot milk slowly. Heat to boiling point; boil 2 minutes, stirring constantly.
4. Combine white sauce, salt, pepper, sugar, and corn; mix well.
5. Pour melted butter over crumbs.
6. Arrange alternate layers of corn and crumbs in well-greased baking pans, finishing with crumbs.
7. Bake in moderate oven (350° F.) about 15 minutes or until crumbs are brown.

NO. 648. SAUTEED CORN

Yield: 100 servings, approximately ½ cup each.

Ingredients	100 servings	.... servings
Corn	100 ears*	
Salt		
Water, boiling		
Bacon, diced	1½ pounds	
Peppers, green, chopped	8 ounces (½ No. 56 dipper)	
Pimientos, chopped	7 ounces (¼ mess kit cup)	
Salt	1 ounce (2 mess kit spoons)	
Pepper		

*Four No. 10 cans whole kernel corn may be substituted for the 100 ears of fresh corn.

1. Remove husks and silk from corn. Clean thoroughly; cut corn from cob.
2. Add a small amount of boiling salted water to corn. Cover and heat to boiling point; reduce heat and simmer 10 to 12 minutes or until corn is tender.
3. Mix corn, bacon, green peppers, and pimientos together; fry until peppers are tender.
4. Add salt and pepper.

NO. 649. SUCCOTASH
Yield: 100 servings, approximately ½ cup each.

Ingredients	100 servings	.... servings
Beans, lima, dry	3 pounds*	
Water, cold		
Salt		
Corn	2 No. 10 cans	
Onion juice	2 ounces (4 mess kit spoons)	
Paprika		
Butter	12 ounces (½ mess kit cup)	

*One No. 10 can lima beans may be substituted for the 3 pounds dry lima beans.

1. Wash beans thoroughly. Cover with cold water; soak 3 to 4 hours.
2. Add salt. Cover and heat to boiling point; reduce heat and simmer 1½ hours or until tender but not split or mushy. Drain.
3. Combine beans, corn, salt, onion juice, paprika, and butter; mix well. Heat slowly to serving temperature.

NO. 650. FRIED EGGPLANT
Yield: 100 servings, approximately 2 to 3 slices per serving.

Ingredients	100 servings	.... servings
Eggplant	25 pounds	
Eggs, slightly beaten	19 eggs (1 No. 56 dipper)	
Water	¾ pint (½ mess kit cup)	
Salt	2½ ounces (5 mess kit spoons)	
Bread crumbs or flour, sifted	12 ounces (1 mess kit cup)	
Fat (for frying)		

1. Wash eggplant; cut into slices ¼ inch thick. Pare slices.
2. Combine beaten egg, water and ½ of the salt.
3. Add remaining salt to bread crumbs or flour.
4. Dip slices of eggplant into egg mixture, drain. Dip into crumbs or flour.
5. Fry in deep hot fat (350° F.) until golden brown and tender.
6. Drain on absorbent paper.

NO. 651. SCALLOPED EGGPLANT
Yield: 100 servings, approximately ½ cup each.

Ingredients	100 servings	.... servings
Eggplant	25 pounds	
Salt		
Water, boiling		
Bread crumbs, moist	2 pounds (4 No. 56 dippers)	
Butter, melted	12 ounces (½ mess kit cup)	
Onions, chopped	12 ounces (¾ No. 56 dipper)	
Parsley, chopped	2½ ounces (⅓ mess kit cup)	
Salt	4 ounces (8 mess kit spoons)	
Pepper	¼ ounce (1 mess kit spoon)	
Milk, evaporated	5—14½-ounce cans	
Water (for milk)	2 quarts (2 No. 56 dippers)	
Cheese, finely chopped	6 ounces (½ mess kit cup)	

1. Wash eggplant; pare and cut into cubes.
2. Add boiling salted water to eggplant. Cover and heat to boiling point; reduce heat and simmer 5 minutes or until tender. Drain well.
3. Pour $\frac{3}{4}$ of the melted butter over crumbs; cook until light brown.
4. Fry onions and parsley in remaining butter. Add to crumbs.
5. Arrange alternate layers of eggplant and crumb mixture in well-greased baking pans, beginning and finishing with crumbs. Sprinkle each layer with salt and pepper.
6. Mix milk and water; heat. Pour over layers in baking pans. Sprinkle with cheese.
7. Bake in moderate oven (350° F.) 1 hour.

NO. 652. SCALLOPED EGGPLANT AND TOMATOES

Yield: 100 servings, approximately $\frac{1}{2}$ cup each.

Ingredients	100 servings	.... servings
Eggplant..................	25 pounds.........................	....
Salt......................		....
Water, boiling.............		
Sugar, granulated...........	2 ounces (4 mess kit spoons)........	....
Salt......................	$\frac{3}{4}$ ounce (1$\frac{1}{2}$ mess kit spoons).......	....
Pepper....................		
Tomatoes..................	1$\frac{1}{2}$ No. 10 cans....................	....
Onions, chopped............	3 pounds (3 No. 56 dippers).........	....
Butter, melted.............	12 ounces ($\frac{1}{2}$ mess kit cup).........	....
Bread crumbs, moist........	12 ounces (2 mess kit cups)..........	....

1. Wash eggplant; pare and dice.
2. Add boiling salted water to eggplant. Cover and heat to boiling point; reduce heat and simmer 5 minutes or until tender. Drain well.
3. Combine sugar, salt, pepper, and tomatoes; heat.
4. Fry onions in butter; add crumbs and continue frying until crumbs are light brown.
5. Combine eggplant, tomatoes, and crumb mixture.
6. Place in well-greased baking pans. Bake in moderate oven (350° F.) about 30 minutes.

NO. 653. GREENS AND EGGS AU GRATIN

Yield: 100 servings, approximately $\frac{1}{2}$ cup each.

Ingredients	100 servings	.... servings
Spinach or other greens.......	25 pounds*.....................	....
Salt......................		....
Water, boiling..............		
Eggs, hard-cooked, sliced......	24 eggs........................	....
White sauce................	1 gallon (4 No. 56 dippers).........	....
Cheese, chopped............	1 pound (1 No. 56 dipper)..........	....

*Three No. 10 cans spinach or other greens may be substituted for the fresh spinach or other greens.

1. Cut roots from spinach or other greens. Wash leaves several times to remove all sand. Drain well.

2. Add small amount boiling salted water to greens. Heat to boiling; reduce heat and simmer 5 to 10 minutes or until just tender. Drain.

3. Line bottom of greased baking pans with ½ of the sliced eggs.

4. Prepare white sauce. (See recipe No. 548.)

5. Pour ½ of the white sauce over eggs in baking pans. Place spinach or other greens on top of eggs and cover with remaining white sauce. Arrange remaining slices of eggs on top and sprinkle with cheese.

6. Bake in moderate oven (375° F.) 40 minutes.

NO. 654. SIMMERED GREENS AND BACON

Yield: 100 servings, approximately ½ cup each.

Ingredients	100 servings	.... servings
Spinach or other greens.......	40 pounds...........................	....
Salt.................		....
Water, boiling..............	4 gallons (16 No. 56 dippers).........	....
Bacon.....................	4 pounds..........................	....
Beef stock..................	1 quart (1 No. 56 dipper)...........	....
Salt..................		....

1. Cut roots from spinach or other greens. Wash leaves several times to remove all sand. Drain well.

2. Add a small amount of boiling salted water to greens. Add strips of bacon. Heat to boiling point; reduce heat and simmer about 10 minutes or until spinach or greens are tender. Drain well.

3. Add beef stock and salt; heat to serving temperature.

Note. Eighteen sliced, hard-cooked eggs may be placed on top of greens to improve flavor and appearance.

NO. 655. FRIED HOMINY

Yield: 100 servings, ½ cup each.

Ingredients	100 servings	.... servings
Hominy....................	4 No. 10 cans....................	....
Peppers, green, chopped (optional).	1¼ pounds (1¼ No. 56 dippers).....	....
Pimientos, chopped (optional).	10 ounces (½ mess kit cup).........	....
Salt................		....
Pepper.................		....
Butter or bacon fat, melted...	1¼ pounds (¾ mess kit cup)........	....

1. Drain hominy; combine hominy, peppers, pimiento, salt, and pepper.

2. Fry in butter or bacon fat until brown.

NO. 656. HOMINY (CANNED)

Yield: 100 servings, ¼ cup each.

Ingredients	100 servings	.... servings
Salt	2 ounces (4 mess kit spoons)	
Pepper		
Hominy	3 No. 10 cans	

Add salt and pepper to hominy; heat slowly, without draining, 20 minutes.

Note. A small amount of butter may be added to the hominy.

NO. 657. WILTED LETTUCE.

Yield: 100 servings, approximately ½ cup each.

Ingredients	100 servings	.... servings
Lettuce, trimmed	20 heads	
Onions, chopped	8 ounces (½ No. 56 dipper)	
Bacon, diced	3 pounds	
Vinegar	2½ quarts (2½ No. 56 dippers)	
Water	1½ quarts (1½ No. 56 dippers)	
Fat, bacon	12 ounces (⅓ mess kit cup)	
Flour, sifted	6 ounces (½ mess kit cup)	
Sugar, granulated	1¼ pounds (⅔ No. 56 dipper)	
Salt	½ ounce (1 mess kit spoon)	
Pepper	½ ounce (2 mess kit spoons)	

1. Wash lettuce; separate leaves. Dry thoroughly.
2. Stack leaves together; roll and cut crosswise into medium sized pieces.
3. Fry onions and bacon together; drain and reserve fat.
4. Mix vinegar and water; heat to boiling point.
5. Mix bacon fat and flour; stir until smooth. Add slowly to hot vinegar. Heat to boiling point; boil 2 minutes, stirring constantly.
6. Add sugar, salt, and pepper.
7. Combine lettuce, onions, and bacon. Pour hot vinegar mixture over lettuce just before serving.

NO. 658. ONIONS AU GRATIN

Yield: 100 servings, approximately ½ cup each.

Ingredients	100 servings	.... servings
Onions	25 pounds	
Salt		
Water, boiling		
White sauce	1 gallon (4 No. 56 dippers)	
Mustard, dry	2¼ ounces (9 mess kit spoons)	
Cheese, finely chopped	1 pound (1 No. 56 dipper)	
Butter, melted	4 ounces (8 mess kit spoons)	
Bread, coarsely chopped	1¼ pounds (2 No. 56 dippers)	

1. Wash onions; peel. Cut into halves or quarters.
2. Add boiling salted water to onions. Heat to boiling point; reduct heat and simmer, uncovered, 5 to 7 minutes or until tender. Drain.
3. Prepare white sauce (recipe No. 548); add mustard and ¾ of the cheese; stir until cheese is melted.
4. Pour melted butter over crumbs.
5. Arrange layers of onions and cheese sauce in well-greased baking pans. Cover with crumbs and remaining cheese.
6. Bake in moderate oven (350° F.) until crumbs are brown and cheese is melted.

NO. 659. FRIED ONIONS

Yield: 100 servings, approximately ½ cup each.

Ingredients	100 servings	.... servings
Onions	30 pounds	
Salt	2 ounces (4 mess kit spoons)	
Fat, bacon, melted	2½ pounds (1¼ No. 56 dippers)	

1. Wash onions; peel. Cut crosswise into slices ¼ to ⅓ inch thick.
2. Sprinkle with salt and pepper.
3. Cover and fry in bacon fat until brown and tender, stirring frequently.

NO. 660. FRENCH FRIED ONIONS

Yield: 100 servings, approximately ½ cup each.

Ingredients	100 servings	.... servings
Onions, large	30 pounds	
Milk, evaporated	5—14½-ounce cans	
Flour, sifted	1¼ pounds (1¼ No. 56 dippers)	
Salt	1½ ounces (3 mess kit spoons)	
Pepper	(¼ mess kit spoon)	
Shortening (for frying)		

1. Wash onions; peel. Cut into slices ¼ inch thick. Separate slices into rings.
2. Dip onion rings in milk; drain thoroughly.
3. Mix flour, salt, and pepper together; dip onion rings in flour mixture.
4. Fry in deep hot fat (375° F.) until golden brown.
5. Drain on absorbent paper.

NO. 661. GLAZED ONIONS

Yield: 100 servings, approximately ⅓ cup each.

Ingredients	100 servings	.... servings
Onions	25 pounds	
Salt (for onions)		
Water, boiling (for onions)		
Sugar, brown	1½ pounds (1 No. 56 dipper)	
Water, boiling (for sugar)	1¾ quarts (1¾ No. 56 dippers)	
Salt	1½ ounces (3 mess kit spoons)	
Butter	12 ounces (½ mess kit cup)	

1. Wash onions; peel. Cut into halves or leave whole.
2. Add boiling salted water to onions. Heat to boiling point; reduce heat and simmer, uncovered, 5 to 7 minutes or until tender. Drain.
3. Mix sugar and water, stirring only until sugar is dissolved. Heat to boiling point; boil, without stirring, until a thin sirup is formed. Add salt and butter.
4. Place onions in baking pans; pour sirup over onions.
5. Bake in hot oven (400° F.) about 30 minutes, basting frequently with sirup.

NO. 662. SAVORY ONIONS

Yield: 100 servings, approximately ⅓ cup each.

Ingredients	100 servings	.... servings
Onions...................	25 pounds.......................	....
Salt....................	....	....
Water, boiling.............	....	....
Sugar, brown..............	1 pound (1 mess kit cup)............	....
Salt.....................	2½ ounces (5 mess kit spoons).......	....
Pepper...................	....	....
Chili sauce................	2½ quarts (2½ No. 56 dippers)......	....
Butter...................	12 ounces (½ mess kit cup).........	....

1. Wash onions; peel. Cut into halves or leave whole.
2. Add boiling salted water to onions. Heat to boiling point; reduce heat and simmer, uncovered, 5 to 7 minutes or until tender.
3. Arrange in baking pans.
4. Combine sugar, salt, pepper, chili sauce and butter; pour over onions.
5. Bake in moderate oven (375° F.) until onions are tender.

NO. 663. SCALLOPED ONIONS

Yield: 100 servings, approximately ½ cup each.

Ingredients	100 servings	.... servings
Onions...................	25 pounds.......................	....
Salt....................	....	....
Water, boiling.	....	....
Butter, melted..............	4 ounces (8 mess kit spoons)........	....
Bread crumbs, moist..........	1 pound (2 No. 56 dippers)..........	....
White sauce................	4½ quarts (4½ No. 56 dippers)......	....

1. Wash onions; peel. Cut into halves or quarters.
2. Add boiling salted water to onions. Heat to boiling point; reduce heat and simmer, uncovered, 5 to 7 minutes or until tender. Drain.
3. Pour melted butter over crumbs.
4. Prepare white sauce. (See recipe No. 548.)
5. Arrange layers of onions, white sauce and crumbs in well-greased baking pans, finishing with crumbs.
6. Bake in moderate oven (375° F.) 20 to 30 minutes or until crumbs are brown.

NO. 664. FRIED PARSNIPS Yield: 100 servings.

Ingredients	100 servings	.... servings
Parsnips...................	25 pounds.........................	....
Salt......................	....	....
Water, boiling.............	....	....
Milk, evaporated...........	¼—14½-ounce can...............	....
Water (for milk)...........	¼ pint (8 mess kit spoons).........	....
Eggs, slightly beaten........	13 eggs (⅔ No. 56 dipper).........	....
Salt......................	1½ ounces (3 mess kit spoons)......	....
Bread crumbs, dry..........	1¼ pounds (1¼ No. 56 dippers).....	....
Fat (for frying)............	....	....

1. Wash parsnips; scrape to remove skins. Cut into halves or quarters.

2. Add boiling salted water to parsnips. Cover and heat to boiling point; reduce heat and simmer until tender. Drain and cool.

3. Mix milk and water; add beaten eggs. Mix well.

4. Mix salt and crumbs.

5. Dip parsnips in milk and egg mixture; drain. Dip in crumbs.

6. Fry in deep hot fat (375° F.) about 3 to 4 minutes or until brown.

Note. Parsnips may be baked in moderate oven (350° F.). Place in well-greased baking pans; brush with melted butter or beef fat and bake until brown.

NO. 665. SAVORY CREAMED PARSNIPS

Yield: 100 servings, approximately ½ cup each.

Ingredients	100 servings	.... servings
Parsnips...................	25 pounds.....................	....
Salt......................	....	....
Water, boiling.............	....	....
Parsley, chopped...........	2 ounces (¼ mess kit cup).......	....
Pepper....................	(¼ mess kit spoon).............	....
Pork, salt, diced...........	2 pounds	....
White sauce................	1¼ gallons (5 No. 56 dippers)......	....

1. Wash parsnips; scrape to remove skins. Cut into quarters.

2. Add boiling salted water to parsnips. Cover and heat to boiling point; reduce heat and simmer until tender. Drain.

3. Add parsley and pepper.

4. Fry salt pork until brown and crisp. Drain and reserve fat.

5. Prepare white sauce (recipe No. 548) using fat from salt pork.

6. Add salt pork to white sauce. Pour over parsnips just before serving.

NO. 666. BAKED PEAS
Yield: 100 servings, approximately ½ cup each.

Ingredients	100 servings	.... servings
Peas	40 pounds*	
Salt		
Water, boiling		
Tomatoes	1 No. 10 can	
Flour, sifted	3 to 5 pounds (3 to 5 No. 56 dippers)	
Peppers, green, chopped	12 ounces (¾ No. 56 dipper)	
Onions, chopped	4 ounces (¼ No. 56 dipper)	
Pimientos, chopped	2 ounces (4 mess kit spoons)	
Sugar, brown	4 ounces (¼ mess kit cup)	
Salt	1½ ounces (3 mess kit spoons)	
Butter, melted	2 ounces (4 mess kit spoons)	
Bread crumbs, dry	1¼ pounds (1¼ No. 56 dippers)	

*Three No. 10 cans peas may be substituted for the 40 pounds fresh peas.

1. Shell peas; wash in cold water.
2. Barely cover peas with boiling salted water. Heat to boiling point; reduce heat and simmer until tender. Drain and reserve liquid.
3. Drain tomatoes. Combine liquids from peas and tomatoes; measure.
4. Mix flour and a small amount of liquid. using 3 ounces (12 mess kit spoons) flour to each quart (1 No. 56 dipper) liquid measured; stir until smooth.
5. Heat remaining liquid; add flour mixture slowly. Heat to boiling point, boil 2 minutes, stirring constantly.
6. Add peas, tomatoes, green peppers, onions, pimientos, sugar and salt, mix well.
7. Pour melted butter over crumbs.
8. Pour vegetables into baking pans. Sprinkle with buttered crumbs.
9. Bake in moderate oven (375° F.) 20 to 30 minutes.

NO. 667. CREAMED PEAS
Yield: 100 servings, approximately ½ cup each.

Ingredients	100 servings	.... servings
Peas	40 pounds*	
Salt		
Water, boiling		
Flour, sifted	6 ounces (½ mess kit cup)	
Salt	2 ounces (4 mess kit spoons)	
Pepper		
Mustard, dry		
Butter, melted	8 ounces (¼ No. 56 dipper)	
Milk, evaporated	6—14½-ounce cans	

*Three No. 10 cans peas may be substituted for the 40 pounds fresh peas.

1. Shell peas; wash in cold water.
2. Barely cover peas with boiling salted water. Heat to boiling point; reduce heat and simmer until tender. Drain and reserve liquid.

3. Mix flour, salt, pepper, mustard and melted butter together. Add a small amount of liquid; stir until smooth.
4. Heat 2 quarts (2 No. 56 dippers) liquid to boiling point. Add flour mixture slowly. Heat to boiling point; boil 2 minutes, stirring constantly.
5. Reduce heat; add milk and simmer about 5 minutes.
6. Add peas and continue simmering until peas are heated through, stirring frequently to prevent scorching.

NO. 668. HOPPING JOHN

Yield: 100 servings, 3 ounces each.

Ingredients	100 servings	.... servings
Peas, blackeyed...............	6 pounds...........................	....
Water, boiling.................		
Ham bones or rind............		
Onions, sliced................	1 pound (1 N . 56 dipper)...........	
Pepper, black.................	¼ ounce (1 mess kit spoon)..........	
Rice, uncooked...............	6 pounds (3 No. 56 dippers).........	
Water, boiling.................		

1. Cover peas with boiling water. Add ham bones or rind, onions and pepper.
2. Cover and heat to boiling point; boil 1 hour.
3. Place rice on top of other ingredients. Add enough water to cover rice.
4. Cover and heat to boiling point; reduce heat and simmer, without stirring, about 30 minutes or until rice is tender.

NO. 669. POTATOES AU GRATIN

Yield: 100 servings, approximately ⅔ cup each.

Ingredients	100 servings	servings
Potatoes, white...............	40 pounds..........................	....
Salt.........................		....
Water, boiling.................		
White sauce..................	1¼ gallons (5 No. 56 dippers).......	
Cheese, finely chopped.......	1½ pounds (1½ No. 56 dippers).....	
Mustard, dry.................	¼ ounce (1 mess kit spoon)..........	
Butter, melted................	6 ounces (¼ mess kit cup)..........	
Bread crumbs, dry..........	1¼ pounds (1¼ No. 56 dippers).....	

1. Wash potatoes thoroughly.
2. Cover potatoes with boiling salted water. Cover and heat to boiling point; reduce heat and simmer 20 to 30 minutes or until tender. Drain and cool. Peel; cut into ¾-inch cubes.
3. Prepare white sauce (recipe No. 548); add cheese and mustard. Stir until cheese is melted.
4. Pour melted butter over crumbs.
5. Arrange alternate layers of potatoes and cheese sauce in well-greased baking pans. Cover with buttered crumbs.
6. Bake in moderate oven (375° F.) 10 to 25 minutes.

NO. 670. POTATOES AU GRATIN WITH CURRY

Reduce cheese to 10 ounces (½ No. 56 dipper) in recipe for potatoes au gratin. Add ¼ ounce (1 mess kit spoon) curry powder to white sauce. Omit crumbs.

NO. 671. POTATOES BAKED IN MILK   Yield: 100 servings, approximately ⅔ cup each.

Ingredients	100 servings	.... servings
Potatoes, white	45 pounds	
Salt		
Water, boiling		
Milk, evaporated	5—14½-ounce cans	
Water (for milk)	2 quarts (2 No. 56 dippers)	
Salt	3 ounces (6 mess kit spoons)	

1. Wash potatoes; pare and dice.
2. Cover potatoes with boiling salted water. Cover and heat to boiling point; reduce heat and simmer 20 to 30 minutes or until nearly tender. Drain.
3. Mix milk, water, and salt together; add to potatoes and mix well.
4. Place in baking pans. Bake in slow oven (325° F.) until potatoes are tender and milk is absorbed, stirring occasionally.

Note. Use water drained from potatoes as the water for diluting the milk.

NO. 672. BAKED POTATOES   Yield: 100 servings, 1 potato each.

Ingredients	100 servings	.... servings
Potatoes, white, medium size	100 potatoes	
Beef fat, melted	1 pound (½ No. 56 dipper)	

1. Scrub potatoes thoroughly; dry.
2. Brush skins with beef fat to keep them soft.
3. Place in baking pans. Bake in hot oven (450° F.) 1 to 1½ hours or until tender when pierced. Remove from oven.
4. Prick each potato with a fork or break open to allow steam to escape.

Note. Potatoes may be cut crosswise and lengthwise on the top. Press both ends until potatoes break open. Place lump of butter and sprinkle paprika in opening in each potato.

NO. 673. FRENCH BAKED POTATOES   Yield: 100 servings, 1 potato each.

Ingredients	100 servings	.... servings
Potatoes, white, large	100 potatoes	
Salt		
Beef stock	1 gallon (4 No. 56 dippers)	
Beef fat	2 pounds (1 No. 56 dipper)	

1. Scrub potatoes; pare and cut into halves lengthwise.
2. Place in well-greased baking pans; add salt, stock, and fat.
3. Bake in moderate oven (350° F.) about 1 hour without stirring.

NO. 674. HASHED BROWN POTATOES

Yield: 100 servings, approximately ⅔ cup each.

Ingredients	100 servings	.... servings
Potatoes, white, cooked, chopped.	45 pounds............................	....
Beef fat, melted..............	2 pounds (1 No. 56 dipper).........	....
Salt.......................	3 ounces (6 mess kit spoons)........	....
Pepper....................	(½ mess kit spoon).................	....

1. Place chopped potatoes in baking pans; pour beef fat over potatoes.
2. Sprinkle with salt and pepper.
3. Fry on top of stove or bake in hot oven (450° to 500° F.) 20 to 25 minutes or until brown, stirring occasionally.

NO. 675. FRANCONIA POTATOES

Yield: 100 servings, approximately ⅔ cup each.

Ingredients	100 servings	.... servings
Potatoes, white..............	45 pounds............................	....
Salt.......................	....	....
Water, boiling..............	....	....
Butter, melted..............	2 pounds (1 No. 56 dipper).........	....
Salt.......................	3 ounces (6 mess kit spoons)........	....
Pepper....................	....	....

1. Wash potatoes; pare and cut into quarters.
2. Cover potatoes with boiling salted water. Cover and heat to boiling point; reduce heat and simmer 20 to 30 minutes or until tender. Drain.
3. Place in well-greased baking pans. Pour melted butter over potatoes; sprinkle with salt and pepper.
4. Bake in hot oven (400° F.) until brown.

NO. 676. FRENCH FRIED POTATOES

Yield: 100 servings, approximately ⅔ cup each.

Ingredients	100 servings	.... servings
Potatoes, white..............	50 pounds............................	....
Fat (for frying).............	....	....
Salt.......................	3 ounces (6 mess kit spoons)........	....

1. Wash potatoes; pare and cut into long narrow strips.
2. Cover with water; allow to stand 30 to 45 minutes. Drain, roll in a cloth to dry.

3. Fry in deep hot fat (350° F.) about 4 to 6 minutes, or until brown and tender.

4. Drain on absorbent paper. Sprinkle with salt.

Note. Cook potatoes just before serving as they cool very quickly.

NO. 677. HOME FRIED POTATOES   Yield: 100 servings, 3 to 5 ounces each.

Ingredients	100 servings	.... servings
Potatoes...................	40 pounds........................	....
Salt.......................	To taste.........................	....
Pepper....................	To taste.........................	....
Lard......................	4 pounds (2 No. 56 dippers).........	....

1. Boil potatoes in the jackets.

2. Cool, peel, and slice crosswise.

3. Season with salt and pepper to taste.

4. Fry on top of range until nicely browned.

NO. 678. LYONNAISE POTATOES   Yield: 100 servings, approximately ⅔ cup each.

Ingredients	100 servings	.... servings
Potatoes, white..............	45 pounds........................	....
Salt.......................		....
Water, boiling..............		
Onions, chopped.............	1 pound (1 No. 56 dipper)..........	....
Bacon fat..................	2 pounds (1 No. 56 dipper)..........	....
Salt......................	3 ounces (6 mess kit spoons)........	....
Pepper....................		....
Parsley, chopped (optional)...	¼ pound (½ mess kit cup)..........	....

1. Wash potatoes; pare and cut into ½-inch cubes.

2. Cover potatoes with boiling salted water. Cover and heat to boiling point; reduce heat and simmer 20 minutes or until tender. Drain.

3. Fry onions in bacon fat until tender but not brown.

4. Combine potatoes, onions, salt, and pepper.

5. Place potato mixture in well-greased baking pans. Bake in moderate oven (350° F.) until light brown.

6. Place parsley over potatoes just before serving.

NO. 679. POTATOES IN JACKETS   Yield: 100 servings, 1 to 2 each.

Ingredients	100 servings	.... servings
Potatoes, white..............	40 pounds........................	....
Salt.......................		....
Water, boiling..............		....

1. Wash potatoes thoroughly.
2. Cover potatoes with boiling salted water. Cover and heat to boiling point; reduce heat and simmer 20 to 30 minutes or until tender. Drain.
3. Allow potatoes to stand uncovered until steam escapes and potatoes are dry and mealy.

Note. Potatoes may be pared before cooking if desired.

NO. 680. PARSLEY POTATOES

Mix 12 ounces (½ mess kit cup) melted butter and 4 ounces finely chopped parsley. Pour over peeled potatoes, mixing until each potato is coated with butter.

NO. 681. MASHED POTATOES

Yield: 100 servings, approximately ⅔ cup each.

Ingredients	100 servings	.... servings
Potatoes, white.............	40 pounds............................	....
Salt........................	....	....
Water, boiling..............	....	....
Milk, evaporated...........	6—14½-ounce cans..................	....
Water, potato (for milk).....	2½ quarts (2½ No. 56 dippers).....	....
Butter.....................	6 ounces (¼ mess kit cup)..........	....
Salt........................	....	....
Pepper.....................	....	....

1. Wash potatoes; pare.
2. Cover potatoes with boiling salted water. Cover and heat to boiling point; reduce heat and simmer 20 to 30 minutes or until tender. Drain.
3. Mash well.
4. Mix milk and potato water; heat.
5. Add milk and butter to potatoes; beat well. Add salt and pepper; mix well.

NO. 682. POTATOES O'BRIEN

Yield: 100 servings, approximately ⅔ cup each.

Ingredients	100 servings	.... servings
Potatoes, white.............	45 pounds............................	....
Fat (for frying).............	....	....
Salt........................	3 ounces (6 mess kit spoons)........	....
Pimientos, chopped*.........	1 pound............................	....
Peppers, green, chopped......	1 pound (1 No. 56 dipper)..........	....
Bacon fat..................	8 ounces (¼ No. 56 dipper).........	....

*If pimientos are not available increase amount of green peppers to 2 pounds (2 No. 56 dippers).

1. Wash potatoes; pare and cut into ¾-inch cubes.
2. Cover potatoes with cold water; allow to stand 30 to 45 minutes. Drain; roll in a cloth to dry.

3. Fry in deep hot fat (350° F.) about 4 to 6 minutes or until brown and tender.
4. Drain on absorbent paper; sprinkle with salt.
5. Fry pimientos and peppers in bacon fat.
6. Combine potatoes, pimientos, and pepper just before serving.

Note. Potato cubes, pimientos, and peppers may be baked in the oven instead of fried. Place in baking pans in a small amount of bacon fat. Bake in moderate oven (350° F.) turning frequently.

NO. 683. POTATO PUFF
Yield: 100 servings, approximately ⅔ cup each.

Ingredients	100 servings	.... servings
Milk, evaporated	1¼—14½-ounce cans	
Water (for milk)	1 pint (½ No. 56 dipper)	
Potatoes, white, mashed	32 pounds (16 No. 56 dippers)	
Egg yolks, beaten	15 yolks (⅓ No. 56 dipper)	
Butter, melted	¾ pound (½ mess kit cup)	
Salt		
Pepper		

1. Combine milk, water, potatoes, egg yolks, ¾ of the butter, salt, and pepper; mix well.
2. Place potato mixture in well-greased baking pans. Pour remaining butter over top.
3. Bake in moderate oven (375° F.) until light brown.

Note. Chopped chives, pimientos or green peppers may be added to the potato mixture.

NO. 684. SCALLOPED POTATOES
Yield: 100 servings, approximately ⅔ cup each.

Ingredients	100 servings	.... servings
Potatoes, white	30 pounds	
White sauce	2 gallons (8 No. 56 dippers)	

1. Wash potatoes; pare. Cut into thin crosswise slices.
2. Prepare thin white sauce. (See recipe No. 548.)
3. Place potatoes in well-greased baking pans. Pour white sauce over potatoes.
4. Bake in moderate oven (350° F.) 2 hours or until tender.

Note. Potato slices may be simmered 10 minutes to reduce baking time. A few minced onions and additional salt and pepper may be added to the white sauce if desired.

NO. 685. BAKED SWEET POTATOES
Yield: 100 servings, 1 potato each.

Ingredients	100 servings	.... servings
Potatoes, sweet, medium size	100 potatoes	
Beef fat, melted	8 ounces (¼ No. 56 dipper)	

1. Scrub potatoes thoroughly; dry.
2. Brush skins with beef fat to keep them soft.
3. Place in baking pans. Bake in hot oven (450° F.) 45 minutes or until tender. Remove from oven.
4. Prick each potato with a fork or break open to allow steam to escape.

NO. 686. BAKED SWEET POTATOES AND APPLES

Yield: 100 servings, approximately ½ cup each.

Ingredients	100 servings	.... servings
Potatoes, sweet..............	32 pounds.......................	....
Salt......................	2½ ounces (5 mess kit spoons).......	....
Water, boiling..............		
Sugar, brown................	2½ pounds (2 No. 56 dippers).......	....
Apples, tart, sliced...........	8 pounds (8 No. 56 dippers)........	....
Butter....................	6 ounces (¼ mess kit cup)..........	....

1. Wash sweet potatoes; pare and cut into crosswise slices ¼-inch thick.
2. Cover sweet potatoes with boiling salted water. Cover and heat to boiling point; reduce heat and simmer until tender. Drain.
3. Arrange potato slices overlapping one another in well-greased baking pans.
4. Sprinkle with salt and ½ the sugar.
5. Cover potato slices with a layer of sliced apples.
6. Sprinkle apples with remaining sugar. Place pieces of butter on top of apples.
7. Bake in moderate oven (350° F.) until apples are tender.

NO. 687. BAKED SWEET POTATOES WITH APPLES AND MARSHMALLOWS

Add 1 pound marshmallows to recipe for baked sweet potatoes and apples. Cut marshmallows into quarters and place on top of layers of sweet potatoes and apples in baking pans.

NO. 688. BAKED SWEET POTATOES AND PINEAPPLE

Substitute 2 No. 2 cans sliced or diced pineapple for apples in recipe for baked sweet potatoes and apples. Reduce brown sugar to 1¼ pounds (1 No. 56 dipper).

NO. 689. BROWN SWEET POTATOES

Yield: 100 servings, approximately 2 halves per serving.

Ingredients	100 servings	.... servings
Potatoes, sweet..............	40 to 50 pounds....................	....
Salt......................		
Water, boiling..............		
Sugar, brown................	1 pound (1 mess kit cup)...........	....
Salt......................	3 ounces (6 mess kit spoons)........	....
Butter or bacon fat..........	1 pound (½ No. 56 dipper).........	....

1. Wash sweet potatoes.
2. Cover sweet potatoes with boiling salted water. Cover and heat to boiling; reduce heat and simmer until tender. Drain; cool and peel.
3. Cut potatoes into halves lengthwise or into slices crosswise, ¼ inch thick.
4. Place in baking pans; sprinkle with sugar and salt.
5. Place pieces of butter or pour melted bacon fat over potatoes.
6. Bake in moderate oven (375° F.) about 1 hour or until brown.

NO. 690. GLAZED SWEET POTATOES   Yield: 100 servings, approximately 4 to 6 slices per serving.

Ingredients	100 servings	.... servings
Potatoes, sweet	45 pounds	
Salt		
Water, boiling		
Sugar, brown	3½ pounds (3½ mess kit cups)	
Water, boiling (for sugar)	2 quarts (2 No. 56 dippers)	
Salt	½ ounce (1 mess kit spoon)	
Butter	8 ounces (¼ No. 56 dipper)	

1. Wash sweet potatoes.
2. Cover sweet potatoes with boiling salted water. Cover and heat to boiling point; reduce heat and simmer until tender. Drain; cool and peel.
3. Cut potatoes into crosswise slices; place slices in well-greased baking pans.
4. Mix sugar and boiling water, stirring only until sugar is dissolved. Heat to boiling point; boil without stirring until a thin sirup is formed.
5. Add salt and butter. Pour sirup over potatoes.
6. Bake in moderate oven (350° F.) 30 minutes.

Note. One-half quart (½ No. 56 dipper) corn sirup may be substituted for ½ of the brown sugar in recipe for glazed sweet potatoes. Reduce water to 1 quart (1 No. 56 dipper).

NO. 691. MASHED SWEET POTATOES

Yield: 100 servings, approximately ½ cup per servnig.

Ingredients	100 servings	.... servings
Potatoes, sweet	40 pounds	
Salt		
Water, boiling		
Milk, evaporated	3—14½-ounce cans	
Water, potato (for milk)	½ to 1½ pints (⅓ to 1 mess kit cup)	
Butter	8 ounces (¼ No. 56 dipper)	
Sugar, granulated	6 to 8 ounces (¼ to ⅓ mess kit cups)	
Salt	3 to 4 ounces (6 to 8 mess kit spoons)	
Pepper		

1. Wash sweet potatoes; pare.
2. Cover sweet potatoes with boiling salted water. Cover and heat to boiling point; reduce heat and simmer until tender. Drain.
3. Mash well.
4. Mix milk and potato water; heat.
5. Add milk, butter, and sugar to potatoes; beat well. Add salt and pepper; mix well.

NO. 692. BAKED PUMPKIN
Yield: 100 servings, approximately ⅓ cup each.

Ingredients	100 servings	.... servings
Eggs, beaten	20 eggs (1 No. 56 dipper)	
Sugar, brown	1½ pounds (1½ mess kit cups)	
Mace	¼ ounce (1 mess kit spoon)	
Salt	1¼ ounces (2½ mess kit spoons)	
Pumpkin	3 No. 10 cans	
Butter, melted	1½ pounds (1 mess kit cup)	

1. Mix beaten egg, sugar, mace, and salt together.
2. Add pumpkin and melted butter; pour into baking pans.
3. Bake in moderate oven (375° F.) about 1 hour.

NO. 693. HOT SAUERKRAUT
Yield: 100 servings, approximately ⅜ cup each.

Ingredients	100 servings	.... servings
Sauerkraut	3 No. 10 cans	
Butter, melted	8 ounces (¼ No. 56 dipper)	
Salt	2 ounces (4 mess kit spoons)	

1. Heat sauerkraut to boiling point in liquid from the can; reduce heat and simmer about 30 minutes.
2. Drain part of liquid from sauerkraut; add butter and salt.

Note. Beef stock may be substituted for sauerkraut liquid in recipe for hot sauerkraut.

NO. 694. BAKED HUBBARD SQUASH
Yield: 100 servings, approximately ⅓-inch square per serving.

Ingredients	100 servings	.... servings
Squash, hubbard	40 pounds	
Water, boiling		
Butter, melted	1 ounce (2 mess kit spoons)	
Salt		
Pepper		

1. Wash squash.
2. Cover squash with boiling water. Cover and heat to boiling point; boil about 10 minutes to soften skin.
3. Cut squash into halves; remove seeds. Cut halves into 3-inch squares.
4. Brush with melted butter. Sprinkle with salt and pepper.
5. Bake in moderate oven (350° F.) 1 hour or until tender.

NO. 695. BAKED HUBBARD SQUASH AND MOLASSES

Prepare squash as in recipe for baked hubbard squash. Cover each piece of squash with ½ mess kit spoon molasses before baking. Add salt and pepper. Allow 1½ pints (1 mess kit cup) molasses for 100 servings.

NO. 696. CREOLE SUMMER SQUASH Yield: 100 servings, approximately ½ cup each.

Ingredients	100 servings	.... servings
Squash, summer	20 pounds	
Salt		
Water, boiling		
Onions, chopped	3 pounds (3 No. 56 dippers)	
Butter or bacon fat	1 pound (½ No. 56 dipper)	
Tomatoes	½ No. 10 can	
Sugar, granulated	2 ounces (4 mess kit spoons)	
Salt	1½ ounces (3 mess kit spoons)	
Pepper		

1. Wash squash thoroughly; cut into 1-inch cubes.
2. Add boiling salted water. Cover and heat to boiling point; reduce heat and simmer about 6 minutes or until tender. Drain.
3. Fry onions in butter or bacon fat until tender.
4. Add cooked squash, tomatoes, sugar, salt, and pepper; mix well.
5. Cover and heat to boiling point; reduce heat and simmer 15 minutes.

NO. 697. FRIED SUMMER SQUASH Yield: 100 servings, approximately ½ cup each.

Ingredients	100 servings	.... servings
Squash, summer, young	25 pounds	
Flour, sifted	1 pound (1 No. 56 dipper)	
Salt	3 ounces (6 mess kit spoons)	
Pepper		
Eggs, slightly beaten	20 eggs (1 No. 56 dipper)	
Bread crumbs, dry	2 pounds (2 No. 56 dippers)	
Fat (for frying)		

1. Wash squash; slice without paring.
2. Mix flour, salt, and pepper. Dip squash in flour mixture.
3. Dip in beaten egg; drain well and dip in bread crumbs.
4. Fry in deep hot fat (350° F.) until tender and golden brown.
   Note. Eggs and crumbs may be omitted if desired.

NO. 698. MASHED HUBBARD SQUASH   Yield: 100 servings, 3 ounces each.

Ingredients	100 servings	.... servings
Squash, hubbard.............	40 pounds............................	....
Water, boiling.............		
Butter.....................	1¼ pounds (¾ mess kit cup)........	....
Salt......................	3 ounces (6 mess kit spoons)........	....
Pepper....................		
Sugar, granulated...........	2 to 3 ounces (4 to 6 mess kit spoons).	....

1. Cover squash with boiling water. Cover and heat to boiling point; boil 10 minutes to soften skin. Drain.
2. Cut squash into medium sized pieces; pare. Remove seeds.
3. Cover with boiling salted water. Cover and heat to boiling point; reduce heat and simmer until very tender. Drain.
4. Mash squash thoroughly. Add butter, salt, pepper and sugar; beat well.

Note. If mixture is too moist, place in well-greased baking pans and bake in moderate oven (350° F.) 30 minutes.

NO. 699. BAKED TOMATOES   Yield: 100 servings, 3 ounces each.

Ingredients	100 servings	.... servings
Tomatoes..................	3 to 4 No. 10 cans.................	....
Bread, cubed...............	2 pounds (4 No. 56 dippers)........	....
Salt......................	2 ounces (4 mess kit spoons)........	....
Pepper....................		
Sugar, granulated...........	8 ounces (¼ No. 56 dipper)........	....
Butter....................	1 pound (½ No. 56 dipper)........	....

1. Heat tomatoes in the liquid from the can.
2. Combine tomatoes, bread, salt, pepper, and sugar. Place in baking pans, place small pieces of butter on top of tomatoes.
3. Bake in moderate oven (375° F.) 30 to 45 minutes.

NO. 700. BAKED, STUFFED TOMATOES   Yield: 100 servings, 1 tomato each.

Ingredients	100 servings	.... servings
Tomatoes..................	100 tomatoes....................	....
Peppers, green, chopped......	1 pound (1 No. 56 dipper)..........	....
Onions, chopped.............	8 ounces·(½ No. 56 dipper)........	....
Parsley, chopped............	1½ ounces (8 mess kit spoons).......	....
Bacon, diced...............	2 pounds.....................	....
Butter, melted..............	1 pound (½ No. 56 dipper)........	....
Bread crumbs, moist.........	3 pounds (6 No. 56 dippers)........	....
Salt......................	1½ ounces (3 mess kit spoons).......	....
Pepper....................	(⅛ mess kit spoon).............	....

1. Wash tomatoes. Cut piece from top of each tomato; scoop out pulp.
2. Fry green peppers, onions, parsley and bacon together.

3. Pour butter over crumbs; combine crumbs, green pepper and bacon mixture, salt, pepper, and tomato pulp. Mix well.
4. Fill tomatoes with mixture.
5. Bake in moderate oven (350° F.) about 20 to 30 minutes or until tender but not soft.

NO. 701. FRENCH FRIED TOMATOES   Yield: 100 servings, 2 to 3 ounces each.

Ingredients	100 servings	.... servings
Tomatoes (green or half ripe)..	40 pounds.........................	
Flour, sifted.................	2 pounds (2 No. 56 dippers).........	
Eggs......................	10 eggs...........................	
Milk, evaporated............	1 pint (½ No. 56 dipper)...........	
Water (for milk)............	1 pint (½ No. 56 dipper)...........	
Bread crumbs..............	2 pounds (2 No. 56 dippers).........	
Salt......................	3 ounces (6 mess kit spoons)........	

1. Clean and cut tomatoes in thick slices.
2. Cover with flour and salt mixture.
3. Dip in egg and milk mixture.
4. Cover with bread crumbs.
5. Fry in deep fat at 360° F. until golden brown.

Note. Salt and pepper may be added to egg and milk mix.

NO. 702. GRILLED TOMATOES   Yield: 100 servings, 2 halves per serving.

Ingredients	100 servings	.... servings
Tomatoes...................	100 tomatoes......................	
Butter, melted..............	2 pounds (1 No. 56 dipper).........	
or		
French dressing.............	1 quart (1 No. 56 dipper)..........	
Salt......................		
Pepper....................		

1. Wash tomatoes; cut into halves.
2. Place in well-greased baking pans. Brush with melted butter or French dressing. (See recipe No. 525.) Sprinkle with salt and pepper.
3. Bake in moderate oven (350° F.) about 20 minutes or until thoroughly heated but not soft.

Note. Dry bread crumbs may be sprinkled over tomatoes before baking.

NO. 703. TOMATO-CORN RAREBIT   Yield: 100 servings, 3 ounces each.

Ingredients	100 servings	.... servings
Onions.....................	4 ounces (⅛ mess kit cup)..........	
Butter or lard..............	2 pounds (1 No. 56 dipper).........	
Flour, sifted................	1½ pounds (1½ No. 56 dippers).....	
Tomatoes...................	2½ No. 10 cans or 19 pounds fresh...	
Corn, whole grain, drained....	2½ No. 10 cans....................	
Salt......................	2½ ounces (5 mess kit spoons)......	
Cheese, cheddar............	12 pounds (12 No. 56 dippers)......	

1. Chop the onions and saute in shortening until tender.
2. Blend in the flour, add the tomatoes, corn and salt. Cook slowly until thickened, stirring frequently.
3. Add the cheese (shredded) and cook slowly, stirring frequently, until the cheese is melted.
4. Serve on toast.

Note. When fresh tomatoes are used, they should be cored, cut into pieces, and cooked until tender.

NO. 704. SCALLOPED TOMATOES   Yield: 100 servings, approximately ½ cup each.

Ingredients	100 servings	.... servings
Tomatoes*..................	4 No. 10 cans........................	....
Sugar, granulated...........	6 ounces (¼ mess kit cup).........	....
Salt......................	1½ ounces (3 mess kit spoons).......	....
Pepper....................	....	....
Flour, sifted...............	6 ounces (½ mess kit cup).........	....
Onions, chopped............	4 ounces (¼ No. 56 dipper).........	....
Bread, chopped.............	3 pounds (6 No. 56 dippers)........	....
Butter, melted.............	1 pound (½ No. 56 dipper).........	....

*Thirty pounds cooked fresh tomatoes may be substituted for the 4 No. 10 cans tomatoes.

1. Combine tomatoes, sugar, salt, pepper, flour, and onions; mix well.
2. Pour melted butter over crumbs.
3. Arrange alternate layers of tomato mixture and crumbs in well-greased baking pans, finishing with crumbs.
4. Bake in moderate oven (375° F.) 30 to 40 minutes.

NO. 705. STEWED TOMATOES   Yield: 100 servings, approximately ½ cup each.

Ingredients	100 servings	servings
Tomatoes..................	4 No. 10 cans........................	....
Onions, chopped............	8 pounds (8 No. 56 dippers).........	....
Sugar, granulated...........	8 ounces (¼ No. 56 dipper).........	....
Salt......................	3 ounces (6 mess kit spoons)........	....
Pepper....................	....	....
Bread, cubed, dry...........	5 pounds (5 No. 56 dippers)........	....
Butter....................	12 ounces (½ mess kit cup).........	....

1. Combine tomatoes, .onions, sugar, salt, pepper, bread cubes, and butter; Mix well.
2. Heat to boiling point; reduce heat and simmer 10 minutes.

NO. 706. STEWED TOMATOES AND ONIONS

Reduce tomatoes to two No. 10 cans and increase onions to 12 pounds (12 No. 56 dippers) in recipe for stewed tomatoes. Peel onions; cut into halves or quarters. Cover with boiling salted water. Heat to boiling point; reduce heat and simmer until tender. Drain. Combine tomatoes, onions and remaining ingredients.

NO. 707. STEWED TOMATOES AND CELERY

Reduce tomatoes to two No. 10 cans in recipe for stewed tomatoes. Substitute 8 pounds (8 No. 56 dippers) diced celery for the onions. Cover celery with boiling salted water. Heat to boiling point; reduce heat and simmer until tender. Drain. Combine tomatoes, celery and remaining ingredients.

NO. 708. STEWED TOMATOES AND CORN

Reduce tomatoes to two No. 10 cans in recipe for stewed tomatoes. Heat one No. 10 can corn in liquid from the can; drain. Combine tomatoes, corn and remaining ingredients.

NO. 709. BOILED TURNIPS AND SALT PORK

Yield: 100 servings, approximately ½ cup each.

Ingredients	100 servings	.... servings
Turnips....................	25 pounds.......................	....
Pork, salt, cut in chunks......	5 pounds........................	....
Salt........................	....	....
Water, boiling..............	....	....
Salt........................	....	....
Pepper.....................	....	....

1. Wash turnips; pare and slice. Add salt pork.
2. Cover with boiling salted water. Heat to boiling point; reduce heat and simmer, uncovered, until turnips are tender. Drain.
3. Add salt and pepper.

NO. 710. MASHED TURNIPS

Yield: 100 servings, approximately ½ cup each.

Ingredients	100 servings	.... servings
Turnips, white or rutabagas...	25 pounds.......................	....
Salt........................	....	....
Water, boiling..............	....	....
Milk, evaporated............	1—14½-ounce cans...............	....
Water (for milk)............	1 pint (½ No. 56 dipper)........	....
Butter.....................	4 ounces (8 mess kit spoons).......	....
Salt.......................	2 ounces (4 mess kit spoons).......	....
Pepper.....................	(½ mess kit spoon)...............	....

1. Wash turnips or rutabagas; pare and slice.
2. Add boiling salted water to turnips. Heat to boiling point; reduce heat and simmer, uncovered, about 40 minutes or until tender. Drain.
3. Mash well.
4. Mix milk and water; heat.
5. Add milk and butter to turnips or rutabagas; beat well. Add salt and pepper.

NO. 711. BUTTERED MIXED VEGETABLES

Yield: 100 servings, approximately ½ cup each.

Ingredients	100 servings	.... servings
Vegetables, mixed	3 to 4 No. 10 cans	
Butter	1 pound (½ No. 56 dipper)	
Salt	½ ounce (1 mess kit spoon)	
Pepper		

1. Drain liquid from vegetables.

2. Combine vegetables, butter, salt, pepper, and 1½ quarts (1½ No. 56 dippers) liquid; mix well.

3. Heat to boiling point; reduce heat and simmer about 15 minutes or until heated through, stirring frequently.

Note. Use remaining vegetable liquid in soups.

NO. 712. CREAMED VEGETABLES

Yield: 100 servings, approximately ½ cup each.

Ingredients	100 servings	.... servings
Peas	1 No. 10 can	
Corn, kernel	1 No. 10 can	
Beans, green	⅓ No. 10 can	
Onions, chopped	3 ounces (¼ mess kit cup)	
Butter or bacon fat	3 ounces (6 mess kit spoons)	
White sauce	5⅓ quarts (5⅓ No. 56 dippers)	
Celery, cooked, diced	3¼ pounds (3¼ No. 56 dippers)	
Carrots, cooked, diced	2¾ pounds (2 No. 56 dippers)	
Salt		
Pepper		

1. Mix peas, corn, and beans together; heat. Drain.

2. Fry onions in butter or bacon fat.

3. Prepare white sauce (recipe No. 548) using liquid from canned vegetables.

4. Combine all vegetables; add salt and pepper. Pour white sauce over vegetables just before serving.

Note. Use any remaining vegetable liquid in soups.

NO. 713. VEGETABLE PIE

Yield: 100 servings, approximately ¾ cup vegetables and 1 biscuit per serving.

Ingredients	100 servings	.... servings
Carrots, cooked, diced........	6 pounds (4½ No. 56 dippers).......	....
Potatoes, cooked, diced.......	9 pounds (5½ No. 56 dippers).......	....
Celery, cooked, diced.........	5 pounds (5 No. 56 dippers)........	....
Peas......................	1 No. 10 can....................	....
Meat stock.................	1¼ gallons (5 No. 56 dippers)........	....
Salt.......................	4 ounces (8 mess kit spoons).........	....
Sugar, granulated...........	....	....
Tomatoes..................	1⅓ No. 10 cans.................	....
Onions, chopped............	1 pound (1 No. 56 dipper).........	....
Butter or beef fat...........	2½ pounds (1¼ No. 56 dippers)....	....
Flour, sifted................	4½ pounds (4½ No. 56 dippers)....	....
Baking powder..............	4 ounces (¼ mess kit cup)........	....
Salt.......................	1 ounce (2 mess kit spoons)........	....
Shortening.................	1 pound (½ No. 56 dipper).........	....
Milk, evaporated............	1½—14½-ounce cans.............	....
Water (for milk).............	1¼ pints (¾ No. 56 dipper).......	....

1. Drain cooked carrots, potatoes, and celery.

2. Drain peas. Mix peas, meat stock, salt, sugar, and tomatoes together; heat.

3. Fry onions in butter or beef fat; add ½ pound (½ No. 56 dipper) flour slowly; mix well. Add to tomato mixture. Heat to boiling point; boil 2 minutes or until thick, stirring constantly.

4. Combine all vegetables. Place in well-greased baking pans.

5. Sift remaining flour, baking powder, and salt together for biscuit dough.

6. Add shortening; mix well.

7. Mix milk and water; add gradually to flour mixture, mixing until soft dough is formed.

8. Place dough on floured board; roll ½-inch thick. Cut into biscuits 2 inches in diameter.

9. Heat vegetables slowly in moderate oven (350° F.).

10. Place biscuits on top of vegetables and bake in hot oven (425° F.) until biscuits are done.

Note. Use vegetable liquids in soups.

NO. 714. VEGETABLE STEW

Yield: 100 servings, approximately ½ cup each.

Ingredients	100 servings	.... servings
Carrots, cooked, diced........	3¾ pounds (2¾ No. 56 dippers).....	....
Potatoes, cooked, diced.......	3¾ pounds (2¼ No. 56 dippers).....	....
Celery, cooked, diced.........	3 pounds (3 No. 56 dippers)........	....
Beans, wax..................	1 No. 10 can.....................	....
Peas........................	1 No. 10 can.....................	....
Flour, sifted.................	6 ounces (½ mess kit cup)..........	....
Sugar, granulated............	3 ounces (6 mess kit spoons)........	....
Salt........................	1½ ounces (3 mess kit spoons).......	....
Pepper......................	(¼ mess kit spoon)................	....
Tomatoes...................	1 No. 10 can.....................	....
Butter or bacon fat...........	12 ounces (½ mess kit cup).........	....

1. Drain cooked carrots, potatoes and celery.

2. Mix beans and peas; heat. Drain.

3. Combine flour, sugar, salt, pepper and tomatoes; mix well. Heat.

4. Combine all vegetables; add butter or bacon fat. Heat thoroughly.

Note. Use vegetable liquids in soups.

SECTION XX

LEFT-OVERS

31. GENERAL. Every effort should be made to prevent left-overs. However, every cook knows that no matter how carefully he plans, left-overs frequently occur. It is impossible to judge the appetites to the exact serving. Therefore this inevitable problem must be considered and solved to the best possible advantage. There are many good uses for left-overs, some of which will be shown in the following recipes. Undoubtedly the good cook, who is familiar with the tastes of those he serves, will think of many more uses for those left-overs he cannot possibly avoid. He must remember to use them while they are still good. Do not keep left-overs too long—and always keep them under refrigeration.

32. USES FOR STALE BREAD. a. Toast. Use bread that is at least a day old. Cut slices ¼ to ½ inch thick. Heat bread quickly until brown for soft toast; slowly for crisp toast. Serve hot.

b. Melba toast. Slice bread very thin. Bake in slow oven (300° F.) about 20 minutes or until brown. Serve unbuttered with soup.

c. Oven toast. Butter slices of bread. Bake in slow oven (300° F.) until brown.

d. Milk toast. Heat milk; add butter and salt. Pour over slices of toast just before serving.

e. Cinnamon toast. Butter toast; sprinkle with mixture of sugar and cinnamon. Heat in slow oven (300° F.) until sugar melts.

f. Croutons. Cut stale bread into cubes. Fry in fat until brown, turning frequently, or fry in deep hot fat. Bread may also be buttered, cut into cubes and baked in a slow oven (300° F.) until brown. Use in soups or on top of creamed dishes.

g. Bread crumbs. Rub slices of soft bread together to break into crumbs. Roll, grind, or grate dry bread into crumbs. Use soft crumbs in scalloped potatoes; dry crumbs for covering foods to be fried.

33. MEAT. The following recipes are for left-over meat using bread crumbs made from left-over bread. The recipes using cooked vegetables may very well use vegetables which have been left over.

NO. 715. BAKED HASH

Any left-over meat—including liver, frankfurters, and cold cuts—chopped, mixed with equal parts of chopped boiled potato, and seasoned with a sautee of onion, green pepper and celery, moistened with left-over gravy or stock and tomatoes. Bake in a moderate oven so that hash becomes piping hot and slightly crusted. See that only lean meat, free of gristle and fat, is used.

NO. 716. BREADED MEAT SLICES

Moisten slices of left-over beef, veal, pork, or lamb with catsup or mustard, then dip and bread. Fry in deep fat or in shallow fat. Serve with barbecue, creole or tomato sauce—or with spiced left-over gravy.

NO. 717. CROQUETTES

Meat—vegetables—fish—fowl, any of these, when left over, may be ground with a sautee of minced onions, celery, and green pepper as the base for croquettes. With a suitable binder and filler, the mix is shaped into cones, cylinders, or balls, breaded and fried in deep fat fried for cutlets.

NO. 718. ESCALLOPED MACARONI AND MEAT

Diced left-over meats mixed with cooked macaroni and a thin cream sauce or a tomato sauce. Sprinkle with bread crumbs and butter or fat. Bake in a moderate oven until brown. Grated cheese makes the dish "au gratin." Spaghetti or noodles may be substituted for macaroni.

NO. 719. ESCALLOPED PORK (OR HAM) AND APPLES

Layers of diced cooked pork or ham alternating with layers of thinly sliced apples sprinkled with sugar and a dash of nutmeg, covered with buttered crumbs (or pie dough) and baked in a moderate oven. Left-over apples or applesauce may be used. Moisten filling if necessary with fruit juice or pork gravy.

NO. 720. HAM AND HOMINY CASSEROLE

Mix cooked hominy with thin cream sauce, adding diced ham (or diced pork, beef, frankfurters, or luncheon loaf), sprinkle with bread crumbs and brown in a moderate oven.

NO. 721. HAMBURG POT PIE
Yield: 100 servings, 6½ ounces each.

Ingredients	100 servings	.... servings
Bacon, diced fine	4 pounds	
Onions, chopped fine	16 onions	
Meat, LEFT-OVER, ground	20 pounds	
Catsup, tomato	3 pints	
Mustard, prepared	½ mess kit cup	
Salt and pepper	To taste	
Gravy of thick soup, LEFT-OVER (if not available, add 2 gallons of stock or water and thicken with smooth flour batter).	2 gallons (8 No. 56 dippers)	

1. Fry bacon and onions together in ration pan.
2. Add left-over ground meat.
3. Add tomato catsup, prepared mustard, salt, and pepper.
4. Add left-over gravy or thick soup.
5. Cover with biscuit dough, ¾" thick or pie dough, ⅛" thick.

NO. 722. MANHATTAN MEAT ROLL

Roll cut biscuit dough on floured surface. Spread evenly, about ½ inch deep, with a moist croquette mixture. Roll up like a jelly roll; cut off 1-inch slices. Lay slices in a greased bakepan, and bake in a moderate oven. This dish should be served with a gravy or sauce. Pie dough may be similarly used.

NO. 723. MEAT AND RICE AU GRATIN

Mix equal quantities of left-over diced meat and left-over cooked rice, seasoned with salt, pepper, mace or nutmeg. Moisten with stock or left-over gravy. Sprinkle generously with grated cheese and bake until cheese is melted and browned.

NO. 724. MEAT BIRDS

Slices of left-over roast meat that will stand rolling are used. The slices should be at least 4 inches in diameter. Put a spoonful of a moist savory bread dressing, flavored with onion or sage, on each meat slice. Roll up the slice, skewering it with a toothpick. Place the birds in a bakepan with a little fat, brown them briefly and finish off in a moderate oven after adding a half inch of stock. Left-over dressing may be used to an advantage in this dish, as may uncooked beef, veal and lamb.

NO. 725. MEAT PATTIES

Ground left-over meat and a filler of mashed potato and, if necessary, a binder, seasoned with a sautee of minced onion, green pepper, celery, salt, and pepper. Put into shape of cakes and wrap with bacon strips skewered with a toothpick. Put bakepan of patties in a moderate oven. When bacon is cooked, the patties are ready to serve.

NO. 726. MEAT SALAD

Any left-over meat can be used for salad. It should be diced or chopped. Mix 60 percent meat with 40 percent diced or chopped celery, season with salt and pepper and moisten with mayonnaise. Serve with lettuce and with suitable garnish or hard-boiled eggs or tomato.

NO. 727. MEAT TURNOVERS

Cut thinly rolled pie dough into 6-inch squares or rounds. Fill well with moist croquette meat mixture in the center of each. Fold over, crimp edges to seal the turnover, brush with milk-and-egg wash, and bake in a moderate oven. A sauce or gravy may be served over the turnovers.

NO. 728. MULLIGATAWNY SOUP

Sautee minced onion, celery, and green peppers in fat. Add flour to take up fat, cooking slowly until well blended. Add left-over lean meat, diced. and season with salt, pepper, Worcestershire sauce, and thyme if available. Add hot beef, veal or chicken stock to make up quantity desired. There should be about 1 pound of meat to every 2 quarts of liquid.

NO. 729. PEPPER STEAK

Make green pepper sauce by sauteeing chopped peppers in fat until tender. Add sufficient flour to take up the fat and cook briefly over a slow flame. Add hot stock to thin down to sauce consistency. Season with salt and pepper. Shape chopped left-over meat into patties, brown in a pan and pour sauce over the meat.

NO. 730. SHEPHERD'S PIE

Shepherd's pie consists of a layer of left-over ground or diced cooked meats, seasoned with sauteed onion, green pepper, and celery and moistened with left-over gravy or sauce, topped by a layer of mashed potatoes garnished with paprika or parsley. The dish is browned in a moderate oven.

NO. 731. FISHERMAN'S PIE

Substituting fish for meat, consists of layers of boneless fish, sliced hard-cooked eggs moistened with cream sauce if necessary and mashed potatoes, with garnish. Bake in a moderate oven.

NO. 732. STUFFED PEPPERS

1. Clean green peppers to form cups, dice the end trimmings for use in the filling.
2. Parboil in covered ration pan with one inch water to tenderize. Drain off water.
3. Stuff peppers with any one of the following mixtures and brown in medium oven.

A. Meat

Ground left-over cooked meat mixed with bread crumbs, sauteed chopped onions, celery, and pepper trimming, salt and pepper to taste. Moisten with left-over gravy or stock. Small amounts of left-over cooked vegetables may be included.

B. Fish

Ground or flaked left-over cooked fish or shrimp, blended with equal parts of left-over mashed or finely diced potatoes; onions, celery, pepper sauteed, salt and pepper. Top with bread crumbs.

C. Rice

Use left-over Spanish rice, or prepare left-over boiled rice with a Spanish sauce for stuffing peppers.

D. Macaroni

Use left-over cooked macaroni or spaghetti, mixed with thin tomato or cream sauce. Stuff into peppers, top with grated cheese and bread crumbs and brown in the oven. Chopped cooked meat can be added.

NO. 733. TEXAS TACOS

Mix left-over cornmeal with water and salt to taste to make a thick batter. Spoon onto hot griddle to make cakes, browning on both sides. Cover cakes in bakepan with left-over chili con carne (or fold over cakes stuffed with meat), bake in oven until piping hot. Serve with Mexican hot sauce or tomato sauce.

34. DESSERT. The cook does not have to be a genius to save that left-over fruit, cake, or pie to be served as a delicious dessert at the next meal. Here are a few recipes showing how it can be used.

NO. 734. ALL-GONE PUDDING

Chop fruit pie or left-over cake and mold into a pan by moistening with fruit juice or milk if necessary. Serve with a custard sauce (recipe No. 538) or, add eggs and milk to make a custard, bake in moderate oven, serve hot with fruit sauce.

NO. 735. BROWN BETTY
Yield: 100 servings, 3 ounces each.

Ingredients	100 servings	.... servings
Bread, diced	10 pounds (10 No. 56 dippers)	
Sugar, brown	6 pounds (6 mess kit cups)	
Raisins	2 pounds (2 mess kit cups)	
Water	2 gallons (8 No. 56 dippers)	
Apples, cooked, LEFT-OVER	2 to 4 quarts	
Cinnamon	To taste	

Dice bread and brown in oven. Mix brown sugar (or caramelized granulated), to water. Add cinnamon. Pour over diced bread and add apples and raisins. Bake in oven. Serve with a fruit sauce. (See recipe No. 536.)

NO. 736. GELATIN SALADS (DESSERTS)

1. These consist of left-over salads (or fruits) jelled in a suitable flavored liquid with plain gelatin. Or, such "ready" gelatins as lemon, lime, orange, and berry flavor may be used. In case the already flavored variety is desired, follow package directions, adding solid food when it is partially set in shallow pans.

2. With plain gelatin, the liquid must be flavored distinctively. Use vinegar and sugar, clear vegetable or meat stocks; fruit juice and grated lemon rind; tomato juice and seasonings. Four mess kit spoons

of plain gelatin will jell a quart of liquid. The liquid should be very hot. Dissolve gelatin in enough *cold* water to allow pouring, add it to the hot liquid, stirring thoroughly. Cool, pour into shallow pans. When beginning to set, add left-over vegetable salad, cabbage salad, carrot salad, apple salad or fruit salad. (If mayonnaise or thick dressings were used on the left-over, wash it away before adding to jell.) Chill. Garnish with salad dressing, lettuce. Left-over fruits may be stretched into a dessert by this means.

35. Fish. Left-over fish can also be used in appetizing dishes if the cook is ingenious. Fish must be used promptly. It will not keep long and should always be kept under refrigeration.

NO. 737. COCKTAIL SAUCE

1. Thin tomato catsup or chili sauce with vinegar, adding a little sugar to cut vinegar "edges." Use about 2 parts catsup to $\frac{1}{2}$ part vinegar.
2. Season with salt or garlic salt, red pepper, Worcestershire sauce, horseradish. Hot—but *not* burning.
3. Serve with seafood.

NO. 738. FISH CHOWDER (10 gallons)   Yield: 100 servings, 1 bowl each.

Ingredients	100 servings	servings
Celery....................	4 bunches.............................	....
Onions, medium.............	12 onions.............................	....
Peppers, green..............	6 peppers.............................	....
Fat.......................	1 pound ($\frac{1}{2}$ No. 56 dipper).........	....
Flour.....................	1 pound (1 No. 56 dipper)...........	....
Milk, hot..................	10 gallons (40 No. 56 dippers).......	....
Potatoes...................	60 potatoes........................	....
Fish or sea food, flaked and diced, LEFT-OVER.	10 to 20 pounds.....................	....
Salt and pepper.............	To taste............................	....
Parsley, chopped............	To taste............................	....
Butter....................	....	....

1. Chop and sautee celery, onions, and green peppers with chopped bacon or salt pork until tender. Remove vegetables.
2. Make roux (add fat if necessary)—1 pound or 1 pint of fat and 1 pound of flour.
3. Slowly add 10 gallons hot milk to roux, stirring constantly. Keep over low heat.
4. Add sauteed vegetables.
5. Add diced boiled potatoes (about 60 potatoes).
6. Add 10 to 20 pounds of left-over flaked or diced fish or sea food.
7. Season with salt and pepper and garnish with chopped parsley and butter.

36. SANDWICHES. There is frequently a need for sandwiches. Here is a good way to use that left-over.

NO. 739. DEVILED SANDWICH SPREAD

Any ground left-over meat mixed with catsup, prepared mustard and a drop of tabasco sauce to make a smooth, meaty spread. Minced pickle relish may be added.

NO. 740. SALAD RELISH

Mince left-over salad ingredients—lettuce, cabbage, tomato, cucumber, onion, green pepper, pickles, celery, carrots, olives—and make into spicy table relish by moistening it with vinegar and sugar, with dashes of combinations of such seasonings as dry mustard, paprika, salt, red pepper, allspice, and celery salt. Chopped parsley, chili sauce, catsup, and prepared mustard may be used. Good for sandwich making.

37. VEGETABLES. Vegetables are not necessarily a loss because they are not used the first time served. There are many uses for good cooked vegetables. They may even be served in the same style at the next meal.

NO. 741. CORN O'BRIEN

Corn with sauteed bacon, minced green pepper and onions, with tomatoes, seasoned with salt, pepper, butter.

NO. 742. ESCALLOPED MIXED VEGETABLES

Diced left-over cooked vegetables, mixed with a thin cream sauce, seasoned with sauteed chopped onion and pepper, seasoned with salt, pepper, mace, and celery salt. Sprinkle with crumbs and butter and brown in the oven. For variations add diced left-over meat, or sprinkle with grated cheese for au gratin dish.

NO. 743. ESCALLOPED VEGETABLES WITH HAM

Any one of these vegetables when left over—asparagus, cauliflower, corn, hominy, lima beans—may be escalloped with ham (or another diced meat) for a delicious baked dish. Mix with a thin cream sauce, season, sprinkle with crumbs, and bake in a moderate oven.

(For using left-over mashed potatoes.)
NO. 744. POTATO PUFFS

Yield: 100 5-ounce servings or 2 serving spoons each.

Ingredients	100 servings	.... servings
Milk, evaporated.............	1—14½-ounce can.....................	....
Water, for milk..............	1 pint (½ No. 56 dipper)...........	....
or		
Milk, powdered..............	4 ounces (¼ No. 56 dipper).........	
Water, for milk..............	1 quart (1 No. 56 dipper)..........	
Eggs, powdered..............	6 ounces (½ No. 56 dipper)........	
Water, for eggs..............	1 pint (½ No. 56 dipper)...........	
Preserved butter.............	1 pound (½ No. 56 dipper).........	
Potatoes, white, mashed......	32 pounds (16 No. 56 dippers)......	
Salt......................	To taste......................	
Pepper....................	To taste......................	

1. Combine evaporated milk and water or reconstitute milk.
2. Add egg powder to ⅓ of the water beating constantly to make a smooth paste. Add remainder of the water and mix until smooth.
3. Melt the preserved butter.
4. Combine milk, eggs, ½ of the preserved butter, mashed potatoes. salt, and pepper. Mix well. Place potato mixture in well-greased roasting pan. Pour remaining preserved butter over top.
5. Bake in moderate oven 20 to 30 minutes.

NO. 745. POTATO CAKES OR BALLS

Yield: 2 to 4 ounces each serving.

Use 16 No. 56 dippers (32 pounds) of potatoes, white, mashed. (See recipe No. 681.) Form into small cakes or balls, roll in cracker crumbs (3½ No. 56 dippers) and pan- or deep-fat fry.

NO. 746. SUCCOTASH

Succotashes are corn in combinations with other vegetables, lima beans (dry fresh types), peas, string beans. Made either with butter or light cream sauce. Tomatoes may be added to corn and lima bean succotash for variation. Season with salt, pepper, dash of onion, and celery salt. Bread crumbs may be sprinkled on top.

NO. 747. WILTED LETTUCE

Lettuce cut or shredded. Pour over the lettuce a piping hot dressing made as follows—fry diced bacon until crisp, add mixture of vinegar and sugar with dash of mustard. Serve at once.

SECTION XXI

DEHYDRATED FOODS

38. DEHYDRATED FOODS. a. General. This section gives directions for the preparation and cooking of dehydrated foods. These recipes will be a value in the mess in the field, either in training on maneuvers or in the theaters of operations during actual combat.

b. Powdered eggs. Powdered eggs are prepared by removing the eggs from the shell and drying the eggs by the spray method. By the newer methods of dehydration egg yolks and whites are dried separately and then combined. Reconstituted powdered eggs have approximately the same food value as fresh eggs.

(1) *Egg conversion table.*

Fresh eggs	Powdered whole eggs		Water Measure No. 56 dippers
	Measure No. 56 dippers	Weight	
1 dozen.................	⅓	5⅓ ounces	⅓
2 dozen.................	⅔	10⅔ ounces	⅔
3 dozen.................	1	1 pound	1
4 dozen.................	1⅓	1⅓ pounds	1⅓
8 dozen.................	2⅔	2⅔ pounds	2⅔
12 dozen.................	4	4 pounds	4
24 dozen.................	8	8 pounds	8

(2) *Reconstituting powdered eggs.* Stir powdered eggs to remove lumps. Add measured water slowly, stirring until a smooth mixture is obtained. If possible, refrigerate reconstituted eggs for several hours. Any remaining lumps can easily be removed by beating the cold eggs. If means of refrigeration are not available, use reconstituted eggs within 10 to 15 minutes after mixing powder with water. In preparing cooked foods, powdered eggs may be added to other dry ingredients without first being reconstituted. Combine thoroughly before adding liquids.

c. Powdered milk. Powdered milk is fresh milk dried by the spray or roller process. A solution can easily be made of powdered milk and cold water. Warm water is better for rolled processed milk.

(1) *Milk conversion table.*

Fresh liquid milk	Evaporated milk	Water	Powdered whole milk	Water
1 quart.......	1—14½-ounce can	½ No. 56 dipper.	¼ No. 56 dipper (¼ lb.).	1 No. 56 dipper.
1 gallon.......	4—14½-ounce cans	2 No. 56 dippers.	1 No. 56 dipper (1 lb.).	4 No. 56 dippers.
5 gallons......	2¼ gallons (2—8-lb. cans).	6 No. 55 dippers.	5 No. 56 dippers (5 lb.).	11½ No. 55 dippers.
10 gallons......	5 gallons (5—8-lb. cans).	11½ No. 55 dippers.	10 No. 56 dippers (10 lb.).	23 No. 55 dippers.

(2) *Reconstituting powdered milk.* Sprinkle the powdered milk on top of the water; mix vigorously with a wire whisk. Scrape the caked powder from the whisk occasionally. If a mechanical mixer is available, add the powdered milk gradually to the water in the mixing bowl and mix at low speed. Continue mixing until powder is completely dissolved and the chalky flavor is lost. When in complete solution the milk will have the flavor and appearance of fresh milk. Handle reconstituted powdered milk in the same manner as fresh milk. Keep it cold. The flavor is improved by refrigerating for a few hours.

39. BREAKFAST FOODS. Breakfast foods are still the same even with only dehydrated foods available. The following recipes show the preparation of dehydrated food in the pattern of the average American breakfast.

NO. 748. GRIDDLE CAKES

Yield: 100 servings, 3 to 4 each.

Ingredients	100 servings	servings
Flour, wheat, sifted..........	15 pounds (15 No. 56 dippers).......	....
Eggs, powdered..............	1 pound (1⅓ 3-pound cans).........	....
Sugar, granulated...........	1½ pounds (¾ No. 56 dipper).......	....
Baking powder..............	20 ounces (⅝ No. 56 dipper)........	....
Salt.......................	2 ounces (4 mess kit spoons)........	....
Milk, powdered, whole........	1½ pounds (1½ No. 56 dippers).....	....
Water (for milk).............	13 quarts (13 No. 56 dippers).......	....
or		
Milk, evaporated.............	6—14½-ounce cans................	....
Water (for milk).............	10 quarts (10 No. 56 dippers).......	....
Fat drippings...............	3 pounds (1½ No. 56 dippers).......	....

1. Combine flour, powdered eggs, sugar, baking powder, and salt.
2. Mix milk and water.
3. Combine dry ingredients, milk mixture and fat. Stir only until dry and liquid ingredients are mixed and most of the lumps beaten out.
4. Drop batter by spoonfuls onto hot, greased griddle. Cook cakes on one side until top is full of bubbles. Turn and cook on other side. Turn cakes only once.

NO. 749. SCRAMBLED EGGS

Yield: 25 servings, 2 to 3 ounces each.

Ingredients	25 servings	.... servings
Water, cold.................	2½ quarts (2½ No. 56 dippers)......	....
Eggs, powdered..............	1½ pounds (½ 3-pound can)........	....
Salt.......................	To taste.........................	....
Pepper.....................	To taste.........................	....
Lard or bacon fat...........	1 pound (½ No. 56 dipper)........	....

1. Sift eggs. Pour ⅓ of the water into a utensil suitable for mixing eggs. Add powdered eggs. Stir vigorously with whip or slit spoon until mixture is absolutely smooth. Tip utensil while stirring.
2. Add salt, pepper, and remaining water slowly to eggs, stirring until eggs are completely dissolved.
3. Melt fat in baking pan. Pour liquid eggs into hot fat.
4. Stir as eggs begin to thicken. Continue stirring slowly until eggs are cooked slightly less than desired for serving.
5. Take eggs from fire while soft, as they will continue to thicken after being removed from heat.

Note. Reconstituted milk, powdered, whole or evaporated, may be used instead of part of the water in the recipe for scrambled eggs. Seasonings, meats, cheese, tomatoes or Spanish sauce add flavor and variety to scrambled eggs.

NO. 750. DICED HAM (OR BACON) AND SCRAMBLED EGGS

1. Add 3 pounds of ham or bacon to basic recipe for scrambled eggs; omit lard. Fry ham or bacon until crisp and brown.
2. Pour egg solution over meat and fat. Stir and cook as in basic recipe. Additional fat may be needed if ham is used.

NO. 751. LUNCHEON MEAT AND SCRAMBLED EGGS

1. Add 3 pounds diced luncheon meat to basic recipe for scrambled eggs, just after eggs begin to set.
2. Stir and cook as in basic recipe.

NO. 752. PORK SAUSAGE AND SCRAMBLED EGGS

1. Add 4 pounds diced pork sausage to basic recipe for scrambled eggs. Substitute 1 pound pork sausage fat for lard or bacon fat.
2. Pour egg solution over melted sausage fat. Stir and cook as in basic recipe, adding sausage just after eggs begin to eat.

NO. 753. CHEESE AND SCRAMBLED EGGS

Add 2 pounds diced cheese to basic recipe for scrambled eggs just after eggs begin to set. Stir and cook as in basic recipe.

NO. 754. SPANISH SAUCE FOR SCRAMBLED EGGS

Yield: 1 ounce each serving.

Ingredients	100 servings	.... servings
Onions, dehydrated	1 pound (1⅔ No. 56 dippers)	
Water, cold	3½ quarts (3½ No. 56 dippers)	
Lard, melted	2 pounds (1 No. 56 dipper)	
Tomatoes	2 No. 10 cans	
Salt	To taste	
Pepper	To taste	
Paprika	To taste	

1. Soak onions in cold water 20 minutes.
2. Fry onions in hot lard until brown.
3. Add tomatoes and seasonings; let simmer 30 minutes.
4. Pour sauce over plain scrambled eggs just before serving.

NO. 755. INDIVIDUAL HAM OMELETS   Yield: 25 servings,
2 to 3 ounces each.

Ingredients	25 servings	.... servings
Eggs, powdered, whole........	1½ pounds (½—3-pound can).......	....
Flour, sifted.................	½ pound (½ No. 56 dipper).........	....
Baking powder..............	1¼ ounces (3 mess kit spoons).......	....
Water.....................	2 quarts (2 No. 56 dippers).........	....
Ham, ground, cooked........	(3 No. 56 dippers)................	....

1. Follow recipe for jelly omelets.
2. Add ham to batter.
3. Cook as directed in above recipe and serve plain or with jelly or syrup.

NO. 756. INDIVIDUAL JELLY OMELETS   Yield: 25 servings,
2 to 3 ounces each.

Ingredients	For 25 men	.... servings
Eggs, dehydrated, whole......	1½ pounds (½ 3-pound can)........	....
Flour, sifted.................	½ pound (½ No. 56 dipper).........	....
Salt.......................	¾ ounce (1½ mess kit spoons).......	....
Baking powder..............	1¼ ounces (3 mess kit spoons).......	....
Water.....................	2 quarts (2 No. 56 dippers).........	....

1. Mix the powdered eggs, flour, salt, and baking powder thoroughly.
2. Add this mixture to ⅓ of the cold water. Stir until smooth. Add the remainder of the water.
3. Drop batter on a hot, greased grill, using a large mixing spoon. Fry until light brown on both sides.
4. Jelly or jam may be spread on top and the pancake rolled and served with syrup.

NO. 757. FRENCH TOAST   Yield: 100 servings,
1 slice each.

Ingredients	100 servings	.... servings
Eggs, dehydrated, whole......	3 pounds (1—3-pound can).........	....
Water, for eggs.............	2¾ quarts (2¾ No. 56 dippers)......	....
Milk, whole, dry.............	9 ounces (½ No. 56 dippers)........	....
Water (for milk).............	2¼ quarts (2¼ No. 56 dippers)......	....
or		
Milk, evaporated............	2—14½-ounce cans.............	....
Water (for milk).............	1½ quarts (1½ No. 56 dippers)......	....
Salt.......................	1 ounce (2 mess kit spoons)........	....
Bread.....................	100 thick slices................	....
Lard......................	6 pounds (3 No. 56 dippers).......	....

1. Reconstitute eggs.
2. Reconstitute milk. Add milk and salt to egg solution; stir briskly.

3. Pour mixture into shallow pan; dip slices of bread in egg mixture. Soak 2 or 3 minutes.
4. Heat lard until quite hot. Put soaked bread in lard, fry until golden brown. Turn and fry on other side.

40. DESSERT. The soldier's heart grows lighter and his eating satisfaction is complete when he is served a properly prepared dessert from dehydrated food. Here are some recipes that will help the cook to accomplish this.

NO. 758. BAKING POWDER FRENCH COFFEE CAKE

Yield: 100 servings, approximately 3 ounces each.

Ingredients	100 servings	.... servings
Lard...................	2½ pounds (1¼ No. 56 dippers).....	....
Sugar, granulated...........	4½ pounds (2¼ No. 56 dippers)....	....
Eggs, powdered, whole........	1 pound (1 No. 56 dipper)...........	....
Water (for eggs).............	1¼ quarts (1¼ No. 56 dippers)......	....
Salt...................	1 ounce (2 mess kit spoons).........	....
Vanilla..................	1 ounce (2 mess kit spoons).........	....
Milk, evaporated............	1 pound (1—14½-ounce can or ½ No. 56. dipper.)	....
Water (for milk)............	1 quart (1 No. 56 dipper)...........	....
or		
Milk, powdered, whole........	4 ounces (¼ No. 56 dipper)........	....
Water (for milk).............	2⅓ quarts (2⅓ No. 56 dippers)......	....
Flour..................	4½ quarts (4½ No. 56 dippers)....	....
Baking powder.............	3 ounces (6 mess kit spoons)........	....
Raisins..................	2 pounds (1⅓ No. 56 dippers)......	....
Water..................	1 pint (¼ No. 56 dipper)...........	....

1. Mix lard and sugar until smooth and fluffy.
2. Add the reconstituted eggs and mix well.
3. Add salt, vanilla, and reconstituted milk and stir.
4. Add flour and baking powder and mix well.
5. Last, add raisins which have been soaked in the 8 ounces of water.
6. Divide in 2 baking sheet cakepans and bake until golden brown.

NO. 759. SPICE COOKIES

Yield: 100 servings, 2 cookies each.

Ingredients	100 servings	.... servings
Flour, sifted...............	3 pounds (3 No. 56 dippers)........	....
Baking powder.............	1⅛ ounces (3 mess kit spoons).......	....
Salt....................	½ ounce (1 mess kit spoon).........	....
Cinnamon.................	½ ounce (2 mess kit spoons)........	....
Nutmeg..................	¼ ounce (1 mess kit spoon)........	....
Shortening................	1½ pounds (1 mess kit cup)........	....
Sugar, granulated...........	2 pounds 12 ounces (1¾ No. 56 dippers).	....
Eggs, powdered............	3 ounces (12 mess kit spoons).......	....
Water (for eggs)............	6 ounces (12 mess kit spoons).......	....
Vanilla..................	½ ounce (1 mess kit spoon)........	....
Water..................	1½ pounds (1 mess kit cup).......	....

1. Sift flour with baking powder, salt, cinnamon, and nutmeg.
2. Stir shortening and sugar together until light and fluffy.
3. Reconstitute eggs and add to shortening and sugar.
4. Add vanilla.
5. Add flour mixture and water alternately, mixing well after each addition.
6. Drop by spoonfuls onto greased baking sheets.
7. Bake in a moderate oven (375° F.) for 12 to 15 minutes.

NO. 760. DEVILS FOOD CAKE

Yield: 100 servings, 1 piece each, 2½"x3".

Ingredients	100 servings	.... servings
Sugar, granulated	7 pounds (3½ No. 56 dippers)	
Lard	2 pounds (1 No. 56 dipper)	
Flour, sifted	5 pounds (5 No. 56 dippers)	
Salt	1½ ounces (3 mess kit spoons)	
Soda	1¼ ounces (2½ mess kit spoons)	
Baking powder	3¼ ounces (6½ mess kit spoons)	
Cocoa	1 pound 4 ounces (1½ No. 56 dippers)	
Water	2 quarts (2 No. 56 dippers)	
Vanilla	To taste	
Eggs, powdered	1 pound 2 ounces (1¼ No. 56 dippers)	
Water (for eggs)	1½ quarts (1½ No. 56 dippers)	

1. Cream sugar and shortening until light and fluffy.
2. Reconstitute eggs and fold into above mix.
3. Combine flour, salt, soda, cocoa, and baking powder. Mix to the above.
4. Add water and vanilla and mix thoroughly.
5. Turn into greased bakepans and bake at 350° F. 28 to 30 minutes.

NO. 761. YELLOW LAYER CAKE

Yield: 100 servings, 1 piece each, 2½"x3".

Ingredients	100 servings	.... servings
Sugar, granulated	7 pounds 4 ounces (3¾ No. 56 dippers)	
Lard	2 pounds (1 No. 56 dipper)	
Flour	5½ pounds (5½ No. 56 dippers)	
Salt	2 ounces (4 mess kit spoons)	
Baking powder	4 ounces (8 mess kit spoons)	
Milk, evaporated	¾ quart (¾ No. 56 dipper)	
Water (for milk)	¾ quart (¾ No. 56 dipper)	
or		
Milk, powdered	6 ounces (⅓ No. 56 dipper)	
Water (for milk)	1½ quarts (1½ No. 56 dippers)	
Eggs, powdered	10 ounces (¾ No. 56 dipper)	
Water (for eggs)	¾ quarts (¾ No. 56 dipper)	
Water	1 quart (1 No. 56 dipper)	
Vanilla	To taste	

1. Cream sugar and shortening until light and fluffy.
2. Reconstitute eggs and fold in above mix.
3. Add evaporated milk and water or reconstituted whole milk and mix thoroughly.
4. Add water and vanilla and mix to above.
5. Combine flour, salt, and baking powder and fold into above.
6. Turn into greased bakepans and bake at 350° F. for 45 minutes.

NO. 762. APPLE CRISP

Yield: 100 servings, 3 sheet pans, 16½x24½ inches.

Ingredients	100 servings	.... servings
Apple nuggets, dehydrated....	3¾ pounds (5 No. 56 dippers).......	....
Water......................	11½ quarts (11½ No. 56 dippers)....	....
Sugar, granulated...........	2 pounds (1 No. 56 dipper).........	....
Nutmeg....................	¼ ounce (2 mess kit spoons)........	....
Cinnamon..................	¼ ounce (2 mess kit spoons)........	....
Sugar, granulated...........	6 pounds (3 No. 56 dippers)........	....
Flour.....................	3¾ pounds (3 No. 56 dippers)......	....
Salt......................	¾ ounce (1½ mess kit spoons)......	....
Fat, melted...............	2 pounds (1 No. 56 dipper).........	....

1. Add apple nuggets to water and bring slowly to a boil. Simmer for 10 minutes. Add 2 pounds of sugar and simmer for an additional 10 minutes or until apples are tender. Cool.
2. Combine 6 pounds of sugar, spices, flour, salt, and melted fat and mix until crumbly. Line bottom of bakepan with ½ mixture.
3. Add layer of cold applesauce and sprinkle remainder of sugar over the top.
4. Bake in moderate oven for 45 minutes or until sugar mixture is browned.

NO. 763. APPLE PIE OR COBBLER

Yield: 100 servings, 1 piece each, 2½"x3".

Ingredients	100 servings	.... servings
Apple nuggets, dehydrated....	4 pounds (7 No 56 dippers)........	....
Water......................	13 quarts (13 No. 56 dippers).......	....
Sugar, granulated...........	4 pounds (2 No. 56 dippers)........	....
Cinnamon (optional)........	½ ounce (2 mess kit spoons)........	....

1. Place apple nuggets in water and bring to a boil over a slow fire.
2. Simmer for 20 minutes.
3. Add the sugar and cinnamon.
4. For cobbler, roll out 4½ pounds (2 No. 56 dippers) of pie dough to the size of a baking sheet. Pour seven No. 56 dippers of apple pie filling into the pan. Roll out 4 pounds of pie dough and cover the whole baking sheet. Dock the top crust and bake in a hot oven for about 45 minutes. Prepare two pans for 100 men.

5. For pie, prepare a two-crust pie as described in 4 above, and fill with the apple pie filling. Butter and nutmeg may be used to give a superior flavor to both apple and sweet potato pies.

NO. 764. CREAM PIE FILLING

Yield: 100 servings, 18 9-inch pies, 6 cuts per pie.

Ingredients	100 servings	.... servings
Milk, evaporated	14 pounds (15—14½-ounce cans or 7 No. 56 dippers).	
Water (for milk)	7 quarts (7 No. 56 dippers)	
or		
Milk, powdered, whole	4 pounds (4 No. 56 dippers)	
Water (for milk)	12 quarts (12 No. 56 dippers)	
Sugar, granulated	7 pounds (3½ No. 56 dippers)	
Salt	1 ounce (2 mess kit spoons)	
Cornstarch	1 pound 12 ounces (1⅓ No. 56 dippers)	
Eggs, powdered, whole	1 pound 12 ounces (2 No. 56 dippers)	
Water (for eggs)	2¼ quarts (2¼ No. 56 dippers)	
Butter	14 ounces (½ No. 56 dipper)	
Vanilla	To taste	

1. Bring reconstituted milk, sugar, and salt to a boil.
2. Mix powdered eggs and cornstarch together. Add water slowly to the mixture and stir vigorously to prevent lumps. Pour into the boiling milk solution and stir vigorously until it thickens.
3. Add butter and vanilla and allow it to cool until it is lukewarm.
4. Place one dipper of filling in each baked pie shell. Top with meringue if fresh eggs are available. Bake to a delicate brown.

NO. 765. VANILLA CREAM SLICES (NAPOLEONS)

1. Roll pie dough to the size of a large baking sheet. Approximately 4½ pounds of pie dough are required. Roll 1 sheet for the bottom and 1 sheet for the top. Dock with a fork and bake until crisp and brown. Prepare 2 pans for 100 men.
2. After rolling to the proper thickness, coil pie dough around the rolling pin. Place on the pan and unroll.
3. The baked pastry should be golden brown and free from blisters. Unless it is properly docked, it will not bake to a uniform appearance and shape.
4. Fill the pie shell with vanilla cream filling. The filling should be poured to a thickness of ½ inch. Fresh fruit of any type may be added at this stage if desired.
5. The second layer of the baked pie shell should be placed on top of the cream filling. The completed slice should be chilled if refrigeration is available.
6. The complete cream slice may either be served plain or it may be finished with water icing, made by mixing together powdered sugar (6 No. 56 dippers) and water (⅔ No. 56 dipper). Flavor to taste.

NO. 766. CUSTARD PIE
Yield: Enough for 18 9-inch pies, 6 cuts per pie.

Ingredients	100 servings	.... servings
Sugar, granulated	6 pounds (3 No. 56 dippers)	
Salt	½ ounce (1 mess kit spoon)	
Eggs, powdered, whole	2½ pounds (3 No. 56 dippers)	
Water (for eggs)	5 pounds (2½ No. 56 dippers)	
Milk, evaporated	11 pounds (12—14½-ounce cans or 5½ No. 56 dippers).	
Water (for milk)	6½ quarts (6½ No. 56 dippers)	
or		
Milk, powdered, whole	3 pounds (3 No. 56 dippers)	
Water (for milk)	10½ quarts (10½ No. 56 dippers)	
Vanilla	To taste	
Butter (melted)	6 ounces (12 mess kit spoons)	
Nutmeg	To taste	

1. Sift or blend dry ingredients together.
2. Mix the dehydrated eggs with the water. Be sure a smooth mixture is obtained. Add to the dry ingredients and mix smooth.
3. Mix the reconstituted milk, vanilla, butter, and nutmeg thoroughly. Add slowly to the egg mixture, and mix well. Place unbaked pie shells in oven and into each pour one No. 56 dipper of filling.

NO. 767. PUMPKIN PIE
Yield: Enough for 18 9-inch pies, 6 cuts per pie.

Ingredients	100 servings	.... servings
Sugar, brown	6½ pounds (3¾ No. 56 dippers)	
Cinnamon	1½ ounce (6 mess kit spoons)	
Nutmeg	½ ounce (2 mess kit spoons)	
Salt	1 ounce (2 mess kit spoons)	
Eggs, powdered	1 pound (1 No. 56 dipper)	
Water (for eggs)	1¼ quarts (1¼ No. 56 dippers)	
Pumpkin	13 pounds (2 No. 10 cans or 6½ No. 56 dippers).	
Milk, evaporated	6½ pounds (7—14½-ounce cans or 3¼ No. 56 dippers).	
Water (for milk)	3¼ quarts (3¼ No. 56 dippers)	
or		
Milk, powdered, whole	1 pound 12 ounces (1¾ No. 56 dippers)	
Water (for milk)	5¾ quarts (5¾ No. 56 dippers)	

1. Sift or blend dry ingredients together.
2. Add part of the water to the eggs and mix to a smooth paste. Add the remainder of the water and mix smooth.
3. Stir eggs into the sugar-spice mixture and beat well.
4. Add pumpkin to egg-sugar mixture. Stir thoroughly until entirely free of lumps.
5. Stir reconstituted milk into pumpkin mixture. Mix well just before using to keep the pumpkin in suspension.
6. Pour into unbaked pie shells and bake in hot oven until the filling sets.

NO. 768. SWEET POTATO PIE

Yield: 100 servings, 2 sheet pans, 16½" x 24" x 1½".

Ingredients	100 servings	.... servings
Sweet potatoes, dehydrated, diced.	4 pounds (4 No. 56 dippers)	
Water (for potatoes)	6 quarts (6 No. 56 dippers)	
Sugar, granulated	6 pounds (3 No. 56 dippers)	
Cinnamon	1 ounce (4 mess kit spoons)	
Nutmeg	1 ounce (4 mess kit spoons)	
Salt	1½ ounces (3 mess kit spoons)	
Milk, evaporated	5—14½-ounce cans	
Water, potato (for milk)	2½ quarts (2½ No. 56 dippers)	
or		
Milk, powdered	1¼ pounds (1¼ No. 56 dippers)	
Water, potato (for milk)	4¼ quarts (4¼ No. 56 dippers)	
Eggs, powdered	15 ounces (1¼ No. 56 dippers)	
Water (for eggs)	1¼ quarts (1¼ No. 56 dippers)	

1. Soak potatoes in water for 20 minutes. Bring slowly to a boil in a covered stockpot (about 45 minutes). Simmer 20 to 30 minutes or until tender. Drain (save water) and mash thoroughly.
2. Combine sugar, spices, and salt. Mix well and add to mashed sweet potatoes.
3. Combine evaporated milk and water or reconstituted milk. Add to the sweet potato mixture. Mix thoroughly.
4. Add egg powder to ⅓ of the water. Mix until smooth. Add remaining to above mixture.
5. Pour mixture into raw pie shell and bake in 375° oven for approximately 45 minutes.

NO. 769. SWEET POTATO PIE

Yield: 100 servings, 1 piece each, 2½" x 3".

Ingredients	100 servings	.... servings
Sweet potatoes, dehydrated	4 pounds 2 ounces (5½ No. 56 dippers)	
Water (for potatoes)	9 quarts (9 No. 56 dippers)	
Sugar, granulated	3 pounds (1½ No. 56 dippers)	
Milk, evaporated	3 pounds 10 ounces (4—14½-ounce cans or 2 No. 56 dippers)	
or		
Milk, powdered, whole	1 pound (1 No. 56 dipper)	
Water (for milk)	1¼ quarts (1¼ No. 56 dippers)	
Nutmeg (optional)	To taste	
Pie dough*	17 pounds (8 No. 56 dippers)	

*See recipe No. 407 for pie crust.

1. Soak the sweet potatoes in the water for 40 to 60 minutes.
2. Cook until tender or about 1 hour 20 minutes. When cold, add sugar and reconstituted milk and mix to a mushlike consistency.
3. Roll out pie dough to the size of a large baking sheet cakepan. Pour half of the filling into the pan.

NO. 770. BREAD AND RAISIN PUDDING Yield: 100 servings,
3 to 5 ounces each.

Ingredients	100 servings	.... servings
Eggs, powdered, whole........	1 pound (1 No. 56 dipper)...........	....
Water (for eggs).............	1 quart (1 No. 56 dipper)...........	....
Milk, evaporated.............	8 pounds (9—14½-ounce cans or 4 No. 56 dippers).	....
Water (for milk).............	8 quarts (8 No. 56 dippers)..........	....
or		
Milk, powdered, whole........	2½ quarts (2½ No. 56 dippers)......	....
Water (for milk).............	10½ quarts (10½ No. 56 dippers)....	....
Sugar, granulated............	6 pounds (3 No. 56 dippers).........	....
Bread......................	5 pounds (16 No. 56 dippers)........	....
Raisins....................	3 pounds (2 No. 56 dippers)........	....
Vanilla....................	2 ounces (4 mess kit spoons)........	....

1. Add part of the water to the powdered eggs to make a paste. Add remainder of the water and mix smooth. Stir vigorously to prevent lumping.

2. Heat reconstituted milk until lukewarm and then dissolve the sugar in it. Pour over the egg solution and stir briskly.

3. Cut or tear the bread into small cubes or pieces (dry bread is best).

4. Pour the warm egg solution over the bread and stir until it is well soaked (10 to 15 minutes). Add the raisins and vanilla.

5. Pour into a large Army baking pan.

6. The pudding should be baked until it is firm and golden brown (approximately 40 minutes to 1 hour). If the oven is too hot, the pudding should be stirred once or twice to prevent scorching. Bake at 350° F.

Note. Do not hold overnight.

NO. 771. RICE PUDDING WITH RAISINS Yield: 100 servings,
3 to 5 ounces each.

Ingredients	100 servings	.... servings
Water......................	12 quarts (12 No. 56 dippers)........	....
Salt.......................	1½ ounces (3 mess kit spoons).......	....
Rice.......................	3½ pounds (1¾ No. 56 dippers).....	....
Water (for eggs).............	2¾ quarts (2¾ No. 56 dippers)......	....
Eggs, powdered, whole........	2 pounds (2⅓ No. 56 dippers)......	....
Water (for milk).............	5½ quarts (5½ No. 56 dippers)......	....
Milk, evaporated.............	5 pounds (6—14½-ounce cans or 2½ No. 56 dippers).	....
or		
Milk, powdered, whole........	1½ pounds (1½ No. 56 dippers).....	....
Water (for milk).............	7¼ quarts (7¼ No. 56 dippers).....	....
Sugar......................	3½ pounds (1¾ No. 56 dippers).....	....
Raisins....................	2 pounds (1⅓ No. 56 dippers)......	....
Vanilla....................	To taste...............	....

1. Bring the salted water to a boil. Add rice and cook about 20 minutes or until tender. Drain and cool.

2. Add the 2¾ quarts of water to the eggs and mix to a smooth paste. Add the reconstituted milk, sugar, and raisins and stir well.

3. Add the cooked and drained rice and the vanilla. Stir until well mixed.

4. Pour the entire mass into a deep baking pan and bake at a moderate temperature until set.

41. MEATS. Meats may not present the same variety in dehydrated form as in fresh, but with some care and thought given to the preparation they can be made palatable.

NO. 772. CORNED BEEF HASH   Yield: 100 servings, 3 to 4 ounces each.

Ingredients	100 servings	.... servings
Potatoes, dehydrated.........	6 pounds (9 No. 56 dippers).........	....
Water (for potatoes)..........	15½ quarts (15½ No. 56 dippers)....	....
Onions, dehydrated..........	8 ounces (¾ No. 56 dipper).........	....
Water (for onions)..........	1¾ quarts (1¾ No. 56 dippers)......	....
Lard......................	1 pound (½ No. 56 dipper).........	....
Corned beef...............	18 pounds (3—6-pound cans)........	....
Pepper....................	¾ ounce (3 mess kit spoons)........	....

1. Soak the potatoes for 40 to 60 minutes and then bring to a boil. Cook until tender. This should require about 45 minutes. Drain off the surplus water but do not discard it.

2. Soak onions for 20 to 40 minutes and bring to a boil. Drain immediately. Do not discard the surplus onion water.

3. Fry the drained, reconstituted onions in the lard until they begin to color.

4. Break up the corned beef and mix with the potatoes. Add the fried onions and then follow with all of the surplus onion water and enough of the potato water to moisten the hash (most of it will be needed).

5. When cooking small portions, brown the hash in a frying pan on top of the stove until it is crusty. For large quantities place the hash in a deep baking pan and bake in a hot oven for 45 minutes or until a brown crust is formed.

NO. 773. EGGS AND BEEF (HUNTER'S STYLE)
Yield: 100 servings, 3 to 4 ounces each.

Ingredients	100 servings	.... servings
Water......................	10 quarts (10 No. 56 dippers)........	....
Eggs, dehydrated............	6½ pounds (7½ No. 56 dippers).....	....
Onions, dehydrated..........	12 ounces (1⅓ No. 56 dippers)......	....
Water, hot.................	2 quarts (2 No. 56 dippers).........	....
Lard......................	2 pounds (1 No. 56 dipper).........	....
Boiled beef diced or beef scraps.	6 pounds (9 No. 56 dippers).........	....
Pepper....................	¼ ounce (1 mess kit spoon)........	....
Salt......................	3 ounces (6 mess kit spoons)........	....

1. Slowly add the first part of the water to the dehydrated eggs. Stir until a smooth mixture is formed.
2. Soak dehydrated onions in the hot water for 20 to 40 minutes.
3. Heat the lard in the large baking pan and fry onions for a few minutes. Use all surplus onion water.
4. Add the diced boiled beef, the egg solution, pepper, and salt, and bake in oven at approximately 400° F.
5. Stir occasionally (as for scrambled eggs) until properly set. Smaller portions can be cooked in the frying pan on top of the stove.

Note. Any left-over meats or canned corned beef can be used to prepare this dish.

42. SALADS. Salads may test the ingenuity of the cook. Here are a few examples of preparing salad from dehydrated food.

NO. 774. COLE SLAW
Yield: 100 servings, 2 to 3 ounces each.

Ingredients	100 servings	.... servings
Cabbage, dehydrated.........	2½ pounds (10 No. 56 dippers)......	....
Water, cold (for cabbage).....	12 quarts (12 No. 56 dippers).......	....
Vinegar....................	2½ quarts (2½ No. 56 dippers)......	....
Onions, dehydrated..........	10 ounces (1 No. 56 dipper).........	....
Water (for onions)..........	2 quarts (2 No. 56 dippers).........	....
Salt.......................	7½ ounces (15 mess kit spoons)......	....
Pepper....................	½ ounce (2 mess kit spoons)........	....

1. Pour cold water over the cabbage and allow it to soak for 2½ to 4 hours. Avoid overheating. For best results, place soaking cabbage in a refrigerator; long soaking at high temperature may ruin the cabbage flavor. If a refrigerator is available, use it. If ice is available, a small piece may be added to the cabbage and water while soaking. This will have approximately the same effect as refrigeration.
2. Soak onions in water 20 minutes.
3. Pour the vinegar over the reconstituted onions, salt and pepper and let it stand until the cabbage is ready.
4. Drain all surplus water from the cabbage, then combine with the onion-vinegar mixture.
5. Serve cold.

Note. Do not allow to soak overnight. Poor flavor and texture will result. If no refrigeration is available and the weather is warm, cole slaw should not be made.

NO. 775. POTATO SALAD
Yield: 100 servings, 3 to 5 ounces each.

Ingredients	100 servings	.... servings
Potatoes, dehydrated, julienne style.	5 pounds (7 No. 56 dippers).........	....
Water (for potatoes)..........	15 quarts (15 No. 56 dippers).......	....
Onions, dehydrated..........	8 ounces (¾ No. 56 dipper)........	....
Water (for onions)..........	1¾ quarts (1¾ No. 56 dippers)......	....
Vinegar....................	1½ quarts (¾ No. 56 dipper).......	....
Salt.......................	3 ounces (6 mess kit spoons)........	....
Pepper....................	½ ounce (2 mess kit spoons)........	....

1. Soak potatoes 40 to 60 minutes in cool water, then heat to the boiling point.

2. Slowly cook until the potatoes are very tender. This should take 40 to 50 minutes.

3. Drain off all surplus water and cool.

4. Reconstitute onions and drain well. Add to the potatoes.

5. Pour on the vinegar, salt, and pepper. Stir until mixed. (If mayonnaise is available, leave out vinegar. Add 1 quart of mayonnaise to the 100-portion recipe.)

6. If fresh eggs are available, add 20 sliced, hard-boiled eggs. Cold, scrambled, dehydrated eggs may be added instead.

43. SOUPS. Soups are a nourishing as well as an appetite-stimulating food. Dehydrated foods easily lend themselves to the preparation of soups.

NO. 776. BEEF STEW

Yield: 100 servings, 1 bowl each.

Ingredients	100 servings	.... servings
Boneless beef chuck, 1½-inch cubes, fresh or frozen.	35 pounds (25 No. 56 dippers).......	....
Salt......................	4½ ounces (9 mess kit spoons).......	....
Pepper....................	½ ounce (2 mess kit spoons)........	....
Lard......................	2 pounds (1 No. 56 dipper)..........	....
Onions, dehydrated.........	9 ounces (1 No. 56 dipper)..........	....
Water (for onions)..........	1½ quarts (1½ No. 56 dippers)......	....
Tomatoes (canned)..........	6 pounds 4 ounces (1 No. 10 can or 3 No. 56 dippers).	....
Carrots, dehydrated.........	1 pound 2 ounces (1 No. 56 dipper)...	....
Water (for carrots)..........	3 quarts (3 No. 56 dippers).........	....
Potatoes, dehydrated, julienne style.	4 pounds (6 No. 56 dippers)........	....
Water (for potatoes)..........	8 quarts (8 No. 56 dippers).........	....

1. Season beef with salt and pepper. Dump into large bakepan and brown in the lard. A hot stove is necessary.

2. Bring 1½ quarts of water to a boil and pour over the dehydrated onions. Allow to stand for 20 minutes.

3. Place meat, onions, tomatoes, and water in the large stockpot. Cover and cook on top of the stove or in the oven. Allow to stew or boil for approximately 1½ hours.

4. Soak carrots and potatoes for 40 to 60 minutes either separately or together. Bring to a boil then add them to the stew and continue cooking until they become tender (approximately 1 hour).

NO. 777. ONION SOUP

Yield: 100 servings,
1 bowl each.

Ingredients	100 servings	.... servings
Onions, dehydrated.........	1 pound 2 ounces (1¾ No. 56 dippers)	....
Water (for onions)..........	4 quarts (4 No. 56 dippers).........	....
Lard or substitute...........	2 pounds (1 No. 56 dipper).........	....
Flour.....................	2 pounds (1⅔ No. 56 dippers).......	....
Water, hot................	20 quarts (20 No. 56 dippers).......	....
Bouillon cubes..............	(70 cubes)...................	....
Salt......................	3 ounces (6 mess kit spoons).........	....

1. Soak dehydrated onions in water for 20 to 40 minutes.

2. Bring them to a boil and simmer for 35 minutes or more.

3. Melt the lard in a deep frying pan and add the simmered onions (with surplus water). Allow to fry until they begin to brown.

4. Add the flour to the fried onions and stir until the flour is distributed.

5. Dissolve bouillon cubes in hot water.

6. Add some of the stock to thin out the onion flour paste; then combine with the remainder of the stock. Add salt and simmer for 1 hour before serving.

NO. 778. CREAM OF POTATO SOUP

Yield: 100 servings,
1 bowl each.

Ingredients	100 servings	.... servings
Water.....................	25 quarts (25 No. 56 dippers).......	....
Salt......................	4 ounces (8 mess kit spoons)........	....
Pepper....................	¼ ounce (1 mess kit spoon).........	....
Onions, dehydrated..........	4 ounces (⅓ No. 56 dipper).........	....
Potatoes, dehydrated, pre-cooked shreds.	4 pounds (6 No. 56 dippers).........	....
Milk, evaporated............	9 pounds (10—14½-ounce cans or 4½ No. 56 dippers).	....
or		
Milk, powdered, whole.......	2½ pounds (2½ No. 56 dippers).....	....
Water (for milk).............	3 quarts (3 No. 56 dippers).........	....
Butter....................	2 pounds (1 No. 56 dipper).........	....

1. Put water, salt, pepper, dehydrated onions, and shredded potatoes in a kettle and bring to a boil.

2. Simmer for about 30 minutes.

3. Add evaporated or reconstituted milk and butter and let simmer for 20 minutes more.

4. Serve hot.

Note. If soup is not the main dish of the meal, prepare only ½ of the recipe.

NO. 779. VEGETABLE SOUP (Made with dehydrated vegetables and beef shank)

Yield: 100 servings, 1 bowl each.

Ingredients	100 servings	.... servings
Beef shank................	15 pounds (9 No. 56 dippers)........	....
Boiling beef (brisket, neck or shank meat), fresh or frozen.	10 pounds (6 No. 56 dippers)........	....
Water....................	18 quarts (18 No. 56 dippers)........	....
Salt.....................	2 ounces (4 mess kit spoons)........	....
Dehydrated:		
Carrots................	12 ounces (¾ No. 56 dipper)........	....
Julienne potatoes........	1 pound (2 No. 56 dippers)..........	....
Onions................	6 ounces (½ No. 56 dipper)..........	....
Cabbage...............	5 ounces (1 No. 56 dipper)..........	....
Rice.....................	12 ounces (⅓ No. 56 dipper)........	....
Salt.....................	3 ounces (6 mess kit spoons)........	....
Water...................	9 quarts (9 No. 56 dippers)..........	....
Tomatoes................	13 pounds (2 No. 10 cans or 7 No. 56 dippers).	....
Pepper..................	¼ ounce (1 mess kit spoon)........	....

1. Place beef shank, meat, and water in a kettle and add salt. Bring the water to a boil and allow to simmer until meat is tender (about 4 hours for the large batch).

2. Add the second portion of water to all of the other ingredients, mix, and then add to the beef shank, meat, and water mixture. Simmer for another hour.

3. Remove the bone, meat, and excess fat, if any. Cut lean meat in small pieces and return it to the soup.

4. If available, 5 pounds of dehydrated beef may replace boiling beef and shank.

44. VEGETABLES. Vegetables in dehydrated form are easily prepared. The following recipes will aid the cook in reconstituting and cooking these foods.

NO. 780. BUTTERED BEETS

Yield: 100 servings, 2 to 3 ounces each.

Ingredients	100 servings	.... servings
Beets, dehydrated...........	3½ pounds (4 No. 56 dippers).......	....
Water, cool (for beets)........	12 quarts (12 No. 56 dippers).......	....
Salt....................	1½ ounces (3 mess kit spoons).......	....
Pepper.................	½ ounce (2 mess kit spoons)........	....
Butter.................	1 pound (½ No. 56 dipper)..........	....

1. Soak beets 20 to 40 minutes. Bring slowly to a boil and cook 15 to 20 minutes after they reach the boiling point. The 100-portion recipe should require 50 to 60 minutes total time, the smaller portions, 25 to 35 minutes.

2. Drain the beets and season while hot with salt, pepper, and melted butter.

298

NO. 781. PICKLED BEETS

Yield: 100 servings,
2 ounces each.

Ingredients	100 servings	.... servings
Beets, dehydrated.............	3½ pounds (4 No. 56 dippers).......	....
Water, cool (for beets)........	12 quarts (12 No. 56 dippers)........	....
Onions, dehydrated..........	5 ounces (½ No. 56 dipper).........	....
Water (for onions)...........	1 quart (1 No. 56 dipper)...........	....
Sugar, granulated............	8 ounces (¼ No. 56 dipper)..........	....
Salt.......................	1½ ounces (3 mess kit spoons).......	....
Pepper.....................	¾ ounce (3 mess kit spoons)........	....
Vinegar....................	1½ quarts (1½ No. 56 dippers)......	....

1. Soak beets and onions separately 20 to 40 minutes.
2. Bring beets to a boil and cook 15 to 20 minutes after they reach the boiling point. The 100-portion recipe should require 50 to 60 minutes total time, the smaller portion, 25 to 35 minutes.
3. Bring vinegar to a boil and pour over the reconstituted onions, sugar, salt, and pepper. Drain the beets and add to the onion-vinegar mixture. Cool for 4 hours. Serve as cold as possible.

NO. 782. SWEET-SOUR BEETS

Yield: 100 servings,
2 to 3 ounces each.

Ingredients	100 servings	.... servings
Beets, dehydrated.............	3½ pounds (4 No. 56 dippers).......	....
Water, cool (for beets)........	12 quarts (12 No. 56 dippers)........	....
Vinegar....................	⅔ quart (⅔ No. 56 dipper).........	....
Sugar, granulated............	8 ounces (¼ No. 56 dipper)..........	....
Salt.......................	1½ ounces (3 mess kit spoons).......	....
Pepper.....................	½ ounce (2 mess kit spoons)........	....

1. Soak beets 20 to 40 minutes. Bring slowly to a boil and cook 15 to 20 minutes after they reach the boiling point. The 100-portion recipe should require 50 to 60 minutes total time, the smaller portion, 25 to 35 minutes.
2. Drain the cooked beets and then bring the vinegar, sugar, salt, and pepper to boil. Add to the beets and stir well.

NO. 783. CORNED BEEF AND CABBAGE

Yield: 100 servings,
4 to 6 ounces each.

Ingredients	100 servings	.... servings
Cabbage, dehydrated.........	3½ pounds (14 No. 56 dippers)......	....
Water, cold (for cabbage).....	16 quarts (16 No. 56 dippers)........	....
Corned beef, canned..........	36 pounds or 6—6-pound cans........	....

1. Follow the directions in recipe for boiled cabbage. (See recipe No. 784.)
2. Break up corned beef and add to the boiling cabbage.

299

NO. 784. BOILED CABBAGE   Yield: 100 servings,
2 to 4 ounces each.

Ingredients	100 servings	.... servings
Cabbage, dehydrated.........	3½ pounds (14 No. 56 dippers)......	....
Water, cold (for cabbage).....	16 quarts (16 No. 56 dippers)........	....
Salt........................	4½ ounces (9 mess kit spoons).......	....
Bacon, diced................	3 pounds (2 No. 56 dippers).........	....
Pepper.....................	½ ounce (2 mess kit spoons)........	....

1. Soak cabbage 10 to 20 minutes in cool water.

2. Bring it slowly to a boil; this will take approximately 40 minutes. Add salt and simmer for an additional 10 to 15 minutes for a total cooking time of approximately 55 minutes.

3. Drain, leaving about half the liquid on the cabbage.

4. Fry diced bacon until it is lightly brown.

5. Add bacon, bacon grease, and pepper to cabbage and serve.

Note. For a different flavor the bacon may be diced and boiled in the water later used with the cabbage. Avoid overcooking cabbage. It will discolor, lose moisture and develop a poor flavor. A small pinch of sugar improves the cabbage flavor. Use only two (2) mess kit spoons for 100 portions.

NO. 785. SWEET-SOUR CABBAGE

1. Cook as boiled cabbage.

2. After draining, add 1½ pounds (1 mess kit cup) of vinegar and 6 ounces (¼ mess kit cup) of sugar.

NO. 786. BUTTER CARROTS   Yield: 100 servings,
2 to 3 ounces each.

Ingredients	100 servings	.... servings
Carrots, dehydrated..........	4 pounds (4 No. 56 dippers)........	....
Water, cool (for carrots)......	12 quarts (12 No. 56 dippers)........	....
Sugar, granulated............	2 ounces (4 mess kit spoons)........	....
Butter.....................	1 pound (½ No. 56 dipper).........	....
Salt.......................	3 ounces (6 mess kit spoons)........	....
Pepper.....................	¼ ounce (1 mess kit spoon).........	....

1. Soak carrots in cool water for 45 to 60 minutes.

2. Slowly bring to a boil. This requires 45 minutes for the entire recipe. Simmer for 10 minutes more or until tender.

3. Remove from the stove; add the sugar, butter, salt, and pepper, and stir until thoroughly mixed.

4. For creamed carrots see directions for white sauce. (See recipe No. 797.)

NO. 787. SMOTHERED ONIONS (for steak, liver, and other meats)

Yield: 100 servings, 2 ounces each.

Ingredients	100 servings	.... servings
Onions, dehydrated..........	2 pounds (3¼ No. 56 dippers).......	....
Water (for onions)..........	7 quarts (7 No. 56 dippers)........	....
Lard or substitute...........	1 pound (½ No. 56 dipper).........	....
Salt......................	1½ ounces (3 mess kit spoons)......	....

1. Stir onions into cool water and allow to soak for 20 minutes.
2. Bring to a boil and allow to simmer (not boil vigorously) for 35 minutes, or until tender. The onions should be very tender at this stage.
3. Heat the lard to frying temperature, add the reconstituted onions (with surplus water) and allow to stew until slightly brown and very tender. Add salt and serve as a dressing for smothered meats.

NO. 788. POTATOES AU GRATIN

Yield: 100 servings, 2 to 4 ounces each.

Ingredients	100 servings	.... servings
Potatoes, dehydrated........	7½ pounds (11 No. 56 dippers)......	....
Water, cool (for potatoes)....	19 quarts (19 No. 56 dippers).......	....
Milk, powdered, whole........	1 pound (1 No. 56 dipper).........	....
Water (potato), (for milk).....	3 quarts (3 No. 56 dippers).........	....
or		
Milk, evaporated............	3 pounds 10 ounces (4—14½-ounce cans or 2 No. 56 dippers).	....
Water (potato), (for milk)....	2 quarts (2 No. 56 dippers).........	....
Salt......................	6 ounces (12 mess kit spoons)........	....
Pepper....................	¼ ounce (1 mess kit spoon).........	....
Cheese (sliced)*............	2 pounds (1¼ No. 56 dippers, broken, cubed, or sliced).	....
Dry bread crumbs...........	8 ounces (½ No. 56 dipper)........	....
Butter....................	1 pound (½ No. 56 dipper).........	....

*When dehydrated cheese is used, reconstitute 1 pound of dehydrated cheese with 1 pound of water, or sprinkle the 1 pound of dehydrated cheese over potatoes.

1. Soak the potatoes in cool water for 40 to 60 minutes.
2. Bring to a boil with pot covered. This should require 40 to 50 minutes.
3. Simmer 10 minutes longer, or until tender.
4. Drain well. Use surplus water in cooking.
5. Reconstitute milk using cold potato water.
6. Place the cooked and drained potatoes in a deep baking pan. Add milk, salt, and pepper. Stir well.
7. Slice cheese into thin slices. Scatter the slices over the potatoes.
8. Sprinkle bread crumbs over the cheese. Dot with pieces of butter.
9. Bake in moderate oven (350° F.) until a rich brown crust has formed. This should require 30 minutes.

NO. 789. HASHED BROWNED OR FRIED POTATOES

Yield: 100 servings,
2 to 4 ounces each.

Ingredients	100 servings	.... servings
Potatoes, dehydrated.........	7 pounds (10 No. 56 dippers).......	....
Water (for potatoes)..........	18 quarts (18 No. 56 dippers).......	....
Salt.......................	4 ounces (8 mess kit spoons)........	....
Lard......................	2 pounds (1 No. 56 dipper).........	....

1. Soak dehydrated potatoes in cool water for 40 to 60 minutes.
2. Bring to a boil. This will require about 40 to 50 minutes.
3. Add salt; simmer for 10 more minutes. (Small portions take less time.)
4. Drain off water and cool.
5. Place 2 pounds of lard in frying pan and heat to frying temperature
6. Add potatoes and mix lightly with fat.
7. Turn the potatoes after those on the bottom have been frying for about 10 to 15 minutes and are browned.
8. Continue frying about 20 minutes more, occasionally turning potatoes.

Note. Be sure to drain potatoes well. Soggy potatoes will not brown well. When cooking smaller batches, the cooking or simmering time should be reduced. Only enough time is required to make the potatoes tender. Twenty minutes simmering is usually enough for small portions.

The ingredients for hashed browned potatoes are proportioned at the rate of three servings per pound of finished product. For men who are not exercising vigorously the portions should be reduced to four servings per pound.

NO. 790. LYONNAISE POTATOES.

1. Prepare exactly like hashed browned potatoes, reconstituting separately 12 ounces (1¼ No. 56 dippers) dehydrated onions in 6 pounds (3 No. 56 dippers) water. Fry onions, using onion water, then add to potatoes.
2. Cook 100-portion quantities inside the oven, using a high temperature (450° F.).

NO. 791. HASHED POTATOES PREPARED FROM JULIENNE OR CUBED POTATOES

Yield: 100 servings,
2 to 4 ounces each.

Ingredients	100 servings	.... servings
Potatoes, dehydrated.........	7 pounds (10 No. 56 dippers).......	....
Water (for potatoes)..........	17 quarts (17 No. 56 dippers).......	....
Milk, evaporated.............	1½ pounds (1½—14½-ounce cans or ¾ No. 56 dippers).	....
Water, potato (for milk)......	¾ quart (¾ No. 56 dipper).........	
or		
Milk, powdered, whole........	5 ounces (⅓ No. 56 dipper).........	
Water, potato (for milk)......	1½ quarts (1½ No. 56 dippers)......	
Salt.......................	4 ounces (8 mess kit spoons)........	
Butter.....................	1 pound (½ No. 56 dipper).........	

1. Soak potatoes for 40 to 60 minutes.
2. Simmer to a boil. This should require 40 to 50 minutes.
3. Simmer 10 minutes longer or until tender.
4. Drain off surplus water. This should give 25 pounds of potato pieces and approimatexly 1½ gallons (6 No. 56 dippers) of surplus potato water.
5. Mash the drained potato pieces until as smooth as possible. All lumps cannot be removed.
6. Reconstitute milk with cool potato water and bring to a boil. Add salt and butter.
7. Slowly stir the hot milk mixture into the mashed potatoes. Beat well.

NO. 792. MASHED POTATOES PREPARED FROM PRECOOKED, SHREDDED POTATOES

Yield: 100 servings,
2 to 4 ounces each.

Ingredients	100 servings	.... servings
Water, boiling	7 quarts (7 No. 56 dippers)	
Dehydrated potato shreds, precooked.	4½ pounds (7 No. 56 dippers)	
Salt	3 ounces (6 mess kit spoons)	
Butter	1 pound (½ No. 56 dipper)	
Milk, evaporated	3 pounds (3—14½-ounce cans)	
Water (for milk)	1½ quarts (1½ No. 56 dippers)	
or		
Milk, powdered, whole	12 ounces (¾ No. 56 dipper)	
Water (for milk)	2½ quarts (2½ No. 56 dippers)	

1. Have water boiling vigorously.
2. Measure accurately and pour over the shredded potatoes. Let stand in covered container on back of stove for 15 minutes or over a low flame for 10 minutes.
3. Add salt and stir vigorously for 15 to 20 minutes in order to work out lumps.
4. After working smooth, add *hot* reconstituted milk and melted butter. Whip until fluffy.

NO. 793. BUTTERED SWEET POTATOES (BAKED)

Yield: 100 servings,
2 to 4 ounces each.

Ingredients	100 servings	.... servings
Sweet potatoes, dehydrated	7½ pounds (10 No. 56 dippers)	
Water, cool	15 quarts (15 No. 56 dippers)	
Salt	1 ounce (2 mess kit spoons)	
Butter	2 pounds (1 No. 56 dipper)	

1. Soak potato slices for 40 to 60 minutes.
2. Slowly bring to a boil. This should require 40 to 50 minutes. It is important that the potatoes be tender and moist at this stage. Be sure to cook sufficiently.

3. Drain off the surplus water (there should be only a small quantity), add salt and butter, and mash by stirring vigorously.

4. Place in large baking pan, add the surplus water which was previously drained off, stir, and bake for 20 minutes in a moderate oven.

NO. 794. CANDIED OR GLAZED SWEET POTATOES

Yield: 100 servings,
2 to 4 ounces each.

Ingredients	100 servings	.... servings
Sweet potatoes, dehydrated...	7½ pounds (10 No. 56 dippers)......	....
Water, cool (for potatoes).....	15 quarts (15 No. 56 dippers)........	....
Sugar, granulated............	5 pounds (2½ No. 56 dippers).......	....
Butter....................	1 pound (½ No. 56 dipper).........	....

1. Soak potatoes in cool water for 40 to 60 minutes.

2. Slowly simmer to a boil. This should require 40 to 50 minutes.

3. Drain off surplus water (do not throw away), being careful to leave slices whole.

4. Make a sirup by adding sugar to the surplus water and boiling for 5 minutes.

5. Place the sweet potato slices in a baking pan. Pour the sirup over the sweet potatoes and dot with butter. Bake for 30 minutes in a moderate oven.

NO. 795. BAKED TURNIPS AND POTATOES

Yield: 100 servings,
2 to 4 ounces each.

Ingredients	100 servings	.... servings
Turnips, dehydrated..........	1½ pounds (2½ No. 56 dippers).....	....
Water, cool (for turnips)......	5 quarts (5 No. 56 dippers).........	....
White potatoes, dehydrated...	4½ pounds (6½ No. 56 dippers).....	....
Water, cool (for potatoes).....	11 quarts (11 No. 56 dippers).......	....
Salt.....................	6 ounces (12 mess kit spoons).......	....
Pepper....................	½ ounce (2 mess kit spoons)........	....
Bacon....................	3 pounds (1½ No. 56 dippers).......	....

1. Measure the dehydrated turnips and potatoes into two portions of cold water and soak for 40 to 60 minutes.

2. Bring each batch to a boil. Boil for 40 to 50 minutes and then drain off surplus water. The potato water may be discarded or held for soup but the turnip water should be poured back on the mixture. This is the only reason for reconstituting the two vegetables separately.

3. Mix potatoes and turnips and place in baking pan. Season with salt and pepper and then strip with bacon.

4. Bake in the oven until the bacon is crisp on both sides.

NO. 796. TURNIPS SEASONED WITH BACON

Method No. 1

Yield: 100 servings,
2 to 3 ounces each.

Ingredients	100 servings	.... servings
Turnips, dehydrated	4 pounds (6½ No. 56 dippers)	
Water (for turnips)	12 quarts (12 No. 56 dippers)	
Salt	4½ ounces (9 mess kit spoons)	
Pepper	½ ounce (2 mess kit spoons)	
Bacon	3 pounds (1½ No. 56 dippers)	

1. Soak dehydrated turnips in cool water for 40 to 50 minutes.
2. Bring to a boil uncovered. This will require approximately 40 to 50 minutes. Simmer uncovered for 10 minutes more. Be sure the turnips are tender.
3. Take stockpot from stove and add salt and pepper.
4. Fry 3 pounds of diced bacon in frying pan until lightly browned.
5. Add to cooked turnips.
6. Mix well and serve.

Method No. 2

Reconstitute 4 pounds dried turnips as suggested in method No. 1. Place in baking pan complete with juice. Strip 3 pounds bacon on top of the turnips and bake in a moderate oven. Turn the bacon after 10 minutes baking in order to brown on both sides. One-quarter pound of sugar sprinkled over the bacon and turnips before baking will improve both its flavor and appearance.

NO. 797. WHITE SAUCE FOR VEGETABLES

Yield: 100 servings,
1 to 2 ounces each.

Ingredients	100 servings	.... servings
Milk, evaporated	2 pounds 11 ounces (3—14½-ounce cans or 1⅛ No. 56 dippers).	
Water (for milk)	2 quarts (2 No. 56 dippers)	
or		
Milk, powdered	12 ounces (1 mess kit cup)	
Water (for milk)	3 quarts (3 No. 56 dippers)	
Flour	8 ounces (⅓ No. 56 dipper)	
Salt	½ ounce (1 mess kit spoon)	
Butter	1 pound (½ No. 56 dipper)	

1. Make a paste of flour and ¾ dipper of milk.
2. Boil reconstituted milk and stir into flour paste. Stir until sauce becomes white and thick.
3. Add butter.

"B" RATION RECIPES

45. FIELD RATIONS. It will be necessary under conditions in the field to have only "B" rations or a similar canned ration. At such times the cook will find it convenient to have recipes to vary an otherwise monotonous menu.

46. BEVERAGES. These recipes for preparing beverages are simple but if followed will produce palatable drinks.

NO. 798. CHOCOLATE MILK Yield: 6 gallons, 100 servings of approximately ½ mess kit cup each.

Ingredients	100 servings	.... servings
Cocoa	2½ pounds (3 No. 56 dippers)	
Sugar, granulated	5 pounds (2½ No. 56 dippers)	
Salt	½ ounce (1 mess kit spoon)	
Milk, powdered	8 pounds (8 No. 56 dippers)	
Water (for milk)	28 quarts (28 No. 56 dippers)	

1. Combine cocoa, sugar, salt, and powdered milk. Mix thoroughly. Beat dry mixture with a wire whip in order to break up any lumps.
2. Add this dry mix to the water by floating it on top.
3. Beat constantly with a wire whip while adding the milk. Stir until all of the milk powder is thoroughly dissolved.
4. Chill if possible.
5. Beat again with a wire whip just before serving.

NO. 799. COFFEE MILK Yield: 8 gallons, 100 servings, approximately ½ mess kit cup each.

Ingredients	100 servings	.... servings
Milk, powdered	6 pounds (6 No. 56 dippers)	
Sugar, granulated	3½ pounds (1¾ No. 56 dippers)	
Coffee, brewed	10 quarts (10 No. 56 dippers)	
Water	21 quarts (21 No. 56 dippers)	

1. Combine powdered milk and sugar and mix thoroughly. Beat vigorously with a wire whip to break up any lumps.
2. Allow coffee to cool at room temperature. Combine coffee and water. Add dry milk powder to the coffee mixture by floating it on top. Beat constantly with a wire whip while adding the milk. Continue stirring until all the milk powder is thoroughly dissolved.
3. Chill if possible. Beat again with a wire whip just before serving.

NO. 800. EGG NOG

Yield: Approximately 8 gallons, 10 ounces each serving.

Ingredients	100 servings	.... servings
Eggs, powdered, whole	2¼ pounds (3 No. 56 dippers)	
Milk, powdered, whole	5¼ pounds (5¼ No. 56 dippers)	
Sugar, granulated	2½ pounds (1¼ No. 56 dippers)	
Salt	1¾ ounces (3½ mess kit spoons)	
Cinnamon	¾ ounce (3 mess kit spoons)	
Nutmeg	¾ ounce (3 mess kit spoons)	
Water	28 quarts (28 No. 56 dippers)	
Vanilla tablets	21 tablets	
Water (for vanilla tablets)	1 pint (½ No. 56 dipper)	

1. Combine all dry ingredients and mix until well blended.
2. Add water gradually to the blended dry mix, stirring constantly.
3. Crush tablets so that they will dissolve more readily and add to the water. Stir until vanilla tablets are thoroughly dissolved, add this to the milk mixture. Chill this beverage if possible and whip thoroughly before serving.

NO. 801. LEMONADE

Yield: 8 gallons, approximately ½ mess kit cup per serving.

Ingredients	100 servings	.... servings
Lemon juice powder, synthetic.	1 pound (1⅓-ounce can)	
Sugar, granulated	6⅔ pounds (3⅓ No. 56 dippers)	
Water	32 quarts (32 No. 56 dippers)	

1. Combine the lemon juice powder, synthetic, and the sugar and mix well. Add gradually to the water.
2. Stir until sugar and lemon powder are thoroughly dissolved. Chill if possible before serving.

NO. 802. LEMON JUICE

Yield: 1 gallon.

Ingredients	100 servings	.... servings
Lemon juice powder, synthetic.	1 12-ounce can	
Water	1 gallon (4 No. 56 dippers)	

Add the lemon juice powder, synthetic, to the water and use in same proportion as fresh lemon juice (1 gallon equaling approximately 92 lemons).

NO. 803. PINEAPPLE MILK

Yield: 100 servings, approximately ½ mess kit cup each.

Ingredients	100 servings	.... servings
Milk, powdered	8 pounds (8 No. 56 dippers)	
Sugar, granulated	2 pounds (1 No. 56 dipper)	
Water	14 quarts (14 No. 56 dippers)	
Pineapple juice	5 No. 10 cans	

1. Combine powdered milk and sugar and beat thoroughly with a wire whip to break up any lumps.
2. Add powdered milk mixture to the water by floating it on top. Beat with a wire whip.
3. Add pineapple juice to milk mixture. Stir constantly to prevent lumping.
4. Chill if possible. Beat with a wire whip just before serving.

NO. 804. VANILLA ICE CREAM MIX

Yield: 8 gallons, approximately
⅓ mess kit cup each.

Ingredients	100 servings	.... servings
Milk, powdered	2⅔ pounds (2⅔ No. 56 dippers)	
Ice cream mix	5⅓ pounds (5⅓ No. 56 dippers)	
Water	8 gallons (32 No. 56 dippers)	
Salt	1 ounce (2 mess kit spoons)	

1. Add milk and ice cream mix powder to water. Mix thoroughly with a wire whip to break up all lumps in the milk.
2. Chill if possible and beat again with a wire whip just before serving.

NO. 805. VANILLA MILK (Evaporated milk)

Yield: 8 gallons, 100 servings, approximately ½ mess kit cup each.

Ingredients	100 servings	.... servings
Milk, evaporated	35—14½-ounce cans	
Water (for milk)	16 quarts (16 No. 56 dippers)	
or		
Milk, powdered	7 pounds (7 No. 56 dippers)	
Water (for milk)	28 quarts (28 No. 56 dippers)	
Vanilla pudding powder	(2 No. 56 dippers)	

1. Combine evaporated milk and water or reconstitute milk by floating powdered milk on the water and beating constantly with a wire whip until milk is thoroughly dissolved.
2. Add pudding powder and whip until dissolved. Chill if possible and whip again just before serving.

Variations.

NO. 806. CHOCOLATE MILK

Add four No. 56 dippers of chocolate pudding powder in place of two No. 56 dippers of vanilla pudding powder.

NO. 807. BUTTERSCOTCH MILK

Add four No. 56 dippers of butterscotch pudding powder in place of two No. 56 dippers of vanilla pudding powder.

NO. 808. VANILLA MILK (Powdered milk)
Yield: 8 gallons, 100 servings of
approximately ½ mess
kit cup each.

Ingredients	100 servings	.... servings
Milk, powdered............	8 pounds (8 No. 56 dippers)........	....
Salt....................	1 ounce (2 mess kit spoons).........	....
Vanilla.................	15 tablets (5 mess kit spoons).......	....
Water..................	28 quarts (28 No. 56 dippers).......	....

1. Beat powdered milk with a wire whip before adding to water in order to break up any lumps in the milk.
2. Add the powdered milk to the water by floating it on top. Beat constantly with a wire whip while adding milk.
3. Add salt and vanilla.* Continue stirring until all the milk powder is thoroughly dissolved.
4. Chill if possible. Beat again with a wire whip just before serving.

*Dissolve vanilla tablets in a small quantity of water before adding to milk.

47. DESSERTS. Desserts are a welcome end to every good meal. They can be prepared from rations. Some recipes follow.

NO. 809. APPLESAUCE CAKE
Yield: 100 servings, 2 sheet pans 16½"x24"x1½".

Ingredients	100 servings	.... servings
Flour, sifted...............	1⅓ pounds (1⅓ No. 56 dippers).....	....
Shortening..............	2 pounds (1 No. 56 dipper).........	....
Applesauce..............	6⅔ pounds (6⅔ No. 56 dippers).....	....
Flour, sifted...............	2⅓ pounds (2⅓ No. 56 dippers).....	....
Sugar, granulated..........	3½ pounds (3½ No. 56 dippers).....	....
Baking soda..............	2¼ ounces (5 mess kit spoons)......	....
Cinnamon................	¾ ounce (3 mess kit spoons).......	....
Cloves..................	(⅔ mess kit spoon)...............	....
Nutmeg.................	½ ounce (2 mess kit spoons).......	....
Salt...................	(¼ mess kit spoon)...............	....
Water, hot..............	2½ ounces (7 mess kit spoons)......	....
Raisins................	2⅓ pounds (2⅓ No. 56 dippers).....	....
Apple nuggets, dehydrated....	1¼ pounds (1¼ No. 56 dippers)....	....
Water.................	3¾ quarts (3¾ No. 56 dippers).....	....
Sugar.................	½ pound (½ No. 56 dipper).......	....

1. Mix flour and shortening together until smooth and light.
2. Add applesauce and mix well.
3. Sift together the flour, sugar, baking soda, cinnamon, nutmeg, cloves, and salt.
4. Add the sifted dry ingredients to the above applesauce mixture and mix well.
5. Add hot water and raisins and beat until light.

6. Measure out the batter into two well-greased bakepans. (Approximately 4-quart dippers of batter per pan.) Bake in moderate oven for 1¼ to 1¾ hours.
7. Add apple nuggets to water and bring slowly to a boil in a covered stockpot. Simmer for approximately 15 minutes. Add sugar and cool.

NO. 810. CHOCOLATE CAKE

Yield: 100 servings, 3 sheet pans.

Ingredients	100 servings	.... servings
Flour, sifted	2 pounds 6 ounces (2 No. 56 dippers)	
Shortening	2 pounds (1 No. 56 dipper)	
Sugar, granulated	5 pounds (5 No. 56 dippers)	
Eggs, powdered	12 ounces	
Cocoa	13 ounces (1 No. 56 dipper)	
Water	1 quart (1 No. 56 dipper)	
Vanilla tablets	9 tablets	
Water	1½ quarts (1½ No. 56 dippers)	
Flour, sifted	1½ pounds (1½ No. 56 dippers)	
Salt	2 ounces (4 mess kit spoons)	
Soda	1 ounce (2 mess kit spoons)	
Baking powder	3 ounces (8 mess kit spoons)	

1. Cream shortening and flour in mixing bowl until light.
2. Sift sugar, powdered eggs, and cocoa together. Add to the creamed mixture.
3. Add one dipper of water gradually and mix well. Crush vanilla tablets and dissolve in 1½-quart dippers of water.
4. Add the remaining sifted dry ingredients and water alternately to the creamed mixture.
5. Bake in greased and flour-dusted sheet cakepans. Bake in moderate oven (375°) for 28 to 30 minutes. (Three-quarters No. 56 dipper of batter per pan.)

NO. 811. SPONGE CAKE FOR JELLY ROLL

Yield: 100 servings, 3 sheet pans 16½" x 24" x 1½".

Ingredients	100 servings	.... servings
Eggs, powdered	1 pound 2 ounces (1 No. 56 dipper)	
Water, lukewarm	¾ quart (¾ No. 56 dipper)	
Sugar, granulated	2 pounds (2 No. 56 dippers)	
Water, hot	¾ quart (¾ No. 56 dipper)	
Vanilla or lemon flavor	(¾ mess kit spoon)	
Flour, sifted	1½ pounds (1½ No. 56 dippers)	
Baking powder	1½ ounces (4½ mess kit spoons)	
Salt	1 ounce (2 mess kit spoons)	

1. Mix the powdered eggs and sugar together and sift together two or three times. Add the water and beat with a wire whip until the mixture is somewhat fluffy and thick.
2. Combine water and flavor and add to egg mixture.

311

3. Sift the flour, baking powder, and salt together twice, fold into the above mixture, mixing only enough to incorporate the egg mixture and flour.
4. Grease sheet pans lightly and preferably line with paper. Bake 10 to 12 minutes in a hot oven. After removing from open, turn sheets out onto a cloth bag or piece of paper which has been previously dusted with sugar. Spread jelly and roll.

NO. 812. YELLOW CAKE

Yield: 100 servings, 3 sheet pans.

Ingredients	100 servings	.... servings
Flour, sifted...............	2 pounds (2 No. 56 dippers).........	....
Shortening.................	2 pounds (2 No. 56 dippers).........	....
Sugar, granulated...........	5 pounds (5 No. 56 dippers).........	....
Eggs, powdered.............	12 ounces (¾ No. 56 dippers).......	....
Water.....................	1 quart (1 No. 56 dipper)...........	....
Vanilla tablets.............	9 tablets...........................	....
Water.....................	1½ quarts (1½ No. 56 dippers)......	....
Flour, sifted...............	3 pounds (3 No. 56 dippers).........	....
Salt......................	2¾ ounces (5½ mess kit spoons).....	....
Baking powder.............	5 ounces (13 mess kit spoons).......	....
Milk, powdered............	8 ounces (½ No. 56 dipper).........	....

1. Cream shortening and flour until light.
2. Sift together and add to creamed mixture.
3. Add one dipper of water gradually and mix well.
4. Crush vanilla tablets and dissolve in water.
5. Sift the dry ingredients and add alternately with the water to the creamed mixture.
6. Bake in greased and flour-dusted sheet cakepans. Bake in moderate oven (375°) for 28 to 30 minutes. (Three-quarters No. 56 dipper of batter per pan.)

NO. 813. BOSTON CREAM CAKE

Prepare yellow cake recipe. Slit layers and pour cream filling between, using cream filling recipe No. 818. Sprinkle top of cake with sugar. Prepared vanilla, butterscotch, or chocolate pudding may be used for this filling.

NO. 814. APPLE BROWN BETTY

Yield: 100 servings, 4 ounces each.

Ingredients	100 servings	.... servings
Apple nuggets, dehydrated....	2¼ pounds (3 No. 56 dippers)......	....
Water (for apples)..........	6½ quarts (6½ No. 56 dippers).....	....
Raisins....................	3 pounds (2¼ No. 56 dippers)......	....
Bread, cubed...............	6 pounds........................	....
Sugar, granulated...........	6 pounds (3 No. 56 dippers).......	....
Salt.......................	¾ ounces (1½ mess kit spoons).....	....
Cinnamon..................	1½ ounces (6 mess kit spoons).....	....
Lemon juice, powder, synthetic	(2 mess kit spoons)...............	....
Water.....................	4 quarts (4 No. 56 dippers)........	....

1. Add apple nuggets to water and bring slowly to a boil in a covered stockpot. Simmer for 15 to 20 minutes or until apples are tender. Cool.

2. Add raisins to apples. Arrange apples and bread in layers in large bakepans.

3. Combine sugar, salt, cinnamon, lemon powder, and water, and sprinkle between layers of apple and bread crumbs.

4. Bake for 45 minutes in a moderate oven (350°).

NO. 815. BREAD AND RAISIN PUDDING

Yield: 100 5-ounce servings, or approximately 2 serving spoons each.

Ingredients	100 servings	.... servings
Eggs, powdered..............	9 ounces (¾ No. 56 dipper).........	....
Water (for eggs).............	⅔ quarts (⅔ No. 56 dipper)........	....
Milk, evaporated.............	6—14½-ounce cans................	....
Water (for milk).............	6 quarts (6 No. 56 dippers)........	....
or		
Milk, powdered..............	3 pounds (3 No. 56 dippers)........	....
Water (for milk).............	11¼ quarts (11¼ No. 56 dippers)....	....
Sugar......................	5 pounds (2½ No. 56 dippers).......	....
Bread, dry..................	5 pounds (10 No. 56 dippers).......	....
Vanilla, extract.............	(4 mess kit spoons)................	....
or		
Vanilla tablets..............	12 tablets.......................	....
Raisins.....................	3¼ pounds (2½ No. 56 dippers).....	....

1. Add eggs to ⅓ of the water and beat until smooth. Add remaining water gradually, stirring constantly.

2. Combine evaporated milk and water or reconstituted powdered milk. Heat until milk is lukewarm.

3. Dissolve sugar in milk and pour into egg mixture. Cube bread and place in a large bakepan. Pour the egg mixture over the bread and stir until the bread mixture is well soaked.

4. Add vanilla and raisins.

5. Bake in a moderate oven for 40 minutes or until firm.

NO. 816. APPLE PIE OR COBBLER FILLING

Yield: 100 servings, 2 sheet pans, 16½" x 24" x 1½".

Ingredients	100 servings	.... servings
Apple nuggets, dehydrated....	3¾ pounds (6⅔ No. 56 dippers).....	....
Water......................	11 quarts (11 No. 56 dippers).......	....
Sugar, granulated...........	3¼ pounds (1⅔ No. 56 dippers).....	....
Cinnamon...................	½ ounce (2 mess kit spoons)........	....

1. Add apple nuggets to water and bring slowly to a boil. Simmer for 10 minutes.
2. Add sugar and simmer for an additional 10 minutes or until apples are tender. Add cinnamon and cool.
3. Pour into pastry-lined sheet pans, and cover with a top crust.
4. Bake for approximately 45 minutes in hot oven.

NO. 817. CARROT PIE FILLING   Yield: 100 servings, 2 sheet pans 16½" x 24" x 1½".

Ingredients	100 servings	.... servings
Carrots, dehydrated	2¾ pounds (2½ No. 56 dippers)	....
Water (for carrots)	7½ quarts (7½ No. 56 dippers)	....
Sugar, granulated	3 pounds (1½ No. 56 dippers)	....
Salt	2 ounces (4 mess kit spoons)	....
Cinnamon	(2½ mess kit spoons)	....
Nutmeg	(2½ mess kit spoons)	....
Cornstarch	2½ ounces (⅛ No. 56 dipper)	....
Milk, evaporated	5—14½-ounce cans	....
Water (for milk)	2½ quarts (2½ No. 56 dippers)	....
or		
Milk, powdered	1¼ pounds (1¼ No. 56 dippers)	....
Water (for milk)	4½ quarts (4½ No. 56 dippers)	....
Eggs, powdered	12 ounces (1 No. 56 dipper)	....
Water (for eggs)	1⅛ quarts (1⅛ No. 56 dippers)	....

1. Soak carrots in water 20 to 40 minutes. Bring slowly to a boil in a covered container (about 45 minutes). Simmer 15 to 25 minutes or until tender. Drain and mash thoroughly. Strain mixture through a coarse sieve if possible.
2. Combine sugar, salt, spices, and cornstarch. Mix well and add to mashed carrots.
3. Combine evaporated milk to water or reconstitute powdered milk. Add to the carrot mixture; stir until smooth.
4. Add egg powder to ⅓ of the water. Mix until smooth. Add remaining water gradually. Add to carrot mixture. Allow to stand about 1 hour before pouring into pastry-lined pans. Bake in moderate oven 30 to 45 minutes.

NO. 818. CREAM PIE FILLING   Yield: 2 sheet pans, 16½" x 24" x 1½".

Ingredients	100 servings	.... servings
Milk, evaporated	11—14½-ounce cans	....
Water (for milk)	5 quarts (5 No. 56 dippers)	....
or		
Milk, powdered	2½ pounds (2½ No. 56 dippers)	....
Water (for milk)	9 quarts (9 No. 56 dippers)	....
Sugar, granulated	5 pounds (2½ No. 56 dippers)	....
Cornstarch	1¼ pounds (1 No. 56 dipper)	....
Salt	¾ ounce (1½ mess kit spoons)	....
Eggs, powdered	18 ounces (1½ No. 56 dipper)	....
Water	1½ quarts (1½ No. 56 dippers)	....
Shortening	½ pound (¼ No. 56 dipper)	....
Vanilla	24 tablets	....

1. Combine evaporated milk and water or reconstitute powdered milk. Add sugar and bring to the boiling point.
2. Mix cornstarch, salt, and powdered eggs together. Add water slowly, stirring constantly to prevent lumping. Add approximately 3 quarts of the hot milk gradually to cornstarch mixture. Add this mixture to remaining hot milk and cook until thick, stirring constantly.
3. Add shortening and vanilla. Cool (refrigerate if not used immediately). Pour into sheet pans of baked pie shells.

NO. 819. MOCK CHERRY PIE FILLING

Yield: 100 servings, 2 sheet pans
16½" x 24" x 1½".

Ingredients	100 servings	.... servings
Apple nuggets, dehydrated....	3 pounds (4 No. 56 dippers).........	....
Cranberries, dehydrated, whole	1 pound (3 No. 56 dippers)..........	....
or		
Cranberries, dehydrated, sliced	20 ounces (1 No. 56 dipper).........	....
Water, cold................	13 quarts (13 No. 56 dippers).......	....
Sugar, granulated...........	12 pounds (6 No. 56 dippers).......	....

1. Combine apple nuggets and cranberries. Add water, bring slowly to a boil and simmer for 15 minutes.
2. Add sugar and mix well, and heat for an additional 5 minutes. Allow to cool. Pour into pastry-lined tins or baking sheets, cover with top crust.
3. Bake in a quick oven for 40 to 45 minutes.

NO. 820. CUSTARD (For baked custard or pie filling)

Yield: 100 servings, approximately 5 ounces each, 2 sheet pans, 16½" x 24½".

Ingredients	100 servings	.... servings
Sugar, granulated...........	4 pounds (2 No. 56 dippers)........	....
Salt.....................	½ ounce (1 mess kit spoon).........	....
Eggs, powdered.............	2¼ pounds (3 No. 56 dippers)......	....
Milk, powdered.............	3 pounds (3 No. 56 dippers)........	....
Water (for milk)............	13 quarts (13 No. 56 dippers).......	....
or		
Milk, evaporated............	12—14½-ounce cans..............	....
Water (for milk)............	9 quarts (9 No. 56 dippers)........	....
Nutmeg...................	8 ounces (2 mess kit spoons)........	....
Vanilla...................	12 tablets or 4 mess kit spoons.......	....

1. Sift together sugar, salt, powdered eggs, and powdered milk (if used).
2. Add dry mixture to water gradually, beating constantly with a wire whip.

315

3. If evaporated milk is used, combine milk and water and add egg mixture gradually, beating constantly.

4. Add nutmeg and vanilla.

5. Pour into bakepans and place pans in top of roasting pan. Pour water into roasting pan top to give a double boiler effect. Bake in slow oven for 30 to 45 minutes or until firm. A good test is to insert a knife into custard and if it comes out clean the custard is done.

Note. For pies, pour custard into unbaked pie shells and bake approximately 45 minutes in a moderate oven until firm.

NO. 821. LEMON PIE FILLING   Yield: 100 servings, 6 cuts per pie, 2 sheet pans, 16½" x 24" x 1½".

Ingredients	100 servings	.... servings
Cornstarch	2½ pounds (2 No. 56 dippers)	
Sugar, granulated	9 pounds (4½ No. 56 dippers)	
Salt	1½ ounces (3 mess kit spoons)	
Water	8 quarts (8 No. 56 dippers)	
Eggs, powdered	15 ounces (1¼ No. 56 dippers)	
Water (for eggs)	1½ quarts (1½ No. 56 dippers)	
Lemon juice powder, synthetic	5 ounces (9 mess kit spoons)	
Water	1 pint (½ No. 56 dipper)	

1. Mix cornstarch, sugar, and salt. Add water gradually to make a smooth paste. Bring to a boil and cook until thick.

2. Add egg powder to ⅓ of the water, beating constantly to make a smooth paste. Add remainder of water and mix until smooth. Add slowly to the filling, stirring constantly. Continue beating for approximately 5 minutes, beating constantly. Remove from heat.

3. Dissolve powder in water. Add to thickened filling. Stir well. Cool. Pour into baked pie shells.

NO. 822. MINCEMEAT FORMULA NO. 1

Yield: 100 servings, 2 sheet pans, 16½" x 24" x 1½".

Ingredients	100 servings	.... servings
Bouillon cubes	36 cubes	
Water, boiling	9 quarts (9 No. 56 dippers)	
Corned beef, canned	4 pounds	
Fat	2 pounds (1 No. 56 dipper)	
Apple nuggets, dehydrated	2½ pounds (3¼ No. 56 dippers)	
Sugar, granulated	3 pounds (1½ No. 56 dippers)	
Raisins	7 pounds (5⅓ No. 56 dippers)	
Cinnamon	¾ ounce (3 mess kit spoons)	
Pepper	(⅓ mess kit spoon)	
Nutmeg	¼ ounce (1 mess kit spoon)	
Salt	(⅓ mess kit spoon)	

1. Dissolve bouillon cubes in boiling water.
2. Add remaining ingredients. Simmer on a slow fire for approximately 45 minutes or until apples and raisins are tender. The addition of gravy coloring or caramelized sugar will improve the appearance. Remove from fire and cool. Pour into pastry-lined sheet pans.
3. Cover with a top crust and make in hot oven 40 to 45 minutes or until crust is golden brown.

Note. This mix should be prepared just prior to using.

NO. 823. MINCEMEAT FORMULA NO. 2

Yield: 100 servings, 2 sheet pans, 16½″ x 24‴x 1½″.

Ingredients	100 servings	.... servings
Bouillon cubes...............	28 cubes........................	....
Water, boiling...............	7 quarts (7 No. 56 dippers).........	....
Corned beef, canned..........	4 pounds........................	....
Fat.........................	2 pounds (1 No. 56 dipper).........	....
Apple nuggets, dehydrated....	2½ pounds (3¼ No. 56 dippers).....	....
Sugar, granulated............	4 pounds (2 No. 56 dippers)........	....
Raisins.....................	4 pounds (3 No. 56 dippers)........	....
Prunes, dried (diced)........	¾ pound (½ No. 56 dipper).........	....
Apricots, dried (diced).......	1¾ pounds (1½ No. 56 dippers).....	....
Cinnamon..................	¾ ounce (3 mess kit spoons)........	....
Salt........................	(⅓ mess kit spoon)...............	....
Pepper.....................	(⅓ mess kit spoon)...............	....
Nutmeg....................	¼ ounce (1 mess kit spoon).........	....
Cherries, sour (with juice)....	1 No. 10 can....................	....

1. Dissolve bouillon cubes in boiling water.
2. Add remaining ingredients and simmer on a slow fire for approximately 45 minutes or until dried fruit is soft. Remove from fire and cool.
3. Pour into pastry-lined sheet pans. Cover with a top crust and bake in hot oven 40 to 50 minutes or until crust is golden brown.

Note. This mix should be prepared just prior to using.

NO. 824. TOPPING FOR PIES

Yield: 100 servings or topping for 2 sheet pans.

Ingredients	100 servings	.... servings
Water......................	2 quarts (2 No. 56 dippers).........	....
Gelatin dessert powder, lemon flavor.	1½ pounds (1⅛ No. 56 dippers).....	....
Milk, evaporated............	4½—14½-ounce cans..............	....
Vanilla tablets..............	5 tablets.......................	....
Water (for tablets)..........	1½ ounces (3 mess kit spoons)......	....

1. Heat water to boiling point. Dissolve gelatin powder in hot water, set aside to cool, then add milk and mix thoroughly. Chill till mixture is consistency of egg whites.
2. Dissolve vanilla tablets in water, add to thickened mixture and beat vigorously with wire whip until light and fluffy. Spread over pie filling.

Note. If brown top is desired, cracker crumbs, cookie crumbs, or crushed dry cereal flakes may be sprinkled over the topping.

NO. 825. HARD CANDY ICE CREAM   Yield: 2½ gallons.

Ingredients	100 servings	.... servings
Hard candy, crushed.........	¼ No. 56 dippers......................	....
Ice cream mix powder........	4½ pounds (1 can)....................	....
or		
Ice cream mix paste..........	6 pounds (½ can).....................	....
Water.....................	3½ quarts (3½ No. 56 dippers)......	....

1. Crush hard candy to consistency of a coarse powder. Put through a sieve if possible, to get out large pieces.

2. Add water to the ice cream mix. Prepare and freeze in the usual manner.

3. Add crushed candy to the ice cream as it is being drawn from the freezer.

Caution. Do not put candy into freezer until ice cream is being drawn.

NO. 826. CHOCOLATE ICE CREAM   Yield: 2½ gallons.

Ingredients	100 servings	.... servings
Cocoa.....................	6 ounces (½ No. 56 dipper).........	....
Sugar, granulated............	8 ounces (¼ No. 56 dipper)........	....
Ice cream mix powder........	4¼ pounds (1 can).................	....
or		
Ice cream mix paste..........	6 pounds (½ can)..................	....

1. Combine cocoa and sugar.

2. Mix dry sugar and cocoa with ice cream mix powder. If ice cream paste is used, reconstitute before adding cocoa mix. Prepare and freeze in usual manner.

NO. 827. COFFEE ICE CREAM   Yield: 2½ gallons.

Ingredients	100 servings	.... servings
Water.....................	2 quarts (2 No. 56 dippers).........	....
Coffee, ground..............	(10 mess kit spoons)	....
Water.....................	1½ quarts (1½ No. 56 dippers)......	....
Ice cream mix powder........	4¼ pounds (1 can).................	....
or		
Ice cream mix paste..........	6 pounds (½ can)..................	....

1. Add coffee to water and let simmer for 10 minutes. Strain and cool before using. Add the water to the 2 dippers of coffee.

2. Reconstitute powder or paste with the coffee mixture and freeze in the usual manner.

Note. Coffee may be put into cheesecloth bag before putting it into the water.

NO. 828. FRUIT COCKTAIL ICE CREAM   Yield: 2½ gallons.

Ingredients	100 servings	.... servings
Fruit cocktail, canned........	⅔ No. 10 can (2 No. 56 dippers).....	....
Water and juice..............	3½ quarts (3½ No. 56 dippers)......	....
Ice cream mix powder........	4¼ pounds (1 can)..................	....
or		
Ice cream mix paste..........	6 pounds (½ can)...................	....

1. Drain juice from fruit after measuring.
2. Use water and juice to make a total of 3½ No. 56 dippers. Use above liquid to reconstitute powder or paste.
3. Add fruit to mix in freezer after freezing and overrun has been obtained. Let freeze several minutes more with refrigerant on, then turn off refrigerant and drain.

NO. 829. LEMON ICE CREAM   Yield: 2½ gallons.

Ingredients	100 servings	.... servings
Lemon juice powder, synthetic.	5 mess kit spoons.................	....
Sugar.....................	1½ pounds (¾ No. 56 dippers)......	....
Water.....................	3½ quarts (3½ No. 56 dippers)......	....
Ice cream mix powder........	4¼ pounds (1 can)..................	....
or		
Ice cream mix paste..........	6 pounds (½ can)...................	....

1. Combine lemon juice powder and sugar.
2. Dissolve the above mixture in the water.
3. Reconstitute the ice cream mix with the lemon juice powder solution and freeze in the usual manner.

NO. 830. MAPLE ICE CREAM   Yield: 2½ gallons.

Ingredients	100 servings	.... servings
Maple tablets................	2 tablets........................	....
Water, boiling...............	1 quart (½ No. 56 dipper)..........	....
Water.....................	3 quarts (3 No. 56 dippers).........	....
Ice cream mix powder........	4¼ pounds (1 can)..................	....
or		
Ice cream mix paste..........	6 pounds (½ can)...................	....

1. Dissolve maple tablets in boiling water.
2. Add dissolved maple tablets to the remaining water and reconstitute ice cream mix. Freeze in the usual manner.

NO. 831. PEACH ICE CREAM   Yield: 2½ gallons.

Ingredients	100 servings	.... servings
Peaches, diced, canned........	2 No. 56 dippers...................	....
Water.....................	3½ quarts (3½ No. 56 dippers)......	....
Ice cream mix powder........	4¼ pounds (1 can)..................	....
or		
Ice cream mix paste..........	6 pounds (½ can)...................	....

1. Drain juice from fruit after measuring. Use water and juice to make a total of 3½ No. 56 dippers.

2. Use water and juice to reconstitute powder. Add fruit to mix in freezer after freezing and overrun has been obtained. Let freeze several minutes more with refrigerant on, then turn off refrigerant and drain.

NO. 832. PINEAPPLE ICE CREAM   Yield: 2½ gallons.

Ingredients	100 servings	.... servings
Pineapple slices, canned.......	1¾ No. 56 dippers................	....
Pineapple juice...............	¾ quart (¾ No. 56 dipper)........	....
Water....................	2¾ quarts (2¾ No. 56 dippers)......	....
Ice cream mix powder........	4¼ pounds (1 can)................	....
or		
Ice cream mix paste..........	6 pounds (½ can)................	....

1. Drain pineapple before measuring.

2. Cut pineapple into small pieces.

3. Use water and pineapple juice to make a total of 3½ No. 56 dippers. Use above liquid to reconstitute powder or paste.

4. Add cut slices of pineapple to mix in freezer after freezing and overrun has been obtained. Let freeze several more minutes with refrigerant on, then turn off refrigerant and drain.

NO. 833. VANILLA ICE CREAM   Yield: 2½ gallons.

Ingredients	100 servings	.... servings
Ice cream mix powder........	4¼ pounds (1 can)................	....
or		
Ice cream mix paste..........	6 pounds (½ can)................	....
Water....................	3½ quarts (3½ No. 56 dippers)......	....

1. Add the entire contents of the can of ice cream mix to the water and mix thoroughly. The powder or paste will go into solution readily. It is not necessary to thoroughly reconstitute the mix as it will reconstitute while freezing.

2. If possible chill the mix before putting into freezer. Pour the mix into freezer and freeze in the usual manner.

48. POWDERED EGGS. Powdered eggs are a necessary part of a concentrated, packed ration. They can be made edible with a little effort in careful preparation.

NO. 834. APPLE FRITTERS

Yield: 100 servings,
2 fritters each.

Ingredients	100 servings	.... servings
Apple nuggets, dehydrated....	1½ pounds (2 No. 56 dippers)......	....
Water (for nuggets)..........	4½ quarts (4½ No. 56 dippers)......	....
Flour, sifted................	4½ pounds (4½ No. 56 dippers).....	....
Sugar, granulated............	1¾ pounds (⅞ No. 56 dipper).......	....
Baking powder..............	2¼ ounces (6 mess kit spoons).......	....
Salt.......................	2¼ ounces (4½ mess kit spoons).....	....
Milk, evaporated.............	1—14½-ounce can...................	....
Water (for milk).............	1 pint (½ No. 56 dipper)...........	....
or		
Milk, powdered..............	4 ounces (¼ No. 56 dipper).........	....
Water (for milk).............	1 quart (1 No. 56 dipper)...........	....
Eggs, powdered..............	6 ounces (½ No. 56 dipper).........	....
Water (for eggs).............	⅔ quart (⅔ No. 56 dipper)........	....
Shortening, melted..........	6 ounces (⅛ No. 56 dipper)........	....

1. Add apple nuggets to water and bring slowly to a boil in a covered container. Simmer for 10 minutes or until apples are tender. (Drain off any excess liquid.)
2. Sift flour, sugar, baking powder, and salt together.
3. Combine milk and water or reconstitute powdered milk.
4. Reconstitute eggs by adding powder to ⅓ of the water and stirring to make a smooth paste. Add the remaining water and mix thoroughly. Combine milk, eggs, and shortening; mix well. Add to the flour mixture, stir until smooth.
5. Add applesauce to mixture. Drop a spoonful into deep hot fat and fry about 6 or 7 minutes, turning frequently to cook them evenly. Drain on absorbent paper. Serve hot.

Note. Any of the "B" ration fruits may be used instead of apples.

NO. 835. CORN FRITTERS

Yield: 100 servings,
200 fritters, 2 each.

Ingredients	100 servings	.... servings
Eggs, powdered............	8 ounces (⅔ No. 56 dipper)..........	....
Corn, canned, cream style.....	2½ No. 10 cans....................	....
Milk, evaporated.............	1—14½-ounce can...................	....
Water (for milk).............	1 pint (½ No. 56 dipper)...........	....
or		
Milk, powdered..............	¼ pound (¼ No. 56 dipper)........	....
Water (for milk).............	1 quart (1 No. 56 dipper)...........	....
Flour......................	4⅓ pounds (3⅓ No. 56 dippers).....	....
Sugar, granulated............	1 pound (½ No. 56 dipper).........	....
Salt.......................	3 ounces (6 mess kit spoons)........	....
Baking powder.............	2¼ ounces (6 mess kit spoons).......	....
Shortening, melted..........	½ pound (¼ No. 56 dipper)........	....
Fat (for frying).............	4 pounds (2 No. 56 dippers)........	....

1. Combine eggs and corn and mix until the eggs are smooth.
2. Combine milk and water or reconstitute milk and add to the corn and egg mixture.

3. Sift dry ingredients together. Add milk and egg mixture gradually to sifted dry ingredients. Add melted shortening and beat until smooth.
4. Drop batter with spoon onto greased griddles. Fry till brown (approximately 3 minutes on each side). Serve with sirup or jelly.

NO. 836. EGG MACARONI CUTLETS

Yield: 100 servings, 1 cutlet each.

Ingredients	100 servings	.... servings
Thick white sauce............	1 to 2 No. 56 dippers...............	
Eggs, powdered..............	1½ pounds (2 No. 56 dippers).......	
Water (for eggs).............	2 quarts (2 No. 56 dippers).........	
Macaroni, dry..............	4½ pounds (4 No. 56 dippers).......	
Water....................	16 quarts (16 No. 56 dippers)........	
Salt.....................	2 ounces (4 mess kit spoons)........	
Onions, dehydrated...........	4 ounces (½ No. 56 dipper)........	
Water (for onions)...........	1 quart (1 No. 56 dipper)...........	
Fat......................	8 ounces (¼ No. 56 dipper)........	
Salt.....................	3 ounces (6 mess kit spoons)........	
Kitchen sauce..............	1 mess kit spoon...............	
Pepper...................	To taste...................	
Crumbs, bread or cracker.....	3 pounds (3 No. 56 dippers)........	

1. Prepare white sauce, using preserved butter. (See recipe No. 906.)
2. Add egg powder to ⅓ of the water, beating constantly to make a smooth paste. Add remainder of the water and mix until smooth. Pour into a greased stockpot, stirring eggs as they thicken. Remove from fire while still a little soft.
3. Add macaroni to boiling salted water and boil for 15 minutes or until tender. Drain.
4. Soak onions in water for 20 minutes. Add onions to fat and fry until lightly brown.
5. Combine seasoning, onions, cooked macaroni, and cooked eggs and white sauce (add sufficient white sauce to make the mixture of good consistency). Form into cutlets or patties. Roll cutlets in crumbs and fry in fat (about 2 inches deep in large bakepan) until brown. Serve with tomato or cheese sauce.

NO. 837. OMELET

Yield: 25 omelets.

Ingredients	25 servings	.... servings
Eggs, powdered..............	1 pound 2 ounces (1½ No. 56 dippers)	....
Milk, evaporated.............	2¼—14½-ounce cans............	
Water (for milk).............	1 quart (1 No. 56 dipper)...........	
or		
Milk, powdered.............	½ pound (½ No. 56 dipper)........	
Water (for milk).............	1¾ quarts (1¾ No. 56 dippers)......	
Salt.....................	½ ounce (1 mess kit spoon)........	
Pepper...................	½ mess kit spoon................	
Baking powder.............	1 mess kit spoon................	

1. Combine evaporated milk and water, or reconstitute powdered milk.
2. Add egg powder to ⅓ of the milk, beating constantly to make a smooth paste. Add remainder of milk and mix until smooth.
3. Add salt and pepper to egg mixture. Add baking powder just before cooking.
4. Pour individual portions on a hot, greased griddle. Turn one time and fold. Serve hot.

NO. 838. WESTERN OMELET — Yield: 25 omelets.

Ingredients	25 servings	.... servings
Eggs, powdered..............	1 pound 2 ounces (1½ No. 56 dippers)	....
Milk, evaporated.............	2¼—14½-ounce cans.................	....
Water (for milk).............	1 quart (1 No. 56 dipper)...........	....
or		
Milk, powdered..............	½ pound (½ No. 56 dipper)........	....
Water (for milk).............	1¾ quarts (1¾ No. 56 dippers).....	....
Luncheon meat, ground.......	1½ pounds	....
Onion flakes.................	¼ No. 56 dipper.............	....
Water.....................	1 pint (½ No. 56 dipper)...........	....
Salt......................	½ ounce (1 mess kit spoon).........	....
Pepper....................	½ mess kit spoon...............	....
Baking powder.............	½ mess kit spoon...............	....

1. Combine evaporated milk and water or reconstitute powdered milk.
2. Add egg powder to ⅓ of the milk, beating constantly to make a smooth paste. Add remainder of milk and mix until smooth.
3. Soak onions in water 20 to 40 minutes. Add onions, meat, salt, and pepper to egg mixture.
4. Add baking powder just before cooking.
5. Pour individual portions on hot, greased griddle. Turn once and serve hot.

NO. 839. PANCAKES — Yield: 100 servings, 2 to 3 cakes each.

Ingredients	100 servings	.... servings
Eggs, powdered..............	12 ounces (1 No. 56 dipper)........	....
Sugar, granulated...........	3 pounds (2½ No. 56 dippers)......	....
Salt......................	5 ounces (10 mess kit spoons).......	....
Milk, powdered..............	3 pounds (3 No. 56 dippers)......	....
Water, warm (for milk).......	11 quarts (11 No. 56 dippers)......	....
or		
Milk, evaporated.............	13—14½-ounce cans...........	....
Water, warm (for milk).......	6 quarts (6 No. 56 dippers).........	....
Shortening, melted..........	2½ pounds (1¼ No. 56 dippers).....	....
Flour, sifted................	15 pounds (15 No. 56 dippers)......	....
Baking powder.............	15 ounces (40 mess kit spoons).......	....

1. Mix eggs, sugar, salt, and powdered milk (if used) together thoroughly. Add enough water to make a smooth paste. Add remaining water and beat until smooth.

2. If evaporated milk is used, omit powdered milk in dry mix. Combine milk and water and add to dry ingredients gradually making a smooth paste. Add melted shortening and beat until smooth.
3. Mix flour and baking powder and add to batter. Mix only until smooth.
4. Fry on hot, greased griddle until brown on both sides.

NO. 840. FRENCH PANCAKES Yield: 100 servings, 4 ounces each or 2 pancakes each.

Ingredients	100 servings	.... servings
Eggs, powdered...............	6 pounds (8 No. 56 dippers).........	....
Flour, sifted.................	2½ pounds (2½ No. 56 dippers).....	....
Salt........................	3 ounces (6 mess kit spoons).........	....
Baking powder..............	4½ ounces (12 mess kit spoons)......	....
Water.....................	8¼ quarts (8¼ No. 56 dippers)......	....

1. Mix thoroughly the dried eggs, flour, salt, and baking powder.
2. Add this mixture to ⅓ of water. Stir until smooth. Add the remainder of water and beat till smooth.
3. Drop batter on a hot, greased grill using a large serving spoon. Fry till brown on one side, turn on the other side and brown.

NO. 841. POTATO OMELET Yield: 100 servings, 5 ounces each or ⅓-inch square per serving.

Ingredients	100 servings	.... servings
Potatoes, dehydrated, diced or julienne.	2 pounds (3 No. 56 dippers).........	....
Water (for potatoes).........	5½ quarts (5½ No. 56 dippers)......	....
Bacon.....................	10 pounds	....
Eggs, powdered..............	3 pounds (4 No. 56 dippers).........	....
Water (for eggs).............	4½ quarts (4½ No. 56 dippers)......	....
Salt.......................	4 ounces (8 mess kit spoons)........	....
Pepper....................	⅔ mess kit spoon...................	....
Milk, evaporated............	2—14½-ounce cans.................	....
or		
Milk, powdered.............	4 ounces (¼ No. 56 dipper).........	....
Water (for milk)............	1 quart (1 No. 56 dipper)...........	....

1. Soak potatoes in water 20 to 40 minutes. Bring slowly to a boil for about 45 minutes, in a covered stockpot, and simmer for 10 to 15 minutes or until tender. Drain.
2. Arrange slices of bacon in large baking pan. Fry until crisp. Remove and keep warm till served.
3. Add diced potatoes to bacon fat and fry until brown. (Use only 1 quart dipper of bacon fat. Drain off any excess.)
4. Add egg powder to ⅓ of the water and beat until all lumps are removed. Add remaining water gradually and continue mixing until smooth. Beat until light.

5. Add seasonings and milk to eggs and beat vigorously. Pour the egg and milk mixture over the potatoes.

6. Bake in a moderate oven for approximately 30 minutes. (Do not overcook the eggs.)

7. Cut into 3-inch squares. Place a slice of bacon on top of each serving.

NO. 842. BASIC RECIPE FOR SCRAMBLED EGGS

Yield: 25 3½-ounce servings or
1 serving spoon each.

Ingredients	25 servings	.... servings
Eggs, powdered	2½ pounds (3⅓ No. 56 dippers)	
Water (for eggs)	2½ quarts (2½ No. 56 dippers)	
Salt	To taste	
Pepper	To taste	
Fat	1 pound (½ No. 56 dipper)	

1. Pour ⅓ of the water into a 10-gallon stockpot insert. Add powdered eggs. Stir vigorously with whip to eliminate all lumps. Tip pot while stirring to obtain a smooth mixture.

2. When smooth, add remaining water gradually. Add salt and pepper.

3. Melt fat and heat to frying temperature. Pour in liquid eggs. Stir as eggs begin to set and continue stirring until eggs are about ready to serve. Remove from fire while eggs are still soft for they will continue to set slightly after removing from the fire.

NO. 843. DICED BACON AND SCRAMBLED EGGS
Fry 2 No. 56 dippers (3 pounds) of diced bacon in ration pans. The bacon fat may be used in place of the fat in the above recipe. Pour the reconstituted eggs over the diced fried bacon and cook till the eggs are of desired firmness.

NO. 844. LUNCHEON MEAT AND SCRAMBLED EGGS
Add 2 No. 56 dippers (3 pounds) of diced luncheon meat to the scrambled eggs as they begin to thicken.

NO. 845. PORK SAUSAGE AND SCRAMBLED EGGS
Omit fat in the above recipe and use pork sausage fat. Add 1¾ No. 56 dippers (2 pounds) of diced pork sausage as eggs begin to thicken.

NO. 846. SPANISH SAUCE AND SCRAMBLED EGGS
Use Spanish sauce recipe. No. 895. Serve scrambled eggs with the hot sauce.

NO. 847. FRENCH TOAST   Yield: 100 servings, 1 slice each.

Ingredients	100 servings	.... servings
Eggs, powdered...............	2 pounds (2⅔ No. 56 dippers).......	
Water (for eggs).............	3 quarts (3 No. 56 dippers).........	
Milk, evaporated............	2—14½-ounce cans.................	
Water (for milk).............	1 quart (1 No. 56 dipper)...........	
or		
Milk, powdered..............	8 ounces (½ No. 56 dipper)........	
Water (for milk).............	1¾ quarts (1¾ No. 56 dippers)......	
Salt.......................	1 ounce (2 mess kit spoons)........	
Bread.....................	100 slices.......................	
Fat (for frying).............	3 pounds (1½ No. 56 dippers).......	

1. Pour ⅓ of the water into a stockpot.

2. Add eggs and stir vigorously with a whip to eliminate all lumps. When smooth add remaining water, salt, and milk. Stir until well mixed.

3. Pour liquid into shallow pans and dip slices of bread into the egg mixture.

4. Fry in fat until brown, turn and brown on other side.

49. MEATS AND FISH. Meats and fish become the main part of the meal in the field just as in the garrison mess.

NO. 848. CORNED BEEF AND CABBAGE
Yield: 100 9-ounce servings or
approximately ½ mess kit cup each.

Ingredients	100 servings	.... servings
Cabbage, dehydrated........	3½ pounds (11 No. 56 dippers)......	
Water (for cabbage).........	17 quarts (17 No. 56 dippers).......	
Salt......................	4½ ounces (9 mess kit spoons).......	
Corned beef, canned........	5—6-pound cans....................	

1. Soak cabbage in water for 20 minutes. Bring slowly to a boil (about 45 minutes in an uncovered stockpot). Add salt and simmer for 10 minutes or until tender. Drain, leaving about ½ of the liquid on the cabbage.

2. Break up corned beef into large pieces and add to the cabbage. (Avoid overmixing.) Reheat and serve.

NO. 849. CORNED BEEF CASSEROLE

Yield: 100 7-ounce servings
or approximately ⅓ mess kit
cup each.

Ingredients	100 servings	.... servings
Fat	2 pounds (1 No. 56 dipper)	
Flour	2½ pounds (2 No. 56 dippers)	
Milk, evaporated	11—14½-ounce cans	
Water (for milk)	5 quarts (5 No. 56 dippers)	
or		
Milk, powdered	2½ pounds (2½ No. 56 dippers)	
Water (for milk)	9 quarts (9 No. 56 dippers)	
Salt	1½ ounces (3 mess kit spoons)	
Pepper	¼ ounce (1 mess kit spoon)	
Corned beef, canned	2—6-pound cans	
Corn, whole kernel	2 No. 10 cans	

1. Melt the fat in large stockpot. Add the flour and stir until smooth.

2. Combine milk and water or reconstitute milk, add to the above flour mixture and cook until it thickens, stirring constantly.

3. Add salt, pepper, corned beef, and drained corn. (The liquid from the corn should be used as part of the liquid necessary to reconstitute milk.) Serve on crackers or toast.

NO. 850. CORNED BEEF CUTLETS

Yield: 100 5½-ounce servings or
approximately 1½ cutlet per
serving.

Ingredients	100 servings	.... servings
Fat	1½ pounds (¾ No. 56 dippers)	
Flour	1¾ pounds (1¼ No. 56 dippers)	
Salt	2 ounces (4 mess kit spoons)	
Milk, evaporated	4—14½-ounce cans	
Water (for milk)	2 quarts (2 No. 56 dippers)	
or		
Milk, powdered	1 pound (1 No. 56 dipper)	
Water (for milk)	3½ quarts (3½ No. 56 dippers)	
Cheese, shredded	2 pounds (2 No. 56 dippers)	
Onion, dehydrated	2 ounces (¼ No. 56 dipper)	
Water (for onions)	1 pint (½ No. 56 dipper)	
Macaroni, dry	1⅔ pounds (1½ No. 56 dippers)	
Water, boiling (for macaroni)	6 quarts (6 No. 56 dippers)	
Salt (for macaroni)	½ ounce (1 mess kit spoon)	
Corned beef	2—6-pound cans	

1. Melt fat in a large stockpot. Remove from heat, add flour and salt and blend well.

2. Combine milk and water or reconstitute milk. Add milk to flour mixture. Cook until very smooth and thick, stirring constantly. Remove sauce from heat. Add cheese and stir until melted. Cool.

3. Soak onions in water for 20 minutes.

4. Add macaroni to boiling salted water and cook approximately 15 minutes or until tender. Drain.

5. Remove corned beef from can and break up into small pieces. (Grind if possible.) Add reconstituted onions, cooked macaroni, and corned beef to sauce. Pour into shallow pans to cool (chill if possible).

6. Form meat mixture into patties or cutlets and dip in egg mixture and roll in cracker crumbs. Fry in fat, about 2 inches deep, until brown.

NO. 851. EGG MIXTURE

Ingredients	100 servings	.... servings
Eggs, powdered...............	12 ounces (1 No. 56 dipper)..........	....
Water (for eggs).............	1 quart (1 No. 56 dipper)............	....
Bread or cracker crumbs......	4 pounds (4 No. 56 dippers).........	....

Reconstitute eggs. (See par. 38.)

NO. 852. CORNED BEEF WITH MACARONI

Yield: 100 servings, 8 ounces each, or approximately ⅓ mess kit cup each.

Ingredients	100 servings	.... servings
Macaroni, dry...............	4½ pounds (4 No. 56 dippers)......	....
Water, boiling (for macaroni)..	16 quarts (16 No. 56 dippers).......	....
Salt.......................	2½ ounces (5 mess kit spoons).......	....
Corned beef.................	3—6-pound cans....................	....
Eggs, powdered..............	12 ounces (1 No. 56 dipper).........	....
Milk, powdered*.............	12 ounces (¾ No. 56 dipper)........	....
Water (for milk).............	3 quarts (3 No. 56 dippers).........	....
Cheese, shredded.............	4 pounds (4 No. 56 dippers)........	....
Salt.......................	1½ ounces (3 mess kit spoons).......	....

*If evaporated milk is substituted, use three 14½-ounce cans of evaporated milk and only 1½ No. 56 dippers of water.

1. Add macaroni to boiling salted water. Boil 10 to 15 minutes or until tender. Drain well.

2. Break up corned beef into medium size pieces.

3. Add powdered eggs (milk in dry form), water, cheese, and salt. Mix all ingredients thoroughly. Bake in large bakepan in moderate oven for approximately 1 hour or until brown.

Note. Vienna sausages cut in 1-inch pieces may be substituted for the corned beef in the above recipe.

NO. 853. CORNED BEEF AND MASHED POTATOES

Yield: 100 8-ounce servings or ⅓ inch square per serving.

Ingredients	100 servings	.... servings
Potatoes, dehydrated (julienne or diced).	5 pounds (7 No. 56 dippers)........	....
Water (for potatoes).........	13 quarts (13 No. 56 dippers).......	....
Salt......................	1 ounce (2 mess kit spoons).........	....
Milk, evaporated.............	4—14½-ounce cans................	....
Water (for milk).............	1½ quarts (1½ No. 56 dippers)......	....
or		
Milk, powdered..............	12 ounces (¾ No. 56 dipper).......	....
Water (for milk).............	3 quarts (3 No. 56 dippers)........	....
Preserved butter.............	1 pound (½ No. 56 dipper)........	....
Corned beef, canned..........	3—6-pound cans................	....
Onions, dehydrated...........	4 ounces (½ No. 56 dippers).......	....
Water (for onions)...........	1 quart (1 No. 56 dipper).........	....
Cracker or bread crumbs......	2 pounds (2 No. 56 dippers)........	....
Eggs, powdered (to be added in dry form).	6 ounces (½ No. 56 dipper)........	....

1. Add potatoes to the water and soak for 20 minutes. Bring slowly to a boil (about 45 minutes). Simmer for 10 minutes in a covered stock-pot or until potatoes are tender. Drain.
2. Add to the potatoes.
3. Combine milk and water or reconstitute powdered milk.
4. Add preserved butter to the milk and heat until the preserved butter is melted. Add ½ of the milk mixture to the potatoes and mash by beating vigorously with a wire whip. (The amount of milk to be used may vary. Use only enough to make the potatoes of the right consistency.)
5. Grind meat or break up into small pieces.
6. Soak onions for approximately 20 minutes. Add to corned beef.
7. Add remaining ingredients to the corned beef with the remainder of the milk.
8. Place mixture into greased baking pan in layers 1 to 2 inches thick and cover with a layer of mashed potatoes.
9. Bake in hot oven for about ½ hour or until potatoes are brown.

NO. 854. BEEF POTTED WITH VEGETABLES

Yield: 100 10-ounce servings or approximately ½ mess kit cup each.

Ingredients	100 servings	.... servings
Onions, dehydrated..........	4 ounces (½ No. 56 dipper)........	....
Potatoes, dehydrated (julienne or diced).	6 pounds (8¾ No. 56 dippers).......	....
Carrots, dehydrated.........	1 pound 5 ounces (1½ No. 56 dipper).	....
Water.....................	20 quarts (20 No. 56 dippers).......	....
Beef and gravy, canned*......	16—30-ounce cans................	....
Salt......................	3 ounces (6 mess kit spoons)........	....
Pepper....................	¼ ounce (1 mess kit spoon)........	....

*Roast beef, canned, may be substituted.

1. Add water to combined vegetables and soak 20 to 40 minutes. Bring slowly to the boiling point (about 45 minutes) in a covered stockpot. Simmer 15 to 25 minutes or until vegetables are tender. Drain.
2. Place beef and gravy in bakepan and heat slowly. Do not stir any more than necessary. Add drained vegetables, salt, and pepper, heat to boiling point. Serve.

NO. 855. CORNED BEEF ROLL

Yield: 100 6-ounce servings or approximately 1½ slices, ¼ inch thick each.

Ingredients	100 servings	.... servings
Onions, dehydrated	8 ounces (1 No. 56 dipper)	
Water (for onions)	2 quarts (2 No. 56 dippers)	
Bread cubes (loose pack)	2 pounds (4 No. 56 dippers)	
Water	1 pint (½ No. 56 dipper)	
Corned beef, canned	4—6-pound cans	
Eggs, powdered	12 ounces (1 No. 56 dipper)	
Milk, powdered	1 pound (1 No. 56 dipper)	
Fat, melted	½ pound (¼ No. 56 dipper)	
Pepper	½ ounce (2 mess kit spoons)	
Pie crust	See recipe No. 407	

1. Soak onions in water for 20 minutes.
2. Moisten bread cubes with water.
3. Combine all ingredients and mix thoroughly. (Do not reconstitute the powdered milk and eggs.)
4. Roll the pie crust in a long rectangular shape, form the meat into a loaf in the center of the crust and joint crust at the top.
5. Bake in a quick oven in an uncovered bakepan until crust is brown. Slice and serve with tomato sauce.

NO. 856. ROAST BEEF AND GRAVY

Yield: 100 7-ounce servings or approximately ⅓ mess kit cup of beef and gravy each.

Ingredients	100 servings	.... servings
Roast beef, canned	5—6-pound cans	
Brown gravy	12 No. 56 dippers	

Separate canned roast beef into large pieces. Place in a large bakepan and cover with brown gravy. (See recipe No. 907.) Heat to a serving temperature. Serve with mashed potatoes or boiled rice.

NO. 857. ROAST BEEF AND GRAVY

Yield: 100 7-ounce servings or approximately ⅓ mess kit cup of beef and gravy each.

Ingredients	100 servings	.... servings
Roast beef and gravy	20—34-ounce cans	

Place beef and gravy into bakepans in 2-inch layers. Heat to serving temperature. Serve with mashed potatoes or boiled rice.

NO. 858. CORNED BEEF AND SPANISH RICE

Yield: 100 9-ounce servings or approximately ½ mess kit cup.

Ingredients	100 servings	.... servings
Onions, dehydrated.........	1 pound (2 No. 56 dippers).........	....
Water (for onions)..........	4 quarts (4 No. 56 dippers).........	....
Fat......................	1½ pounds (¾ No. 56 dipper).......	....
Corned beef, canned.........	2—6-pound cans................	....
Rice, dry.................	6 pounds (3 No. 56 dippers)........	....
Tomatoes, canned.........	3 No. 10 cans.................	....
Water (preferably hot).......	(10 No. 56 dippers).............	....
Pepper....................	⅜ ounce (1½ mess kit spoons).......	....
Salt......................	½ ounce (1 mess kit spoon).........	....

1. Soak onions in water for 20 minutes and melt fat in stockpot. Add onions and fry until brown.

2. Combine browned onions, corned beef, dry rice, tomatoes, water, and seasonings. Bring to a boil and allow to simmer slowly in a covered pan 25 to 35 minutes or until rice is tender. Stir occasionally to prevent burning.

NO. 859. BEEF STEW (Using canned roast beef and gravy)

Yield: 100 8-ounce servings, or approximately ⅓ mess kit cup each.

Ingredients	100 servings	.... servings
Onions, dehydrated.........	8 ounces (1 No. 56 dipper).........	....
Carrots, dehydrated.........	14 ounces (1 No. 56 dipper)........	....
Potatoes, dehydrated (julienne or dried).	4 pounds (6 No. 56 dippers)........	....
Water (for vegetables).......	13 quarts (13 No. 56 dippers).......	....
Tomatoes, canned..........	1 No. 10 can.................	....
Roast beef and gravy, canned.	27½ pounds (13—34-ounce cans).....	....
Salt......................	4½ ounces (9 mess kit spoons).......	....
Pepper....................	¼ ounce (1 mess kit spoon).........	....

1. Soak onions, carrots, and potatoes in water for 20 to 40 minutes. Bring slowly to the boiling point in covered stockpot. Combine with onions and tomatoes and simmer for approximately 30 minutes or until vegetables are tender but not mushy.

2. Add meat and seasonings and heat to a serving temperature. Avoid stirring vigorously after meat has been added as it breaks up readily.

NO. 860. BEEF STEW (Using fresh or frozen meat)

Yield: 100 9-ounce servings or
approximately ½ mess kit
cup each.

Ingredients	100 servings	.... servings
Boneless beef chuck (1½-inch cubes, fresh or frozen).	35 pounds (21 No. 56 dippers).......	....
Salt.	4½ ounces (9 mess kit spoons).......	....
Pepper.	¼ ounce (1 mess kit spoon)..........	....
Fat.	2 pounds (1 No. 56 dipper).........	....
Tomatoes, canned.	1 No. 10 can..................	....
Onions, dehydrated.	8 ounces (1 No. 56 dipper).........	....
Carrots, dehydrated (julienne or dried).	14 ounces (1 No. 56 dipper).........	...............:
Potatoes, dehydrated.	4 pounds (6.No. 56 dippers).........	....
Water.	13 quarts (13 No. 56 dippers).......	....

1. Season beef with salt and pepper. Melt fat in stockpot and brown the meat in the hot fat.

2. Add tomatoes to browned meat. Cover and simmer for approximately 1½ hours.

3. Soak onions, carrots, and potatoes in water for 20 to 40 minutes. Bring slowly to the boiling point. Combine with the meat and tomatoes and continue cooking for about 1 hour or until the meat and vegetables are tender. (Add more water if necessary.)

NO. 861. CHICKEN PIE

Yield: 100 8-ounce servings or
approximately ⅓ mess kit
cup per serving.

Ingredients	100 servings	.... servings
Onions, dehydrated...........	8 ounces (1 No. 56 dipper).........	....
Carrots, dehydrated..........	14 ounces (1 No. 56 dipper)........	....
Potatoes, dehydrated (julienne or dried).	4 pounds (5 No. 56 dippers)........	....
Water..................	13 quarts (13 No. 56 dippers).......	....
Chicken, or turkey, canned....	9—35-ounce cans................	....
Flour, sifted................	6 ounces (⅓ No. 56 dipper).........	....
Salt.....................	2½ ounces (5 mess kit spoons).......	....
Pepper...................	¼ ounce (1 mess kit spoon)........	....

1. Soak onions, carrots, and potatoes in water for 20 to 40 minutes. Bring slowly to the boiling point in a covered stockpot. Simmer for 30 minutes or until vegetables are tender.

2. Drain chicken. Save broth and add enough water to make 3 quarts of total liquid. Add a small amount of the broth to the flour and stir until a smooth paste is formed.

3. Add paste to chicken broth and cook until thick. Add gravy, seasonings, and vegetables to chicken. Place in baking pans and cover with a pie crust or biscuit topping.

NO. 862. CHOP SUEY

Yield: 100 12-ounce servings or approximately ½ mess kit cup each.

Ingredients	100 servings	.... servings
Bouillon cubes[1]	32 cubes (4½ ounces)	
Onions, dehydrated	20 ounces (2½ No. 56 dippers)	
Water	13 quarts (13 No. 56 dippers)	
Flour	3 pounds (2¼ No. 56 dippers)	
Water	2 quarts (2 No. 56 dippers)	
Roast beef, canned[2]	3—6-pound cans	
Pepper	¼ ounce (1 mess kit spoon)	
Salt	3 ounces (6 mess kit spoons)	
Soy sauce (optional)	(½ No. 56 dipper)	
Rice, dry	10 pounds (5 No. 56 dippers)	
Salt (for rice)	3½ ounces (7 mess kit spoons)	
Water (for rice)	20 quarts (20 No. 56 dippers)	

[1] An equal quantity of meat stock may be substituted for the water and bouillon cubes.
[2] Roast beef and gravy, canned, may be substituted.
[3] Salt should be eliminated if soy sauce is used.

1. Add bouillon cubes and dehydrated onions to the water. Heat to the boiling point.
2. Add water to the flour gradually. Mix until smooth. Add gradually to the bouillon mixture. Add roast beef. (The meat will break up in mixing so it does not require breaking up beforehand.)
3. Add pepper, salt[3] and soy sauce. (If soy sauce is not available, use burnt sugar or gravy coloring for darkening.) Continue heating until the mixture thickens, stirring occasionally.
4. Add rice to rapidly boiling salted water. Boil uncovered for 15 to 20 minutes or until tender. Drain well.
5. Serve with chop suey mixture.

NO. 863. MEAT PATTIES OR CROQUETTES

Yield: 100 6-ounce servings or approximately 2 patties per serving.

Ingredients	100 servings	.... servings
Onions, dehydrated	4 ounces (½ No. 56 dipper)	
Water (for onions)	1 quart (1 No. 56 dipper)	
Fat	1 pound (½ No. 56 dipper)	
Flour	1¼ pounds (1 No. 56 dipper)	
Milk, evaporated	4—14½-ounce cans	
Water (for milk)	1½ quarts (1½ No. 56 dippers)	
or		
Milk, powdered, whole	12 ounces (¾ No. 56 dipper)	
Water (for milk)	3 quarts (3 No. 56 dippers)	
Salt	3½ ounces (7 mess kit spoons)	
Pepper	½ ounce (2 mess kit spoons)	
Roast beef, canned*	4—6-pound cans	
Crackers or bread crumbs	2¼ pounds (2¼ No. 56 dippers)	
For dipping:		
Egg, powder, whole	12 ounces (1 No. 56 dipper)	
Water (for eggs)	1 quart (1 No. 56 dipper)	
Bread crumbs	3 pounds (3 No. 56 dippers)	

*Roast beef and gravy, canned, may be substituted.

1. Soak onions for 20 minutes.
2. Melt fat. Add onions and fry until brown.
3. Add flour to onions and fat, stirring to make a smooth paste.
4. Combine milk and water or reconstitute milk. Add to the above mixture, stirring constantly.
5. Add salt and pepper. Cook until smooth and thick, stirring frequently. Remove from heat.
6. Grind meat or break up into small pieces and add to the above mixture.
7. Add crumbs to the meat mixture and mix the whole thoroughly. (Chill if refrigeration is available.)
8. Reconstitute egg powder. (See par. 38.) Shape meat into patties and dip in egg mixture and bread crumbs. Fry in fat until brown.

Note. This mixture may also be formed into croquettes and fried in deep fat (375° F.) for about 3 or 5 minutes.

NO. 864. SPAGHETTI AND MEAT SAUCE

Yield: 100 10-ounce servings or approximately ½ mess kit cup each.

Ingredients	100 servings	.... servings
Onions, dehydrated...........	8 ounces (1 No. 56 dipper)..........	....
Water (for onions)...........	2 quarts (2 No. 56 dippers).........	....
Bacon, diced, ½-inch pieces...	2 pounds (1⅓ No. 56 dippers).......	....
Tomatoes, canned...........	2 No. 10 cans....................	....
Flour......................	⅛ No. 56 dipper................	....
Salt......................	2 ounces (4 mess kit spoons)........	....
Pepper....................	½ ounce (2 mess kit spoons)........	....
Roast beef*................	1—6-pound can..................	....
Spaghetti, dry..............	10 pounds.....................	....
Water (for spaghetti)........	40 quarts (40 No. 56 dippers).......	....
Salt......................	5 ounces (10 mess kit spoons).......	....

*Roast beef and gravy, canned, may be substituted.

1. Add water to the dehydrated onions and soak in a covered stockpot for approximately 20 minutes. Drain and save surplus liquid.
2. Fry bacon in roast pan. Add drained onions and fry until light brown.
3. Add tomatoes to fried bacon and onions. Mix flour with enough water to make a smooth paste and add to tomato mixture. Add liquid drained from onions, salt, pepper, and roast beef. Simmer the sauce slowly for approximately 30 minutes, stirring occasionally.
4. Add spaghetti to rapidly boiling salted water in a covered stockpot. Cook spaghetti for approximately 15 minutes or until tender. Drain well.
5. Pour hot sauce over spaghetti and serve.

NO. 865. LUNCHEON MEAT

This product comes packed in 6-pound cans.

It can be sliced cold or heated and served. However, if it is to be included often on a menu it should be combined with other ingredients. This method of preparation will help to vary the serving of the meat which will become monotonous after frequent repetition.

NO. 866. BAKED LUNCHEON MEAT WITH MUSTARD SAUCE

Yield: 100 5-ounce servings or
approximately 1 slice per serving.

Ingredients	100 servings	.... servings
Luncheon meat, canned.......	5—6-pound cans.....................	....
Sugar, granulated...........	1 pound (½ No. 56 dipper).........	....
Mustard, dry..............	1 ounce (4 mess kit spoons).........	....
Cinnamon..................	¼ ounce (1 mess kit spoon).........	....
Vinegar...................	50 gram (½ No. 56 dipper).........	....
Water....................	1 pint (½ No. 56 dipper).........	....

Note. Luncheon meat may be sliced in serving slices. The slices should be cut ¾ of the way but not completely so that the loaf will hold together. Pour the sauce over all and bake for ½ hour in a moderate oven.

NO. 867. BREADED LUNCHEON MEAT

Yield: 100 6-ounce servings or
approximately 1½ slices, ¼-inch
thick each.

Ingredients	100 servings	.... servings
Eggs, powdered..............	1½ pounds (2 No. 56 dippers).......	....
Water (for eggs).............	2 quarts (2 No. 56 dippers).........	....
Luncheon meat..............	5—6-pound cans....................	....
Crumbs, dry (bread or cracker)	4 pounds (2 No. 56 dippers)........	....
Fat (for frying).............	4 pounds (2 No. 56 dippers)........	....

1. Add egg powder to approximately ⅓ of the water, stirring until all the lumps are removed. Add the remaining water, stirring constantly.

2. Cut luncheon meat into ¼-inch slices. Dip slices of meat into egg mixture and then in crumbs. Fry in fat until light brown.

NO. 868. CREAMED LUNCHEON MEAT

Yield: 100 7-ounce servings or
approximately ⅓ mess kit cup each.

Ingredients	100 servings	.... servings
Fat......................	2 pounds (1 No. 56 dipper).........	....
Flour....................	2½ pounds (2 No. 56 dippers).......	....
Milk, evaporated............	11—14½-ounce cans.................	....
Water (for milk)............	5 quarts (5 No. 56 dippers).........	....
or		
Milk, powdered.............	2½ pounds (2½ No. 56 dippers).....	....
Water (for milk)............	9 quarts (9 No. 56 dippers).........	....
Salt.....................	1½ ounces (3 mess kit spoons).......	....
Pepper...................	¼ ounce (1 mess kit spoon).........	....
Luncheon meat, canned.......	2—6-pound cans....................	....
Fat (for frying)............		....
Peas, canned...............	2 No. 10 cans.....................	....

1. Melt the fat in large stockpot. Remove from heat and add the flour. Stir until smooth.
2. Combine milk and water or reconstitute milk. Add to the above mixture and cook until it thickens, stirring constantly. (The liquid from the peas should be used as part of the liquid necessary to reconstitute milk).
3. Add salt and pepper to sauce.
4. Cut luncheon meat into ½-inch cubes. Fry meat in roast pan until light brown. Add to cream sauce.
5. Add drained peas. Mix thoroughly. Serve on crackers or toast.

NO. 869. LUNCHEON MEAT CREAMED WITH CHEESE

Yield: 100 8-ounce servings
or approximately ⅓ mess kit
cup each.

Ingredients	100 servings	.... servings
Luncheon meat, canned.......	3—6-pound cans.....................	....
Macaroni, dry...............	5½ pounds (5 No. 56 dippers).......	....
Water, boiling..............	20 quarts (20 No. 56 dippers)........	....
Salt.......................	3 ounces (6 mess kit spoons).........	....
White sauce, medium.........	6 No. 56 dippers....................	....
Cheese, shredded.............	2 pounds (2 No. 56 dippers)........	....
Salt.......................	2 ounces (4 mess kit spoons)........	....
Pepper.....................	¼ ounce (1 mess kit spoon).........	....

1. Cut luncheon meat into ½-inch cubes.
2. Add macaroni to rapidly boiling salted water. Cook uncovered for approximately 15 minutes or until tender. Drain.
3. Prepare white sauce. (See recipe No. 905.) Add ½ of the cheese and allow cheese to melt in the sauce.
4. Add salt and pepper. Combine luncheon meat, macaroni, and cheese sauce. Place in large bakepan and sprinkle remainder of cheese over the top.
5. Bake in moderate oven for 1 hour.

NO. 870. LUNCHEONBURGER

Yield: 100 5-ounce servings or
approximately 1½ 3-inch patties
per serving.

Ingredients	100 servings	.... servings
Onions, dehydrated..........	4 ounces (½ No. 56 dipper)........	....
Water (for onions)..........	1 quart (1 No. 56 dipper).........	....
Apple nuggets, dehydrated....	12 ounces (1 No. 56 dipper)........	....
Water.....................	2 quarts (2 No. 56 dippers)........	....
Luncheon meat, canned.......	4—6-pound cans....................	....
Milk, powdered..............	1 pound (1 No. 56 dipper).........	....
Eggs, powdered.............	12 ounces (1 No. 56 dipper)........	....
Pepper.....................	¼ ounce (1 mess kit spoon)........	....

1. Soak onions for 20 minutes. Drain.
2. Soak apples for 20 minutes.
3. Break up and mash luncheon meat by hand. Add dry powdered milk, dry powdered eggs, pepper, reconstituted onions and apple nuggets and mix well. Form into patties and fry on a griddle. Serve with tomato sauce.

NO. 871. MACARONI LUNCHEON LOAF

Yield: 100 7-ounce servings
or 1½ slices, ¼-inch thick each.

Ingredients	100 servings	.... servings
Luncheon meat, canned	3—6-pound cans	
Sausage, Vienna	6—30-ounce cans	
Macaroni, dry	3½ pounds (3 No. 56 dippers)	
Water, boiling	12 quarts (12 No. 56 dippers)	
Salt	1 ounce (2 mess kit spoons)	
Milk, powdered	1½ pounds (1½ No. 56 dippers)	
Eggs, powdered	12 ounces (1 No. 56 dipper)	
Bread or cracker crumbs	3 pounds (3 No. 56 dippers)	
Cheese, shredded	1½ pounds (1½ No. 56 dippers)	

1. Break up and mash luncheon meat and Vienna sausage by hand. Combine and mix thoroughly.
2. Add macaroni to rapidly boiling salted water. Cook uncovered for 15 minutes or until tender. Drain and cool.
3. Combine dry powdered milk, dry powdered eggs, cracker crumbs, cheese, and cooked macaroni with mashed meat mixture. Form into loaves or place in layer about 3 inches deep in large bakepans.
4. Bake in moderate oven for 1 hour. Serve with tomato sauce.

NO. 872. RICE MEAT LOAF

Yield: 100 5-ounce servings or approximately 1½ slices, 1 inch thick per serving.

Ingredients	100 servings	.... servings
Rice, dry	2⅔ pounds (1⅛ No. 56 dippers)	
Salt (for rice)	2 ounces (4 mess kit spoons)	
Water (for rice)	10 quarts (10 No. 56 dippers)	
Onions, dehydrated	4 ounces (½ No. 56 dipper)	
Water (for onions)	1 quart (1 No. 56 dipper)	
Luncheon meat, canned	4—6-pound cans	
Milk, powdered	1 pound (1 No. 56 dipper)	
Eggs, powdered	18 ounces (1½ No. 56 dippers)	
Pepper	½ ounce (2 mess kit spoons)	

1. Add rice to rapidly boiling salted water. Boil uncovered for 20 minutes until tender. Drain well.
2. Soak onions in water for 20 minutes.
3. Slip luncheon meat loaf from can and place in large container for mixing. Mash the meat thoroughly.

337

4. Add the cooked and drained rice, the reconstituted onions, dried milk, dried eggs and pepper. Mix thoroughly. (Do not add any water to reconstitute eggs or milk.) Place in 3-inch layer in bottom of greased roasting pan or form into loaves. Meat should be formed well to make good solid loaves.

5. Bake uncovered for 1 hour in moderate oven.

Note. Meat should be removed from the oven at least ½ hour before serving. This allows time for meat to set so that it can be easily sliced. Slice in 1-inch slices and serve with tomato sauce.

NO. 873. SWISS HAM SLICES

Yield: 100 7-ounce servings or 2 slices each.

Ingredients	100 servings	.... servings
Luncheon meat.............	4—6-pound cans.......................	....
Flour......................	2 pounds (1½ No. 56 dippers)........	....
Fat.......................	2 pounds (1 No. 56 dipper).........	....
Onions, dehydrated..........	4 ounces (½ No. 56 dipper)..........	....
Water (for onions)..........	1 quart (1 No. 56 dipper)...........	....
Flour......................	1 pound (¾ No. 56 dipper)..........	....
Water......................	8 quarts (8 No. 56 dippers).........	....
Bouillon cubes*.............	32 cubes...........................	....
Tomatoes, canned............	1 No. 10 can.......................	....
Pepper......................	½ mess kit spoon....................	....

*An equal quantity of meat stock may be substituted for the water and bouillon cubes.

1. Slip luncheon meat loaf from the can and cut in half lengthwise. Then cut in ½-inch slices crosswise. Dip the slices in the flour and fry in fat in large roasting pan until brown. (Remove slices from pan after browning.)

2. Soak onions in water for 20 minutes. Then simmer onions (do not brown) in roasting pan in which meat was fried, adding extra fat if necessary.

3. Add flour and mix well.

4. Combine water and bouillon cubes and add gradually to the flour and onions. Stir until smooth.

5. Add tomatoes and pepper and allow sauce to cook for about 15 minutes or until it begins to thicken. Add browned meat slices.

6. Cover and bake for 30 minutes in a moderate oven.

NO. 874. SCALLOPED SALMON

Yield: 100 6-ounce servings or approximately ¼ mess kit cup each.

Ingredients	100 servings	.... servings
Onions, dehydrated...........	4 ounces (½ No. 56 dipper)..........	....
Water (for onions)..........	1 quart (1 No. 56 dipper)...........	....
Bread, or cracker crumbs.....	6 pounds (6 No. 56 dippers).........	....
Fat, melted.................	2 pounds (1 No. 56 dipper)..........	....
Salt.......................	2 ounces (4 mess kit spoons)........	....
Pepper.....................	¼ mess kit spoon...................	....
Salmon, canned..............	24—1-pound cans....................	....
Milk, evaporated............	8—14½-ounce cans..................	....
or		
Milk, powdered..............	1½ No. 56 dippers.................	....
Water (for milk)............	3½ quarts (3½ No. 56 dippers).....	....

1. Soak onions in water for 20 minutes.
2. Mix bread crumbs, melted fat, salt, and pepper. Spread a layer of bread crumbs over the bottom of a large bakepan.
3. Flake salmon and mix with onions. Cover crumbs with a layer of salmon and salmon liquor. Repeat with a layer of crumbs and salmon.
4. Pour milk over the top and cover all with a layer of crumbs.
5. Bake for approximately 30 minutes in moderate oven.

NO. 875. VEGETABLE LUNCHEON PATTIE

Yield: 100 5-ounce servings or
approximately 1½ 3-inch
patties per serving.

Ingredients	100 servings	.... servings
Cornmeal, yellow*	1⅓ pounds (1 No. 56 dipper)	
Water, boiling	3 quarts (3 No. 56 dippers)	
Salt	½ ounce (1 mess kit spoon)	
Carrots, dehydrated	7 ounces (1 No. 56 dipper)	
Water (for carrots)	1½ quarts (1½ No. 56 dippers)	
Luncheon meat, canned	2—6-pound cans	
Meat and vegetable hash, canned.	2 No. 10 cans	
Eggs, powdered	12 ounces (1 No. 56 dipper)	
Flour	2½ pounds (2 No. 56 dippers)	
Fat (for frying)		

*Any cooked cereal may be substituted.

1. Add cornmeal gradually to rapidly boiling salted water. Cook until thick, stirring occasionally.
2. Soak carrots 20 to 40 minutes. Bring slowly to a boil (45 minutes) and simmer in a covered stockpot 15 to 25 minutes or until carrots are tender. Drain.
3. Break up and mash luncheon meat and combine with meat and vegetable hash, powdered eggs, cornmeal mush, and carrots. Mix thoroughly. Form in patties, roll in flour and fry. Serve with tomato sauce.

NO. 876. PORK AND RICE CASSEROLE (BULK PORK SAUSAGE)

Yield: 100 8-ounce servings or
approximately ⅓ mess kit
cup each.

Ingredients	100 servings	.... servings
Onions, dehydrated	4 ounces (½ No. 56 dipper)	
Water (for onions)	1 quart (1 No. 56 dipper)	
Bacon	1 pound (¾ No. 56 dipper)	
Rice, dry	6 pounds (3 No. 56 dippers)	
Tomatoes, canned	1 No. 10 can	
Bouillon cubes	32 cubes	
Water	8 quarts (8 No. 56 dippers)	
Pepper	¼ ounce (1 mess kit spoon)	
Salt	1 ounce (2 mess kit spoons)	
Pork sausage, bulk, canned	12—34-ounce cans (25—½-pounds)	
Fat	½ pound (¼ No. 56 dipper)	

339

1. Soak onions in water for 20 minutes in large stockpot.

2. Chop bacon very fine. Fry until slightly brown. Add bacon to reconstituted onions.

3. Add dry rice, tomatoes, bouillon cubes, water, salt, and pepper to the onion and bacon mixture. Mix thoroughly and cook until rice is tender, but not mushy. Stir occasionally to prevent burning.

4. Dice pork sausage into 1-inch cubes. Melt fat in large bakepans. Add sausage and heat thoroughly. Stir occasionally but do not overmix. Pour rice mixture over meat and bake in moderate oven for 25 minutes.

NO. 877. PORK MEAT BALLS—RICE CREOLE

Yield: 100 8-ounce servings or approximately ¼ mess kit cup rice and 2 to 3 meat balls each.

Ingredients	100 servings	.... servings
Luncheon meat, canned.......	3—6-pound cans.....................	....
Sausage, Vienna, canned......	4—30-ounce cans....................	....
Milk, powdered..............	1 pound (1 No. 56 dipper)..........	....
Eggs, powdered..............	12 ounces (1 No. 56 dipper)........	....
Onions, dehydrated...........	4 ounces (½ No. 56 dipper)........	....
Water (for onions)..........	1 quart (1 No. 56 dipper)..........	....
Bacon, diced.................	1½ pounds (1 No. 56 dipper).......	....
Tomatoes, canned............	1 No. 10 can......................	....
Water......................	10 quarts (10 No. 56 dippers)......	....
Bouillon cubes..............	40 cubes..........................	....
Salt.......................	2 ounces (4 mess kit spoons).......	....
Pepper.....................	¼ mess kit spoon.................	....
Rice, dry..................	6 pounds (3 No. 56 dippers).......	....

1. Break up luncheon meat and Vienna sausage, mash and combine thoroughly. Grind, if possible.

2. Add powdered milk and eggs to the meat. (Add them in their dry form. Do not add water.) Form into small meat balls, place in baking pans and bake in hot oven until brown, approximately 45 minutes. The meat balls may be floured and fried in fat.

3. Soak onions in water for 20 minutes.

4. Fry bacon in large stockpot until lightly brown. Add onions and brown with bacon.

5. Add tomatoes, water, bouillon cubes, and seasoning to onions. Bring to a boil.

6. Add rice to boiling sauce and cook covered for 20 minutes or until rice is tender and sauce is thick. Serve meat balls on top of rice.

NO. 878. PORK SAUSAGE AND SWEET POTATOES

Yield: 100 8-ounce servings or
approximately ⅓ mess kit
cup each.

Ingredients	100 servings	.... servings
Sweet potatoes, dehydrated, diced.	8 pounds (8 No. 56 dippers)........	....
Water (for potatoes).........	(12 No. 56 dippers)............	....
Salt......................	½ ounce (1 mess kit spoon)........	....
Sugar, granulated...........	3 pounds (1½ No. 56 dippers)......	....
Pork sausage, bulk, canned....	15—34-ounce cans................	....
Milk, powdered.............	1 pound (1 No. 56 dipper)..........	....
Eggs, powdered.............	12 ounces (1 No. 56 dipper)........	....

1. Soak potatoes in water for 20 minutes. Bring slowly to a boil (about 45 minutes) in a covered stockpot. Simmer 20 to 30 minutes or until tender. Drain and save liquid.

2. Add salt. Combine 2 quarts of drained liquid with sugar and simmer for 5 minutes. Add to the sweet potatoes.

3. Break up pork sausage by hand (grind, if possible). Add powdered milk and eggs in dry form to the meat. Do not add water. Form into small meat balls. Place on baking pans and bake in hot oven until brown. Serve meat balls on top of sweet potatoes.

NO. 879. VIENNA SAUSAGE WITH BARBECUE SAUCE

Yield: 100 6-ounce servings or
4 sausages per serving.

Ingredients	100 servings	.... servings
Onions, dehydrated...........	4 ounces (½ No. 56 dipper)........	....
Water (for onions)..........	1 quart (1 No. 56 dipper)..........	....
Fat......................	2 pounds (1 No. 56 dipper)........	....
Vinegar (50 grain)............	1 quart (1 No. 56 dipper)..........	....
Water....................	1 quart (1 No. 56 dipper)..........	....
Mustard, dry...............	(5 mess kit spoons).............	....
Tomatoes, canned...........	2 No. 10 cans.................	....
Pepper...................	(2 mess kit spoons).............	....
Sugar, granulated...........	5 ounces (10 mess kit spoons).......	....
Salt.....................	1 ounce (2 mess kit spoons)........	....
Kitchen sauce..............	(10 mess kit spoons)............	....
Flour....................	1 pound (¾ No. 56 dipper)........	....
Water....................	1 quart (1 No. 56 dipper).........	....
Vienna sausage.............	15—30-ounce cans...............	....

1 Soak onions in water for 20 minutes. Fry onions in fat in large stockpot until tender and slightly brown.

2. Combine vinegar, water, mustard, tomatoes, pepper, salt, sugar, and sauce with onions and heat to the boiling point. Combine water and flour gradually and stir until smooth. Add to tomato mixture.

3. Add Vienna sausage to the sauce. Simmer about 20 minutes or until sauce thickens.

NO. 880. VIENNA SAUSAGE AND BEANS

Yield: 100 9-ounce servings or approximately ½ mess kit cup.

Ingredients	100 servings	.... servings
Beans, white (issue)..........	10 pounds (5¾ No. 56 dippers)......	....
Water.....................	To cover....................	....
Water, boiling..............	8 quarts (8 No. 56 dippers).........	....
Onions, dehydrated..........	4 ounces (½ No. 56 dipper).........	....
Water (for onions)..........	1 quart (1 No. 56 dipper).........	....
Bacon, diced...............	1½ pounds (1 No. 56 dipper).......	....
Tomatoes, canned...........	2 No. 10 cans...................	....
Tomato puree, canned.......	1 No. 10 can..................	....
Sugar.....................	8 ounces (¼ No. 56 dipper)........	....
Mustard, dry..............	¾ ounce (3 mess kit spoons).......	....
Salt......................	6 ounces (12 mess kit spoons)......	....
Pepper....................	¼ ounce (1 mess kit spoon)........	....
Vienna sausage.............	12 pounds (8—30-ounce cans)......	....

1. Pick over and wash beans thoroughly. Soak in cool water about 6 hours. Do not drain. Add boiling water to cover and heat to boiling temperature. Let simmer about 1 hour, until tender but not mushy.
2. Soak onions in water for 20 minutes.
3. Fry bacon and onions in stockpot until lightly browned.
4. Add tomatoes, tomato puree, sugar, mustard, salt, and pepper. Combine tomato mixture with beans. Cook 20 to 30 minutes.
5. Cut Vienna sausage in 1-inch lengths and mix with beans. Simmer sausages and beans together for 20 minutes.

NO. 881. VIENNA SAUSAGE AND SWEET POTATOES

Yield: 100 8-ounce servings or approximately ⅓ mess kit cup each.

Ingredients	100 servings	.... servings
Sweet potatoes, dehydrated, diced.	8 pounds (8 No. 56 dippers)........	....
Water (for potatoes)..........	12 quarts (12 No. 56 dippers).......	....
Sugar, granulated...........	3 pounds (1½ No. 56 dippers)......	....
Vienna sausage.............	20—30-ounce cans................	....
Fat......................	½ pound (¼ No. 56 dipper)........	....

1. Soak potatoes in water for 20 minutes. Bring slowly to a boil (about 45 minutes) in a covered stockpot. Simmer 20 to 30 minutes or until tender. Drain and save surplus liquid.
2. Combine 2 quarts of drained liquid and sugar and simmer for 5 minutes. Add to the sweet potatoes. Place a layer of Vienna sausages in large bakepan, then a layer of sweet potatoes, and finally a layer of Vienna sausages on top.
3. Dot with fat and bake in a moderate oven for 45 minutes.

NO. 882. PIGS IN BLANKETS

Yield: 100 6-ounce servings or approximately 3 sausages per serving.

Ingredients	100 servings	.... servings
Flour, sifted..............	3½ pounds (3½ No. 56 dippers).....	....
Sugar, granulated..........	⅔ pound (⅓ No. 56 dipper)........	....
Salt.....................	1 ounce (2 mess kit spoons)........	....
Eggs, powdered............	4 ounces (⅓ No. 56 dipper)........	....
Shortening................	8 ounces (¼ No. 56 dipper)........	....
Milk, evaporated...........	3½—14½-ounce cans.............	....
Water (for milk)...........	1½ quarts (1½ No. 56 dippers).....	....
or		
Milk, powdered............	(¾ No. 56 dipper)...............	....
Water (for milk)...........	2¾ quarts (2¾ No. 56 dippers).....	....
Sausage, Vienna or pork links*.	15—30-ounce cans................	....
Fat (for frying)............		

*Pork links, canned, may be substituted.

1. Sift flour, sugar, salt, and powdered eggs together. Add shortening and mix well.
2. Combine evaporated milk and water or reconstitute milk and add slowly to the flour mixture. Beat until the batter is smooth.
3. Place fat about 2 inches deep in bakepan. Dip sausages in batter and drop in hot fat. (Have fat at a temperature at which a piece of day old bread will brown in 60 seconds.) Fry 8 to 10 minutes or until a golden brown.

NO. 883. VIENNA SAUSAGE, POTATOES AND TOMATOES

Yield: 100 8-ounce servings or approximately ⅓ mess kit cup each.

Ingredients	100 servings	.... servings
Potatoes, dehydrated, diced...	5½ pounds (8 No. 56 dippers).......	....
Water (for potatoes).........	15 quarts (15 No. 56 dippers).......	....
Onions, dehydrated.........	4 ounces (½ No. 56 dipper)........	....
Water (for onions)..........	1 quart (1 No. 56 dipper)..........	....
Fat......................	½ pound (¼ No. 56 dipper)........	....
Tomatoes, canned..........	1 No. 10 can....................	....
Salt.....................	2½ ounces (5 mess kit spoons)......	....
Pepper...................	⅛ ounce (½ mess kit spoon)........	....
Vienna sausage............	15—30-ounce cans................	....

1. Soak potatoes in water 20 to 40 minutes. Bring slowly to the boiling point (about 45 minutes) in a covered container. Simmer for 10 to 15 minutes or until tender but not mushy. Drain.
2. Soak onions in water 20 to 40 minutes.
3. Place fat in large bakepan. Fry onions in fat but do not brown. Add tomatoes, potatoes, salt, and pepper and bring mixture to a boil.
4. Add Vienna sausage to the potato combination. Bake in moderate oven for 1 hour.

50. SALADS. Salads in the field ration add color as well as vitamins and other nourishment.

NO. 884. JELLIED BEET SALAD Yield: 100 servings, 2½ by 2 by 1½-inch squares each.

Ingredients	100 servings	.... servings
Beets, dehydrated, cubed.....	1½ pounds (2 No. 56 dippers).......	....
Water (for beets)............	7 quarts (7 No. 56 dippers).........	....
Onions, dehydrated..........	4 ounces (½ No. 56 dipper).........	....
Water (for onions)...........	1 quart (1 No. 56 dipper)...........	....
Gelatin, lemon flavor.........	3¼ pounds (2½ No. 56 dippers).....	....
Water, boiling..............	4 quarts (4 No. 56 dippers).........	....
Salt......................	½ ounce (1 mess kit spoon).........	....
Beet juice.................	4 quarts (4 No. 56 dippers).........	....
Vinegar, 50 grain............	½ pint (¼ No. 56 dipper)..........	....

1. Soak beets in water 20 to 40 minutes. Bring slowly to a boil (about 45 minutes) in a covered stockpot. Simmer 15 to 25 minutes or until tender. Drain (save beet juice) and cool.
2. Soak onions for 20 minutes. Drain.
3. Dissolve gelatin in boiling water.
4. Add salt, vinegar, and beet juice. (If there is not sufficient beet juice add water to make 4 quarts.) Cool until slightly thickened.
5. Add beets and onions, mix well and pour into shallow pans. Chill until firm. Cut into squares.

NO. 885. PICKLED BEET SALAD Yield: 100 4-ounce servings or approximately 1½ serving spoons each.

Ingredients	100 servings	.... servings
Beets, dehydrated, diced......	3¼ pounds (4 No. 56 dippers).......	....
Water (for beets)............	14 quarts (14 No. 56 dippers).......	....
Onions, dehydrated..........	8 ounces (½ No. 56 dipper).........	....
Water (for onions)...........	1 quart (1 No. 56 dipper)...........	....
Vinegar, 50 grain............	2½ quarts (2½ No. 56 dippers)......	....
Sugar, granulated...........	8 ounces (¼ No. 56 dipper).........	....
Salt......................	1½ ounces (3 mess kit spoons)......	....
Pepper....................	¼ ounce (1 mess kit spoon)........	....
Cinnamon..................	(½ mess kit spoon)...............	....
Cloves....................	(½ mess kit spoon)...............	....

1. Soak beets 20 to 40 minutes. Bring slowly to boiling point (about 45 minutes) in a covered stockpot. Simmer for 20 to 30 minutes or until tender. Drain and cool.
2. Soak onions for 20 minutes. Drain.
3. Combine beets, onions, vinegar, sugar, and seasonings. Cool thoroughly before serving.

NO. 886. CABBAGE, APPLE, AND PINEAPPLE SALAD

Yield: 100 servings, 1 square, 2½ by 2 by 1½ inches each.

Ingredients	100 servings	.... servings
Cabbage, dehydrated.........	10 ounces (2 No. 56 dippers).........	....
Water (for cabbage)..........	4 quarts (4 No. 56 dippers)..........	....
Gelatin, lemon flavored.......	3¼ pounds (2½ No. 56 dippers).....	....
Water, boiling...............	4 quarts (4 No. 56 dippers).........	....
Pineapple, canned...........	1 No. 10 can.....................	....
Lemon juice powder, synthetic.	(1 mess kit spoon).................	....
Water, cold, and pineapple juice.	4 quarts (4 No. 56 dippers).........	....
Salt.......................	½ ounce (1 mess kit spoon).........	....
Apple nuggets, dehydrated....	12 ounces (1 No. 56 dipper).........	....

1. Soak cabbage in cold water for 40 minutes. Drain.
2. Dissolve gelatin powder in boiling water.
3. Drain pineapple and save juice. Cut pineapple into 1-inch pieces.
4. Add cold water to pineapple juice to make 4 quarts. Dissolve lemon powder in this cold water and add with salt to the gelatin mixture. Chill until slightly thickened.
5. Add drained cabbage, cut pineapple and add with dry apple nuggets to the gelatin mixture. Pour into shallow pans. Chill until firm. Cut into squares.

NO. 887. CABBAGE-CARROT SALAD

Yield: 100 servings, 1 square, 2½x2x1½ inches each.

Ingredients	100 servings	.... servings
Carrots, dehydrated.........	14 ounces (1 No. 56 dipper).........	....
Water (for carrots)..........	3½ quarts (3½ No. 56 dippers)......	....
Cabbage, dehydrated........	5 ounces (1 No. 56 dipper).........	....
Water (for cabbage).........	2 quarts (2 No. 56 dippers).........	....
Gelatin, lemon flavored......	3¼ pounds (2½ No. 56 dippers).....	....
Water, boiling..............	4 quarts (4 No. 56 dippers).........	....
Salt.......................	½ ounce (1 mess kit spoon).........	....
Lemon juice powder, synthetic.	(1 mess kit spoon).................	....
Water, cold................	4 quarts (4 No. 56 dippers).........	....

1. Soak carrots in water for 20 to 40 minutes. Bring slowly to a boil (about 45 minutes) in a covered container. Simmer for 15 to 25 minutes, or until tender. Remove from heat, drain and cool.
2. Soak cabbage in cold water for 40 minutes. Drain.
3. Dissolve gelatin powder in boiling water.
4. Dissolve lemon powder, synthetic, in the cold water. Add cold water and the salt to the gelatin. Chill until slightly thickened.
5. Add drained carrots and cabbage and mix well. Pour into shallow pans. Chill until firm. Cut into squares.

NO. 888. CABBAGE SLAW

Yield: 100 5-ounce servings or 2 serving spoons each.

Ingredients	100 servings	.... servings
Cabbage, dehydrated.........	3 pounds (9½ No. 56 dippers)......	....
Water, cold (for cabbage).....	15 quarts (15 No. 56 dippers)........	....
Onions, dehydrated...........	8 ounces (1 No. 56 dipper)...........	....
Water (for onions)...........	2 quarts (2 No. 56 dippers)...........	....
Vinegar, 50 grains............	1 pint (½ No. 56 dipper).............	....
Salt........................	4 ounces (8 mess kit spoons).........	....
Pepper.....................	½ ounce (2 mess kit spoons).........	....
Sugar, granulated............	12 ounces (⅓ No. 56 dipper)........	....
Salad dressing or mayonnaise..	(2 No. 56 dippers)...................	....

1. Pour cold water over the cabbage and allow to soak for 3½ to 4 hours. For best results place soaking cabbage in a refrigerator; long soaking at high temperature is to be avoided. If ice is available, add a small piece to the cabbage while it is soaking.

2. Soak onions in water for 20 minutes. Drain and add vinegar, salt, pepper, and sugar to the onions and let stand until the cabbage is ready.

3. Drain all surplus water from the cabbage and combine with onions and vinegar mixture.

4. Add mayonnaise, or salad dressing and serve.

NO. 889. CRANBERRY SALAD

Yield: 100 servings, 2½ x 2 x 1½-inch squares each.

Ingredients	100 servings	.... servings
Gelatin, plain...............	4 ounces (¼ No. 56 dipper)........	....
Water, cold.................	1 pint (½ No. 56 dipper)...........	....
Cranberries, dehydrated*, sliced,	1 pound (¾ No. 56 dipper)........	....
or		
Cranberries, dehydrated, whole.	1 pound (3 No. 56 dippers)..........	....
Sugar, granulated............	8 pounds (4 No. 56 dippers)........	....
Water (for cranberries).......	8 quarts (8 No. 56 dippers).........	....
Apple nuggets, dehydrated....	8 ounces (⅔ No. 56 dipper)........	....
Water (for apple nuggets).....	1¼ quarts (1¼ No. 56 dippers)......	....

*If compressed cranberry slices are used, do not use volume measurements. Note weight given on box.

1. Soak gelatin in cold water.

2. Add cranberries to water. Bring to a boil over a slow fire and simmer 15 minutes. Add sugar and continue boiling for 5 to 10 minutes. Pour over soaked gelatin. Cool.

3. Soak apples in water 20 to 40 minutes. Add apples and juice to cooled gelatin mixture. Mold and serve.

NO. 890. POTATO SALAD

Yield: 100 5-ounce servings or approximately 2 serving spoons each.

Ingredients	100 servings	.... servings
Potatoes, dehydrated, julienne or diced.	4¾ pounds (7 No. 56 dippers).......	....
Water (for potatoes).........	14 quarts (14 No. 56 dippers).......	....
Onions, dehydrated..........	6 ounces (¾ No. 56 dipper).........	....
Water (for onions)..........	1½ quarts (1½ No. 56 dippers)......	....
Vinegar, 50 grain............ or	¾ quart (¾ No. 56 dipper).........	....
Mayonnaise or salad dressing..	(½ No. 56 dipper)...............	....
Salt......................	3 ounces (6 mess kit spoons)........	....
Pepper....................	½ ounce (2 mess kit spoons)........	....
Eggs, hard-cooked, chopped...	20 eggs....................	....

1. Soak potatoes in water for 20 to 40 minutes. Bring slowly to the boiling point (about 45 minutes) in a covered stockpot. Simmer for 10 to 15 minutes or until potatoes are tender but not mushy. Drain and spread out on trays to cool.

2. Soak onions in water 20 minutes. Drain.

3. Add onions, vinegar or mayonnaise, salt, pepper, and eggs (if available) to cooled potatoes and mix well.

NO. 891. SALMON SALAD

Yield: 100 5-ounce servings or approximately 2 serving spoons each.

Ingredients	100 servings	.... servings
Onions, dehydrated..........	¾ pound (1½ No. 56 dippers).......	....
Water (for onions)..........	2½ quarts (2½ No. 56 dippers)......	....
Salmon....................	17—1-pound cans...............	....
Salt......................	½ ounce (1 mess kit spoon).........	....
Peas, canned..............	2 No. 10 cans.................	....
Lemon juice powder, synthetic.	(2 mess kit spoons)...............	....
Water....................	½ pint (¼ No. 56 dipper)...........	....
Salad dressing or mayonnaise..	(2 No. 56 dippers)...............	....

1. Soak onions in water for 20 minutes. Drain.

2. Flake salmon into a large mixing container.

3. Add salt, drained peas, and onions.

4. Dissolve lemon juice powder, synthetic, in the water and add to the salmon.

5. Add dressing and mix until well blended.

51. SAUCES, DRESSING, AND GRAVIES. Sauces, dressing and gravies are a welcome addition to the dish. They can add food value as well as eye appeal.

NO. 892. APPLESAUCE

Yield: 100 4-ounce servings or approximately 1½ serving spoons per serving.

Ingredients	100 servings	.... servings
Apple nuggets, dehydrated....	4 pounds (5¼ No. 56 dippers).......	....
Water.....................	12 quarts (12 No. 56 dippers)........	....
Sugar, granulated............	3 pounds (1½ No. 56 dippers).......	....
Cinnamon...................	(2 mess kit spoons)..................	....
or		
Nutmeg....................	(2 mess kit spoons)..................	....
Lemon powder, synthetic.....	(1 mess kit spoon)...................	....

1. Add apple nuggets to water and bring slowly to a boil in a covered stockpot. Simmer for 10 minutes.
2. Add sugar and simmer for an additional 10 minutes or until apples are tender.
3. Add spices and lemon powder and cool.

NO. 893. APPLE CRANBERRY SAUCE

Yield: 100 3-ounce servings or 1½ serving spoons each.

Ingredients	100 servings	.... servings
Apple nuggets, dehydrated....	2¼ pounds (3 No. 56 dippers).......	....
Water (for apples)...........	6½ quarts (6½ No. 56 dippers)......	....
Cranberries, dehydrated, whole,	½ pound (1½ No. 56 dippers).......	....
or		
Cranberries, dehydrated, sliced*.	½ pound (⅓ No. 56 dipper)........	....
Water.....................	2½ quarts (2½ No. 56 dippers)......	....
Sugar, granulated............	5 pounds (2½ No. 56 dippers).......	....

*If compressed cranberry slices are used, do not use volume measurements. Note weight given on box.

1. Soak apples in water 20 to 40 minutes.
2. Add cranberries and water to apple nuggets.
3. Bring to a boil over a slow fire and simmer 15 minutes. Add sugar and continue boiling for 5 minutes. Cool and serve.

NO. 894. CRANBERRY SAUCE

Yield: 100 2-ounce servings or 1 serving spoon each.

Ingredients	100 servings	.... servings
Cranberries, dehydrated, whole*,	1 pound (3 No. 56 dippers)..........	....
or		
Cranberries, dehydrated, sliced.	1 pound (¾ No. 56 dipper)........	....
Water.....................	5 quarts (5 No. 56 dippers).........	....
Sugar, granulated............	7 pounds (3½ No. 56 dippers).......	....

*If compressed cranberry slices are used, do not use volume measurements. Note weight given on box.

1. Add water to cranberries. Bring to a boil over a slow fire and simmer 15 minutes.
2. Add sugar and continue boiling for 5 minutes. Pour into shallow pans and chill.

NO. 895. SPANISH SAUCE

Yield: 100 2½-ounce servings or approximately 1 serving spoon each.

Ingredients	100 servings	.... servings
Onions, dehydrated	13 ounces (1⅔ No. 56 dippers)	
Water (for onions)	3½ quarts (3½ No. 56 dippers)	
Fat	2 pounds (1 No. 56 dipper)	
Tomatoes, canned	2 No. 10 cans (6½ No. 56 dippers)	
Salt	To taste	
Pepper	To taste	
Paprika	To taste	

1. Soak onions in water for 20 minutes.
2. Fry reconstituted onions in fat in a large stockpot until browned.
3. Add tomatoes and seasoning and simmer for 30 minutes.

NO. 896. TOMATO SAUCE NO. 1

Yield: 100 2-ounce servings or approximately 1 serving spoon each.

Ingredients	100 servings	.... servings
Onions, dehydrated	4 ounces (½ No. 56 dipper)	
Water	1 quart (1 No. 56 dipper)	
Fat	½ pound (¼ No. 56 dipper)	
Flour	10 ounces (½ No. 56 dipper)	
Tomatoes, canned	2 No. 10 cans	
Sugar, granulated	3 ounces (6 mess kit spoons)	

1. Soak onions in water in a stockpot for 20 minutes.
2. Add fat and simmer onions for 10 minutes (do not brown).
3. Add flour and mix thoroughly.
4. Combine sugar, tomatoes, flour and onion mixture. Bring to a boil slowly and simmer for 30 minutes. Serve hot.

NO. 897. TOMATO SAUCE NO. 2

Yield: 100 servings, 3 ounces or approximately 1 serving spoon each.

Ingredients	100 servings	.... servings
Onions, dehydrated	2 ounces (¼ No. 56 dipper)	
Water (for onions)	1 pint (½ No. 56 dipper)	
Fat	1 pound (½ No. 56 dipper)	
Flour	20 ounces (1 No. 56 dipper)	
Tomatoes	1½ No. 10 cans	
Bouillon cubes	16 cubes	
Water, boiling	4 quarts (4 No. 56 dippers)	
Sugar	4 ounces (8 mess kit spoons)	
Pepper	¼ ounce (1 mess kit spoon)	
Salt	1½ ounces (3 mess kit spoons)	

1. Soak onions 20 minutes. Add fat to onions. Simmer until onions are slightly brown.

2. Add flour and tomatoes to fried onions.

3. Add bouillon cubes, boiling water, sugar, salt, and pepper, to mixture and continue to simmer for 1 hour. Serve hot.

NO. 898. BOILED SALAD DRESSING   Yield: Approximately 1 gallon.

Ingredients	100 servings	.... servings
Sugar, granulated...........	1½ pounds (¾ No. 56 dipper).......	....
Salt.......................	1½ ounces (3 mess kit spoons).......	....
Mustard, dry...............	½ ounce (2 mess kit spoons).........	....
Eggs, powdered.............	9 ounces (¾ No. 56 dipper).........	....
Flour.....................	5 ounces (¼ No. 56 dipper).........	....
Milk, evaporated............	14½-ounce can (3½ No. 56 dippers)..	....
Water (for milk)............	1¾ quarts (1¾ No. 56 dippers)......	....
or		
Milk, powdered, whole.......	12 ounces (¾ No. 56 dipper).........	....
Water (for milk).............	3 quarts (3 No. 56 dippers).........	....
Vinegar, 50 grain............	1 quart (1 No. 56 dipper)...........	....
Fat.......................	8 ounces (¼ No. 56 dipper).........	....

1. Mix sugar, salt, mustard, eggs, and flour together.

2. Combine water and milk or reconstitute milk. Combine slowly with dry ingredients. Mix until smooth.

3. Add vinegar very slowly, cook until thick, stirring constantly. Remove from heat.

4. Add fat, mix thoroughly. Cool.

NO. 899. COLE SLAW DRESSING

Prepare recipe for boiled salad dressing, cool and add ½ No. 56 dipper prepared mustard.

NO. 900. PEANUT BUTTER DRESSING

Prepare recipe for boiled salad dressing, cool and add ½ No. 56 dipper peanut butter.

NO. 901. SAVORY DRESSING

Prepare recipe for boiled salad dressing, cool and add one No. 56 dipper pickle relish or chopped sweet pickles.

NO. 902. HAWAIIAN DRESSING

Prepare recipe for boiled salad dressing, cool and add 1½ No. 56 dippers pineapple juice.

NO. 903. MAYONNAISE

Yield: 5 quarts.

Ingredients	100 servings	.... servings
Eggs, powdered	3 ounces (¼ No. 56 dipper)	
Water (for eggs)	½ pint (¼ No. 56 dipper)	
Mustard, dry	¾ ounce (3 mess kit spoons)	
Salt	1 ounce (2 mess kit spoons)	
Sugar, granulated	6 ounces (⅕ No. 56 dipper)	
Milk, evaporated	1—14½-ounce can	
or		
Milk, powdered	4 ounces (¼ No. 56 dipper)	
Water (for milk)	1 pint (½ No. 56 dipper)	
Oil, salad	(4 No. 56 dippers)	
Vinegar, 50 grain	10 ounces (⅓ No. 56 dipper)	
Lemon juice powder, synthetic	(2 mess kit spoons)	

1. Add egg powder to ⅓ of the water and stir to make a smooth paste. Add remainder of the water and mix thoroughly.
2. Add mustard, salt, and sugar and mix well.
3. Add milk and blend well with egg mixture.
4. Add ½ of the oil very slowly, stirring constantly with a wire whip. Add half the vinegar slowly, continue stirring. Add last half of the oil slowly.
5. Dissolve lemon juice powder in remaining vinegar and add to the mixture. Continue beating 5 to 6 minutes after everything has been added.

Note. If it separates, make a small batch of new mayonnaise and slowly beat the separated batch into it.

NO. 904. TARTAR SAUCE

Prepare the recipe for mayonnaise. Soak ¼ No. 56 dipper of onions in ½ No. 56 dipper of water for 20 minutes. Add reconstituted onions and ½ No. 56 dipper of pickle relish. Serve cold.

NO. 905. WHITE SAUCE

Yield: 1 gallon.

Ingredients	*Thin* For cream soups	*Medium* For scalloped dishes and creamed vegetables	*Thick* For croquettes, etc.
Fat	8 ounces (¼ No. 56 dipper).	1 pound (½ No. 56 dipper).	2 pounds (1 No. 56 dipper).
Flour	4 ounces (⅙ No. 56 dipper).	10 ounces (½ No. 56 dipper).	1 pound (¾ No. 56 dipper).
Salt	½ ounce (1 mess kit spoon).	½ ounce (1 mess kit spoon).	½ ounce (1 mess kit spoon).
Pepper	(⅓ mess kit spoon)	(⅓ mess kit spoon)	(⅓ mess kit spoon)
Milk, evaporated	4—14½-ounce cans	4—14½-ounce cans	4—14½-ounce cans
Water	(2 No. 56 dippers)	(2 No. 56 dippers)	(2 No. 56 dippers)
or			
Milk, powdered	1 pound (1 No. 56 dipper).	1 pound (1 No. 56 dipper).	1 pound (1 No. 56 dipper).
Water	(3½ No. 56 dippers).	(3½ No. 56 dippers).	(3½ No. 56 dippers)

1. Melt the fat.
2. Add the flour, stirring until a smooth paste is formed.
3. Add water to the evaporated milk or reconstitute the powdered milk by floating the milk on the water and beating with a wire whip. Add seasonings. Gradually add the milk to the fat and flour paste, stirring constantly. Cook until smooth and thick.

NO. 906. WHITE SAUCE USING PRESERVED BUTTER

Yield: 1 gallon.

Ingredients	*Thin* For cream soups	*Medium* For scalloped dishes and creamed vegetables	*Thick* For croquettes, etc.
Milk, evaporated	4—14½-ounce cans	4—14½-ounce cans	4—14½-ounce cans
Water	(2 No. 56 dippers)	(2 No. 56 dippers)	(2 No. 56 dippers)
or			
Milk, powdered	1 pound (1 No. 56 dipper).	1 pound (1 No. 56 dipper).	1 pound (1 No. 56 dipper).
Water	(3½ No. 56 dippers).	(3½ No. 56 dippers).	(3½ No. 56 dippers)
Flour	4 ounces (⅕ No. 56 dipper).	10 ounces (½ No. 56 dipper).	1 pound (¾ No. 56 dipper).
Preserved butter	8 ounces (¼ No. 56 dipper).	1 pound (½ No. 56 dipper).	2 pounds (1 No. 56 dipper).
Salt	½ ounce (1 mess kit spoon).	½ ounce (1 mess kit spoon).	½ ounce (1 mess kit spoon).
Pepper	(¼ mess kit spoon)	(¼ mess kit spoon)	(¼ mess kit spoon)

1. Add a small quantity of milk gradually to the flour, making a smooth paste.
2. Add the remainder of the milk, preserved butter, and seasoning.
3. Cook until smooth and thick.

NO. 907. BOUILLON GRAVY

Yield: 2 gallons.

Ingredients	100 servings	.... servings
Fat	1½ pounds (¾ No. 56 dipper)	....
Flour	1½ pounds (1⅕ No. 56 dippers)	....
Bouillon cubes	40 cubes	....
Water	8 quarts (8 No. 56 dippers)	....
Salt	½ ounce (1 mess kit spoon)	....
Pepper	(½ mess kit spoon)	....

1. Melt fat in a large stockpot. Add flour gradually, stirring until all lumps are removed.
2. Add water and bouillon cubes and stir until bouillon cubes are dissolved.
3. Add salt and pepper. Heat to boiling point and boil 2 minutes or until thick, stirring constantly.
4. Add gravy coloring if a darker color is desired.

NO. 908. CHOCOLATE SIRUP NO. 1   Yield: 3½ quarts.

Ingredients	100 servings	.... servings
Cocoa beverage powder (from combat ration).	9—10-ounce packages (5½ pounds)...	....
Water.....................	1½ quarts (1½ No. 56 dippers)......	....

Add water gradually to cocoa beverage powder, beating until all lumps are removed. Cook for 1 hour until thick. Serve either hot or cold. (A double boiler should be used to prevent scorching.)

NO. 909. CHOCOLATE SIRUP NO. 2   Yield: 3½ quarts.

Ingredients	100 servings	.... servings
Cocoa beverage powder (from combat ration).	9—10-ounce packages (5½ pounds)...	....
Sugar, granulated............	3 pounds (1½ No. 56 dippers).......	....
Water.....................	2¾ quarts (2¾ No. 56 dippers)......	....
Shortening.................	6 ounces (12½ mess kit spoons)......	....

1. Mix sugar with cocoa beverage powder.
2. Add water gradually, beating to remove all lumps. Add shortening. Bring mixture to a boil and cook, stirring constantly for 10 to 15 minutes or until desired thickness. Serve either hot or cold.

NO. 910. LEMON SAUCE   Yield: 100 2-ounce servings or 1 serving spoon each.

Ingredients	100 servings	.... servings
Sugar, granulated............	3 pounds (1½ No. 56 dippers)......	....
Cornstarch................	10 ounces (½ No. 56 dipper)........	....
Eggs, powdered, whole........	24 ounces (6 mess kit spoons).......	....
Water.....................	5 quarts (5 No. 56 dippers)........	....
Lemon juice powder, synthetic.	5 ounces (¼ No. 56 dipper)........	....
Water.....................	1 pint (½ No. 56 dipper)...........	....
Salt......................	(⅔ mess kit spoon)................	....

1. Combine sugar, cornstarch, and powdered eggs. Add 1 quart of water. Stir until smooth. Heat the remaining water to the boiling point and gradually add the cornstarch mixture. Boil for 10 minutes or until the mixture thickens. Stir constantly. Remove from heat.
2. Dissolve lemon juice powder, synthetic, in the water and add with the salt to the cornstarch mixture. Mix well, serve hot.

NO. 911. MAPLE SIRUP   Yield: 1 gallon.

Ingredients	100 servings	.... servings
Water.....................	2 quarts (2 No. 56 dippers)........	....
Sugar, granulated............	8 pounds (4 No. 56 dippers)........	....
Maple tablets..............	8 tablets.........................	....

1. Bring water to a boil. Add sugar and stir until dissolved. Heat to the boiling point, boil 10 minutes or until a thin sirup is formed.
2. Crush tablets and dissolve in a small quantity of warm water. Add to sirup and cool. (Do not cook sirup after adding tablets as boiling of tablets and sirup will cause the sirup to have a greenish off-color.)

52. SOUPS. Soups are a good start for the meal. For the light meal a heavy soup adds the extra food needed while for a heavy meal a light soup is right to start the dinner.

NO. 912. BORSCHT

Yield: 100 servings, approximately ⅓ mess kit cup each 6¼ gallons.

Ingredients	100 servings	.... servings
Beets, dehydrated, diced......	13 ounces (1 No. 56 dipper).........	....
Carrots, dehydrated..........	14 ounces (1 No. 56 dipper).........	....
Onions, dehydrated..........	8 ounces (1 No. 56 dipper).........	....
Water.....................	28 quarts (28 No. 56 dippers)........	....
Fat........................	½ pound (¼ No. 56 dipper).........	....
Bouillon cubes..............	32 cubes.......................	....
Tomatoes, canned...........	2 No. 10 cans....................	....
Cabbage, dehydrated........	5 ounces (1 No. 56 dipper)...........	....
Salt.......................	3 ounces (6 mess kit spoons)........	....
Pepper....................	½ ounce (2 mess kit spoons)........	....

1. Combine the beets, carrots, and onions and add to the water. Bring slowly to a boil and simmer until vegetables are tender.
2. Add bouillon cubes and fat.
3. Add tomatoes, cabbage, salt, and pepper. Simmer for 30 minutes.

NO. 913. CREAM OF CARROT SOUP

Yield: 6¼ gallons, 100 servings of approximately ⅓ mess kit cup each.

Ingredients	100 servings	.... servings
Onions, dehydrated..........	4 ounces (½ No. 56 dipper).........	....
Carrots, dehydrated.........	1¾ pound (2 No. 56 dippers).......	....
Water.....................	8 quarts (8 No. 56 dippers).........	....
Milk, evaporated............	19—14½-ounce cans................	....
Water.....................	8 quarts (8 No. 56 dippers).........	....
or		
Milk, powdered..............	4 pounds (4 No. 56 dippers).........	....
Water.....................	14 quarts (14 No. 56 dippers)........	....
Preserved butter............	1 pound (½ No. 56 dipper).........	....
Salt.......................	4 ounces (8 mess kit spoons)........	....
Pepper....................	(½ mess kit spoon)...............	....
Flour.....................	20 ounces (1 No. 56 dipper).........	....
Water.....................	1 quart (1 No. 56 dipper)...........	....

1. Soak onions and carrots for 20 minutes in a large stockpot. Bring slowly to a boil. This should require about 30 minutes. Simmer for 15 to 20 minutes more or until tender.

2. Add evaporated milk and water or reconstituted powdered milk.
3. Add preserved butter, salt, and pepper. Mix well. Cover and heat to boiling.
4. Mix water and flour together to make a smooth paste. Add to the hot soup mixture and stir until smooth. Simmer for about 20 minutes or until slightly thick, stirring constantly.

NO. 914. CORN CHOWDER

Yield: 6¼ gallons, 100 servings of ⅓ mess kit cup each.

Ingredients	100 servings	.... servings
Onions, dehydrated...........	4 ounces (½ No. 56 dipper).........	....
Potatoes, dehydrated, julienne or dried.	3½ pounds (5 No. 56 dippers).......	....
Water.....................	11 quarts (11 No. 56 dippers)........	....
Corn, cream style............	3 No. 10 cans.....................	....
Milk, evaporated*............	14—14½-ounce cans.................	....
or		
Milk, powdered..............	3 pounds (3 No. 56 dippers).........	....
Water (for milk).............	5 quarts (5 No. 56 dippers).........	....
Water.....................	7 quarts (7 No. 56 dippers).........	....
Salt......................	4 ounces (8 mess kit spoons)........	....
Pepper....................	¼ ounce (1 mess kit spoon).........	....

*Do not dilute with water.

1. Soak onions, and potatoes in water for 20 to 40 minutes. Bring slowly to a boil (about 45 minutes) in a covered stockpot.
2. Add corn, milk, water, salt, and pepper to potatoes and onions. Cover and heat to a boiling point. Simmer about 40 minutes.

NO. 915. FRENCH ONION SOUP

Yield: 6¼ gallons, 100 servings of approximately ⅓ mess kit cup each.

Ingredients	100 servings	.... servings
Onions, dehydrated...........	2¼ pounds (4½ No. 56 dippers).....	....
Water.....................	9 quarts (9 No. 56 dippers).........	....
Fat.......................	2½ pounds (1¼ No. 56 dippers).....	....
Bouillon cubes*..............	85 cubes.........................	....
Water.....................	24 quarts (24 No. 56 dippers)........	....
Salt......................	3½ ounces (7 mess kit spoons).......	....
Flour.....................	26 ounces (2 No. 56 dippers)........	....
Water.....................	2 quarts (2 No. 56 dippers).........	....

*An equal quantity of meat stock may be substituted for the water and bouillon tubes.

1. Soak onions in water for 20 minutes. Drain, saving onion water. Heat fat to frying temperature in large pan. Fry onions until they are a golden brown.
2. Add bouillon cubes, water, and surplus onion water to fried onions.
3. Add salt.
4. Add flour to the water gradually making a smooth paste and stir into the soup. Simmer covered for 30 minutes.

VARIATION.

Cut left-over bread slices into ½-inch cubes. Toast and serve several on top of each bowl of soup.

NO. 916. GREEN OR YELLOW PEA OR NAVY BEAN

Yield: 6½ gallons, 100 servings of approximately ⅓ mess kit cup per serving.

Ingredients	100 servings	.... servings
Water.....................	24 quarts (24 No. 56 dippers).......	....
Soup powder, dehydrated.....	6 pounds (4¾ No. 56 dippers)......	....

Add soup powder to cold water. Gradually bring to a boiling point, stirring constantly. Cook soup for 3 minutes and serve hot.

VARIATIONS.
NO. 917.

Add 24 bouillon cubes to the soup before it comes to the boiling point. Cook soup 3 minutes and serve.

NO. 918.

Fry 2 pounds of dried bacon and add the bacon and bacon fat to the soup before it comes to the boiling point. Cook 3 minutes and serve.

NO. 919.

Brown 2 pounds of diced Vienna sausage or link pork sausages and add to the soup before it comes to the boiling point. Cook 3 minutes and serve.

NO. 920. CREAM OF POTATO SOUP

Yield: 6 gallons, 100 servings, approximately ⅓ mess kit cup per serving.

Ingredients	100 servings	.... servings
Water.....................	25 quarts (25 No. 56 dippers).......	....
Salt......................	4½ ounces (9 mess kit spoons).......	....
Pepper....................	¼ ounce (1 mess kit spoon).........	....
Onions, dehydrated..........	3 ounces (⅛ No. 56 dipper).........	....
Potatoes, shreds, dehydrated*.	4¾ pounds (7½ No. 56 dippers).....	....
Milk, evaporated............	10—14½-ounce cans...............	....
or		
Milk, powdered.............	2 pounds (2 No. 56 dippers)........	....
Water.....................	3½ quarts (3½ No. 56 dippers).....	....
Preserved butter............	2 pounds (1 No. 56 dipper).........	....

*Six and one-half No. 56 dippers of diced dehydrated potatoes may be substituted for the potato shreds. An additional 3 quarts of water must be added.

1. Put water, salt, pepper, onions, and potatoes in a large stockpot. Bring slowly to a boil and simmer for 30 minutes.
2. Add evaporated milk or reconstituted powdered milk and preserved butter. Simmer for 20 minutes. Serve hot.

NO. 921. VEGETABLE SOUP NO. 1   Yield: 6¼ gallons, 100 servings, approximately ⅓ mess kit cup each.

Ingredients	100 servings	.... servings
Water	24 quarts (24 No. 56 dippers)	
Carrots, dehydrated	10 ounces (¾ No. 56 dipper)	
Potatoes, dehydrated (julienne or diced).	1 pound (1½ No. 56 dippers)	
Onions, dehydrated	4 ounces (½ No. 56 dipper)	
Salt	5 ounces (10 mess kit spoons)	
Rice, dry	1 pound (½ No. 56 dipper)	
Tomatoes, canned	2 No. 10 cans	
Pepper	(½ mess kit spoon)	
Bouillon cubes	72 cubes	

1. Add dehydrated vegetables to water and soak 20 to 40 minutes. Bring gradually to the boiling point in a covered stockpot.
2. Add salt, rice, tomatoes, pepper, and bouillon cubes and continue to simmer for 1 hour or until all vegetables are tender.

NO. 922. VEGETABLE SOUP NO. 2   Yield: 6¼ gallons, 100 servings of approximately ⅓ mess kit cup each.

Ingredients	100 servings	.... servings
Water	24 quarts (24 No. 56 dippers)	
Meat and vegetable stew	15—30-ounce cans or 37—12-ounce cans.	
Tomato juice, canned	1 No. 10 can	
Salt	4 ounces (8 mess kit spoons)	
Pepper	¼ ounce (1 mess kit spoon)	

Use large stockpot (10 gallons). Add water, meat, and vegetable stew, tomato juice and seasonings. Bring to the boiling point and simmer for 20 minutes.

53. VEGETABLES. Vegetables prepared from the dehydrated ration can be edible as well as nourishing. Recipes follow.

NO. 923. BUTTERED BEETS   Yield: 100 4-ounce servings or approximately 1½ serving spoons each.

Ingredients	100 servings	.... servings
Beets, dehydrated	3¼ pounds (4 No. 56 dippers)	
Water (for beets)	14 quarts (14 No. 56 dippers)	
Preserved butter	1 pound (½ No. 56 dipper)	
Salt	2 ounces (4 mess kit spoons)	
Pepper	½ ounce (2 mess kit spoons)	

1. Soak beets 20 to 40 minutes. Bring slowly to a boil (about 45 minutes). Simmer for 20 to 30 minutes in a covered stockpot or until tender. Drain.
2. Melt preserved butter. Add seasoning. Pour over drained beets. Serve hot.

NO. 924. HARVARD BEETS

Yield: 100 4-ounce servings or approximately 1½ serving spoons each.

Ingredients	100 servings	.... servings
Beets, dehydrated............	3¼ pounds (4 No. 56 dippers).......	....
Water (for beets)............	14 quarts (14 No. 56 dippers)........	....
Beet juice..................	4 quarts (4 No. 56 dippers).........	....
Sugar, granulated...........	1 pound (½ No. 56 dipper).........	....
Salt.......................	1½ ounces (3 mess kit spoons).......	....
Cornstarch.................	7 ounces (⅓ No. 56 dipper)........	....
Water.....................	2 quarts (2 No. 56 dippers).........	....
Vinegar...................	1 quart (1 No. 56 dipper)..........	....
Preserved butter............	8 ounces (¼ No. 56 dipper)........	....

1. Soak beets 20 to 40 minutes. Bring slowly to a boil (about 45 minutes) in a covered stockpot. Simmer for 20 to 30 minutes or until beets are tender. Drain and save beet juice.
2. Bring 4 quarts of beet juice to a boil in a large stockpot (add water if necessary to make 4 quarts).
3. Combine sugar, salt, and cornstarch. Add a small quantity of beet juice to cornstarch mixture and mix until smooth. Add this mixture gradually to the remaining hot beet juice. Heat to the boiling point.
4. Add vinegar and preserved butter to the thickened beet juice. Add Drained beets and mix thoroughly.

NO. 925. SWEET SOUR BEETS

Yield: 100 4-ounce servings or approximately 1½ serving spoons each.

Ingredients	100 servings	.... servings
Beets, dehydrated............	3¼ pounds (4 No. 56 dippers).......	....
Water (for beets)............	14 quarts (14 No. 56 dippers)........	....
Vinegar, 50 grain............	1 quart (1 No. 56 dipper)..........	....
Sugar, granulated...........	11 ounces (½ No. 56 dipper)........	....
Salt.......................	1½ ounces (3 mess kit spoons).......	....
Pepper....................	¼ ounce (1 mess kit spoon)........	....

1. Soak beets 20 to 40 minutes. Bring slowly to a boil (about 45 minutes). Simmer for 20 to 30 minutes in a covered stockpot until beets are tender. Drain.
2. Combine vinegar, sugar, salt, and pepper and bring to the boiling point. Add to beets and stir well. Serve hot.

NO. 926. CABBAGE AND BACON
Yield: 100 4-ounce servings or approximately 1½ serving spoons each.

Ingredients	100 servings	.... servings
Cabbage, dehydrated.........	3½ pounds (11 No. 56 dippers)......	....
Water (for cabbage)..........	17 quarts (17 No. 56 dippers)........	....
Salt.......................	4½ ounces (9 mess kit spoons).......	....
Bacon, diced................	3 pounds (2 No. 56 dippers).........	....
Pepper.....................	(½ mess kit spoon).................	....

1. Soak cabbage in water for 20 minutes. Bring slowly to a boil, in an uncovered stockpot (about 45 minutes).
2. Add salt and simmer for 10 minutes, or until tender. Drain, leaving about ½ of the liquid on the cabbage.
3. Fry diced bacon until it is lightly brown. Add bacon, bacon grease, and pepper to the cabbage and mix thoroughly. Serve hot.

NO. 927. CREAMED CABBAGE
Yield: 100 5-ounce servings or approximately 2 serving spoons each.

Ingredients	100 servings	.... servings
Cabbage, dehydrated.........	3 pounds (9½ No. 56 dippers)......	....
Water (for cabbage)..........	15 quarts (15 No. 56 dippers).......	....
Salt.......................	4½ ounces (9 mess kit spoons).......	....
White sauce, medium.........	(8 No. 56 dippers).................	....
Pepper.....................	¼ ounce (1 mess kit spoon).........	....

1. Soak cabbage in water for 20 minutes. Bring slowly to a boil in an uncovered stockpot (about 45 minutes). Add salt and simmer for 10 minutes or until tender. Drain and save surplus water.
2. Prepare white sauce as given in recipe No. 905 or recipe No. 906. (Use drained surplus water as part of liquid to prepare white sauce.)
3. Combine white sauce, cabbage, and pepper.

NO. 928. SCALLOPED CABBAGE
Yield: 100 5-ounce servings or approximately 2 serving spoons each.

Ingredients	100 servings	.... servings
Cabbage, dehydrated.........	3 pounds (9½ No. 56 dippers)......	....
Water (for cabbage)..........	15 quarts (15 No. 56 dippers).......	....
Salt.......................	4½ ounces (9 mess kit spoons).......	....
White sauce, medium.........	(8 No. 56 dippers).................	....
Bread or cracker crumbs......	2 pounds (2 No. 56 dippers)........	....
Fat, melted.................	½ pound (¼ No. 56 dipper)........	....

1. Soak cabbage in water for 20 minutes. Bring slowly to a boil in an uncovered container (about 45 minutes).

2. Add salt and simmer for 10 minutes or until tender. Drain and save the surplus water. Arrange cabbage in layers in bakepan.
3. Prepare medium white sauce given in recipe No. 905. (Use the drained surplus water as part of liquid to prepare white sauce.) Combine cabbage and white sauce. Pour melted fat over bread crumbs and mix. Sprinkle over top of creamed cabbage mixture and bake in moderate oven for 20 to 30 minutes.

NO. 929. BUTTERED CARROTS

Yield: 100 4-ounce servings or approximately 1½ serving spoons each.

Ingredients	100 servings	.... servings
Carrots, dehydrated..........	4 pounds (4½ No. 56 dippers).......	....
Water (for carrots)...........	14 quarts (14 No. 56 dippers).......	....
Preserved butter.............	1½ pounds (¾ No. 56 dipper).......	....
Salt.......................	3 ounces (6 mess kit spoons)........	....
Pepper.....................	To taste............................	....

1. Soak carrots in water for 20 to 40 minutes. Bring slowly to a boil (about 45 minutes) in a covered stockpot. Simmer for 15 to 25 minutes or until tender. Drain.
2. Melt preserved butter. Add preserved butter, salt, and pepper to carrots and mix thoroughly.

NO. 930. CREAMED CARROTS
If creamed carrots are desired use the above recipe but omit preserved butter and use 4 No. 56 dippers of medium white sauce. (See recipe No. 905.) Use surplus water from carrots as part of liquid in preparation of white sauce.

NO. 931. BUTTERED CARROTS WITH CORN

Yield: 100 4-ounce servings or approximately 1½ serving spoons each.

Ingredients	100 servings	.... servings
Carrots, dehydrated..........	1¾ pounds (2 No. 56 dippers).......	....
Water (for carrots)...........	9 quarts (9 No. 56 dippers).........	....
Corn, whole kernel, canned....	2 No. 10 cans....................	....
Salt.......................	3 ounces (6 mess kit spoons)........	....
Pepper.....................	¼ ounce (1 mess kit spoon)........	....
Preserved butter.............	1½ pounds (¾ No. 56 dipper).......	....

1. Soak carrots 20 to 40 minutes. Bring slowly to the boiling point (about 45 minutes) in a covered stockpot and simmer for 15 to 25 minutes or until tender. Drain.
2. Combine carrots and corn and add salt and pepper.
3. Melt preserved butter and pour over mixed carrots and corn before serving.

NO. 932. WHIPPED CREAMED CARROTS

Yield: 100 4-ounce servings or approximately 1½ serving spoons each.

Ingredients	100 servings	.... servings
Carrots, dehydrated.........	4 pounds (4½ No. 56 dippers).......	....
Water (for carrots)..........	14 quarts (14 No. 56 dippers).......	....
Milk, evaporated...........	2—14½-ounce cans................	....
Water (for milk)...........	1 quart (1 No. 56 dipper)...........	....
or		
Milk, powdered.............	½ pound (½ No. 56 dipper)........	....
Water (for milk)..........	¾ quart (¾ No. 56 dipper)........	....
Preserved butter............	1 pound (½ No. 56 dipper)........	....
Salt......................	1½ ounce (3 mess kit spoons).......	....
Pepper...................	To taste................	....

1. Soak carrots in water for 20 to 40 minutes. Bring slowly to a boil in a covered stockpot (about 45 minutes). Simmer for 15 to 20 minutes or until tender. Drain and save surplus water.

2. Combine milk and water (use surplus water) or reconstituted powdered milk.

3. Add preserved butter and heat milk until preserved butter is completely melted. Add milk mixture, salt, and pepper to mashed carrots. Beat well.

4. Place in a greased pan and bake in a moderate oven for 30 minutes.

NO. 933. GLAZED CARROTS

Yield: 100 4-ounce servings or approximately 1½ serving spoons each.

Ingredients	100 servings	... servings
Carrots, dehydrated.........	4 pounds (4½ No. 56 dippers).......	....
Water (for carrots)..........	14 quarts (14 No. 56 dippers).......	....
Sugar, granulated...........	2½ pounds (1¼ No. 56 dippers).....	....
Water, boiling..............	¾ quart (¾ No. 56 dipper)........	....
Salt......................	1 ounce (2 mess kit spoons)........	....
Preserved butter............	1 pound (½ No. 56 dipper).......	....

1. Soak carrots in water for 20 to 40 minutes. Bring slowly to a boil in a covered stockpot (about 45 minutes). Simmer for 15 to 25 minutes or until tender. Drain.

2. Add the sugar to the boiling water. Stir until sugar is dissolved. Reheat to the boiling point, boil, without stirring, until a thin sirup is formed (boil about 3 minutes).

3. Add salt and preserved butter. Stir until preserved butter is completely melted.

4. Place carrots in greased bakepan and pour sirup over carrots.

5. Bake in moderate oven about 20 minutes, basting frequently with sirup.

NO. 934. LYONNAISE CARROTS Yield: 100 4-ounce servings or 1½ serving spoons each.

Ingredients	100 servings	.... servings
Carrots, dehydrated.........	3½ pounds (4 No. 56 dippers).......	....
Water (for carrots)..........	12½ quarts (12½ No. 56 dippers)....	....
Onions, dehydrated.........	8 ounces (1 No. 56 dipper)...........	....
Water (for onions)..........	2 quarts (2 No. 56 dippers)..........	....
Fat.......................	1½ pounds (¾ No. 56 dipper).......	....
Salt......................	2½ ounces (5 mess kit spoons).......	....
Pepper...................	To taste................	....
Sugar....................	8 ounces (¼ No. 56 dipper).........	....

1. Soak carrots in water for 20 to 40 minutes. Bring slowly to a boil in a covered stockpot (about 45 minutes). Simmer for 15 to 25 minutes or until tender. Drain.

2. Soak onions in water for 20 minutes.

3. Melt fat and add onions. Fry onions until light brown.

4. Combine onions and fat used in frying, salt, pepper, and sugar and pour over carrots. Mix lightly.

NO. 935. CARROTS AND PEAS Yield: 100 4-ounce servings or approximately 1½ serving spoons each.

Ingredients	100 servings	.... servings
Carrots, dehydrated.........	1¾ pounds (2 No. 56 dippers).......	....
Water (for carrots)..........	6 quarts (6 No. 56 dippers)..........	....
Peas, canned................	2 No. 10 cans................	....
Preserved butter............	1½ pounds (¾ No. 56 dipper).......	....
Salt......................	3 ounces (6 mess kit spoons)........	....
Pepper...................	¼ ounce (1 mess kit spoon).........	....

1. Soak carrots 20 to 40 minutes. Bring slowly to the boiling point (about 45 minutes) in a covered stockpot and simmer for 15 to 25 minutes or until tender. Drain.

2. Combine carrots and peas.

3. Melt preserved butter.

4. Mix melted preserved butter, salt, and pepper with peas and carrots, and serve hot.

NO. 936. CREAMED CARROTS AND PEAS

If creamed carrots and peas are desired, use the above recipe but omit preserved butter and use 4 No. 56 dippers of medium white sauce. (See recipe No. 905.) Use surplus water drained from carrots and peas as part of liquid in preparing white sauce.

NO. 937. SWEET SOUR CARROTS

Yield: 100 4-ounce servings or approximately 1½ serving spoons each.

Ingredients	100 servings	.... servings
Carrots, dehydrated	4 pounds (4½ No. 56 dippers)	
Water (for carrots)	14 quarts (14 No. 56 dippers)	
Vinegar, 50 grain	1¼ quarts (1¼ No. 56 dippers)	
Sugar, granulated	2½ pounds (1¼ No. 56 dippers)	
Salt	1½ ounces (3 mess kit spoons)	
Pepper	¼ ounce (1 mess kit spoon)	
Water	¾ quart (¾ No. 56 dipper)	
Cornstarch	5 ounces (¼ No. 56 dipper)	
Preserved butter	1 pound (½ No. 56 dipper)	

1. Soak carrots 20 to 40 minutes. Bring slowly to the boiling point (about 45 minutes) in a covered stockpot and simmer for 15 to 25 minutes or until tender. Drain.

2. Bring vinegar, sugar, salt, and pepper to a boil.

3. Add cornstarch to water gradually and then add to hot vinegar mix. Cook for 5 minutes.

4. Add preserved butter and stir until melted. Pour sauce over carrots and mix well.

NO. 938. CORN PUDDING

Yield: 100 3½-ounce servings or approximately 1½ serving spoons each.

Ingredients	100 servings	.... servings
Milk, evaporated	3—14½-ounce cans	
Water	1½ quarts (1½ No. 56 dippers)	
or		
Milk, powdered	¾ pound (¾ No. 56 dipper)	
Water (for milk)	2¾ quarts (2¾ No. 56 dippers)	
Corn, cream style	2 No. 10 cans	
Bread crumbs, dry	1¾ pounds (1¾ No. 56 dippers)	
Pepper	¼ ounce (1 mess kit spoon)	
Salt	3 ounces (6 mess kit spoons)	
Eggs, powdered	18 ounces (1½ No. 56 dippers)	
Water	1¾ quarts (1¾ No. 56 dippers)	

1. Combine evaporated milk and water or reconstitute powdered milk.

2. Add milk, bread crumbs, salt, and pepper to corn. Mix thoroughly.

3. Add egg powder to ⅓ of the water, beating constantly to make a smooth paste. Add remainder of water and mix until smooth. Add to corn mixture and mix well.

4. Pour into a greased bakepan and bake in moderate oven for 1 hour or until knife inserted in center comes out clean.

NO. 939. ONIONS AU GRATIN   Yield: 100 4-ounce servings or approximately 1½ serving spoons each.

Ingredients	100 servings	.... servings
Onions, dehydrated............	1½ pounds (3 No. 56 dippers).......	....
Water (for onions)...........	7 quarts (7 No. 56 dippers).........	....
White sauce, medium.........	(6 No. 56 dippers)..................	....
Salt........................	3 ounces (6 mess kit spoons)........	....
Mustard, dry................	2¼ ounces (9 mess kit spoons).......	....
Cheese, shredded.............	1 pound (1 No. 56 dipper)..........	....
Fat, melted.................	4 ounces (8 mess kit spoons)........	....
Bread or cracker crumbs......	1½ pounds (1½ No. 56 dippers).....	....

1. Soak onions in water approximately 20 minutes. Cover and simmer for 10 minutes or until tender. Drain and save surplus.
2. Prepare white sauce. (See recipe No. 905.) Use drained surplus water as part of liquid to prepare white sauce. Add mustard and ¾ of the cheese. Stir until the cheese is melted.
3. Pour melted fat over bread crumbs.
4. Arrange layers of onions and cheese sauce in well-greased bakepans, cover with crumbs and remaining cheese. Bake in moderate oven 20 to 30 minutes.

NO. 940. FRIED ONIONS   Yield: 100 2-ounce servings or approximately 1 level serving spoon each.

Ingredients	100 servings	.... servings
Onions, dehydrated...........	2 pounds (4 No. 56 dippers)........	....
Water (for onions)...........	8 quarts (8 No. 56 dippers)........	....
Salt........................	2 ounces (4 mess kit spoons)........	....
Pepper......................	To taste...........................	....
Fat, bacon..................	2½ pounds (1¼ No. 56 dippers).....	....

1. Soak onions in water 20 to 40 minutes.
2. Sprinkle with salt and pepper.
3. Add bacon fat, cover and fry until brown and tender, stirring frequently.

NO. 941. SCALLOPED ONIONS   Yield: 100 4-ounce servings.

Ingredients	100 servings	.... servings
Onions, dehydrated...........	1½ pounds (3 No. 56 dippers).......	....
Water (for onions)..........	7 quarts (7 No. 56 dippers).........	....
Fat.........................	4 ounces (8 mess kit spoons)........	....
Bread crumbs, moist.........	3 pounds (1½ No. 56 dippers)......	....
White sauce, medium........	(6 No. 56 dippers)..................	....
Salt........................	3 ounces (6 mess kit spoons)........	....

1. Soak onions in water approximately 20 minutes. Cover and simmer for 10 minutes or until tender. Drain and save surplus water.
2. Pour melted fat over bread crumbs and mix.

3. Prepare white sauce. (See recipe No. 905.) Use drained surplus water as part of the liquid used to prepare white sauce. Mix reconstituted onion, white sauce, salt, and ½ of the crumbs in well-greased baking dish. Top with remaining crumbs.
4. Bake in moderate oven 20 to 30 minutes.

NO. 942. POTATOES AU GRATIN

Yield: 100 6-ounce servings or approximately 2 serving spoons each.

Ingredients	100 servings	.... servings
Potatoes, dehydrated, diced...	7 pounds (10 No. 56 dippers)........	....
Water (for potatoes)..........	19 quarts (19 No. 56 dippers)........	....
White sauce, medium........	(6 No. 56 dippers)...................	....
Cheese, shredded.............	3 pounds (3 No. 56 dippers)........	....
Mustard, dry................	¼ ounce (1 mess kit spoon)........	....
Salt.....................	3 ounces (6 mess kit spoons)........	....
Fat.......................	8 ounces (¼ No. 56 dipper)........	....
Bread or cracker crumbs, dry..	1 pound (1 No. 56 dipper)........	....

1. Soak potatoes for 20 to 40 minutes. Bring slowly to a boil (about 45 minutes), in a covered stockpot. Simmer for 10 to 15 minutes or until potatoes are tender but not mushy. Drain well, save surplus water.
2. Prepare medium white sauce using preserved butter as in recipe No. 906. Use drained surplus water as part of liquid in preparation of white sauce.
3. Add salt, mustard, and ⅔ of the cheese to the sauce. Stir until cheese is melted.
4. Mix potatoes and cheese sauce and put in well-greased roast pans. Melt fat and mix with bread crumbs and the remainder of the cheese. Sprinkle over bread crumbs.
5. Bake in moderate oven for approximately 20 minutes.

NO. 943. CREAMED POTATOES

Yield: 100 4-ounce servings or approximately 1½ serving spoons each.

Ingredients	100 servings	.... servings
Potatoes, dehydrated, diced...	7 pounds (10 No. 56 dippers)........	....
Water (for potatoes)..........	19 quarts (19 No. 56 dippers)........	....
White sauce, medium........	(4 No. 56 dippers)...................	....
Salt.......................	4½ ounces (9 mess kit spoons)........	....
Pepper....................	(½ mess kit spoon).................	....

1. Soak potatoes in water 20 to 40 minutes. Bring slowly to a boil (about 45 minutes) in a covered stockpot and simmer for 10 minutes or until potatoes are tender, but not mushy. Drain well. Save surplus water.
2. Prepare medium white sauce using recipe No. 905. Use drained surplus water as part of liquid in preparation of white sauce. Add salt, pepper, and white sauce to drained potatoes and serve.

NO. 944. HASHED BROWN POTATOES

Yield: 100 5-ounce servings or approximately 2 serving spoons each.

Ingredients	100 servings	.... servings
Potato shreds...............	10 pounds (16 No. 56 dippers).......	....
Water, cool.................	10 quarts (10 No. 56 dippers)........	....
Fat........................	4 pounds (2 No. 56 dippers).........	....
Salt.......................	4 ounces (8 mess kit spoons)........	....
Pepper.....................	¼ ounce (1 mess kit spoon)..........	....

1. Soak potato shreds in cool water for 3 minutes. Drain.

2. Melt fat in roast pan. Add drained potato shreds, salt, and pepper. Fry potatoes for about 10 minutes. Turn and continue frying for about 15 minutes. (Care must be taken not to turn potatoes too often or product will be mushy.)

NO. 945. HASHED BROWNED OR FRIED POTATOES

Yield: 100 5-ounce servings or approximately 2 serving spoons each.

Ingredients	100 servings	.... servings
Potatoes, dehydrated, diced...	7 pounds (10 No. 56 dippers).......	....
Water (for potatoes)..........	19 quarts (19 No. 56 dippers).......	....
Fat........................	4 pounds (2 No. 56 dippers).........	....
Salt.......................	4 ounces (8 mess kit spoons)........	....
Pepper.....................	¼ ounce (1 mess kit spoon)..........	....

1. Soak potatoes for 20 to 40 minutes. Bring slowly to a boil (about 45 minutes) in a covered stockpot. Simmer for 10 to 15 minutes or until potatoes are tender, but not mushy. Drain well and cool.

2. Heat fat in bakepan in frying temperature. Add potatoes and mix lightly with fat. (Divide the potatoes and fat into two or three batches, and fry separately. This will give a better finished product.)

3. Add salt and pepper. Turn potatoes after those on the bottom have been frying about 10 minutes or are a light brown. Continue frying for about 15 minutes more, occasionally turning potatoes.

NO. 946. LYONNAISE POTATOES

Prepare exactly like hashed brown potatoes recipe No. 945. Reconstitute separately 1¼ No. 56 dippers (12 ounces) of dehydrated onions by soaking 20 minutes in 2½ No. 56 dippers of water. When the onions are reconstituted add to the potatoes and fry as directed in recipe No. 945.

NO. 947. MASHED POTATOES PREPARED FROM JULIENNE OR CUBED POTATOES

Yield: 100 5-ounce servings or approximately 2 serving spoons each.

Ingredients	100 servings	.... servings
Potatoes, dehydrated, diced...	7 pounds (10 No. 56 dippers)........	....
Water (for potatoes).........	19 quarts (19 No. 56 dippers)........	....
Milk, evaporated............	1—14½-ounce can (½ No. 56 dipper).	....
Water, potato (for milk)......	1 pint (½ No. 56 dipper)...........	....
or		
Milk, powdered..............	4 ounces (¼ No. 56 dipper).........	....
Water, potato (for milk)......	1 quart (1 No. 56 dipper)..........	....
Salt........................	4 ounces (8 mess kit spoons).......	....
Preserved butter............	2 pounds (1 No. 56 dipper).........	....

1. Soak potatoes for 20 to 40 minutes. Bring slowly to a boil (about 45 minutes) in a covered stockpot. Simmer for approximately 10 to 15 minutes or until potatoes are very tender. Drain and save surplus water. Mash the drained potatoes until they are as smooth as possible. All the lumps cannot be removed.

2. Combine evaporated milk with potato water or reconstitute the powdered milk with cool potato water. Add preserved butter and salt and heat until preserved butter is completely melted. Add hot milk mixture to potatoes, whipping constantly.

NO. 948. MASHED POTATOES FROM PRECOOKED POTATO SHREDS

Yield: 100 5-ounce servings or 2 serving spoons each.

Ingredients	100 servings	.... servings
Potatoes, precooked shreds....	6 pounds (9½ No. 56 dippers).......	....
Water (for potatoes).........	9 quarts (9 No. 56 dippers)........	....
Salt........................	4 ounces (8 mess kit spoons).......	....
Milk, evaporated............	2—14½-ounce cans................	....
Water (for milk)............	2 quarts (2 No. 56 dippers)........	....
or		
Milk, powdered, whole........	1 pound (1 No. 56 dipper).........	....
Water (for milk)............	3¾ quarts (3¾ No. 56 dippers).....	....
Preserved butter............	1½ pounds (¾ No. 56 dipper)......	....

1. Bring water to the boiling point in a large stockpot. Measure the potatoes accurately and pour into the boiling water. Stir potatoes only enough so that all the shreds are submerged in the water. Let stand in covered container in a warm place for 20 minutes or over a low flame for 10 minutes.

2. Add salt.

3. Combine evaporated milk with water or reconstitute the powdered milk.

4. Add the preserved butter to milk mixture and heat until preserved butter is completely melted. Add the hot milk mixture to potatoes gradually, whipping constantly. Beat well.

NO. 949. SWEET POTATOES AND APPLES

Yield: 100 5-ounce servings or approximately 2 serving spoons each.

Ingredients	100 servings	.... servings
Sweet potatoes, dehydrated, diced.	7 pounds (7 No. 56 dippers)........	....
Water (for potatoes)..........	10½ quarts (10½ No. 56 dippers)....	....
Apple nuggets...............	2¼ pounds (3 No. 56 dippers).......	....
Water (for apples)...........	7 quarts (7 No. 56 dippers).........	....
Sugar, granulated............	4 pounds (2 No. 56 dippers)........	....
Salt.......................	1½ ounces (3 mess kit spoons).......	....
Fat, melted.................	10 ounces (⅓ No. 56 dipper)........	....

1. Soak potatoes in water for 20 minutes. Bring slowly to a boil in a covered stockpot (about 45 minutes). Simmer for 20 to 30 minutes or until tender. Drain.

2. Soak apple nuggets for 20 minutes. Bring slowly to a boil and simmer for 10 to 20 minutes or until apples are tender. Add sugar.

3. Add salt to sweet potatoes and place apples and sweet potatoes in layers in a greased bakepan. Pour melted fat over the top.

4. Bake in moderate oven for 30 minutes.

NO. 950. SWEET POTATO BALLS OR CROQUETTES

Yield: 200 1½-inch balls.

Ingredients	100 servings	.... servings
Sweet potatoes, dehydrated, diced.	8 pounds (8 No. 56 dippers)........	....
Water (for potatoes)..........	12 quarts (12 No. 56 dippers).......	....
Milk, evaporated.............	2—14½-ounce cans.................	....
Water, potato (for milk)......	1 pint (½ No. 56 dipper)..........	....
or		
Milk, powdered.............	½ pound (½ No. 56 dipper)........	....
Water, potato (for milk)......	1 quart (1 No. 56 dipper).........	....
Preserved butter.............	1 pound (½ No. 56 dipper)........	....
Salt.......................	2 ounces (4 mess kit spoons)........	....

1. Soak potatoes in water for 20 minutes. Bring slowly to a boil (about 45 minutes) in a covered stockpot. Simmer for 20 to 30 minutes or until tender. Drain, save surplus water, and mash.

2. Combine milk and water or reconstitute powdered milk.

3. Add preserved butter to milk and heat until preserved butter is melted. Add milk mixture and salt to potatoes. Mash by stirring vigorously with a wire whip. Cool and form into balls or croquettes.

NO. 951. EGG MIXTURE   Yield:

Ingredients	100 servings	.... servings
Eggs, powdered.............	12 ounces (1 No. 56 dipper).........	....
Water (for eggs)	1 quart (1 No. 56 dipper)..........	....
Bread crumbs...............	(2½ No. 56 dippers)...............	....

1. Reconstitute the eggs as instructed in paragraph 38.
2. Dip balls or croquettes in egg mixture and roll in bread crumbs. Fry balls or croquettes in deep fat until brown.

NO. 952. BUTTERED SWEET POTATOES (MASHED)

Yield: 100 4-ounce servings or approximately 1½ serving spoons each.

Ingredients	100 servings	.... servings
Sweet potatoes, dehydrated, diced.	8 pounds (8 No. 56 dippers)........	....
Water (for sweet potatoes)....	12 quarts (12 No. 56 dippers).......	....
Milk, evaporated.............	2—14½-ounce cans.............	....
Water, potato (for milk)......	1 pint (½ No. 56 dipper)..........	....
or		
Milk, powdered.............	4 ounces (¼ No. 56 dipper)........	....
Water, potato (for milk)......	1 quart (1 No. 56 dipper).........	....
Preserved butter............	2 pounds (1 No. 56 dipper)........	....
Salt......................	2½ ounces (5 mess kit spoons).:......	....

1. Soak potatoes in water for 20 minutes. Bring slowly to a boil in a covered stockpot (about 45 minutes). Simmer 20 to 30 minutes or until tender. Drain and save surplus water.
2. Combine milk and potato water or reconstitute powdered milk. Add preserved butter to milk and heat until preserved butter melts. Add milk mixture and salt to potatoes. Mash by stirring vigorously with a wire whip.

NO. 953. GLAZED SWEET POTATOES

Yield: 100 4-ounce servings or approximately 1½ serving spoons each.

Ingredients	100 servings	.... servings
Sweet potatoes, dehydrated, diced.	8 pounds (8 No. 56 dippers)........	....
Water (for potatoes).........	12 quarts (12 No. 56 dippers).......	....
Sugar, granulated...........	3 pounds (1½ No. 56 dippers)......	....
Salt......................	2 ounces (4 mess kit spoons)........	....
Preserved butter............	1 pound (½ No. 56 dipper)........	....

1. Soak potatoes in water for 20 minutes. Bring slowly to a boil in a covered stockpot (about 45 minutes). Simmer 20 to 30 minutes. Drain and save surplus water.

2. Mix sugar and 2 quarts of surplus water. Bring slowly to a boil and stir only until sugar is dissolved. Simmer without stirring for approximately 5 minutes.

3. Add preserved butter and salt to hot sirup and heat until preserved butter has completely dissolved. Pour sirup over potatoes and bake in moderate oven for 30 minutes.

Note. Potatoes may be mashed and hot sirup added during whipping. Bake as directed above.

NO. 954. BAKED SWEET POTATOES AND PINEAPPLE

Yield: 100 4-ounce servings or approximately 1½ serving spoons each.

Ingredients	100 servings	.... servings
Sweet potatoes, dehydrated, diced.	7 pounds (7 No. 56 dippers).........	....
Water (for potatoes)..........	10½ quarts (10½ No. 56 dippers)....	....
Pineapple, diced.............	1 No. 10 can........................	....
Preserved butter.............	2 pounds (1 No. 56 dipper).........	....
Salt......................	2 ounces (4 mess kit spoons)........	....

1. Soak potatoes in water for 20 minutes. Bring slowly to a boil (about 45 minutes) in a covered stockpot. Simmer 20 to 30 minutes or until tender. Drain and mash.

2. Drain pineapple and save juice. Cut pineapple into ½-inch pieces.

3. Melt preserved butter.

4. Add pineapple, pineapple juice, preserved butter, and salt to sweet potatoes and mix thoroughly. Place in greased bakepan and bake in moderate oven for 30 minutes.

NO. 955. BAKED SWEET POTATOES WITH RAISINS

Yield: 100 4-ounce servings or approximately 1½ serving spoons each.

Prepare the recipe for baked sweet potatoes and pineapple, substituting 2 No. 56 dippers of raisins for the pineapple. Soak the raisins in water for 30 minutes before using.

TROPICAL FRUITS AND VEGETABLES

54. GENERAL. These recipes are prepared for those messes which may, in the course of changing events, find that these tropical fruits and vegetables are plentiful and therefore are items of issue. If this should occur, these recipes will contain valuable information for the cooks. For that situation only these recipes are presented. They will not be found of value for everyday use everywhere but only in the tropics that produce these vegetables and fruits which to the uninitiated seem strange and unusual but when understood are as commonplace as the sweet potato, cucumber, etc., which are grown in our home gardens. All of these fruits and vegetables may be cooked in combination with each other. It has, however, been noted that the camotes take a longer period of cooking than do the other vegetables. They may be used in stews and casserole dishes. Full advantage should be taken of sauces and seasoning agents.

55. DESCRIPTION. a. Camote. The camote is a root vegetable similar to the sweet potato. It is grown from planting the vine shoots and is ready for harvest in from three to five months after planting. It is good to cook when it is firm and has a bright color. The color combinations of the camote are: red skin with white center, yellow skin with white center, white skin with violet colored center and a pinkish white skin with a darker pink center. The color has nothing to do with the flavor or use of the vegetable. When camotes are soft or shriveled they are not fit for use. The camote may be boiled, fried, or candied in the same manner as the sweet potato.

b. Patola. The patola is a gourd. It is similar to the squash. It grows on a vine similar to the cucumber. It is grown from seeds and is ready for harvest in about three months after planting. When the patola is bright green and soft with a white moist center, it is ready for cooking. If the patola is brown, hard or tough, and the center has a brownish hue and pithy, it is too old and not fit for consumption. The patola is very similar in texture and flavor to the eggplant.

c. Pepino. The pepino is similar to the cucumber. It differs in size, however. It has been found to be most suitable for salads, cold meat garnish, etc. Recipes can be based on ordinary cucumbers.

d. Sayote. The sayote is very similar to the squash in both texture and taste. It can be cooked by the same methods as the squash. It is grown from the vegetable itself. The vegetable is planted with the shriveled end down from which the roots start. It grows on a vine similar to the squash and is ready for harvest in about three months. The size does not impair the eating qualities. When the vegetable is light green in color and solid it is ready for cooking. When the end begins to sprout the vegetable is not fit for use.

e. Sincamas. The edible root of the sincamas has approximately the same shape as does the turnip. The skin is the color of the Irish potato. Its edible contents is white and is most suitable mixed with other vegetables or fruits for slaws and salads. If it is cooked, the cooking time is approximately that of the potato. Sincamas do not become soft if cooked for a long period of time but retain a delicious crispness.

f. Sitaw. Sitaw is similar to the string bean. The approximate length is 1 foot or more. It is characteristically spongy and fibrous which necessitates a longer period of time for cooking.

g. Talong. The talong is like the eggplant in mineral and nutritional value. Its size is smaller than the eggplant but it is much more tender.

h. Tangcoy. Tangcoy is a member of the melon family and looks like a small watermelon. It is adopted from China. It contains few carbohydrates but is very nutritious and is high in mineral content. It is suitable for pies, jams and cake fillings. It may be candied or used in soups.

i. Upo. The upo or Malay apple is similar to the summer squash. It has a fine, smooth texture, high in minerals and is very suitable for boiling, steaming, in meat stews, or cooked with any combinations of meats.

NO. 956. BIG THREE

Yield: 100 servings, 5 ounces each.

Ingredients	100 servings	.... servings
Camote	10 pounds	
Sayote	10 pounds	
Patola	10 pounds	
Bacon	3 pounds	
Water, boiling	To cover	
Onions	3 pounds	

1. Wash, pare, peel, and dice each vegetable separately; add to boiling water in the above order.
2. Saute bacon and onions, drain liquid from vegetables.
3. Season with salt, pepper, Worcestershire sauce and combine bacon and onions. Serve *hot*.

NO. 957. CALABASA CANDIED (Pumpkin)

Yield: 100 servings, 7 ounces each.

Ingredients	100 servings	.... servings
Calabasa	45 pounds	
Salt		
Boiling water		
Sugar, brown	3 pounds (3 mess kit cups)	
Butter	8 ounces (¼ No. 56 dipper)	

1. Pare calabasa, cut open, remove pulp and seeds, cut into small triangular shaped slices about 4 inches long.
2. Cover with boiling water, steam until just tender. Drain.
3. Place in sheet pans, brush with melted butter, sprinkle brown sugar on top.
4. Bake in oven (400° F.) 30 minutes prior to serving time.

NO. 958. CALABASA, SCALLOPED WITH ONIONS

Yield: 100 servings,
7 ounces each.

Ingredients	100 servings	.... servings
Calabasa	40 pounds	
Onions, diced	4 pounds (4 No. 56 dippers)	
Bacon	2 pounds	
Salt	To taste	
Pepper	To taste	
Ginger	⅛ ounce (½ mess kit spoon)	
Stock	2 quarts (2 No. 56 dippers)	

1. Pare and wash calabasa thoroughly, cut open, remove pulp and seeds. Cut into big cubes.
2. Cut bacon in small pieces, add onions fried until brown.
3. Combine calabasa, bacon, onion, salt, pepper, ginger, and stock. Simmer till tender.

NO. 959. CAMOTE CUSTARD (Sweet potato)

Yield: 100 servings,
4½ ounces each.

Ingredients	100 servings	.... servings
Eggs, powdered	1 pound (4½ No. 56 dippers)	
Milk, evaporated	6—14½-ounce cans	
Sugar, granulated	To taste	
Cinnamon	To taste	
Nutmeg	To taste	
Salt	To taste	
Vanilla extract	To taste	
Camote	20 pounds	

1. Reconstitute eggs, add milk, sugar, cinnamon, nutmeg, salt, and vanilla extract.
2. Wash camotes thoroughly and cook until tender. Peel and mash until smooth. Add 1 pound of melted butter to camotes.
3. Combine custard and camote and add 8 ounces of sirup. Place in sheet pans and bake in moderate oven for approximately 45 minutes.

NO. 960. MASHED CAMOTE (Sweet potato)   Yield: 100 servings, 7 ounces each.

Ingredients	100 servings	.... servings
Camote	45 pounds	
Butter	1 pound (½ No. 56 dipper)	
Milk, evaporated	6—14½-ounce cans	
Salt	To taste	
Water, boiling	2 quarts (2 No. 56 dippers)	

1. Peel camote and place in pot.

2. Add 2 quarts of boiling water.

3. Steam until tender.

4. Add butter and salt.

5. Mash thoroughly.

6. Add milk and whip as potatoes.

7. If desired sprinkle cinnamon, sugar (mixture) over camotes prior to serving.

NO. 961. PATOLA BUTTERED (Gourd-like squash)
Yield: 100 servings, 6½ ounces each.

Ingredients	100 servings	.... servings
Patola	45 pounds	
Water, boiling	2 quarts (2 No. 56 dippers)	
Salt	To taste	
Butter	1 pound (½ No. 56 dipper)	

1. Wash and pare patola, slice.

2. Pour boiling water over them. Stew until tender.

3. Drain off excess liquids, season to taste, and add melted butter.

NO. 962. PATOLA FRIED (Gourd-like squash)   Yield: 100 servings, 6 ounces each.

Ingredients	100 servings	.... servings
Patola	45 pounds	
Eggs	19 eggs (slightly beaten)	
Flour, sifted	12 ounces (1 mess kit cup)	

Wash patola and pare. Slice in ¼-inch slices. Dip in eggs and fry in deep fat until golden brown and tender.

NO. 963. PATOLA GUMBO (Gourd-like squash)

Yield: 100 servings,
10 ounces each.

Ingredients	100 servings	.... servings
Patola	40 pounds	
Tomatoes	4 No. 2½ cans	
Bacon	3 pounds (diced)	
Onions	2 pounds (2 No. 56 dippers)	
Chili powder*	2 ounces	
Garlic	1 clove	
Mustard powder	To taste	

*Chili con carne may be substituted.

1. Saute bacon and onions.
2. Add chili powder, chopped up garlic clove, tomatoes and then add patola, peeled and diced. Add mustard.
3. Stir and simmer until slightly thickened and patolas are tender.

NO. 964. PATOLA MARLOW (Gourd-like squash)

Yield: 100 servings,
7 ounces each.

Ingredients	100 servings	.... servings
Patola	40 pounds	
Onions, diced	3 pounds (3 No. 56 dippers)	
Bacon, diced	3 pounds	
Salt	To taste	
Pepper	To taste	
Worcestershire sauce		
Water	1½ quarts (1½ No. 56 dippers)	

1. Saute bacon and onions. Add Worcestershire sauce.
2. Wash, pare, and dice patola, add 1½ quarts of water. Steam until tender. Add onions and bacon mixture to above.
3. Season to taste and simmer for 10 minutes. Serve *hot*.

NO. 965. PEPINO PICKLED (Cucumber)

Yield: 100 servings,
5 ounces each.

Ingredients	100 servings	.... servings
Pepino	30 pounds	
Onions, sliced	2 pounds (2 No. 56 dippers)	
Vinegar	1 pint (½ No. 56 dipper)	
Sugar, granulated	(1 mess kit cup)	
Salt	(1 mess kit spoon)	
Pepper	To taste	

1. Wash, peel and slice pepino.
2. Add all ingredients together and mix 10 minutes before serving.

NO. 966. PEPINO SALAD—HOTEL MANILA (Cucumber)
Yield: 100 servings,
7 ounces each.

Ingredients	100 servings	.... servings
Pepino	30 pounds	
Eggs, hard-boiled	36 eggs	
Onions, sliced	3 pounds (3 No. 56 dippers)	
Salad oil	(½ mess kit cup)	
Vinegar	½ pint (¼ No. 56 dipper)	
Sugar, granulated	1 ounce (2 mess kit spoons)	
Mustard	(½ mess kit cup)	
Salt	To taste	
Pepper	To taste	

1. Wash, peel, and slice pepino.
2. Add hard-boiled eggs (sliced) and onions.
3. Add vinegar, salad oil, sugar, mustard, salt, pepper, and mix; first mixing 10 minutes before serving time.

NO. 967. STUFFED PEPINO—MAIN DISH (Cucumber)
Yield: 100 servings,
8 ounces each.

Ingredients	100 servings	.... servings
Pepino, whole	24 or 30 pepinos (depending on size)	
Ground pork or beef	25 pounds	
Tomatoes	2 No. 2½ cans	
Cooked rice or bread crumbs	4 pounds (2 No. 56 dippers)	
Onions, chopped fine	1 pound (1 No. 56 dipper)	
Eggs	12 eggs	
Flour	5 ounces (¼ No. 56 dipper)	
Ginger	(2 mess kit spoons)	
Salt	To taste	
Pepper	To taste	

1. Pare and wash pepino thoroughly, cut crosswise about 3 inches long, scoop seeds and pulp from pepino, forming into cup.
2. Combine meat, tomatoes, cooked rice or bread crumbs, onions, eggs, flour, ginger, salt, pepper; mix well.
3. Grease bakepans, line pepino cup, stuff with meat mixtures.
4. Bake stuffed pepino in oven (350° F.) for 45 minutes or until pepino is tender.

NO. 968. SAYOTE A LA CREOLE (Like squash)
Yield: 100 servings,
6½ ounces each.

Ingredients	100 servings	.... servings
Sayote	30 pounds	
Bacon (chopped)	3 pounds	
Onions, dehydrated	½ pound	
Onions, fresh	3 pounds (3 No. 56 dippers)	
Tomatoes	2 No. 2½ cans	
Tomato puree	1 No. 2½ can	
Sugar, granulated	4 ounces (⅛ No. 56 dipper)	
Salt	To taste	
Pepper	To taste	

1. Place diced bacon in skillet.
2. When bacon is sauteed, add onions, tomatoes, and seasoning.
3. When sauce starts to thicken, add diced sayote.
4. Simmer slowly until tender.

NO. 969. BAKED SAYOTE (Like squash)   Yield: 100 servings, 7 ounces each.

Ingredients	100 servings	.... servings
Sayote	40 pounds	
Bacon	3 pounds	
Salt	To taste	
Pepper	To taste	

1. Peel and wash sayote. Cut into quarters.
2. Place in well-greased sheet pans.
3. Lay strips of bacon over sayote.
4. Bake in a moderate oven until tender.

NO. 970. BOILED SAYOTE (Like squash)   Yield: 100 servings, 6½ ounces each.

Ingredients	100 servings	.... servings
Sayote	40 pounds	
Salt	To taste	
Pepper	To taste	
Butter	Optional	
Sugar, granulated	4 ounces (⅛ No. 56 dipper)	

1. Peel and slice sayote. Place in pot. Add 2 quarts of water (hot).
2. Add seasoning.
3. Cook with lid on pot, usually for 15 minutes or until tender.
4. Drain water and butter. Serve *hot*.

NO. 971. SAYOTE—ESPANA (Like squash) Yield: 100 servings, 5½ ounces each.

Ingredients	100 servings	.... servings
Sayote	30 pounds	
Bacon	2 pounds (diced)	
Vinegar	1 pint (½ No. 56 dipper)	
Sugar, granulated	3 ounces (⅛ No. 56 dipper)	
Salt	To taste	
Pepper	To taste	

1. Peel and slice sayote, place in pot, add 2 quarts of liquid, 1 pint of water and 1 pint of vinegar.
2. Saute bacon and add to the above.
3. Season to taste.
4. Simmer until tender. Serve *hot*.

NO. 972. MASHED SAYOTE (Like squash)　　Yield: 100 servings, 7 ounces each.

Ingredients	100 servings	.... servings
Sayote	40 pounds	
Water	2 quarts (2 No. 56 dippers)	
Salt	To taste	
Pepper	To taste	
Butter	1 pound (½ No. 56 dipper)	
Sugar, granulated	4 ounces (⅛ No. 56 dipper)	

1. Peel sayote and place in pot. Add 2 quarts of boiling water.
2. Add salt, sugar, and pepper. Cook in covered stockpot until tender.
3. Drain water and mash, adding butter. Serve *hot*.

NO. 973. SAYOTE—SEIDEMAN EN CASSEROLE (Like squash)
Yield: 100 servings,
6½ ounces each.

Ingredients	100 servings	.... servings
Sayote	20 pounds	
Meat*	15 pounds	
Onions	3 pounds (3 No. 56 dippers)	
Soy sauce or Worcestershire	1 pint	
Sugar, granulated	4 ounces (⅛ No. 56 dipper)	
Salt	To taste	
Pepper	To taste	
Water, boiling	1½ quarts (1½ No. 56 dippers)	

*Beef, pork, or canned meats may be used.

1. Saute meat and onions together.
2. Add sayote diced.
3. Add soy sauce or Worcestershire. Stir thoroughly.
4. Add 1½ quarts of boiling water.
5. Then add sugar and seasoning ingredients. Simmer until tender.
6. Tomatoes may be added by decreasing the amount of water.

NO. 974. SINCAMAS SALAD WALDORF
(Edible root with pod-like string bean) Yield: 100 servings,
6 ounces each.

Ingredients	100 servings	.... servings
Sincamas	30 pounds	
Raisins	2 pounds	
Mayonnaise or salad dressing	1 quart	
Chopped nuts	1 pound	
Sugar	1 mess kit cup	
Salt	(½ mess kit spoon)	
Vanilla	(½ mess kit spoon)	

1. Pare sincamas, wash thoroughly and dice into small dices.
2. Combine raisins, sugar, salt, vanilla, mayonnaise or salad dressing, and mix 10 minutes before serving time.
3. Sprinkle chopped nuts on top just before serving.

NO. 975. SINCAMAS SAVORY
(Edible root with pod-like string bean)

Yield: 100 servings,
6½ ounces each.

Ingredients	100 servings	.... servings
Sincamas	30 pounds	
Tomatoes	1 No. 10 can	
Onions, diced	1 pound (1 No. 56 dipper)	
Bacon, cut fine	2 pounds	
Salt	To taste	
Pepper	To taste	
Ginger	(½ mess kit spoon)	
Worcestershire sauce	(1 mess kit cup)	
Stock	1 quart (1 No. 56 dipper)	

1. Pare sincamas, wash thoroughly, cut in half and slice thin.
2. Fry and brown bacon and onions in pot sincamas is to be cooked in.
3. Add sincamas, tomatoes, salt, pepper, Worcestershire sauce, ginger and stock. Bring to boiling point. Reduce heat and allow to simmer for 45 minutes, until tender.
4. Thicken with flour and water mix, heat to serving temperature.

NO. 976. SINCAMAS SLAW (Edible root with pod-like string bean)

Yield: 100 servings,
4½ ounces each.

Ingredients	100 servings	.... servings
Sincamas	30 pounds	
Vinegar	1 pint (½ No. 56 dipper)	
Sugar	(2 mess kit cups)	
Salt	(½ mess kit spoon)	
Cinnamon	(½ mess kit spoon)	

1. Pare sincamas, wash thoroughly and shred.
2. Combine vinegar, salt, sugar, cinnamon and mix 10 minutes before serving time.

NO. 977. SITAW AU GRATIN, TROPICAL (String bean)

Yield: 100 servings,
5 ounces each.

Ingredients	100 servings	.... servings
Sitaw	25 pounds	
Cheese, grated	2 pounds	
Eggs, hard-boiled	12 eggs	
Flour	10 ounces (½ No. 56 dipper)	
Onions	1 pound (1 No. 56 dipper)	
Stock	4 quarts (4 No. 56 dippers)	
Salt and pepper	To taste	
Paprika	To taste	
Milk, evaporated	1—14½-ounce can	

1. Wash sitaw, remove ends, and cut into small pieces.

2. Add boiling stock, simmer until almost tender, add onion and simmer until completely tender, and add salt and pepper.

3. Thicken with flour mixed with water, add milk, and stir until evenly mixed.

4. Sprinkle grated cheese on top, decorate with sliced hard-boiled eggs, and sprinkle sparingly with paprika.

NO. 978. SITAW, BOILED WITH BACON OR SALT PORK

(String bean)   Yield: 100 servings,
5½ ounces each.

Ingredients	100 servings	.... servings
Sitaw..........................	25 pounds........................	....
Bacon or salt pork...........	2 pounds.........................	....
Salt.........................	To taste..........................	....
Pepper......................	To taste..........................	....
Stock.......................	4 quarts (4 No. 56 dippers).........	....

1. Wash sitaw, and remove ends, cut into fine pieces.

2. Cut bacon or salt pork into small pieces, brown in skillet, and strain grease.

3. Combine sitaw, bacon or salt pork, and stock, bring to boiling point; reduce heat, and simmer until tender.

Note. Same recipe may be creamed, using stock to make cream sauce.

NO. 979. SITAW, SAUTE MANILA (String bean)

Yield: 100 servings,
5½ ounces each.

Ingredients	100 servings	.... servings
Sitaw.......................	25 pounds........................	....
Beef, pork, or ham, cut fine...	4 pounds.........................	....
Onions, diced...............	3 pounds (3 No. 56 dippers)........	....
Flour......................	10 ounces (½ No. 56 dipper).......	....
Salt.......................	To taste..........................	....
Pepper.....................	To taste..........................	....
Ginger.....................	(½ mess kit spoon)...............	....
Stock......................	(2 No. 56 dippers)................	....

1. Wash sitaw, and remove ends, cut into fine pieces.

2. Saute meat and onions until brown.

3. Combine sitaw, meats, onion, salt, pepper, ginger, and stock. Bring to boiling point, reduce heat and simmer until tender.

4. Mix flour with water (white wash) and thicken combined ingredients slightly, heat to serving temperature.

NO. 980. FRIED TALONG (Eggplant) Yield: 100 servings, 5 ounces each.

Ingredients	100 servings	.... servings
Talong	25 pounds	
Eggs, slightly beaten	2 pounds (1 No. 56 dipper)	
Milk, evaporated	1—14½-ounce can	
Water	1 pint (½ No. 56 dipper)	
Salt	To taste	
Cornmeal	1 pound 5 ounces (1 No. 56 dipper)	
Flour	3 pounds 12 ounces (3 No. 56 dippers)	
Fat (for frying)	As needed	

1. Wash talong. Pare and dice.

2. Add boiling salted water to talong, cover and heat to boiling point, reduce heat and simmer 5 minutes or until tender; drain well.

3. Combine sugar, salt, pepper, and tomatoes, heat.

4. Fry onions in butter, add crumbs and continue frying until crumbs are light brown.

5. Combine talong, tomatoes, and crumb mixture.

6. Place in well-greased baking pans; bake in moderate oven (350°) about 30 minutes.

NO. 981. TALONG—RAREBITS (Eggplant) Yield: 100 servings, 5½ ounces each.

Ingredients	100 servings	.... servings
Talong	25 pounds	
Fats, from cooking or butter	1 pound (½ No. 56 dipper)	
Flour	1¼ pounds (1 No. 56 dipper)	
Milk, evaporated	8—14½-ounce cans	
Water (for milk)	4 quarts (4 No. 56 dippers)	
Cheese, grated	2 pounds (2 No. 56 dippers)	
Salt	To taste	
Pepper	To taste	

1. Pare and wash talong, cut into big dices, add to boiling salted water, steam until tender, drain well.

2. Pour fats or butter in pan, add flour and stir until smooth, and brown flour slightly.

3. Mix milk and water, heat.

4. Add hot liquid gradually to flour and fat, stir constantly, add salt, pepper, and cheese, stir well.

5. Pour above mix on top of talong and bake in oven (350° F.) for 30 minutes and serve.

NO. 982. TANGCOY (Edible gourd)

Yield: Filling for 18
9-inch pies.

Ingredients	100 servings	.... servings
Tangcoy	45 pounds	
Sugar, granulated	9 pounds (4½ No. 56 dippers)	
Salt	3 ounces (6 mess kit spoons)	
Cinnamon	1 ounce (4 mess kit spoons)	
Nutmeg	½ ounce (2 mess kit spoons)	
Butter	1 pound (½ No. 56 dipper)	
Cracker crumbs	1 pound (1 No. 56 dipper)	
Water	2 quarts (2 No. 56 dippers)	

1. Pare tangcoy and remove heart and seeds, cut into small slices.

2. Add water, bring to boiling point, reduce heat and allow to simmer until tender. Drain water.

3. Combine salt, sugar, nutmeg, cinnamon, butter, cracker crumbs and mix evenly.

4. Use regular pie crust dough (2 crusts).

5. Brush top with egg and milk mixed and bake in oven (425° F.) until crust is evenly browned.

NO. 983. TANGCOY—SUCCOTASH (Edible gourd)

Yield: 100 servings,
3½ ounces each.

Ingredients	100 servings	.... servings
Tangcoy	20 pounds	
Beans, lima, dry	3 pounds	
Water, cold		
Salt	To taste	
Pepper	To taste	
Butter	1 pound	

1. Wash beans thoroughly, cover with cold water, soak 3 to 4 hours.
2. Add salt, cover and heat to boiling point, reduce heat and allow to simmer 1 hour or until tender.

3. Pare tangcoy and wash thoroughly, dice into small cubes. Cover with water, steam until tender, drain water.

4. Combine beans, tangcoy, salt, pepper, and butter. Mix well, heat slowly to serving temperature.

NO. 984. UPO CASSEROLE (Malay apple)   Yield: 100 servings,
5½ ounces each.

Ingredients	100 servings	.... servings
Upo	30 pounds	
Bacon, small dices	2 pounds	
Onion, diced	2 pounds (2 No. 56 dippers)	
Ginger	¼ ounce (1 mess kit spoon)	
Flour	5 ounces (¼ No. 56 dipper)	
Salt	To taste	
Pepper	To taste	
Stock	1 quart (1 No. 56 dipper)	

1. Pare and wash upo thoroughly, cut into thin small slices.

2. Fry bacon and brown onions together.

3. Combine upo, bacon, onions, ginger, salt, pepper, and stock; bring to boiling point, reduce heat, simmer 45 minutes or until tender.

4. Thicken with flour and water mix, heat to serving temperature.

NO. 985. UPO HARVARD STYLE (Malay apple) Yield: 100 servings,
6 ounces each.

Ingredients	100 servings	.... servings
Upo	30 pounds	
Salt	To taste	
Butter, melted	1 pound (½ No. 56 dipper)	
Water, boiling	3 quarts (3 No. 56 dippers)	
Flour	10 ounces (½ No. 56 dipper)	
Vinegar	1 pint (½ No. 56 dipper)	
Sugar, granulated	8 ounces (⅛ No. 56 dipper)	
Pepper	To taste	

1. Pare and wash upo thoroughly, cut into small dices.

2. Steam upo until tender, drain water, heat same water to boiling point, add sugar, vinegar, salt, pepper, thickened with flour and water mix. Combine upo and add butter, mix well.

3. Heat to serving temperature and serve immediately.

   Note. Upo is excellent with meat stew or cooked with any meat combinations.

CENTRAL PASTRY BAKERY RECIPES

56. USE. The recipes in this section are intended primarily for the central pastry bakery; however, the pastry cook in a large mess may find them of value. Inasmuch as the formulas are prepared for use in the large mixing machines, they will be in slightly different form from those recipes for the hand mixer or for the smaller machine usually found in mess kitchens.

NO. 986. APPLE PIE FILLINGS
(Cold process)   Yield: For approximately
                                  100 9-inch pies.
Step No. 1

18 No. 10 cans apples
36 pounds granulated sugar
4 ounces salt   Blend all together thor-
4 ounces cinnamon   oughly.
2 ounces cloves
2 ounces nutmeg

Step No. 2

3 pounds 8 ounces cornstarch

1. Use enough water to dissolve starch into heavy liquid. Pineapple juice may be used in lieu of water. This gives the filling an excellent flavor. Add this dissolved starch to above filling and again blend in thoroughly.
2. Fill into pies and bake at 450°.

NO. 987. PIE DOUGH   Yield: 85 pies or
                                  510 servings
Step No. 1

24 pounds hard wheat flour
14 pounds soft wheat flour   Rub into a medium crumb.
23 pounds shortening

Step No. 2

13 pounds ice water
2 pounds evaporated milk   Dissolve together and add
1 pound 8 ounces sugar   to above. Mix just enough
1 pound 4 ounces salt   to form a dough.

1. This pie dough is suitable for all types of pies, fruit cobblers and turn-overs.
2. Use dough-hook if mixed by machine.

NO. 988. SWEET DOUGH AND COFFEE CAKES

Yield: For 500 servings.

Step No. 1

14 pounds granulated sugar
14 pounds shortening
1 pound 2 ounces salt — Mix thoroughly until light.
4 ounces nutmeg
4 ounces lemon flavor
8 ounces vanilla

Step No. 2

10 pounds whole eggs — Add in three parts and mix in thoroughly.

Step No. 3

25 pounds water
5 pounds 8 ounces yeast — Dissolve thoroughly and add alternately with flour.
6 pounds evaporated milk (7 cans)

Step No. 4

66 pounds hard wheat flour — Add and mix into a smooth semi-stiff dough.
6 pounds soft wheat flour

Dough temperature should be 78° to 82°. Allow to rise for 1½ to 2 hours. Punch thoroughly and take to bench for make-up in 15 minutes.

Note. This dough can be used for all types of coffee cakes, cinnamon rolls, buns, etc., also excellent for raised doughnuts and jelly doughnuts.

NO. 989. GINGERBREAD

Yield: 12 pans or 600 servings.

Step No. 1

8 pounds hard wheat flour
4 pounds soft wheat flour — Mix 3 minutes in second speed. Scrape down well.
12 pounds shortening

Step No. 2

12	pounds granulated sugar	
14	pounds hard wheat flour	
4	pounds soft wheat flour	
6½	ounces soda	
14	ounces baking powder	Add to the above and mix smooth. Scrape down well and then mix for 3 minutes in second speed.
6	ounces salt	
4	ounces cinnamon	
6	ounces ginger	
2	ounces cloves	
15	pounds water	

Step No. 3

12 pounds whole eggs ⎱ Add in three parts and mix until smooth; approximately 3 minutes in low speed.

Step No. 4

24 pounds molasses
1 pound water ⎱ Add in three parts and mix smooth; approximately 3 minutes in low speed.

1. Scale about 9 pounds to a standard pan.
2. This cake does not require any icing.

NO. 990. PLAIN CAKE

Yield: Approximately 600 servings or 12 pans.

Step No. 1

16 pounds soft wheat flour
9 pounds shortening ⎱ Mix to a mass. Then mix for 3 minutes in low speed.

Step No. 2

25 pounds granulated sugar
6 pounds 8 ounces soft wheat flour
10 ounces salt
1 pound 2 ounces baking powder
10 pounds evaporated milk and
  water, half and half ⎱ Add and mix in a few turns. Scrape down well. Then mix for 3 minutes in low speed.

Step No. 3

12 pounds 8 ounces whole eggs ⎱ Add in three parts and mix in until smooth, approximately 3 minutes in low speed.

Step No. 4

5 pounds liquid milk
6 ounces vanilla ⎱ Add and mix in, scrape down well. Mix for 3 minutes in low speed.

Scale approximately 7 pounds to a sheet pan. Bake at 375°. Do not overbake.

Note. Never mix cakes at fast speed.

NO. 991. MARBLE CAKE

Note. Use both the plain cake batter and the devils food for marble cake.

Method

1. Spot squal parts of plain batter and chocolate batter on sheet pan. Streak through batter from end to end and from side to side. Use

a table knife or small spatula to do this. Do not overwork the spreading as this will give the cake a muddy appearance.

2. Serve this cake without icing for better eye appeal.
3. Scale 8 pounds to a sheet pan.

NO. 992. DEVILS FOOD CAKE

Yield: 12 pans or approximately 600 servings.

Step No. 1

| 16 pounds soft wheat flour | Mix to a mass. Then mix |
| 10 pounds shortening | 3 minutes in low speed. |

Step No. 2

24 pounds sugar
4 pounds soft wheat flour
8 ounces salt
5 ounces soda
10 ounces baking powder
5 pounds cocoa
12 pounds water

Add and mix in a few turns. Then scrape down well. Mix for 3 minutes in low speed. *Be sure to sift all dry ingredients.*

Step No. 3

12 pounds whole eggs

Add in three parts. Mix in well for 3 minutes in low speed.

Step No. 4

6 pounds water
6 ounces vanilla
2 ounces almond flavor

Add and mix in for 3 minutes in low speed. Scrape down well.

1. Scale 7 pounds to a sheet pan.
2. Do not overbake; oven temperature 375°.
Note. Never mix cakes at fast speed.

NO. 993. SPONGE CAKE

Yield: Approximately 500 servings.

Step No. 1

12 pounds whole eggs
12 pounds granulated sugar
4 ounces salt

Whip together in second speed until light, approximately 8 minutes. Use wire whip.

Step No. 2

9 pounds warm water (120°)
8 pounds granulated sugar
8 ounces vanilla

Dissolve together thoroughly and stir into the above.

Step No. 3

16 pounds soft wheat flour
1 pound cornstarch
6 ounces baking powder

} Sift together three times and add. Mix in just enough to obtain a smooth batter.

1. Scale 4½ pounds to a sheet pan.
2. Bake at 400°.

Note. For Boston cream pies, scale 8 ounces of this batter into a 9-inch pie plate (greased). Slice through center when baked and then fill with a custard cream and top with a chocolate icing.

NO. 994. CHOCOLATE COOKIES   Yield: 86 dozen or approximately 500 servings.

Step No. 1

12 pounds granulated sugar
3 pounds light brown sugar
10 pounds shortening
6 ounces salt
3 ounces soda

} Cream together until light.

Step No. 2

4 pounds whole eggs
8 ounces vanilla

} Add in three parts and mix smooth.

Step No. 3

4 pounds evaporated milk and water, half and half

} Add and stir in.

Step No. 4

3 pounds 8 ounces cocoa
18 pounds soft wheat flour
4 pounds granulated sugar

} Sift together well and mix in until smooth. Do not overmix.

For proper make-up, scale into 1-pound pieces and roll into a strip. Cut into 12 equal parts. Place on pans and flatten. Wash with regular egg wash.

NO. 995. JELLY ROLL   Yield: 24 pans or approximately 500 servings.

Step No. 1

21 pounds granulated sugar
21 pounds whole eggs
5 ounces salt

} Place in machine and whip for 10 minutes in medium speed, using wire whip.

Step No. 2

9 pounds evaporated milk and water, half and half

6 ounces vanilla

} Add alternately with flour. Run mixer in low speed.

Step No. 3

21 pounds soft wheat flour

1 pound 5 ounces baking powder

} Sift together three times. Add to above alternately with liquid. Mix just enough to form a smooth batter.

1. Scale 3¼ pounds to a sheet pan. Bake at 400°. Do not overbake; baking time approximately 15 minutes. Use greased and papered pans.
2. Roll while warm. Cut each roll into 20 or 22 pieces.
3. Use approximately 1½ pounds of jelly to each roll.

NO. 996. UPSIDE DOWN CAKE

Use regular plain cake batter to cover upside down smear and fruits.

Upside down smear

30 pounds brown sugar

15 pounds granulated sugar

5 ounces salt

14 pounds shortening

6 pounds butter

2 pounds syrup or honey

6 ounces vanilla

1 ounce maple flavor

} Place all together in machine bowl and whip until light.

1. Use 1½ pounds of this preparation to coat each sheet pan. Place desired fruits and nuts on pans and carefully cover with plain cake batter.
2. Bake at 375°.
3. Turn upside down on boards as soon as taken from the oven. Remove pan and allow to cool before serving.

NO. 997. HOT ROLLS (All types)

Step No. 1

4 pounds sugar

7 pounds 8 ounces shortening

1 pound salt

} Place in bowl and cream until smooth.

Step No. 2

32 pounds water

4 pounds evaporated milk

3 pounds yeast

} Dissolve together thoroughly. Add to above and mix in a few turns.

Step No. 3

64 pounds hard wheat flour } Add and mix into a smooth semi-stiff dough.

1. Let rise for 1½ hours and punch. Take to bench in 15 minutes. Cut into 2½-pound pieces for roll divider. Make into desired shapes. Give ¾ proof.
2. Do not overbake.
3. Dough temperature should be 78°–80°.

NO. 998. SUGAR COOKIES

Yield : 100 dozen or approximately 500 servings. Cookies should weigh approximately 1 ounce each.

Step No. 1

22 pounds sugar
8 pounds shortening
4 ounces salt
8 ounces vanilla
2 ounces lemon
} Cream until light. Use second speed.

Step No. 2

5 pounds whole eggs } Add in three parts and mix in smoothly.

Step No. 3

4 pounds evaporated milk and water, half and half } Add and stir in.

Step No. 4

26 pounds soft wheat flour
1 pound baking powder
2 pounds sugar
} Sift together three times. Add and mix in until a smooth dough is obtained. Do not overmix.

Bake on lightly greased pans at 400°.

NO. 999. FRUIT BARS

Yield : 100 dozen or approximately 500 servings.

Step No. 1

12 pounds 8 ounces granulated sugar
6 ounces salt
5 ounces cinnamon
3 ounces cloves
2 ounces allspice
6 ounces soda
9 pounds shortening
} Place in machine and mix until smooth.

Step No. 2

8 pounds whole eggs   ⎫ Add together in three
12 pounds 8 ounces light molasses ⎬ parts. Mix until smooth.

Note. Do not use Karo or syrup in lieu of molasses.

Step No. 3

18 pounds raisins   ⎫ Add and mix in a few
2 pounds chopped nuts (if desired) ⎬ turns.

Step No. 4

20 pounds soft wheat flour   ⎫ Add and mix in until
5 pounds hard wheat flour   ⎬ smooth. Do not overmix.

Bake on lightly greased pans. Wash with egg wash. Bake at 400° for approximately 15 to 18 minutes. Do not overbake. Cut into desired sizes.

NO. 1000. OATMEAL COOKIES

Yield: 100 dozen or approximately 500 servings. Cookies should weigh approximately 1 ounce each.

Step No. 1

16 pounds granulated sugar
4 pounds light brown sugar
8 pounds 8 ounces shortening
4 ounces cinnamon   Place in bowl and cream
6 ounces salt   until light. Use second
10 ounces soda   speed.
3 ounces lemon flavor
4 ounces vanilla

Step No. 2

3 pounds whole eggs   ⎫ Add in three parts and
                            ⎬ mix until light.

Step No. 3

                            Dissolve the ground rais-
5 pounds raisins (ground)   ins thoroughly in the
8 pounds warm water   water. Then add to above
                            and mix in.

Note. Raisins must be ground to permit proper leavening action in the dough.

Step No. 4

9 pounds oatmeal (crushed or fine, ⎫ Add in, stir in thor-
   not flaked)   ⎬ oughly.

Step No. 5

16 pounds soft wheat flour   ⎫ Sift together and add mix
4 pounds hard wheat flour   ⎬ until smooth. Do not over-
1 pound 8 ounces granulated sugar ⎭ mix.

Note. Cut dough into 1-pound pieces and roll into a strip. Cut into 12 equal pieces and place on pans. Flatten out and wash with egg wash. Use greased and dusted pans. Bake at 375°-400° F. Do not overbake.

NO. 1001. CHOCOLATE CREAM PIE FILLING

Step No. 1

72 pounds evaporated milk and water, half and half 10 pounds granulated sugar	Place in kettle and bring to a boil.

Step No. 2

20 pounds granulated sugar 6 pounds cocoa 6 pounds cornstarch 4 ounces salt	Sift together thoroughly and add to egg and milk below.

Step No. 3

20 pounds whole eggs 4 pounds evaporated milk (straight)	Add dry ingredients and mix into a light fluffy consistency.

When milk in kettle comes to a rising boil, add the egg and sugar mix and stir vigorously until thickened and smooth. Remove from kettle at once and add:

Step No. 4

2 pounds butter 10 ounces vanilla	Stir into above until smooth.

Pour into prebaked pie shells and allow to cool before serving.

NO. 1002. BROWNIES (Whole Wheat)

Yield: 8 sheet pans or approximately 500 servings.

Step No. 1

16 pounds granulated sugar 8 pounds brown sugar 5 ounces salt 10 pounds shortening 2 ounces cinnamon 4 ounces soda 5 pounds cocoa	Cream until light. Be sure to sift all dry ingredients.

Step No. 2

4 pounds egg yolks 8 ounces vanilla	Add in three parts and mix until light, approximately 5 minutes in second speed.

Step No. 3

12 pounds evaporated milk and water,
   half and half
8 ounces vinegar
} Add and stir in.

Step No. 4

8 pounds raisins
24 pounds whole wheat flour
4 pounds soft wheat flour
5 ounces baking powder
} Add and stir in. Mix until smooth.

Scale about 11 pounds to a sheet pan. Bake at 350°. Do not overbake. This pastry does not require an icing.

NO. 1003. WHITE OR VANILLA ICING

45 pounds XXXX sugar
8 pounds shortening
2 pounds butter
4 ounces salt
1 pound 8 ounces soft wheat flour
6 pounds evaporated milk
2 pounds ice water
10 ounces vanilla
} Place all together in machine and beat until light in second speed. Never use fast speed.

Note. Other flavors, such as lemon, orange, maple, etc., may be used in lieu of vanilla to produce a variety of icings.

NO. 1004. CHOCOLATE ICING

50 pounds XXXX sugar
12 pounds shortening
6 ounces salt
5 pounds cocoa (sifted)
5 pounds evaporated milk
6 pounds hot water
10 ounces vanilla
} Place all together in machine and beat until light. Use second speed. Never use fast speed.

Note. More or less liquid may be used to bring this icing to desired consistency.

Variation. For mocha icing use hot strong black coffee in lieu of water and omit 1 pound of cocoa.

INDEX

A

D

E

F

N

O

P

S

Made in the USA
Columbia, SC
06 January 2023

75452754R00255